Henry Cadwallader Adams

History of the Jews

From the War with Rome to the present Time

Henry Cadwallader Adams

History of the Jews
From the War with Rome to the present Time

ISBN/EAN: 9783337134907

Printed in Europe, USA, Canada, Australia, Japan

Cover: Foto ©ninafisch / pixelio.de

More available books at **www.hansebooks.com**

THE

HISTORY OF THE JEWS

*FROM THE WAR WITH ROME TO THE
PRESENT TIME.*

THE

HISTORY OF THE JEWS

*FROM THE WAR WITH ROME TO THE
PRESENT TIME.*

BY THE

REV. H. C. ADAMS, M.A.

VICAR OF OLD SHOREHAM.

Author of 'Wykehamica,' 'Schoolboy Honour,' etc., etc.

London:

THE RELIGIOUS TRACT SOCIETY,

56, PATERNOSTER ROW.

—

1887.

BERNARD MOSES

BUTLER & TANNER,
THE SELWOOD PRINTING WORKS
FROME, AND LONDON.

CONTENTS.

..

PART II.

FROM THE BEGINNING OF THE FOURTEENTH CENTURY TO THE PRESENT
TIME.

APPENDICES.

PREFACE.

THE reader will understand that this work does not profess to be anything more than a popular history, with just so much reference to Jewish learning and controversy as may be necessary to a due comprehension of the facts related, and the character of the people treated of. But such references will not, for various reasons, be frequent. Of the vast accumulations of Jewish literature, the most valuable portions are the Commentaries of their doctors on Scripture, and their contributions to grammar, mathematics, and physical science. With these, however, the writer of history has but little concern. The abstruse and intricate speculations of the Rabbins, the subtleties of the Cabbalists, the wild fancies— or what, at all events, the sober Western intellect accounts such—of the Talmuds, the Sepher-Yetzira, and the Zohar, might absorb whole years of study, but would yield the historian only a barren return for the labour. The poetry

of the Hebrews is said to be plaintive and touching, but too
exclusively national to have interest for any but Jews. Their
ancient historians, again, overlay their narratives with exaggeration and fable to such an extent that their statements
cannot be received without the greatest caution. It is mainly
from writers belonging to other races that we must derive
our record of the strange and varied fortunes of the people
of Israel.

This must, of course, place them at some disadvantage.
Yet there is no history so full of striking incident and
mournful pathos as theirs, none which stirs such solemn questions, or imparts so profound a wisdom to those who rightly
study it. As an illustration of the sad interest it awakens,
the words of Leopold Zunz, one of the greatest of modern
Jews, may suffice. 'If there are gradations in suffering,' he
writes, 'Israel has reached its highest acme. If the long
duration of sufferings, and the patience with which they are
borne, ennobles a people, then the Jews may defy the high-
born of any lands.' In truth, again and again, in every succeeding century of their annals, the evidences of a heroism
which no persistence in severity could bend, and no pressure
of persecution could break, engage the attention of the reader.
Whatever may be his estimate of the worth or the demerits
of the Jews, their tragic story at least commands his sympathy.

In these respects other nations, though they may not have
rivalled, at least resemble, them. But there are peculiarities
in their history which separate them from every other people
on the earth. Foremost among these is the question—Are we
still to regard them, as our fathers for so many generations
regarded them, as lying under the special curse of God, a

perpetual monument of His anger? Was the imprecation
uttered before Pilate's tribunal (St. Matt. xxvii. 25), 'His
blood be on us, and on our children!' ratified, so to speak,
by Almighty God? Is the Lord's blood still upon them?
Is that the true explanation of their past miseries and their
present condition?

Let us consider what the guilt of the Jews, who slew
the Lord, really amounted to. They do not, I believe, themselves deny that they are suffering under Divine displeasure,
or that that displeasure has been occasioned by their sin. On
the contrary, they hold that it is their sin that has delayed,
and still delays, the coming of the Messiah. But, far from
thinking that sin to have been the murder of Jesus Christ,
they do not consider that their fathers were guilty in that
matter at all. Their law, so they contend, requires them to
put to death blasphemers and setters up of strange gods.
The assertion of Jesus, 'I and My Father are one,' say they,
was both blasphemy and the setting up of a strange god.
They would only therefore have obeyed a Divine command
if they had put Him to death. But, they add, it was not
they, but the Romans, by whose sentence He died, for declaring Himself King of the Jews. This, they say, is sufficiently
evident from the manner of His death by crucifixion, which
was one never inflicted by Jews, and by the inscription on
the cross, 'This is the King of the Jews.' It is extremely
doubtful, they add, whether their fathers possessed the power
of putting Him to death, but at all events they did not exercise it. The Jewish people, according to their view, had
nothing to do with the matter. Some of the multitude may
have imprecated the blood of Jesus on themselves and their
children; but if so, the curse could only come on those few

persons on whom it had been invoked. Jost and others even deny that the Sanhedrim was ever legally convened, the meeting that condemned Jesus and delated Him to Pilate being, as they hold, merely a tumultuary assembly of the enemies of Christ.

It will, of course, be answered that to charge our Lord with blasphemy and setting up of a strange god, is simply to beg the whole question at issue between Jew and Christian. Indeed, considering that the Hebrew Scriptures distinctly declare the Messiah to be God[1] (Psa. xlv. 6; Isa. vii. 14; ix. 6, etc.), according to this view of the matter, at whatever period He might come, it must be the duty of the Jews to put Him to death, as soon as He declared His true character. It might be asked—How were the Jews to know that Jesus was really what He proclaimed Himself? Our answer is, that in the fulfilment of prophecy in Him, in the exercise of His miraculous powers, and the superhuman holiness of His teaching, they had sufficient evidence that He was indeed the Christ. They had, in fact, *the* evidence of it which Divine wisdom accounted sufficient.

Again, it was doubtless by the order of a Roman magistrate that He was crucified ; and it may perhaps be true that during the Roman Procuratorship the Sanhedrim had no power of pronouncing a capital sentence.[2] But it was the

---

[1] A Jew would doubtless deny this. I do not pursue the question further, as this is not a work of controversial theology : and, besides, the point has been made so clear by Christian divines that there can be no need of any advocacy of mine. Let the reader who may have any doubt on the subject consider Isa. xl. 10; xlv. 24 ; xlviii. 17 ; Jer. xxiii. 6 ; Hosea i. 7 ; Zech. ii. 10, 11 ; Malachi iii. 1, where not the title Elohim only, but that of Jehovah, is given to the Messiah.

[2] No question has been more disputed than whether the Sanhedrim,

Jews who carried our Lord before Pilate and demanded His death. Far from being anxious to condemn Him, Pilate was most reluctant to order the execution. It was only when the dangerous insinuation of disloyalty to Cæsar was suggested that he consented to their wishes. Who can doubt that the guilt was theirs? Pilate might as well have put off the blame on the centurion who commanded the quaternion at Calvary, or he on the three soldiers who put in force the sentence. The statement again, that the Sanhedrim was not convened, is in direct contradiction to that of St. Mark (xv. 1). Nor does it appear that the Evangelist's assertion was ever called in question by contemporary writers.

There can be no reasonable doubt in the mind of any man who accepts the Gospel narrative as a true—I do not here say an inspired—history, that the Jews of that day were guilty of the blood of our Lord, and that it was a deed of the most flagrant wickedness. But it remains to be proved that they slew Him, knowing Him to be their Incarnate God, and

during the rule of the Roman Procurators, possessed the power of putting to death persons convicted of capital crimes. The statement made, St. John xviii. 31, and the action of Albinus, who, A.D. 63, deposed the High Priest Ananus, because the Sanhedrim had put St. James to death without his sanction, seem conclusive that they could not capitally punish persons *convicted of blasphemy*, unless under the Procurator's order. The case of St. Stephen, Acts viii., does not disprove this ; for that was evidently a tumultuary procedure, no sentence having been pronounced. But the Sanhedrim certainly had the power of capitally punishing *some* offenders, as, for instance, any Gentile passing beyond the barrier between the Temple Courts (see Jos. *B. J.* vi. 2, 4), an offence closely resembling blasphemy. Possibly they could inflict death for certain specified crimes, but only for these. It would be quite consistent with the principle of Roman government to allow the High Priests to punish capitally persons convicted of grave moral offences, but not such as were only guilty in matters relating 'to their own superstitions,' as they would phrase it.

I think that would be found extremely difficult of proof. If we are to be guided by Scripture in the matter, we shall entertain a different opinion. St. Peter said to these very men, not many weeks afterwards, 'I wot that ye did it in ignorance,' and then called upon them 'to repent, that their sin might be blotted out.'[1] Our Lord also pleaded their ignorance of the nature of the deed they were perpetrating, in their behalf.[2] Both these passages are inconsistent with the idea of an abiding and inexorable curse. Their guilt was like that of the Athenian people when they condemned Socrates to death, or of that of the Florentines, when they similarly murdered Savonarola, or again of the Romans, when they assassinated Count Rossi—like theirs, though doubtless more aggravated. The sin of rejecting the preachers of holiness, and silencing their voices in their blood, is one of the worst of which a people can be guilty, and must needs draw down the heavy wrath of the All Just; but surely not on their descendants for all after ages.

As regards the other argument advanced, no doubt the slayers of Socrates or Savonarola did not imprecate on themselves and their children the consequences of their deed, as the Jews did. But what then? The Jews at the crucifixion could have had no more power than other men to cut themselves off from repentance, much less to cut their children off from it. The blood of Christ can cleanse men from *any* sin. This, even if it were not the plain declaration of Scripture, would be proved by St. Peter's address to them, already quoted. Even were this otherwise, what claim could these men have had to represent the Jewish people? There

---

[1] Acts iii. 17.   [2] St. Luke xxiii. 34.

were, as is shown elsewhere,[1] probably some six or seven millions of Jews in the world. Of these not one half, in all likelihood, had heard of our Lord till after His death. Many never heard of Him for generations afterwards. Of the two or three millions present in the Holy Land when the crucifixion took place, not the thousandth part could have heard Pilate's protest, or the rejoinder of the crowd. On what principle is this small section to be regarded as representing the whole Jewish people, for whose words and acts it is to be held accountable? When the Cordeliers, with their frantic blasphemies, in the name of the French people disavowed God, doubtless they drew down Divine anger on all concerned; but are we to believe that the guilt of their impiety will rest on the French nation for ever? Such an idea appears to me to be alien alike to the spirit of both natural and revealed religion.

But it will, no doubt, be asked—How, then, is the strange and exceptional condition of the Jews for so many centuries to be accounted for? No careful student of God's Word will have any difficulty in answering this question. Great and enduring blessings had been promised to Abraham, 'the friend of God,' and to his posterity for his sake. These had been repeated to David, 'the man after God's own heart,' with an assurance of still greater mercies. The faithfulness of God to His promises is a thing wholly independent of lapse of time. To us, a promise given nearly 4,000 years ago may seem a thing wholly obsolete; to Him it is as fresh and binding as if it had been made yesterday. Therefore, although any other nation but that which sprung from the loins of

---

[1] See Appendix I.

Abraham would have been destroyed and rooted out for such
a series of rebellious deeds as that which culminated in the
crucifixion of the Lord, the remembrance of Abraham and
David has prevented its entire destruction. We are distinctly
told that this was the case at other periods of their history.
When Jeroboam relapsed into idolatry, he and his whole race
were cut off root and branch. But when Solomon did the
same, the kingdom, though with reduced strength and splendour, was continued to his posterity. When the kingdom of
Israel offended beyond endurance, it was scattered into all
lands, and its nationality perished. When that of Judah was
equally guilty, its dispersion was only for awhile, and then it
was allowed to return and resume its national existence. A
remnant of the nation was preserved for Abraham's sake, that
particular remnant, for the sake of David. Such, it is most
reasonable to conclude, is the true explanation of their mar-
vellous history for the last eighteen hundred years. Their
protracted existence in their present condition is indeed a
miracle, but a miracle, not of wrath, but of mercy. This they
are themselves quick to perceive.

But, as in the cases above alleged, the continuance of the
sceptre to Solomon's descendants, and the restoration of
Judah after the Captivity, did not exempt them from the
penalty of their subsequent disobedience, so now the preservation of Israel through so many centuries of danger and
suffering, does not annul or modify the consequences of their
unbelief. Like all nations which come into contact with
Christianity, but do not accept Christ, they share the benefits
of His sacrifice, in the amended moral tone of the world,
which is the slow growth of His teaching; but they can only
gain, or to speak more correctly, regain, His favour, by taking

Him as their Lord and their God.[1] They cannot rightly be said to be living under a curse, but they assuredly fail to obtain a blessing. But to this they continue persistently blind.

This is the key to their history. This is the explanation of their persistent isolation, their resolute endurance, their unconquerable self-reliance. Descendants of the special favourites of Heaven, fully persuaded that its favour has not been forfeited, but only temporarily withdrawn, this high-spirited and gifted race has ever felt that, supported by this conviction, it could, like 'the charity' of St. Paul, hope and endure all things. Races that had not sprung into existence when theirs had reached the highest point of civilization and glory, might pretend to despise them : but, to use the language which Sir Walter Scott puts into the mouth of the bard, Cadwallon, they knew that the blood which flowed in the veins of their persecutors, when compared with their own, 'was but as the puddle of the highway to the silver fountain.'[2]

Their history is sad and humiliating to read ; and no less sad and humiliating to them, than to those whose ancestors trampled upon and persecuted them. It brings out into strong relief, not only the good, but also the bad points of their national character. The stubborn unbelief of generation after generation ; the way in which business ability, under the pressure of injustice, developed into craft, into the power of

---

[1] 'Ye shall not see Me, until the time come when ye shall say, Blessed is He that cometh in the name of the Lord' (St. Luke xiii. 35) —that is, 'ye shall not apprehend Me, and the blessings I come to bring you, until you acknowledge Me as the true Messiah and Saviour of the world.' To '*see*' the Lord is, in the New Testament phrase, spiritually to discern and understand Him.

[2] *Betrothed*, chap. 31.

heaping up wealth by usury, and relentless exaction of the uttermost farthing; the slow processes by which the most manifest characteristic of a Jew became that of the harsh and merciless creditor;—these are the dark shadows upon a great national character, and a national story of the deepest interest.

On the other hand, their history shows, as no other can, the folly and wickedness of that most deadly, though sometimes most fair-seeming, of all Satanic influences, religious persecution. Our fathers were wont in those evil times to enlarge with horror on the sin of the Jew in obstinately rejecting Christ. In the day when account will be required of all, may it not be found that the deadliest of their own sins was, that by their hideous travesty of the Christian faith they shut out from the Jew the knowledge of the reality?

For centuries the bitterest persecutions came from those who, while robbing and ill-treating the Jews, because they charged them with heaping ridicule upon Christianity and eagerly aiding its enemies, were themselves ignorant of the first principles of the Gospel, and devoted adherents of the Church of those times. As the Reformation of the Church developed, and as the power of evangelical principles has increased, the persecution of the Jew has ceased. More and more has the Church everywhere realized the truth, that Christ died for the Jew no less than for the Gentile, and that He can be better served in this respect by the proclamation of His own loving message of forgiveness, than by any attempts to usurp His function as Judge, or to compel an outward submission, in which the heart has no part.

Israel has, indeed, a heavy account against the Anglo-Saxon race, though, it may be, not so heavy as against the Goth, the Teuton, and the Slav. There is some comfort in reflecting

that we in this century have done somewhat to reduce the
balance that stands against us. May our children learn the
lesson of mercy and toleration in all its fulness, and so make
such reparation as is possible for the mistakes and sins of our
fathers !

PART I.

FROM THE DEPOSITION OF ARCHELAUS TO THE END OF THE THIRTEENTH CENTURY.

CHAPTER I.

FROM THE REVOLT OF JUDAS TO THE SIEGE OF JERUSALEM.

I T is not proposed in these pages to deal with the history of the Jews during the long period which intervened between the origin of the nation in the family of Abraham[1] and their final revolt from the Roman power. The records of those times are to be found in the inspired volume, or in the narrative of Josephus; and we have no further concern with them than to inquire how the various changes in their fortunes— from bondage to freedom, and from freedom to bondage, under

---

[1] It is an error, I think, to connect the name Hebrew with Heber, or Eber, the great-grandson of Shem. Abraham was called the Hebrew, or passer over, ὁ περάτης (Gen. xiv. 13, LXX.), because, in obedience to Divine command, he 'passed over' the Euphrates, leaving his home and people, to settle in a strange land. Heber was the progenitor, not of the Hebrews only, but many other nations. The notion that they were called after him, because at the dispersion of Babel he retained and transmitted the primitive language of the world to one only of his descendants, is a mere fancy. He may have been, and very probably was called the 'passer' or 'carrier away,' because he was the patriarch of the dispersion. But Abraham's name was given to him for a different reason and altogether independently of Heber.

lawgiver, judge and high priest, foreign tyrant and native sovereign, contributed to the formation of their national character—the most strongly marked, it may confidently be affirmed, that ever distinguished any people.

The childhood of the Jewish nation was a hard and harsh one. They grew up into national existence under alien rulers, who feared and hated them, imposed on them intolerable burdens, and would have destroyed them from off the face of the earth, but for the Divine protection extended over them. Delivered by the same visible display of Divine power from these tyrants, they were transported to a rich and genial land, powerful and warlike nations being ejected to make way for them. Their first national, and true, idea must needs have been their special privileges as the favoured people of Heaven ; but to this they added the untrue persuasion that nothing could ever forfeit them ; and this rooted itself so deeply in their belief, that all the experience of after generations was unable to destroy, or even modify it. Their own participation in the sins of neighbouring nations—those very sins which had drawn down Divine vengeance on *them*—did not shake this confidence in their secure possession of Almighty favour. Visited with sharp chastisement for disobedience, they were for the moment alarmed and humbled ; but they resumed their old complacency the moment that deliverance from suffering was vouchsafed. The woes of foreign subjugation, exile and captivity, so far affected them, that they abandoned the idolatry which had been the main cause of their miseries. But it did not abate their sense of ascendency over all other races, and of their special and inalienable possession of the favour of the Most High.

It was impossible, they believed, that they could be under the dominion of any foreign people. They might seem to be so for a while, but they were not really so. The fact that they were for seventy years the vassals of the King of Babylon ; for two hundred more the dependants, to use a mild term, of the sovereigns of Persia ; for several generations afterwards at the mercy of one potentate or another, who dealt with them as his caprice might dictate ; that their own Asmonæan kingdom was, in reality, but a dependency of Imperial Rome, existing only so long as she chose to permit it—all this went for nothing with them. Nay, even the reduction of Judæa to the status of a Roman province, and the residence of a Roman procurator in Judæa, did not prevent them from replying to our Lord that 'they were Abraham's children, and had never been in bondage to any man.' So long as it was possible, on any pretext however transparent, to assert their independence, they persisted in doing so.

At the same time, they were too intelligent not be aware that Imperial Rome would endure neither opposition to her arms nor evasion of her claims It must needs have been long evident to them, that the time must come, sooner or later, when they would have to make their choice between genuine allegiance to, or open rebellion against, the empire of the Cæsars. They were purposed, however, to defer it as long as they could. Requirements might be made, which they would rather perish than comply with ; but until these were advanced, there was no need to anticipate them ; and the mildness which always marked the Roman sway, when unopposed, its strict observance of justice in all its dealings with a conquered people,[1] and its toleration of their customs and prejudices, long delayed the terrible struggle which ensued at last.

The deposition of Archelaus, and the conversion of Judæa into a Roman province, brought about the first overt act of rebellion. Judas, called the ' Galilæan,' raised an insurrection, which was with difficulty put down. He took for his watchword the significant sentence, 'We have no other master

---

[1] In proof of this may be alleged the fact, that in the brief space of sixty years no less than four Roman procurators were summoned before the Imperial Tribunal to answer complaints brought against them by the Jews ; and two of them were punished by banishment for life.

but God.' The reasons already alleged, in all likelihood, restrained the more influential classes of the Jews from lending him the support he expected. He was crushed and put to death. But the spirit he evoked lived long after him, and Josephus attributes to it all the outbreaks which ensued, which culminated at last in the destruction of Jerusalem and the dispersion of the Jews.[1]

Coponius, the first Roman governor, was allowed to take up his abode at Cæsarea without opposition. That city, rather than Jerusalem, was chosen as his seat of government probably out of consideration for the feelings of the Jews. He was succeeded after a short interval by Ambivius and Rufus. After him Valerius Gratus held the reins of power for nearly twelve years. Throughout their prefectures, and for some years afterwards, Judæa remained tranquil. But at Rome, the Jews, who under Augustus had been treated with great indulgence, were expelled from the city by his successor, Tiberius. This act is said to have been really due to the enmity of Sejanus, though the pretext alleged was their extortion of money from Fulvia, a noble matron. Four thousand Jews were forced to enter the army, the greater part of whom died of malaria, in the island of Sardinia. After Sejanus's fall, the edict against the Jews was revoked.

To Gratus succeeded Pontius Pilatus, who held office for ten years. During the government of this procurator, another formidable insurrection occurred, or rather, series of insurrections, caused in the first instance by the removal of the Roman army, with its idolatrous standards, to Jerusalem. On this occasion there was a very general rising of the people; and

---

[1] Judas was born at Gamala, a city of Gaulonitis. He was a brave, able, and eloquent man. Supported by Sadoc, an influential Pharisee, he founded the party of the Gaulonites, who were the predecessors of the Zealots and Assassins of later times. Though multitudes gathered round his standard, he was not supported by the nation generally, and the power of Rome was too great for him to contend with. He was overpowered and put to death. He is referred to in Acts v. 37.

if Pilatus had remained in power, hostilities with Rome might have broken out a generation previously to their actual occurrence. But after committing, with apparent impunity, several sanguinary massacres of Jews, whom his wanton disregard of their feelings had stirred up to insurrection, Pilatus was accused to Vitellius, the Prefect of Syria, by the Samaritans, of a similar outrage on them. Vitellius ordered him to Rome, to take his trial. There he was deposed, and sentenced to exile.

Some time afterwards Judæa was again converted, for a brief space, into a Jewish kingdom under Agrippa I., whose strange and terrible end is recorded in the Acts of the Apostles. Agrippa was the son of Aristobulus, and grandson of Herod the Great. He early attached himself to Caligula, and thereby aroused the suspicion of Tiberius, who threw him into prison. He would probably have been put to death, if the decease of the emperor had not rescued him from the danger. On his succession to the empire, Caligula gave him the tetrarchies formerly held by Lysanias and Philip, together with the title of King. But his reign was soon beset with trouble. The royal dignity bestowed on him roused the jealousy of Herod Antipas, Tetrarch of Galilee. Accompanied by his wife, Herodias, he sailed to Rome, in the hope of ousting Agrippa, by charges of disloyalty, from the Imperial favour. But Agrippa retorted on Antipas with a counter-charge of treasonable correspondence with the Parthians; and the result was the banishment of Antipas, and the addition of his dominions to those already ruled by Agrippa. The latter was a rigid observer of the Mosaic law; and his murder of St. James and persecution of St. Peter were probably due to this, rather than to tyranny or cruelty. During his reign of seven years he seems to have done his best for his kingdom and country. He built the third wall round Jerusalem, and endeavoured to reconcile the contending factions, which were destroying the life of the nation.

It was a short time before his accession that the event

occurred which roused the anger of the Jews to a higher
pitch than had ever before been manifested ; and had the
outrage been pushed further, a civil war would have undoubtedly been the result.   This was the attempt of the
Emperor Caligula to erect his statue as that of 'The
Younger Jupiter,' as he styled himself, in the most sacred
part of the Jewish Temple.

The design seems to have been the result of a mere whim,
conceived by the half-crazy emperor, and pertinaciously
persisted in, when he learned (as he did from both the
Jews themselves, and Petronius, the Procurator of Syria)
that its execution would occasion among the worshippers
of the God of the Hebrews unspeakable horror and alarm.[1]
There can be no doubt that the impiety was intended.   The
statue had been ordered, if not completed ; but the wise
and generous procrastination of Petronius, the earnest
representations of Agrippa, who was a favourite of the
emperor, together with the death of the emperor himself,
which followed almost immediately afterwards, averted the
accomplishment of the design.   The narrative of the transaction is valuable, because it shows that at that time the
Jews were disposed to wise and moderate counsels, which
contrast forcibly with their reckless violence a generation
later.   When the fatal intentions of Caligula were made
known, the whole population, we are told, of all ranks and
ages, from a vast distance round Jerusalem, crowded round
the chair of the Roman procurator, declaring their deter-

---

[1] It was not in Judæa only that these feelings were aroused.   In
Alexandria, the proposal made by the Greeks, to place the emperor's
statue in the Jewish Proseuchæ, provoked riots, in which much property
was wrecked, and terrible carnage took place.   The Roman governor,
Flaccus Aquilius, for many years a wise and able ruler, but who had
grown reckless since the accession of Caligula, towards whom he bore
no good will, made no attempt to repress, but rather encouraged, the
outrages.   He was so unwise as to openly insult the emperor's friend,
Agrippa.   He was arrested by order of Caligula, and put to death with
barbarous cruelty.

mination to die rather than witness so fearful a profanation.[1] Their demeanour so deeply affected Petronius, that he thenceforth strove by every means in his power to avert the dreaded catastrophe; and, aided by circumstances and the intercession of Agrippa, he succeeded in his attempt. Caligula, however, could not forgive his disobedience, and it is said that the emperor's death alone saved Petronius from the consequences of his anger.

Through the favour of Claudius, who now mounted the Imperial throne (and whose reign, notwithstanding one act of severity,[2] was favourable to the Jews), Agrippa succeeded to the whole of the dominions of his grandfather, Herod the Great, and held them for four years, when he died, A.D. 44, in the manner already referred to; and Judæa again became a Roman province, Cuspius Fadus being sent as governor.[3] During his rule, and that of his successor Tiberius Alexander, the peace of Palestine continued undisturbed, except by the outbreaks of one or two of the turbulent incendiaries, of which the land contained great numbers. These were easily put down. But during the procuratorship of Ventidius Cumanus, the animosity between the people and the Roman soldiers, which had long been smouldering, burst out into a flame. During one of the Jewish festivals, a soldier offered a gross insult to the ceremonial in progress, which roused the fury of the Jews against, not only the offender, but Cumanus himself. The latter, hearing the furious cries with which he was assailed, marched his whole force into the Antonia, and commenced an indiscriminate massacre, in which 20,000 perished. For this outrage and his subsequent conduct in a hostile encounter

---

[1] The celebrated Philo came from Alexandria on this occasion to plead the cause of his countrymen.

[2] Banishing the Jews from Rome A.D. 54. Acts xviii. 2 ; Suet. Claud. 25.

[3] During his tenure of office, an impostor named Theudas, who claimed to be a prophet, raised a formidable insurrection. But Fadus, a man of action, arrested and executed him. He is mentioned in Acts v. 36.

between the Jews and Samaritans, Cumanus was tried at Rome, and condemned to banishment.

He was succeeded by the profligate Felix, whose government was worse than that of any of his predecessors. It was, in fact, one long scene of cruelty and treachery. He allied himself with some of the bands of robbers now infesting Judæa, and by their aid murdered, in the very precincts of the Temple, Jonathan, the high priest, who had rebuked his vices. After eleven years of misrule, he was accused by the Jews in Cæsarea of the barbarous slaughter of some of their countrymen. He was tried at Rome, but escaped through the interest of his brother, Pallas. He was, however, a vigorous ruler, and put down the notorious Egyptian Jew, who, with 30,000 followers, had raised a formidable insurrection (Acts xxi. 38).

After his prefecture, and that of his more humane and upright successor Porcius Festus, the inveterate evils which afflicted the whole of Judæa continued to grow in violence and intensity. Banditti overspread the country, and carried on their lawless depredations almost with impunity. Impostors and fanatics started up on every side, and drew after them great multitudes, to whom they preached rebellion against their Roman governors as a religious duty. Riot and bloodshed, and armed encounters with the Roman soldiery, became matters of continual occurrence, which the authority of the procurator was unable to restrain. The evil was aggravated by the succession of the corrupt Albinus to the office vacated by the death of Festus; but it was not until he, in his turn, was superseded by the infamous Gessius Florus that the discontent of the unhappy Jews culminated in the rebellious outbreak which brought on their ruin.

It can hardly be supposed that it was actually Florus's object to drive the Jews into rebellion; yet the course he pursued persistently from the very commencement of his rule could have had no other result. It was not merely that he took bribes from all men who sought his favour or feared his anger. He leagued with robbers and assassins, sharing their gains and countenancing their crimes. He exacted large sums alike from public treasuries and private coffers, on the flimsiest pretexts, and often on no pretext at all. He inflamed the angry feelings, already dangerously excited, by every possible insult and outrage which lawless power could exercise ; and, finally, having by pillage and butchery stirred up the infuriated Jews to refuse obedience to an authority which appeared to exist only for their destruction, he called in Cestius Gallus, the Prefect of Syria, to lead the Roman forces under his command to put down the sedition.

This officer, though a man of narrow views and mediocre ability, was a Roman functionary, and, as such, would not act on *ex parte* evidence. He sent a tribune named Neapolitanus to Jerusalem, to inquire into the truth of Florus's charges ; and Agrippa,[1] who was cognisant of what had passed, and was anxious to avert the ruin that threatened his country, accompanied him to the Jewish capital. Fully convinced of the truth of the charges against Florus, they nevertheless hesitated to uphold his accusers, and endeavoured to persuade the people to make submission to him. But they had been too deeply incensed by Florus's barbarities : and the seditious spirits among them had gained too much ascendency to allow this advice to prevail ; notwithstanding that the upper classes of the citizens, who were still desirous of avoiding war, declared in its favour. They drove Neapolitanus and Agrippa, with insult, from the city, and openly renounced allegiance to Rome.[2]

Shortly afterwards a new adventurer, Menahem, the son of Judas the Gaulonite, appeared, and was gladly welcomed by the people. But he soon provoked the jealousy of Eleazar,

---

[1] This was Agrippa II., son of Agrippa I. It was before him that St. Paul pleaded (Acts xxvi.). Suet. (*Vesp.* 4).

[2] According to Suetonius, Florus was slain by the Jews in a tumultuous outbreak. Josephus has been thought to contradict him. But his language may be interpreted so as to harmonize with Suetonius.

the leader of the Zealots, by whom he was deposed and slain. Eleazar having gained complete mastery in the city, proceeded to murder, with shameless treachery, the Roman garrison, which had surrendered on condition of being spared. Almost coincidently with this shocking deed, one of equal horror was perpetrated at Cæsarea, where 20,000 Jews were slaughtered by the Greek inhabitants. In this atmosphere of treachery and bloodshed the whole nation appears to have gone mad. They were resolved, apparently, that as every man's hand was against them, so should their hand be against every man. They took up arms, plundered several of the Syrian cities, laying waste the whole country round them. The Syrians retaliated with equal barbarity, everywhere slaying without mercy their Jewish fellow-citizens. Neither Agrippa's dominions nor Egypt escaped the contagion. In the former, a feud between Varus, the deputy, to whom Agrippa had committed the government of his kingdom during his absence at Antioch, and Philip, the general of his army, very nearly caused a civil war. At Antioch another quarrel between the Jews and Greeks, relative to the right of the former to attend public assemblies, led, first to a riot, and then to a general rising of the Hebrew population. The governor, Tiberius Alexander—who was by birth a Jew, and had some years previously been Procurator of Judæa, afterwards holding a command in Titus's army at the siege of Jerusalem—sent for the principal men among the Jews, and exhorted them to use their influence in quieting the disturbance. Failing in this attempt, he ordered out the troops, and made an attack on the Jews' quarter, in which 50,000 persons were slain. Throughout the whole of Palestine, Syria, and Egypt, strife and bloodshed prevailed. The advance of the Roman army was anxiously looked for by all who retained their reason, as the only hope of putting an end to the frantic anarchy wherewith the whole land was now overspread.

CHAPTER II.

A.D. 71, 72.

SIEGE OF JERUSALEM BY TITUS.

W AR was now openly declared, and Cestius marched on
Jerusalem with 10,000 Roman soldiers, and a still
larger force of allies, to put down the rebellion and avenge
the murder of his countrymen.   The result was the most
terrible disaster to the Roman arms which they had sustained
since the defeat of Varus.   Unsuccessful in some preliminary
skirmishing, Gallus assaulted the city, and after five days of
indecisive fighting, forced his way on the sixth to the wall
on the north side of the Temple.   Every effort to scale this
having failed, he ordered the legionaries to lock their shields
together and form the testudo, their usual mode of obtaining
a cover, under which they undermined fortifications which
they could not surmount.   The manœuvre was successful.
The wall was all but pierced through, and the garrison on the
point of flight, when Gallus suddenly, without any apparent
reason, ordered a retreat,[1] withdrew in haste, first to his camp,

---

[1] By this the Christians in Jerusalem were enabled to secure their
retreat to Pella, where they remained uninjured by the fearful sufferings
which ensued, so making good the Lord's promise, St. Luke xxi. 20, 21.

and afterwards to Antipatris, losing in his retreat his whole
battering train and 6,000 soldiers.

The Jews had now offended beyond hope of forgiveness,
and both parties braced themselves for the fierce and deadly
struggle which had become inevitable. The rebels recruited
their comparatively scanty numbers by securing the support
of the inhabitants of Idumæa (of whom 20,000 were enlisted),
Peræa, and Galilee. On the other side, Rome summoned into
the field a formidable force, which was placed under the
command of T. Flavius Vespasian, the greatest soldier of
his day. In the hope, apparently, that the Jews, when they
learned the strength of the force sent against them, would
submit without further resistance, Vespasian delayed the
attack on Jerusalem for more than two years, choosing first
to reduce the cities of Galilee—Gadara, Jotapata, Gischala,
and others ; which, indeed, no prudent general could leave
unsubdued in his rear. The whole of this province, which
had been placed under the government of the celebrated
historian, Josephus,[1] remained throughout this period in a
state of internal dissension, fomented in a great measure by
the notorious John of Gischala, giving but little hope of a
successful resistance to Rome when the actual struggle
should begin. Yet some of these cities, notably Gamala
Tarichæa, above all Jotapata, where Josephus commanded in
person, offered a protracted and desperate resistance.[2]

---

[1] Flavius Josephus was born A.D. 37 at Jerusalem, and was connected
on the mother's side with the Asmonæan family. He received a liberal
education, and at the age of 20 attached himself to the sect of the
Pharisees. When the war with Rome broke out he was made Governor
of Galilee, and defended Jotapata for nearly seven weeks against
Vespasian. When it was taken, he fell into the hands of the enemy,
by whom he was favourably received. He now attached himself to the
Romans, and was present in Titus's camp during the siege of Jerusalem.
He accompanied the conquerors to Rome, where he wrote his historical
works. He died about the end of the first century. His countrymen
have generally regarded him as a traitor.

[2] The fall of Jotapata is one of those occurrences, often repeated in
the history of the Jews, which strikingly illustrate their national character.

When the road to Jerusalem had been laid fully open, the civil strife, by which the empire had been distracted, had come to an end. Galba, Otho, and Vitellius, one after another, had succeeded to the Imperial sceptre, only to have it snatched from their grasp ; and, finally, Vespasian had been advanced to the throne of the Cæsars. Leaving to his son Titus the task of reducing to obedience the rebellious city, Vespasian set sail for Italy ; and the Roman army, 60,000 strong,[1] advanced under its new leader to the final encounter in the spring of A.D. 70.

Jerusalem was at that time one of the strongest, as well as one of the most picturesque, cities in the world. It stands upon a rocky plateau about 2,600 feet above the level of the sea. On all sides except one it is surrounded by mountains ; which do not, however, rise to a much greater altitude than the city itself. The plateau consists of two principal emi nences, Zion and Acra, on the former of which stood the Upper City, or the City of David, and on the latter what was called the Lower City. A third—a smaller and somewhat lower hill, called Moriah—was anciently divided from Mount Acra by the Tyropœon, or Valley of the Cheesemongers, which was filled up by the Maccabees, who raised Moriah to the same level as the neighbouring hill. It was on the summit of Moriah that the Temple stood. In later times the suburb called Bezetha was added to the city, and the whole environed by walls.

Of these there were three—one inside another. The first began on the north side at the tower called Hippicus, terminating at the western cloister of the Temple. The

---

After a desperate defence, when the place had been carried by assault, the remnant of the garrison took refuge in a cavern ; and here, rejecting the offers of the Romans, they, by mutual consent, slew one another, until only Josephus and one of his men were left alive. These two then gave themselves up to the mercy of Vespasian.

[1] Titus had four Roman legions, and a large force of Greek and Syrian auxiliaries. The number, 60,000, has been objected to, as an exaggeration, but it is probably rather under than over the mark.

second wall began at the gate called Gennath, enclosing the northern quarter of the city only, and ending at the Tower of Antonia. The third, which was designed to protect Bezetha, was incomplete at the time of the outbreak of the Jewish war, but was then completed, in anticipation of the approaching siege. These walls were strengthened by towers of solid masonry—some of the stones being of enormous size—and rose to a great height above the level of the walls. The Tower of Antonia stood on a rock ninety feet high, the fortress itself being fully seventy feet higher; and at the portions not defended by these walls, the platform of rock itself, sinking down, as it did almost with a sheer descent, into the ravines below, formed an impregnable defence. In times when the use of gunpowder was unknown, it could be captured only by blockade, or after the most frightful waste of human life.

Meanwhile the city was distracted by factions, which appeared to be more likely to destroy one another than to maintain a successful defence against an enemy. After the massacre of the Roman troops, Ananus the High Priest, a wise and good man, gained some authority in the city, and endeavoured to counteract the influence of the Zealots. He might have succeeded in averting the war. But Eleazar, the leader of the Zealots, and John of Gischala,[1] the chief of the Galilæans, conspired against him, and by night introduced the Idumæans, in overwhelming force, into the city. By them Ananus and his friends were murdered, and Jerusalem thenceforth was given up to hopeless anarchy.

Such authority as there was, rested with the chiefs of the

---

[1] John was the son of Levi, and a native of Gischala, who began his career as a robber, and raised a band, it is said, of 4,000 men. In craft, daring, and merciless cruelty he has never been exceeded. He defended Gischala, from which he fled when its capture was imminent. He repaired to Jerusalem, where he gained great ascendency, and with Eleazar and Simon defended it to the last. At its capture, he surrendered to the Romans, and was sentenced to imprisonment for life.

three factions, Eleazar, John, and Simon ;[1] but between these there was not only no accord, but the most bitter and persistent animosity. Of the Zealots there were about 2,500, of the Galilæans 6,000, and of the Assassins (as Simon's followers were called) 10,000 Jews and 5000 Idumæans. Few of these, comparatively speaking, had undergone any military training. But their desperate and fanatical courage, stimulated by their total disregard of all laws, human and Divine, rendered them the most formidable enemies that Rome herself ever encountered. Not only between the three leaders, but their followers also, there subsisted the bitterest hate, which they gratified by continual quarrels and murders ; and had it been in their power, they would gladly have exterminated one another. Yet in the field they combined against the common foe with the most perfect unanimity.

The great bulk of the inhabitants awaited the approach of the Romans with uneasiness and alarm. The city was densely crowded, multitudes having come in from the country to celebrate the Passover. Josephus's numbers are doubtless an exaggeration.[2] But, on the other hand, there has been a tendency among modern writers to err in the opposite direction. It may safely be affirmed that the total of inhabitants, when

---

[1] Simon, the son of Gioras, was a man as fierce and lawless, though hardly as crafty, as his rival John. He was a native of Gerasa, and first appeared in history when he attacked the troops of Cestius Gallus in their retreat from Jerusalem. Driven out of Judæa by Ananus, he took possession with his banditti of Masada, and ravaged the neighbourhood. The Idumæans rose against him and, after several battles, drove him out of the country. Soon afterwards they captured his wife, whom they carried to Jerusalem. Simon repaired thither with his followers, and terrified the citizens, by his barbarities, to surrender her to him. In the spring of the following year, A.D. 69, a party in Jerusalem, headed by Matthias, invited Simon to enter the city. Then ensued an internecine struggle between the three factions, which lasted until the Romans environed the city, and indeed to the end of the siege. When the city was at length captured by the Romans, he surrendered himself prisoner, was conveyed to Rome, figured in the triumphal procession of Vespasian and Titus, and was then put to death.

[2] See Appendix I.

the Roman standards came in sight, could not have been less
than a million, and probably exceeded that amount. There
was much, independently of the terror of the Roman name, to
awaken their apprehensions. There had been signs in heaven
and on earth of approaching disaster. A fiery sword is
said to have hung over Jerusalem, day and night, for many
months. The whole sky on one occasion was full of what
seemed to be chariots and horses of fire, environing Jerusalem.
It was whispered that the great gate of the Temple had opened
of itself at midnight, and a voice had been heard to exclaim,
'Let us depart hence.' A simple herdsman, Jesus, the son
of Hanani, was suddenly seized with the spirit of prophecy,
and for several years went up and down the city exclaiming,
'Woe, woe, to Jerusalem!' He was carried before the Roman
governor, and scourged till his bones were laid bare. But he
never desisted from his mournful chaunt, until one day during
the siege he was struck by a stone from a catapult, and slain.

But nothing daunted the determined spirits of the garrison.
At the very outset of the siege, Titus had a signal proof of the
character of the enemies with whom he had to deal. He had
approached the city for the purpose of surveying it, accompanied by 600 horsemen, never dreaming that they would be
rash enough to assail him, and rather anticipating that his
presence would strike terror into them, and induce them to
capitulate. But the moment he approached the walls the
Jews sallied out, surrounding his troop, and cutting him off
from his supports; and it was only by the most desperate
exercise of personal valour that he escaped being slain. On
the following day they twice attacked the tenth legion, while
engaged in fortifying the camp, and threw it into confusion;
and it was Titus's promptitude alone which averted a great
disaster. Soon afterwards they contrived to allure a body of
Roman soldiers under the walls, by a pretended offer of surrender, and almost entirely cut it off. It became at once
evident that if these men were to be conquered, or even kept in
check, the utmost vigilance and promptitude would be required.

Two fortified camps were accordingly formed, too strong to be attacked even by desperate men; and then the siege proper commenced. After careful survey, Titus resolved to assault the triple wall on the north side of the city; which was, after all, less difficult to surmount than the mighty ramparts, reared by nature and aided by art, which the other parts of the defences presented. He accordingly constructed three great walls, cutting down for the purpose all the timber which was to be found near the city. On these he set up his military engines, which hurled huge stones and darts against the defenders of the wall, and then set the rams at work to batter it down. Towers were also erected, sheeted with iron, so as to be proof against fire, and overtopping the defences, thus rendering it impossible for the defenders to man the ramparts. After a desperate attempt to set the works of the besiegers on fire, the Jews were obliged to abandon the outer wall, and fall back on the second.

This was captured and thrown down in a much shorter space of time than had been spent on the reduction of the former. But the success was not obtained without more than one repulse, and heavy loss; and the defences still to be surmounted appeared so formidable, garrisoned as they were by men whom nothing could daunt or weary out, that Titus resolved to make a display under their eyes of his whole military array, in the hope that by showing the impossibility of ultimate resistance, he might induce them to surrender. He caused all his troops to pass in review before him, in sight of the city, all arrayed in their complete accoutrements and observing the strictest form of military discipline—a splendid but terrible sight to men who knew that it was impossible for them to offer effectual resistance. But Simon, and John, and their fierce followers knew also that they had offended too deeply for forgiveness; they looked sternly and gloomily on, but made no sign; nor would they reply to Josephus, when soon afterwards he offered his intercession. Titus saw that all efforts at conciliation were vain, and the last scene of the fearful tragedy began.

C

So unconquerable was the ferocity of the Jewish soldiery,[1] that it may be doubted whether even the stern discipline, the high military spirit, and the overwhelming numbers of the Romans would not have been compelled ultimately to give way before them, if it had not been that Rome now acquired two new allies, more terrible than any they had yet brought into the field. Jerusalem, at all times a populous city, was now crowded to excess by strangers, who had come over to keep the Jewish Passover, and had been unable to withdraw. The supplies of food soon began to fail, and the famine which ensued grew every hour more pressing. The soldiers had to supply their own wants by making the round of the houses, and tearing their daily meals from the mouths of their starving fellow-citizens. Numbers of these were driven by hunger to steal out of the city by night, to gather herbs and roots, which might afford temporary relief. Titus, hoping to terrify the besieged by a display of severity which would save in the end more lives than he sacrificed, ordered these unhappy wretches to be crucified in the sight of their countrymen ; and the city in which the Lord of Life had undergone the same form of death was surrounded by a multitude of crosses, on which the agonized sufferers slowly yielded up their lives in torment. Others, who implored the protection of the Romans, were ruthlessly ripped open in vast numbers by the barbarous soldiery, who believed that the fugitives had swallowed gold, which they would find in their entrails. The fate of these, dreadful as it was, was less terrible than that of the wretches who remained to perish of famine. Scenes almost too shocking for belief have yet been recorded on authority which cannot be dis-

---

[1] An extraordinary instance of the desperate courage with which the Jews fought occurred about this time. Antiochus, King of Commagene, had arrived in Titus's camp, with a chosen band of youths, armed in the Macedonian fashion. He expressed his surprise that Titus did not take the city by escalade. Titus suggested that he should himself make the attempt with his warriors. This he did ; but though his men fought with the utmost valour, they were all killed or severely wounded.

puted. Husbands saw their wives perishing before their eyes, and were unable to save them; parents snatched the food from the mouths of their starving children; hungry wretches crawled to the walls, and entreated the soldiers to slay them, and failing to obtain this last mercy, lay down by hundreds in the streets, and died. Nay, the last horror of all but too surely was accomplished, and mothers slew and ate their own nursing children! The numbers of the dead lying unburied soon bred pestilence, and added to the horrors of the time. An attempt was made to bury the corpses at the public expense; but the accumulating numbers rendered this impossible, and they were thrown by thousands over the walls in the sight of the horror-stricken Romans.

Through all these frightful scenes the siege of the inner wall went on. The frantic followers of Simon and John continued to fight with unabated ferocity against their enemies without and their countrymen within the wall, undeterred by the sufferings of their fellow-citizens or the near approach of the avenging swords of the besiegers. It was at this time that the judicial murder of the High Priest, Matthias, took place. He was an inoffensive old man, who had introduced Simon into the city, hoping that he would restrain the violence of John. Simon now accused him of a treacherous correspondence with the enemy.[1] He was put to death along with his sons and several of the Sanhedrin.

Titus now built fresh walls on which to plant his engines; but they were undermined or destroyed by fire, and he was compelled to surround the whole city by a vast circumvallation, and then to erect fresh platforms and towers, from which the inner wall, with Antonia and the Temple, might be assailed. After several repulses and severe fighting, this was accomplished. The heights were scaled, Antonia levelled

---

[1] There may have been some grounds for this suspicion. A considerable number of the chief priests (including one of the sons of this same Matthias) effected their escape, and were kindly received by Titus.

with the ground, and the Temple itself laid open to attack. Struck with horror at the profanation of a place dedicated to the service of God, which must ensue if the strife was continued, Titus offered to permit the Jews to come forth and meet him on any other battle ground, promising in that case himself to keep the Temple inviolate from the step of any enemy. He represented that the daily services had already ceased, and the holy ground had been polluted by human blood. He wished to have no share in such impieties, and would prevent them, if he could. His overtures were contemptuously rejected. The Jews themselves set fire to the western cloister, and so laid bare the space between the remains of the Antonia and the Temple.

Another assault was now ordered, and a close and murderous strife, which raged for eight hours, ensued without material gain to either party. It was the 10th of August —the anniversary, always dreaded by the Jews, of the destruction of Solomon's Temple. Both parties seemed to have entertained the idea that the day would prove fatal to the second Temple, as it had to the first. But this apparently had proved fallacious. The Romans had retired, and the guard for the night had been set, when suddenly a cry was raised that the Temple was on fire. Some of the Jews had again provoked a skirmish. The Romans had not only driven them back, but had forced their way into the innermost court, and one of them had hurled a firebrand into the sanctuary itself, which had instantly caught fire. This was contrary to the express order of Titus; and he instantly hurried down, accompanied by his officers, to extinguish the flames. The courts were full of armed men engaged in desperate strife, and his commands were unheard or unheeded. The devouring fire wreathed round the stately pillars and surged within the cedar roofs. Before the resistance of the few survivors had ceased, the Temple was one vast pagoda of roaring flame; and when the morning dawned, the Holy House and the chosen nation had passed away for ever.

CHAPTER III

A.D. 72—131.

THE JEWS UNDER THE EMPERORS TRAJAN AND ADRIAN.

THE destruction of the Temple, though it was the death-
knell of the Jewish people, did not at once put an end
to the siege. The Upper City, into which Simon and John
had retreated, still held out, and was to all appearance
stronger and more difficult to assault than what had been
already captured. But the spirit of the Jewish leaders, fierce
as it was, had been broken by the failure of their cherished
hope—the direct interference of Heaven in behalf of the
Temple. They demanded a parley, which was granted them,
and Titus would have spared their lives, on condition of
absolute surrender. But they required terms which he refused to grant, and hostilities were renewed. After incessant labour, occupying nearly three weeks, Titus raised his
works to a sufficient height to enable him to attack the
walls by which the Upper City was guarded, and an assault
was made. It was almost instantly successful. The determined obstinacy of the defenders had sunk into sullen despair. They gave way on all sides ; their leaders took re-

fuge in the vaults beneath the city, soon afterwards surren-
dering to the mercy of Titus; and the whole city fell into
the hands of the besiegers.

But even this did not put a period to the war.   Three
strong fortresses, Herodion, Machærus, and Masada, garrisoned by men as fierce and resolute as the defenders of Jerusalem itself, still remained unconquered.   The first of these,
indeed, surrendered as soon as summoned ; and the second,
after some fierce conflicts with the Romans, was induced to
do the same.   But the third, Masada, the favourite stronghold of Herod the Great, offered a long and desperate resistance.   It stood on a lofty rock, on the south-west border
of the Dead Sea, and was only accessible by two narrow
paths on the east and west, winding up lofty precipices,
where the slightest slip of the foot would be inevitable death.
When these tracks, which were three or four miles in length,
were surmounted, the fortress of Masada appeared, standing
in the centre of a broad plateau, and surrounded by a wall
twenty-two feet high, defended by massive towers.   It was
strongly garrisoned, and supplied with provisions sufficient
for a siege of almost any duration.   Silva, as the Roman
general sent against it was called, blockaded the place, and
then erected a mound of enormous height, on the top of
which he planted his battering rams.   A breach was made, to
which the besieged opposed an inner wall of timber.   But
this the Romans set on fire and reduced to ashes ; upon
which the besieged, finding it impossible to offer further resistance, and resolved not to surrender, took the desperate
resolution of perishing by their own deed.   They first slew
their wives and children.   Then, appointing ten executioners
for the work, they all submitted their own breasts to the sword :
the ten then fell, each by his neighbour's hand, and finally
the surviving one drove the weapon into his own heart!
This terrible catastrophe forms a fitting conclusion to the long
catalogue of horrors which the Jewish wars record.

Judæa being now completely subdued, it remained for Titus

to determine how the vanquished were to be dealt with. Further severities could hardly be required, even if they were possible. The numbers which had already perished are very variously stated. Those given by Josephus may certainly be regarded as an exaggeration, while the estimate of some later writers clearly fall short of the fact.[1] It is enough to say, that the whole of Galilee and Judæa had become one vast wreck—the fields and vineyards wasted, the woods cut down, the cities heaps of ruins, the land a graveyard. The very soldiers were weary of the work of carnage. Yet even of the miserable remnant of the inhabitants of Jerusalem, such as were old and weakly, and would not therefore realize a price in the auction mart, were put to death. Of those that remained, the tallest and best looking were reserved to grace the triumph of the conqueror at Rome. The rest were sent to labour in the Egyptian mines, or despatched in batches to distant provinces—to work as slaves, or be exhibited in the amphitheatres, as gladiators or combatants with wild beasts. A large proportion of the captives is said to have died of hunger.

As regards the leaders, the life of John was spared, though of all men who took part in the defence of Jerusalem he least deserved mercy. Simon was carried to Rome, and walked in the triumphal procession which Vespasian and Titus led up to the Capitol. This is said to have exceeded in splendour all previous pageants. Among the spoils displayed were the golden table, the silver trumpets, the seven-branched candlestick, and the book of the law; and these, the sole surviving monuments of the glories of the Latter House, still remain sculptured on the entablature of the Arch of Titus, to attest to posterity this terrible tale of crime and suffering.

---

[1] According to Josephus's account, 600,000 perished of hunger during the siege; and the total of those who died during the campaign amounted to little short of a million and half. But that he exaggerates is beyond dispute. See Appendix I.

With the fall of Jerusalem and the overthrow of the Temple, as has been already observed, the national existence of the Jews terminated. Thenceforth, though they were to be found in large numbers in almost every country in the world, they were strangers and sojourners among other nations, no longer themselves a people. It must not, however, be supposed, though the mistake is a common one, that their dispersion dates from the conquest of Judæa by Titus. They had spread into distant lands long before that time, and had formed large and powerful communities. It was only a portion of the Jews that returned from Babylon after the captivity. A large number had remained behind, occupying the homes which they had made for themselves, and enjoying prosperity and peace. In Egypt and Cyrene they were almost as numerous; in Rome, and in other great Italian cities, they constituted no small section of the inhabitants. How widely they were scattered may be gathered from the catalogue given by St. Luke, in his narrative of the doings of the Day of Pentecost.

The real change which now took place consisted in the destruction of their great centre of life and unity. It was like cutting off the main fountain in some system of artificial irrigation. The waters still remained in a hundred reservoirs, but the system itself existed no longer. With any other nation in the world, the result, in the course of a few generations, would have been the disappearance of all the peculiar and distinctive features of the people. They would have become fused with, and incorporated in, the nations among whom they were dwelling, as was the case with the Danes and Saxons among ourselves. But though they have resided among alien races for two thousand years, they have ever dwelt, and still dwell, apart from them. They obey the laws and comply with the customs of the land in which they reside; they converse in its language and respect its religious observances. But they cling to the Jewish laws and customs, so far as it is possible for them to do so. The Hebrew is still their national language ; the ancient worship of Israel the only one they will render. Like the stream of the Rhone at Chalons, which mingles with that of the Saone, yet continues to retain the peculiarity of its colour, they are dwellers among many nations, but Jews after all, and Jews only.

It was this distinctive feature that enabled them, before the lapse of many years, to resume something of the organization which had been, to all appearance, destroyed by the heavy blow they had sustained. The Sanhedrin, which they had always acknowledged as the chief authority of Palestine, had escaped, it was said, the general wreck, and was presently re-established at Jamnia. How far this may have been the case is a moot point in history. But it is certain that a school of theology, commanding very wide and general respect, grew up in that city ; and its presidents exercised considerable influence over their countrymen. The Eastern Jews were under the authority of a chief, known as 'the Prince of Captivity,' while those lying more to the west acknowledged a similar ruler, who assumed the title of 'the Patriarch of the West.' The synagogues also, which had in later generations been set up in every Jewish city, though they could not supply the void caused by the destruction of the Temple, afforded, nevertheless, something of a centre of religious unity. In this manner, before the lapse of two generations, the Jews, with the amazing vitality that has ever distinguished them, had recovered in a great measure their numbers, their wealth, and their unconquerable spirit.

Throughout the reigns of Titus, Domitian, and Nerva, little is heard of them. It is said indeed that Vespasian ordered search to be made for any blood-relations of Jesus, the Son of David, whom he purposed to put to death, as possible aspirants to the crown of Judæa ; and Hegesippus affirms that two grandsons of St. Jude were cited before Domitian for the same reason. But we learn that they were at once dismissed as unworthy of notice. Nor, throughout Nerva's reign, was any burden laid upon them, beyond the didrachma imposed by Vespasian. But during Trajan's Parthian wars, which necessitated the absence of the Roman troops from the garrison towns of Africa, the Jews in Egypt and Cyrene broke out into insurrection, and terrible bloodshed ensued. It began with the massacre of the entire Jewish population at Alexandria by the Greeks, who had taken up arms to oppose them. Maddened by the tidings of this disaster, the Cyrenian Jews are said to have committed unheard-of atrocities; sawing in twain the bodies of their prisoners, or compelling them to fight in the amphitheatres—it was even alleged, feasting on their flesh. They are thought to have slaughtered more than 200,000, some say 600,000 men. The revolt had hardly attained its height, when it was followed by two others, one in Cyprus, and the other in Mesopotamia. They were put down after a little while, with frightful carnage, by the Romans and more particularly by Lucius Quietus, one of the ablest generals of the day. Trajan's anger seems to have been greatly roused by the outbreak, for which he felt that his mild and equitable government had given no adequate cause. He required their total expulsion from Mesopotamia; and it is likely that his death in the ensuing year alone prevented the accomplishment of his purpose.

The Jews, however, fared little better under his successor, Adrian. This emperor had been a witness of the atrocities perpetrated by the Jews during the insurrection in Cyprus; and he had probably some reason for anticipating a similar demonstration in Palestine. Scarcely fifty years had elapsed since that land had been reduced to the condition of a desert.[1] But so irrepressible was the vigour of the Hebrew race, that the fields had been recultivated, the forests replanted, most of the cities rebuilt, and tenanted by large and thriving populations. It was obvious, if Jerusalem should rise from

---

[1] See note at end of chapter.

its ruins, and a new temple crown Mount Moriah, that a repetition of the war, which had cost Rome so much blood and
treasure, would inevitably ensue. It is not known with any
certainty what was the condition of Jerusalem at this time.
When the city fell entirely into the hands of Titus, he ordered
the whole of it to be destroyed, with the exception of the
three stately towers of Hippicus, Phasaelus, and Psephinus,
together with part of the western wall,—which was left as
a shelter to the Roman camp, where about eight hundred
legionaries were stationed, as a garrison, to preserve order
in the neighbouring country. How long they remained there
is uncertain. But no one seems to have interfered with such
persons as chose to return to the deserted spot, and erect
new homes out of the heaps of ruin that lay scattered round.
What numbers may by this time have assembled on the site
of the Holy City we are not told. But Adrian resolved to
put a stop to the fancies which, not improbably, really were
current among the Jews, by establishing a Roman colony on
the spot, and building on Mount Moriah a temple of Jupiter.[1]

It is probable that the emperor did not understand—
indeed, no heathen could understand—the horror and despair
which the publication of the design caused among the unhappy Jews. It was in their eyes the most fearful impiety—
the most horrible profanation. Their only hope lay in the
advent of the long-promised Messiah; who now surely, if ever,
might be expected to appear on earth, and redeem His people
from the depth of degradation and misery to which they had
sunk. In the midst of these alternations of despondency and
reassurance, a rumour suddenly reached them, that the long-
expected deliverer *had* at last made his appearance, and was
even then, on his way, at the head of an armed force, to take
possession of the ruins of Jerusalem, and prevent the per-
petration of the intended impiety. His name, they were

---

[1] He is said at the same time to have issued a decree forbidding the
Jews to circumcise their children.

told, was Barchochebas, 'the son,' that is to say, 'of the star,'—the star predicted by Balaam, 'which was to come out of Jacob, and smite the corners of Moab, and destroy all the children of Sheth.'

It is likely that the faith of the Jewish people in the appearance of a promised Messiah was by this time a good deal shaken. So many impostors had appeared, and lured their thousands to destruction, that even the deeply seated belief in his speedy advent was not sufficient to induce them to admit the pretensions of any fresh aspirant without careful inquiry. But in the present instance there were two considerations, each of which had been enough by itself to remove all doubt or hesitation. The first is, what has been already mentioned, the flagrancy of the insult offered to Almighty God; which, in the judgment of the Jews, was certain to bring down signal and immediate judgment on its authors. The other was the fact that Barchochebas had been accepted as the veritable Messiah by Akiba, the greatest of their Rabbis, and chief of the schools at Bethor. Something should be said of both these men, who played so conspicuous a part at this crisis in Jewish history.

— — —

NOTE TO CHAPTER III. ON THE NUMBER SLAIN IN THE JEWISH WARS.

The numbers of those slain in the Jewish wars, as reported by Josephus, are as under.

At Cæsarea	. . . .	20,000	At Mt. Gerizim	. . .	11,600
„ Scythopolis	. . . .	13,000	„ Jotapata	. . . .	40,000
„ Alexandria	. . . .	50,000	„ Gamala	. . . . .	15,000
„ Damascus	. . . . .	10,000	„ Gadara	. . . . .	15,000
„ Ascalon (3 massacres)	.	20,000	„ Jerusalem	. .	1,100,000
„ Joppa	. . . . . .	15,000			

At other places there were smaller totals, amounting altogether to upwards of 100,000, and making the entire sum of slain something less than a million and a half. But, as is elsewhere intimated (Appendix 1.), Josephus's statements must be received with caution. The large population found in Palestine in Adrian's reign is not easily reconcilable with it. Lightfoot's opinion seems the more probable one. Notwithstanding the great carnage, he says, ' Tantum abfuit gens a totali et consummatâ deletione, ut undique adhuc restaret innumera multitudo, quæ se pacate Romano nutui dedidisset, et pace sedibus suis quiete fruerctur. Ita ut Templum et Metropolim quidem desiderares, verum terram habitatoribus repletam, compositum Synedrii, Synagogarum, Populi statum illico cerneres.'— Lightfoot, vol. xi. 468.

CHAPTER IV.

THE REVOLT OF BARCHOCHEBAS.

R ABBI AKIBA was a proselyte of Canaanitish descent, a herdsman in the employ of a wealthy man named Kalba-Sabua. His master's daughter fell in love with him, and they were married, though without the father's knowledge. When he learned the fact, he drove them from his house ; and Akiba, at the age of forty, began the study of the law. He obtained great reputation in it, being accounted one of the chief authorities of that Rabbinical school of interpretation which upholds the absolute integrity of the received text, and teaches that every word, nay every letter of it, has its special and mystical meaning. After twelve years of study, when he had risen to considerable eminence, he paid a visit to Kalba-Sabua, followed by 12,000 disciples, who attended on his teaching. The old man continuing inflexible, Akiba returned to his studies for twelve years more, when he again appeared at his father-in-law's house, this time accompanied by 24,000 scholars. This evidence of the honour in which his son-in-law was held overcame Kalba-

Sabua's resentment, and he bestowed a large portion of his riches upon him. At the time of the revolt from Adrian, Akiba was nearly 120 years old.[1] He had been recently travelling in Northern Africa and Mesopotamia, where he had witnessed the zeal of his countrymen for the Hope of Israel ; and he was resolved that he and his should not fall behind them in courage and devotion.

His feelings must have been very warmly awakened to allow of his accepting Barchochebas, as he called himself, as the true Messiah that was to come. Who Barchochebas really was, has always been a problem with historians. By some he is said to have been a captain of banditti, notorious for his robberies and murders. But this may, not impossibly, be a calumny. He may have been the leader of one of the bands of wild warriors, who in those lawless times lived, like the more modern Bedouins, after a predatory manner, but are hardly to be regarded as mere robbers. Though undoubtedly an impostor, and conscious of his own imposture,[2] he was nevertheless a man of courage and ability, who might, under more favourable circumstances, have succeeded in establishing the independence of his country.

His first step, as we have seen, was to march with such forces as he could raise to Jerusalem ; where he put a stop to the sacrilegious work which had been already commenced by Adrian's order. He then proceeded to the strong city of Bithor, or Bethor, which lay at no great distance from Jerusalem. Here he was publicly acknowledged by Akiba as the Messiah, and large numbers of Jews, not from Judæa only, but from other neighbouring countries, flocked in to his standard. The levies at his command are said to have

---

[1] So, at least, say the Jewish biographers. But as they labour to assimilate him in all things to Moses, it is not unlikely that they have accommodated his age to their theories.

[2] He is said to have resorted to the expedient, already practised by pretenders before him, of filling his mouth with lighted tow, and so appearing to vomit flame.

amounted at one time to 200,000 men ; a force with which
the Roman troops in Judæa were wholly unable to cope.
The whole country fell under his dominion, and the utmost
zeal and loyalty were displayed in his service. The only
persons throughout the whole of Palestine who stood aloof
were the Christians ; who, knowing that Jesus Christ was the
true Deliverer of the Jewish people, could not acknowledge
any other to be such. Barchochebas is said to have punished
their defection, as he considered it, with the most savage
cruelty, regarding them as rebels and traitors, more criminal
than the Romans themselves.

Adrian, who could not for a long time be induced to
believe that the Jews, after the terrible lesson which their
fathers had learned of the consequences of rebellion against
Rome, would again provoke a mortal quarrel, treated the outbreak as a matter of but small importance. But the tales
that reached him, of large military stores being in the
possession of the Jews, who had for a long time past been
secretly collecting them ; of their countrymen from Egypt
and the East thronging to their standard ; and even of
multitudes of strangers to their faith and nation nevertheless
joining them, in the hope of obtaining plunder, roused him
at length to vigorous action. He sent a reinforcement of
troops to Ticinius, or Tinnius, by some called Turnus Rufus,[1]
who commanded in Judæa, and recalled from Britain Julius
Severus, the ablest officer of his time, to put down, what—it
was now impossible to disguise—had become a dangerous
rebellion.

Severus, on his arrival, found the condition of things so
unfavourable to the Roman arms that he did not venture to
meet Barchochebas in the field. The latter was in possession
of fifty fortified places, and nearly a thousand villages and

---

[1] The Jews often confounded this man, who is the object of their
special enmity, with the Terentius Rufus to whom Titus entrusted the
final demolition of Jerusalem, and who is almost equally detested by
them.

towns. Rufus had done little but exercise the most merciless
severities on all, even women and children, who had fallen
into his power; thus, without really diminishing the strength
of his enemies, increasing tenfold their exasperation. If he
had continued in command, it is far from improbable that the
yoke of Rome would, for a time at all events, have been cast
off. But Severus had learned the art of war in his campaigns
in Britain; and the consequences of the change of the general
in command soon became evident. Avoiding, as has been
already intimated, any decisive engagement, he harassed the
Jews by an endless succession of petty conflicts, in nearly all
of which they were worsted, driving them into their strong
holds, which he then besieged and captured,[1] until nearly all
that had revolted were reduced to submission.[2] By the end
of the third year of the war, the rebels were driven into the
strong city of Bithor, or Bethor, the situation of which is
uncertain, but is generally believed to have been somewhere
in the neighbourhood of Bethhoron. Here Barchochebas and
Akiba sustained, we are told, a long and terrible siege, 'the
rebels being driven,' says Eusebius, 'to the last extremities
by famine.' But there is no historian of this war to record its
particulars with the minuteness and accuracy of a Josephus.
The Rabbins have indeed given many details; but it is
impossible to rely on their statements. Thus, they relate,
that when the prospects of the besieged became gloomy and
threatening, one of the most zealous of their body, Rabbi
Eliezer, the son of Hamadai, following the example of Moses
at Rephidim, remained on his knees in prayer during the

---

[1] It is a doubtful point whether Jerusalem was one of the places so
taken. It appears most probable that it was; and that the work of
demolition, which had been begun by Titus, was completed by Adrian,
and every trace of old Jerusalem destroyed.

[2] There is evidence, however, that these successes were not obtained
without severe reverses. The language of Adrian in his despatches to the
Senate, in which he omits his usual assurance, that all is well with the
army, is significant of this fact.

whole time that the fighting was going on ; and the result of his prayers was, that the Jews fought with signal success, everywhere driving the besiegers back. To avert the disaster which seemed likely to result to the Roman arms, a treacherous Samaritan pretended to be discovered in carrying treasonable communications between the Rabbi and the Romans. Barchochebas, without inquiry, ordered the Rabbi to be slain ; and from that moment, it is said, the courage of the besieged gave way. Bithor was at length taken by storm. Barchochebas, according to some, was killed in action, according to others, put to death with cruel tortures by the conquerors. The slaughter that ensued is described as exceeding anything on record. The streams of blood were so great as to carry heavy stones the whole way from the city to the sea, and the ground for eighteen miles round is said to have been covered with corpses ! These flights of Rabbinical imagination may be dismissed as worthless ; but the more sober historian, Dion Cassius, reports that more than half a million perished by the sword, independently of vast numbers who died by disease and famine. Judæa once more became a barren waste. The cities were reduced to heaps of ruin, and the wild beasts tenanted the streets, The inhabitants who escaped the sword were sold as slaves, and transported to foreign lands.

The fate of the stern old Rabbi Akiba should not be passed over. He was treated with the utmost barbarity by Rufus, who seems to have been in command at the capture of the city. While under examination before the Roman tribunal, the hour of prayer came round, and Akiba, wholly disregarding the presence of his judge, and his own mortal peril, fell on his knees and calmly went through his usual devotions. Only a scanty pittance of water was allowed him in his dungeon ; but though he was consumed with thirst, he applied the water to the customary ceremonial ablutions. He was sentenced to death, and executed with the most barbarous cruelty, some writers affirming that he was flayed alive, and afterwards slain, others that he was torn to pieces with iron combs.[1]

Adrian now carried out his design, the commencement of which had been the immediate cause of the war, and built a heathen city on the site of ancient Jerusalem. This he called Ælia Capitolina—Ælia after his own name Ælius, and Capitolina, because it was dedicated to the Capitoline Jupiter. It was built in the style prevalent among the Romans of that day ; and was enclosed by a wall, which included Mount Calvary and the Holy Sepulchre, but did not take in Mount Zion. In the execution of his plan he was careful to show all possible dishonour to the localities which the Jews and also the Christians regarded with veneration. The temple of Jupiter Capitolinus was erected on the site of the Temple itself ; over the gate which looked towards Bethlehem, the city of David, a marble figure of a hog was set up ; on Mount Calvary was placed a statue of Venus, the foulest of the heathen deities ; and in the grotto at Bethlehem, where the Saviour was born, the worship of Adonis was established. Why Adrian should have been thus studious to profane these latter places, which, though they possessed special sanctity in the eyes of the Christians, had little or none in those of the Jews, does not appear. We can only suppose that the confusion between the Jews and the Christians, who for many generations were regarded as being merely a schismatical Jewish sect, misled the Roman emperor, even at this date and that he regarded Mount Calvary and the Holy Sepulchre as spots especially venerated by Jews. It is certain that no part of his anger was levelled against the Christians. He suffered them to settle within his newly erected city, and carry on their worship there without interruption. Ælia became, not long afterwards, the seat of a Christian bishopric.

---

[1] The Talmud affirms that his cheerful demeanour, while subjected to the most agonizing tortures, amazed his executioners, and that he told them, that having the love of God in his heart, he could not but rejoice.

But to the Jews he extended no such grace. He issued two edicts; one renewing the order which forbade the circumcision of their children; the other interdicting them, on pain of instant death, from entering the newly-built city, or even approaching so near to it as to be able to discern with their eyes the sacred precincts. It would seem that this prohibition was subsequently relaxed, so far as one day in the year was concerned, the anniversary, namely, of the capture of the city in the war with Titus, and again, in that with Barchochebas; for it is a singular fact that the two events occurred in the same month and on the same day.[1] On the recurrence of that day of misery and despair, they were allowed to pass the Roman sentinels, and gaze once more on the ruins of the past. Jerome has given a moving account of the scene, which, it would appear, he himself witnessed, two centuries afterwards—the crowd of dejected exiles, the sobs of the women, the agonized despair of the men, the jeers and scoffs of the bystanders, and the rude demands of the Roman soldiers for bribes of money, as the only condition on which they could be allowed to indulge their sorrow.[2]

---

[1] August 9th. This was also the day of the taking of Jerusalem by Nebuchadnezzar. One cannot but entertain suspicion of the accuracy of these statements.

[2] Their exclusion from Jerusalem is mentioned by many writers earlier than Jerome—Justin Martyr, Eusebius, and Tertullian, amongst others.

CHAPTER V.

THE JEWS UNDER THE ROMAN EMPERORS FROM ADRIAN TO CONSTANTINE.

DEPLORABLE as had been the condition of the Jews after the war with Titus, that of their descendants appeared to be still worse, when their struggle for independence was closed by the fall of Bethor. The devastation of their lands, and the destruction of their cities, could not have been worse than it was on the former occasion. But they were not then forbidden by their conquerors to return to their ancient homes, or practise the initiatory rite of their religion. To all appearance, the total extinction of the nation, by the absorption of its scattered members among the various communities to which they had fled for shelter, must inevitably ensue. Nevertheless, this did not occur. On the contrary, a period of nearly two hundred years now elapsed, during which they continued, undisturbed by Imperial severity or intestine commotion, to recruit their numbers and increase their wealth and influence in almost every portion of the Roman Empire. This appears to have been due in the first instance to the favour of Antoninus, who succeeded to the Imperial purple on the death of Adrian. A story is told of a miraculous cure of the Emperor's daughter by a Jew,[1] in requital of which the edict forbidding circumcision was repealed. But the story rests on no trustworthy authority. The prohibition was renewed by Aurelius, when the Eastern Jews offended him by joining the standard of the rebel Avidius Cassius. But it was soon repealed, if it was ever acted on.

It is evident, however, that, notwithstanding the toleration extended to the Jews, they were closely watched, and little trust was reposed in their good faith. At Jamnia (a town, according to Eusebius, between Diospolis and Azotus), where a great Rabbinical school had been established after the fall of Jerusalem, the jealousy of the Romans was roused by an imprudent speech made by the celebrated Simon (or Simeon) Jochaides, the reputed author of the Book of Zohar, and the person by whom (as the reader is informed in the note) the cure of Antoninus's daughter is said to have been effected. On the occasion of some public debate, he denounced the rapacity and selfishness of the heathen rulers. For this expression of opinion he was condemned to death, which he only escaped by flight ; and the school at Jamnia was suppressed. On another occasion the periodical sounding of the trumpet, in the month Tisri, was mistaken by the governor of the city for the signal of a general revolt.

In Rome itself—indeed, in all the great cities of the Empire—during the reigns of the emperors who succeeded Aurelius, up to the time of Constantine, the Jews were but little interfered with. This was owing partly to their long residence in the capital. The date of their first settlement there is unknown.

---

[1] According to others, it was the daughter of Aurelius who was healed. A deputation had been sent to protest against the severe edicts of Verus. The celebrated mystic, Simon ben Jochai, was the envoy, and he cast an evil spirit out of the Emperor's daughter. The Rabbins assert also that Antoninus received circumcision. But their testimony on this, as on many similar matters, cannot be relied on.

It has been supposed to be coincident with Pompey's victories, which probably did bring a large number of Jewish slaves to Rome. Philo's testimony to this fact, and to their general emancipation by their purchasers, seems trustworthy enough. But it is certain that the Jews had spread far and wide among all nations before that date, and hence it is most unlikely that so great a commercial centre as Rome would be overlooked by them. Josephus says that 8,000 of them attended when Archelaus was received by Augustus ; and though Claudius banished them, it was only temporarily. It is plain that there were great numbers there, when St. Paul was imprisoned at Rome. Juvenal, again, speaks of the mendicant hordes who profaned the grove of Egeria ; and the testimony of Tacitus and Martial is to the same effect. The Jews were regarded with contemptuous dislike, but there was no inclination to persecute them. There was another reason, too, why they were treated with leniency. After Adrian's time, attention was directed to the Christians, as the professors of a faith distinct from, and alien to, Judaism. Thenceforth the Jews were regarded in a different light. As Christianity grew and spread throughout the empire, its converts came to be accounted the deadly enemies of the State ; and the Jews, who disliked them as much as the heathen did, were naturally welcomed as allies against the common enemy. In any persecution of the 'New Superstition,' the Jews were ever ready to take their part ;[1] and their wealth, their numbers, and their zeal rendered their help valuable. The Pagan rulers felt but little inclination to inquire into the shortcomings and offences of such useful partisans.

It will be proper here to say a few words respecting the Sanhedrin, which, during this period, as well previously and subsequently, exercised a certain authority. The origin of

---

[1] Thus it is mentioned that the Jews were more forward than the heathen in bringing faggots to burn the Christian martyr Polycarp—'as is their habit,' says the historian (*Polyc. Martyr.* xiii.).

this National Council is a matter of dispute. By some it is affirmed that it was first instituted by Moses (Num. xi. 16), and is identical with the 'Elders' of Joshua xxiv. 1 and Judges ii. 7. But even if that be so, there is no mention of it in subsequent Jewish history for some 1,200 years, and the absolute power exercised by the kings (as *e.g.* 1 Kings ii. 27-46) is altogether inconsistent with the existence of any such judicial body in their day. Others hold that the Great Synagogue, which Ezra established after the return from the Captivity, gradually developed into the Sanhedrin. But it is denied by writers whose opinion is of weight that there was any connection between the Great Synagogue and the Sanhedrin. Its true origin seems to have been in the time of Judas Maccabæus, or possibly his brother Jonathan. We read how the latter wrote a letter to the Lacedæmonians in the names of 'Jonathan the High Priest, the Elders of the nation, the priests and other people of the Jews.' It is likely that the High Priest and the Elders continued from that time forth to exercise supreme power in judicial matters, including that of life and death, until the time when Judæa became a Roman province, and disputes and jealousies with the Roman procurators on the subject ensued.

The statement has already, been noticed, that the Sanhedrin escaped destruction during the war with Titus. Some of its members were slain, but the greater part were allowed—so it is averred—to depart from Jerusalem, and settle at Jamnia. Thence they removed to Sepphoris, and afterwards to Tiberias, on the Sea of Galilee, whence the President of the Sanhedrin came to be styled 'the Patriarch of Tiberias.' His authority was acknowledged by all Jews residing within the limits of the Roman Empire.[1] How far obedience to him was voluntary, how far a matter of compulsion, it would not be very easy to determine. The Romans in all likelihood would be

---

[1] Origen affirms that the power of the patriarchs was little less than that of a king (Orig., *Epist. ad Afric.*).

tolerant enough of the exercise of any such authority, which did not infringe their Imperial power—nay, would probably refer to it all matters relating to the peculiar usages of the Jews, in the same spirit in which Claudius Lysias wrote to Felix, and Gallio refused to listen to the Jewish disputants. The people on their part would readily submit themselves to the Patriarch of their own nation, if only in protest against the hated rule of the stranger. Hence, for many generations, Gamaliel and his successors wielded a wide and undisputed authority.[1]

The Sanhedrin consisted of seventy-one members, who were chosen entirely for the moral excellence of their characters. No young or unmarried man, no alien, and no one who followed a disreputable calling, was eligible. With these exceptions, membership was open to all ranks and conditions of men.

To this era belongs the Jerusalem Talmud; but of that, and also of the Babylonian Talmud, the reader will find a full account in Appendix II.

---

[1] The Presidents of the Sanhedrin are said to have been—

1. Ezra, who, according to this list, must have survived to the reign of Darius Codomannus, fully 200 years.

2. Simon the Just (identified by some with Jaddua who received Alexander the Great).

3. Antigonus of Soco.

4. Joseph of Zeredah.

5. Joshua, banished by Hyrcanus.

6. Judah, contemporary with A. Jann.

7. Shemaiah.

8. Hillel, the renowned Jewish Doctor.

9. Simeon, son of Hillel, supposed by some to be the same who took Jesus into his arms (St. Luke ii. 25).

10. Gamaliel (St. Paul's teacher).

11. Simeon, son of Gamaliel, killed during the siege of Jerusalem.

12. Jochanan.

13. Gamaliel II., son of Simeon, first Patriarch of Jerusalem.

14. Simeon, called the Just.

15. Judah II., called Hakkadosh.

16. Gamaliel III., in whose time the Sanhedrin is said to have ceased to exist.

17. Judah II.

18. Hillel II., who drew up the permanent Jewish calendar.

19. Judah III.

20. Hillel III.

21. Gamaliel IV., with whom the Patriarchate of Tiberias expired, A.D 429.

To resume our narrative. At the accession of Septimius Severus, who attained the Imperial purple at the close of the struggle which ensued after the murder of Commodus, the Jews are said to have received harsh treatment at his hands ; which may well occasion the reader surprise, as they almost everywhere joined his standard, as the rival of their bitter enemy, Niger. Yet it is certain that he re-enacted the old laws against proselytism, or entering the precincts of Jerusalem ; and, if Eusebius is to be credited, he actually made war on the Jews, and a triumph was decreed him for his successes in the campaign.[1]   But even if this be true, his anger must soon have subsided ; for during his reign they enjoyed a considerable share of his favour, for which writers hint that they had to pay heavily. It would appear again that they prospered under the rule of his depraved and barbarous son Caracalla.[2] This Emperor is said in early life to have been warmly attached to a Jewish playmate, the only person for whom he seems ever to have felt any affection. A few years afterwards they had a still more extraordinary and discreditable patron in Heliogabalus, the very vilest, it may safely be affirmed, of all the Roman emperors. Actuated by the strange caprice which commonly swayed his actions, he adopted the Jewish customs of circumcision and abstinence from swine's flesh. It does not appear, however, that he bestowed any special marks of regard on the Jews, in consequence of the inclination he showed for their peculiar tenets. Their religion, in fact, was only one out of many from which he borrowed one observance or another ; and if it is true that he was on the point of pro-

---

[1] It may be that it was not against the Jews, but the Samaritans, that Severus waged war, and that he temporarily confounded them with the Jews. The Romans continually made such mistakes.

[2] Some of the Rabbins assert that Caracalla received circumcision, but with no more evidence in support of their statement than in the instance of Antoninus. There was, however, something unusual in the education of Caracalla. Tertullian says that he received a Christian education ' lacte Christiano educatus ' (Tertull. *ad Scop.*). If so, he profited but little by it.

claiming himself to be the chief object of all religious worship, which all must render him on pain of death, his murder came only just in time to save them from a sharp persecution. Under his successor, Alexander Severus, they are thought to have experienced unusual kindness,[1] because that prince had imbibed from his mother Mammæa (the disciple, it is said, of Origen) a great prejudice in their favour. He did show some feeling of this kind, in that he set up the statue of Abraham in his private chapel, as one of those worthy of Divine honours.

But it should be borne in mind that this virtuous prince was after all a heathen, and had very vague and imperfect ideas about religion. He regarded all good men as equally worthy of honour, and his theology hardly extended further. In the shrine already referred to, he placed not only the statue of Abraham, but of Orpheus, Apollonius Tyaneus,[2] and Jesus Christ! It is needless to say that the man who did this could have been no proselyte to Judaism (let the Rabbins say what they will), or to Christianity either.

A similar protection was extended to the Jews during the reign of Philip the Arabian—another sovereign about whom similar fancies are entertained by Jewish writers, and with no more reason, apparently, than in the other instances. The Christians also experienced the same merciful sway. But with the accession of Decius, A.D. 249, the persecution of the Christians, which had slumbered, with only some slight and

---

[1] This seems to have been notorious, as the nickname of the 'Ruler of the Synagogue,' given him by the wits of the day, seems to indicate.

[2] This extraordinary man was born at Tyana, in Cappadocia, a year or two before our Lord. Hierocles, A.D. 300, wrote a comparison between him and Jesus Christ, in which the main points of resemblance are his (supposed) miraculous birth and power of working miracles, his attempt to reform the religion of the world, and the voice from heaven, which is said to have summoned him from earth. His history, written by Philostratus is overlaid with exaggeration and fable ; but he is to be regarded rather as an enthusiast and a mystic than as an impostor. His fame was at its zenith in the time of Alexander Severus.

partial renewals, since the time of Aurelius, broke out with greater violence than ever, and continued to rage, with rare intermissions, through the reigns of successive emperors, until the accession of Constantine. There is little or nothing to record respecting the Jews during this period, so far as those of the West are concerned, unless the war waged by one of the most powerful of the later occupants of the Imperial throne, Aurelian, with Zenobia, Queen of Palmyra, may be thought to have some relation to Jewish affairs. This princess is said to have been a descendant of the Asmonæan family, or, at all events, of Jewish birth,[1] and to have been brought up in the Jewish faith. Some go so far as to say she was a zealous professor of it.[2] It is certain that she built splendid synagogues for the use of the Jews, and advanced them to the highest posts of dignity. The celebrated Paul of Samosata,[3] who enjoyed her special favour, has been thought to have attempted to effect a reconciliation between Christianity and Judaism, insisting on the necessity of the rite of circumcision, and teaching that Jesus was, although a man, one in whom the Divine *Λόγος* dwelt. This, it is thought, may have had her approval. If such was really his design, it proved, as might have been expected, a total failure, both parties alike rejecting his teaching. After the fall of Zenobia, he was deprived of his office, and vanished into obscurity.

---

[1] Theodoret, *de Hær. Fab. Athanas, de solit. vit.*

[2] Zenobia has been claimed as an upholder of, if not a convert to, Christianity. She was probably an eclectic with no settled faith. Hence her patronage of Paul.

[3] This notorious heresiarch was a native of Samosata, in Syria. He was made Bishop of Antioch A.D. 260; but his elevation seems to have turned his head. He thenceforth affected great state and splendour. Encouraged by the favour of Zenobia, he usurped great power in the Church. To gain her favour, it is said, he attempted the alleged compromise between Judaism and Christianity. A council was held A.D. 265, to consider his opinions, over which Firmilian presided, and by which he was condemned. He refused to obey the decree; but a second council was thereupon summoned, by which he was deposed, and its sentence was confirmed by Aurelian.

But in any case her history belongs more properly to that of the Eastern Jews, that large section of the Hebrew race which had spread far to the eastward of the great river, and who dwelt under the rule of the Patriarch, known by the title of the 'Prince of the Captivity.' It will be proper now to turn to their affairs.

CHAPTER VI.

THE PRINCES OF THE CAPTIVITY.—MANES.—THE JEWS UNDER THE ROMAN EMPERORS FROM CONSTANTINE TO JULIAN.

IT is probable that the authority exercised by the Patriarchs of the East[1] grew up after the abandonment by Adrian of his predecessor's conquests beyond the Euphrates. The power of the Parthian kings had been broken by the victories of Trajan ; and in the remoter parts of their dominions they exercised but a feeble authority. Hence little opposition would be offered to the rule of the Jewish Patriarch—the less, because the respect and obedience rendered to him did not in any way trench on the allegiance due to the civil ruler.

His power appeared to be everywhere firmly established ; yet in the ensuing generation it was assailed, and in a great measure superseded, by the interference of his Western rival, the Patriarch of Tiberias. Simeon, son of Gamaliel II., called

---

[1] Josephus, who wrote as late as Trajan's reign, evidently knows nothing of them.

'the Just,' was a man of ambitious and restless character. Believing that Jerusalem was the true centre of Jewish unity, and that his Patriarchate was, in reality, the Patriarchate of Jerusalem, he argued that he ought to exercise undivided sway over the whole of the Jewish community, and regarded his brother of Babylon as a usurper. He sent a delegate to him, accordingly, who was instructed to approach him with all possible deference ; but as soon as he had made good his position, to throw off the mask, and demand his submission, His scheme took effect : the delegate was kindly received. and admitted to the confidence of his entertainers ; when he suddenly changed his tone, and sharply censuring some of the prince's acts, required, in the name of the Patriarch of Jerusalem, that they should be rescinded. A scene of angry resistance followed. But the name of Jerusalem had too strong a hold on the heart of every Jew to allow of any successful opposition. The Babylonian potentate was obliged to succumb, and until the Patriarchate of Tiberias ceased to exist continued to hold a place subordinate to his rival.

But in the succeeding century the Prince of the Captivity recovered all, and more than all, the power exercised by his predecessors. Tales are related of his grandeur and magnificence, which it is difficult to credit, and the more so, because they do not seem to have diminished after the accession of the Persian kings,[1] who might reasonably have been expected to be jealous of such subjects. The Patriarch was wont to be installed in his office with the greatest pomp. He was carried in a splendid procession, attended by the Rabbins, and preceded by trumpets, to the Synagogue, where he was formally admitted to his office, amid the prayers and blessings of the people. He then returned in like fashion to his palace, where he entertained his chief officers at a sumptuous banquet. He lived in the seclusion usual among

[1] The Parthian kingdom, after a long decline, may be said to have died out, A.D. 230.

Eastern potentates. But whenever he went abroad or entered a house he was received with every token of respect. He would sometimes, we are told, pay a visit to the king; when one of the royal chariots would be sent for his use—which, however, he would decline, remembering that, after all, he was an alien and a captive. But this studied humility was visible in nothing else. He was robed in the most splendid vestments, and preceded by a guard of fifty soldiers. The way was cleared before him, and all who met him saluted him with the profoundest respect. At the door of the palace he was met by the royal officers, who conducted him to the king's presence; where, after the first reverence had been paid, he was placed on the left hand of the throne, to confer with the sovereign on the affairs of the State.

It seems that intercourse with the Persians, who were fire worshippers,[1] and at least as bigoted in their religious opinions as the Jews, did not bring about enmity and persecution. Yet many of the Jewish practices must have been highly offensive to them. Thus the Jews have always interred their dead, and that practice is an abomination in the eyes of the Ghebirs. Again, there were certain occasions when no lights were permitted to be kindled except in the Fire Temples;[2] and the Jews were, in consequence, obliged to extinguish their household fires. We should naturally have expected that some at least among the Jews would refuse compliance, and so bring themselves into collision with the law. But we do not hear of any disputes of this kind[3] until the time of Sapor, who, at the outset of his reign, had shown the Jews great favour. But having embarked one day in a

---

[1] See note at the end of the chapter.

[2] Such is Jost's statement (ii. 141). He adds that the Jews obeyed the edict, but very unwillingly.

[3] Nothing more, that is, than discontented murmurs. It is related that when Abba bar Huna lay sick at Pumbeditha, and Rabbi Jehuda was attending him, a Magian came into the room and carried off the light : whereupon the Rabbi prayed that the people might pass under the dominion of the Romans again, rather than endure such ignominy.

controversy with the Rabbins on the subject of the burial of
the dead, he required that they should produce some passage
out of their Scriptures in which interment in the earth was
ordered. The doctors, unable to do this, gave some evasive
answer; which so incensed him that he began a fierce persecution. Sapor, however, died A.D. 272, and we do not hear
that the persecution was continued.

This is also the era of the notorious Mani, or Manes, who
founded the sect which caused such widespread strife and
division in the Christian Church. He is said by some to have
held many conferences with Jewish doctors during Sapor's
reign, and to have urged upon them that the acts attributed
to their God in the Old Testament, such as the extirpation
of the nations of Canaan, were inconsistent with the Divine
attribute of mercy. He was, in fact, according to Mani's
teaching, the God of Darkness; from whom they ought to
turn, to worship the God of Light. It is needless to say that
the Jews utterly rejected his teaching. Through their
influence, he lost the favour of Sapor, and was banished from
his dominions.[1]

Turning again to the West, we now come to the era of
Constantine, when the pagan idolatry was abolished by law,
and the religion of Christ publicly recognised. It is obvious
that this was a matter which gravely affected the Jews no
less than the heathen. They were as much opposed to the
newly authorized faith as any pagans could have been—far
more so, in fact, because they had a profound belief in, and
an earnest zeal for, their own creed, which was altogether
wanting in the instance of the heathen. It would seem that
the Roman Emperor contemplated making the religion of
Christ the religion of the world; in which case he must insist

---

[1] The date of Mani's birth seems uncertain. The time when he
attracted notice was circ. 272. He returned to the Persian Court circ.
278, when Hormisdas, or some say Varanes, caused him to be flayed
alive, for failing to cure the king's son; but Beausobre discredits this
story.

E

on its adoption by the Jews, as well as by all the other
subjects of the Roman empire. Whether the idea of compulsory conversion was ever entertained must remain doubtful.
But it is tolerably clear that Constantine did hope for, if he
did not anticipate, their adoption of his own faith. Conferences with Jewish doctors were held in his presence, at which
the disputants on both sides not only upheld their cause by
argument, but endeavoured to prove its truth by resort to
miracles. If Constantine hoped anything from trials like
these,[1] in which anything that appeared to be preternatural
was claimed on the one side as having been effected by
the finger of God, and denounced on the other as due to the
agency of Satan—he was certainly disappointed; and to this
failure perhaps may be imputed the severe laws against the
Jews, some of which he certainly decreed. Thus he issued an
edict that any Jew who imperilled the life of a Christian
should be burned alive ; he forbade proselytizing by the Jews
on the severest penalties ; he prohibited Jews from having
Christian slaves. In one of his Acts he styles the Jews 'the
most hateful of all people.' On the other hand, he has been
unjustly charged with acts of positive cruelty towards them,
which would have soiled the lustre of his name, if they had
been really committed. It is said, for instance, that having
heard that large numbers of them had assembled for the
purpose of rebuilding Jerusalem, he ordered their ears to be
cut off, and themselves banished,[2] and again that he required
them to accept baptism, whether they would or not, and to
eat swine's flesh on Easter Day.[3] But these charges refute

---

[1] To quote an example of these. A disputation was held between the
Rabbins and the Christians, headed by Pope Sylvester. The Jews
brought in an ox, and one of their miracle-mongers whispered the name
of God in its ear, whereupon it instantly fell dead. But Sylvester, no-way
discomposed, ordered the ox, in the name of Jesus Christ, to return to life.
Upon which, we are told, it got up and began feeding !

[2] Chrysost. *Or. in Jud.* - He seems to have confounded Constantine
with Adrian.

[3] Eutych. vol. i. 466.

themselves. Jerusalem was a large and noble city in his day, and it is absurd to talk of the Jews having wished to rebuild it. Nor among all his edicts, preserved in the Theodosian Code, is there a word about cutting off ears or compulsory eating of pork.

During this reign the Jews in Persia are accused of having stirred up a sanguinary persecution against the Christians. The latter had, for a long time past, been making their way into Sapor's dominions, to the great vexation of the Jews. But when at last they had succeeded in converting to their faith Ustazades, one of Sapor's chief officers, the irritation of the Jews rose to so great a height that they persuaded Sapor to put down the growing evil by the severest measures. A long and bloody persecution ensued, in which Simeon, Bishop of Ctesiphon, suffered martyrdom, the newly built churches were destroyed, and every trace of Christianity obliterated.

Constans, the son of Constantine, who succeeded to the throne A.D. 353, far from relaxing any of the severities laid on the Jews by his father, proceeded to greater lengths against them. Provoked by an insurrection they had raised in Judæa, he re-enacted the laws of Adrian and his father—adding to them that any Jew who married a Christian, who circumcised, or even kept, any Christian slave, should be put to death. He also greatly increased the heavy taxes with which they were already loaded.

It is no wonder that the accession of Julian—who, immediately after his assumption of the purple, publicly declared his abnegation of Christianity—should have been hailed by the Jews, as well as the pagans, as the dawn of a new day of freedom and prosperity to them. They hastened to present him with an address, representing, among other grievances, the great wrong done them in their exclusion from Jerusalem, the scene of the ancient glories of their race, the never-forgotten home of their ancestors, though the heathen were permitted to dwell there without molestation. While the most sacred sites were hidden by Christian churches, and devoted to Christian worship, the spot where their own beloved Temple had once stood lay desolate, and they were not even permitted to approach and gaze upon its ruins. Julian replied even more favourably than they could have hoped. He addressed the Jewish patriarch as 'his brother;' he inveighed against the unmerited severity with which they had been treated; he remitted the imposts of which they complained; annulled the decree by which they had been forbidden to enter Jerusalem; and finally gave them permission to rebuild the Temple on Mount Moriah, promising them every help in the execution of the work, and appointing one of his own favourite officers, Alypius, to superintend it.

His motives for this extraordinary step are not difficult to conjecture. He had not the slightest inclination to Judaism, being a devoted follower of the ancient creed of Greece and Rome, as held by the sages, whom he had made his study. But he wished, in the first place, to repair the injustice of past years; in the second, to conciliate the Jews, whose help might be of the greatest service to him in his Persian expedition; and in the third, to confute and establish the falsehood of Christianity. It was well known that the universal belief among 'the Christians was, that the voice of prophecy had declared that the Jewish Temple should never be rebuilt;[1] at all events, never until the Jewish people had accepted Jesus Christ as their God. If then he could prove that their belief was untrue on one point, why might it not be untrue on all?

It is needless to say that this unexpected grace filled the whole Jewish world with wonder and delight. Funds for providing the required materials poured in, in abundance; thousands offered themselves as labourers; men of the highest position and wealth, even delicately nurtured ladies, were seen digging up the ground with pickaxes made of gold and silver,

---

[1] Probably founded on Daniel ix. 26, 27. But that prophecy is obscure, and susceptible of a different interpretation. Even if the Temple had been rebuilt, every one of our Lord's prophecies would still have been fulfilled. (See Appendix iv.)

or carrying away the earth in silken handkerchiefs. The work advanced with great rapidity, till it was suddenly interrupted by flames bursting forth from the ground, accompanied by earthquakes, which repeatedly injured or destroyed the labourers engaged in the undertaking, and ultimately compelled them to desist from it.[1] Other strange circumstances are said to have accompanied this occurrence. Fiery crosses filled the air, and were seen on the dresses of the fugitives, as they escaped from the dangerous precincts. Some of the latter, who fled to the shelter of a neighbouring church, found the doors closed by some unseen power against them.

Doubtless much that has been related must be regarded as idle tales, the result of panic or exaggeration. But to suppose the whole occurrence to be simply attributable to natural causes appears impossible. This, however, is a matter requiring careful and minute inquiry. The reader will find a full examination of it in Appendix IV.

Not long afterwards (on the 26th of June, 363) the death of Julian, in battle with the Persians, put a period—not only to any renewal of this particular undertaking—but to the hopes in which the Jews had indulged, of Imperial favour especially bestowed on them. So ended the last recorded attempt to rebuild the Jewish Temple.

NOTE TO CHAPTER VI. ON THE RELIGION OF THE MAGI.

The origin of this religious belief is lost in the darkness of antiquity. The Magi existed, a body highly honoured, long before the time of Zerdusht or Zoroaster, who lived B.C. 589. He seems to have remodelled and formulated the ancient doctrine. According to his teaching, there are two independent ruling powers, Ormuzd and Ahriman, the principles of good and evil, symbolized by light and darkness.[2] Ormuzd created man good and happy. Ahriman marred his happiness by the introduction of evil. The strife between these two is to continue, until the victory is finally gained by Ormuzd.

Their religious rites are of a very simple character. They had origin-

---

[1] Cyril, it should be remarked, says nothing of these miracles, which are reported by Socrates, Sozomen, and Theodoret.

[2] Comp. Isa. xlv. 6, 7, where the idea is directly confuted.

ally neither temples, altars, nor statues, though later on, fire temples were built. They adored fire, light, and the sun, as the emblems of purity and beneficence. But, in the first instance at all events, they did not regard these as independent deities ; though afterwards, following the rule of all false religions, they offered worship to the symbols themselves, instead of the principles symbolized. They exposed their dead to be devoured by vultures, considering it an abomination to bury them in the earth. They still exist, a numerous people, in India, under the name of Parsees, a name derived from Pars, said to be the ancient designation of Persia. By some it is affirmed that Zoroaster maintained the existence of a third deity, superior to the other two.

CHAPTER VII.

A.D. 365-429.

JOVIAN TO HONORIUS.—MUTUAL JEALOUSIES AND OUT-
RAGES. — SUPPRESSION OF THE PATRIARCHATE OF
TIBERIAS.

JOVIAN, a stern enemy of the Jews, succeeded to the
throne vacated by Julian, but, fortunately for them, reigned
for a few months only. Valens and Valentinian, who followed, reinstated the Jews in the possession of their ancient
rights, but withdrew the exemption from serving public
offices, which they had hitherto enjoyed. Under their rule,
as under that of all succeeding emperors to the time of
Justinian, the main things that attract the reader's notice
are the mutual jealousies of the Jews and Christians, for
ever breaking out into acts of lawless violence, the blame of
which does not lie wholly on one side. The idea seems to have
possessed the minds of the Christians, even of their bishops
(whose training and office should have taught them better),
that the Jews as a race were the personal enemies of Christ,[1]

---

[1] I have elsewhere pointed out how fearfully mistaken is such a belief.
Granting, for the argument's sake, that the Jews who crucified our Lord

71

and, as such, objects of aversion and horror. This was a fruitful source of the wrongs, oppressions, and cruelties with which the pages of their after history are so deeply stained. The emperors strove, to the best of their ability, to hold the balance of justice evenly between the contending parties, but often found it impossible to do so. Thus, a synagogue having been burnt by the Christians at Rome (A.D. 387), Maximus the Usurper, who was at that time in possession of the capital, ordered it to be rebuilt by those who had wrecked it. For this righteous act he was denounced by Ambrose,[1] Bishop of Milan, who attributed his subsequent fall and ruin to that act, and induced Theodosius to revoke the decree. A similar outrage having been committed at Osrhoene, a city of Mesopotamia (A.D. 395), the same order was issued by Theodosius himself. But Ambrose again interfered, and addressed a most indignant letter to the Emperor. Overlooking altogether the wrong committed by the Christians, he argued that it was most unjust to require them to take part in building up a Jewish synagogue ; which was, he says, 'the home of perfidy, the dwelling-place of impiety.' It is said also, by Zonaras, that he preached publicly to the same effect at Milan ; but of that there is no evidence. Theodosius, who entertained the profoundest respect for Ambrose, was overawed, and withdrew his edict.[2] But that his conviction as to the justice of the case was

---

are to be regarded as His enemies, and, as such, just objects of our abhorrence, their genuine descendants, those who should inherit that abhorrence, are not their children according to the flesh, but they (St. John viii. 41, 44) who imitate their deeds. These are their genuine children. These 'crucify the Son of God afresh.' If we must abhor any as the enemies of Christ, let us abhor these.

[1] Ambrose, *Epist.* xxix.

[2] A similar case occurred at Antioch, under Theodosius II. (A.D. 423), where the clergy were ordered to make restitution to the Jews, whose synagogue they had gutted and plundered. The celebrated Simeon Stylites interfered on this occasion, and succeeded, as Ambrose had done, in annulling the Imperial order.

unaltered, we may see by the law which Theodosius promulgated in the last year of his life, which secured protection to
the Jews in the exercise of their religion, and decreed the
punishment of all who assailed them.[1]

On the other hand, the Jews were not behindhand in
displaying a very turbulent and rancorous temper. On all
occasions which offered themselves, and these were neither
few nor trivial, they did their best to harass and mortify the
Christians. The Arian controversy, which so grievously distracted the East, and for so long a period, could not have
concerned them. Yet they were always ready to support the
Arian leaders with their influence, and unite with Arian mobs
in attacking the churches of the Orthodox. Nor were these
the only outrages they committed. At some of their feasts,
when, ' flown with insolence and wine,' they issued forth from
the banqueting chamber, they were wont to insult and attack
any Christians they might meet. At the feast of Purim in
particular such displays were likely to occur. On that occasion it was their practice to erect a gibbet, to which a figure
representing Haman was fastened, and whenever his name
occurred in the service for the day they broke out into furious
execrations against him. On the occasion of one of the
celebrations of this feast at Inmestar, a city of Chalcis, near
Antioch, their insolence was carried to a most shocking height.
Rushing out into the street, some of the drunken Jews seized
on a Christian boy whom they met, and dragging him into
the house, fastened him to the gibbet, from which the figure
of Haman had been removed, and which, in mockery doubtless of the crucifixion, had been fashioned in the shape of
a cross.[2] They then proceeded to scourge the lad so severely
that he is said to have died under their hands. The Christians

---

[1] Cod. Theod. viii. 16.

[2] It is not improbable that the tradition of this occurrence gave rise
to the charge so often made, and which seems so inexplicable, against
the Jews in after ages, of crucifying boys in mockery of the Saviour's
passion, though no evidence of such an act was ever produced.

were roused to fury by the murder, and a bloody fight ensued, in which many lives were lost. This occurred A.D. 412.

Several strange stories are told of occurrences during the early part of the fifth century, which illustrate the temper of the times. They are mostly concerned with conversions ; to effect which great zeal was undoubtedly displayed; but it is not often of a kind that we can either admire or approve. Offers of worldly advantages of one kind or another were made by those who were anxious to secure converts ; and no one will wonder at hearing that many, in consequence, professed themselves willing to submit to baptism. These converts, however, were not inclined to be content with profit-ing once only by so easy a mode of obtaining the good things of life. They presented themselves as candidates for baptism at the churches of every sect in Constantinople. The practice was detected. A tradition relates that when one of these pseudo-converts was brought to the font, the water receded from the sacred vessel, so that the ministrant could not per-form his office. Startled at so strange an occurrence, he set on foot a strict inquiry, and elicited the fact that the man had already been baptized in the churches belonging to every sect in the city, except the one in which this incident was reported to have occurred. Unfortunately, the church be-longed, not to the Orthodox, but to the Novatians. The extent to which the scandal had reached is proved by the enactment of a law, which forbade the baptism of any Jew, until strict inquiry had been made as to his character and motives, and a certain noviciate passed.

Not unfrequently the conversions were what may be termed wholesale, large bodies of men offering themselves at the same time for admission to the Church ; and these were brought about after what most persons would consider a strange fashion. Thus, in the island of Minorca (A.D. 418), Severus, the bishop, had been greatly distressed by the presence of a Jewish synagogue under a Rabbi named Theodorus, and exerted himself to the utmost to effect their conversion. He

had heard that Theodorus was a man of unusual learning and
ability, as well as of the highest character, and well accus-
tomed to controversy—a formidable antagonist, in fact, for
whom, it was to be feared, the bishop himself was no match.
Nevertheless, fortified by the possession of the relics of St.
Stephen, which, it appears, had been left in the island, he
challenged Theodorus to a disputation, which he proposed to
hold in a church at Magona. The Jews declined the contest,
on the ground that it was their Sabbath day, on which they
could enter no unclean place. The bishop then proposed that
the meeting should take place in the Jews' synagogue ; and
when they came up in large numbers to his house, to decline
that suggestion also, he solved the difficulty by marching
with all his followers to the synagogue. A riot broke out
in the street, and the Christians pursued their opponents
into their place of worship, which they plundered and then
burned. This procedure failing to convert the Jews, a disputation was at last held, at which Theodorus made an oration
so learned and powerful that Bishop Severus was unable
to answer him. Happily, however, there was no need for
him to do so. When he had concluded, the whole of the
Christians, anxious to gain so worthy a proselyte, broke out
into a general cry, 'Theodorus, believe in Christ.' The Jews
mistook the words for 'Theodorus *believes* in Christ,' and
straightway, stricken to the heart by this terrible apostasy,
fled into the woods, leaving Theodorus in the hands of the
Christians. The bishop did not fail to point out to him that
the hand of Heaven was plainly discernible in what had
passed ; and Theodorus, perplexed by the position in which
he found himself placed, angered at his desertion by his
countrymen, and possibly influenced by the hopes of worldly
advancement, submitted to baptism ; and his example was
followed by his congregation. The bishop plumed himself
on his victory, and besought his brethren everywhere to adopt
the same method with the Jews. In burning down synagogues,
as Milman remarks, they were ready enough to adopt his advice.

Another general conversion took place in Crete (A.D. 432) where the circumstances, though not exactly similar, were equally strange. An impostor, who had assumed the name of Moses, gained so much influence over the Jews in that island, who, we are told, were numerous and wealthy, as to persuade them that he could open a way for them to the Holy Land through the waters of the Mediterranean, as his namesake had done of old through those of the Red Sea. The delusion spread so far, that the Jews abandoned their houses and lands and all their personal possessions, except such as they could carry with them, and having been led by their conductor to the top of a high rock, threw themselves by his order into the sea. He himself then disappeared,[1] having probably reaped all that he could hope to gain by the transaction. Great numbers were drowned, and more would probably have shared their fate, if it had not chanced that there were some fishing boats lying off that part of the coast, which came to their assistance. The occupants of these boats were Christians ; and this circumstance, added to the fact that the impostor had been a Jew, induced large numbers to adopt Christianity.

Turning to Egypt, always a place of importance in Jewish history, we learn that there were, about the middle of the reign of the Emperor Theodosius II., great disturbances, caused mainly by the continual feuds between the Christians and Jews. The latter had always been conspicuous, not more on account of their wealth and numbers, than of their turbulent spirit. This, however, was in a great measure stirred into action by the accession of Cyril to the bishopric of Alexandria, vacated by Theophilus, A.D. 412. Cyril was a man of great force of character, but vain, hasty, and imperious. He soon obtained a most commanding influence in the city,

---

[1] The historian Socrates is persuaded that the impostor was a demon, who assumed human shape to beguile the Jews. But seeing that the cheat resulted in a numerous conversion to the Christian faith, it is strange that he should have entertained such a notion.

of which the Prefect Orestes was naturally jealous. Desiring to punish the insolence of Cyril's followers, he ordered one of them, Hierax, a schoolmaster, who had committed some breach of the peace, to be publicly scourged. Cyril sent for the Jews who had delated Hierax to Orestes, and threatened them with his anger unless they adopted a different course in their dealings with the Christians. Anticipating that this threat would soon be followed by an open attack upon them, the Jews resolved to be beforehand with him. Having put on rings of bark, in order to be able to distinguish one another in the dark, they raised at midnight the cry that one of the principal churches was on fire. The Christians rushed out in great numbers to extinguish the flames, and the Jews falling upon them, made a great slaughter of them. In the morning Cyril armed his followers, and assailing the Jews in his turn, slew great numbers, plundered and burned their houses, and drove the survivors out of the city. Orestes interfered on their behalf, but was himself attacked, and wounded in the head by a stone. Both parties made their appeal to Theodosius, at that time a boy of fourteen. Whether it was that the Court of Constantinople was too much engaged with affairs of State to attend to troubles in Egypt, or that Cyril's private influence gained the ascendency, we are not told ; but it does not appear that any of the criminals, not even the murderers of Hypatia,[1] were ever punished, or the Jews, who had been expelled from Alexandria, reinstated in their homes.

Some years afterwards (A.D. 429), the Jews received a severe blow in the suppression of the Patriarchate of Tiberias ; which had existed for about three hundred years, but now expired in the person of Gamaliel IV., the ninth patriarch who had

---

[1] Hypatia was a young lady of Alexandria, professing heathenism, and of rare accomplishments, great beauty, and unspotted character. Cyril is said to have been jealous of her influence in the city ; and, in the hope of pleasing him by the deed, the fierce Christian mob tore her from her chariot, and cut her to pieces with oyster shells. This barbarous and revolting murder is the worst deed of those cruel and lawless times.

held that office. The revenue by which the patriarchs had been supported, was derived from certain duties levied upon the Jews residing in all quarters of the empire, the patriarch's collectors being sent everywhere for that purpose. It is probable that the tie which united the Jews to the ancient centre of their faith had for a long time been growing gradually weaker, as the severance itself widened ; and the periodical visits to Jerusalem, which had kept up the bond of attachment, had long ceased to be observed. It is said that petitions were presented to the emperors requesting the abolition of the impost. However that may have been, an edict was issued by Honorius, forbidding the levying of the duty at Rome, and, most probably, in any part of the Western empire. That raised in the East appears to have gone directly into the Imperial treasury. This step did not formally abrogate the patriarchal office, but it was a deathblow to it. Gamaliel retained the name, and some show of authority, during the remainder of his life, but no successor was appointed when he died.

CHAPTER VIII.

A.D. 429–622.

HONORIUS TO HERACLIUS.—JEWISH SLAVE-HOLDERS.—
JUSTINIAN.—CHOSROES.

THE great change in the condition of Europe, the first symptoms of which had appeared a generation or two previously to this era, now began to make itself everywhere felt. The irruption of the barbarian tribes of the North, which resembled at first the few drops of an approaching shower, became, as the century advanced, the heavy downpour of the storm itself. Every year witnessed their further advance into Europe, in vast and irresistible hordes, disorganizing, and, in some instances, wholly changing the face of society. There were new rulers in the seats of Government, new languages spoken in the streets of cities. The armies carried strange standards, and wielded weapons hitherto unknown in European warfare. Even at the plough and by the cottage fireside, there were forms and faces of a type hitherto unknown. In many places the ancient inhabitants had been driven into exile; in many more, they had been put to the sword; in many more, they cowered out of the sight of their new

masters. There must have been terrible and protracted suffering among high and low alike.

But there was one class upon whom these woes fell
harmlessly, and this class was the Jews. It is bitter for
men to be driven from their homes and deprived of their
rights of citizenship. But the Jew had no home to lose,
no right of citizenship to forfeit. His nationality had long
been destroyed, and could not be taken from him. He was
like Ladurlad, in Southey's poem, whom the flood could not
swallow up or the sea-monster destroy, because Kehama's
curse had rendered him secure against all minor ills. If the
country in which the Jew was a sojourner was threatened by
the approach of an invading horde, he simply removed elsewhere, and took his money with him. Nay, the march of the
barbarian armies, which brought terror and destruction to
others, was to him a source of profit. When some bloody
defeat on the battle-field, or some frightful sack of a
populous town, had plunged a whole people in misery and
desolation, the Jew would drive a thriving trade with the
ignorant conquerors, purchasing of them the spoil they had
obtained by the plunder of palaces and churches, for, it
might be, the twentieth part of their value, and conveying
it to lands which were, as yet, safe from invasion; where
they sold it again at an enormous profit. Their establishment in all the great cities of the known world, and the
strong bonds of brotherhood which subsisted among them,
made it easy for them to carry on mercantile transactions
of this kind : nor can the rapidity with which they acquired
wealth—and which was popularly attributed to their alliance
with the Evil One—be any cause of wonder to us. Even
in times when the principles on which commerce is conducted
have become generally understood and acted on, the Jews
have always had the advantage over their Christian neighbours, by reason of their greater astuteness and perseverance.
But in those days, when they alone understood those
principles, even in the rudest manner, it would have been

a marvel indeed, if they had failed to gather riches, almost as easily as a child gathers pebbles on the shore.

One very profitable, but somewhat odious, branch of commerce seems to have fallen almost entirely into their hands. After one of the great victories of the Goths or Huns, when large numbers of captives became the property of the barbarian conquerors, their native ferocity often induced them to put their vanquished enemies to the sword ; and possibly they might always have done so, had it not been that avarice, stimulated by the offer of money in exchange for them, proved the more potent passion of the two. The Jew knew what would be the value of an able-bodied slave in the markets of Alexandria or Constantinople, and was willing to pay, it might be, the sixth part of that price to the Goth or the Hun, for the prisoner whom he had at his disposal. None but the Jews, as has been observed, pursued this particular traffic ; and the consequence was, that large numbers of Christian slaves passed into the possession of Hebrew masters, who in every city exposed them publicly for sale. It would not have been human nature if the Jews, despised and rejected as they were by their Christian fellow-citizens, had not experienced a sense of triumph, at finding themselves in this manner the undisputed owners and masters of those who had long held them in contempt. It is even less wonder that the spectacle should have roused the greatest indignation among the Christians themselves.

By the ancient law it was illegal, nay, a capital offence, for a Jew to keep a Christian in bondage. But either this law was treated from the first as a nullity, or it had been repealed by one of Constantine's successors ; for the edict of Honorius, while it forbids Jews to proselytize their Christian slaves, allows the full right of ownership over them. Now, however, the Jews had become the masters, not of a few Christian bondsmen, but of large numbers of them, many being persons belonging to a higher station, and reduced to their present state of degradation by having been conquered

F

in battle with the barbarians. This appeared an intolerable
scandal ; and it is not unlikely that the old law of Constantine
would have been re-enacted, if it had not been for the pretty
certain fact that, in that case, all prisoners taken in battle
would thenceforth be massacred. Therefore, though many
efforts were made, and especially by the Church, to mitigate
the evil, it was never proposed to prohibit the purchase of
slaves by Hebrew masters. The Council of Macon, A.D. 582,
distinctly lays down that 'the conditions upon which a
Christian—whether as a captive in war or by purchase—has
become the slave of a Jew, must be respected.' All that is
stipulated for by that, or any other of the many Councils
which deal with the subject, is, that the slaves shall have the
right of purchasing their own freedom, or that others shall
have the right of purchasing it for them. The Councils,
further, continually exhort the clergy, indeed, all Christians,
to shelter any slaves who may take refuge with them from
the tyranny of their masters, and even to pay the price which
will redeem them from captivity.

It is needless to add that these injunctions had but little
effect. Neither clergy nor laity have, in any age, except that
of the Apostles, been thus ready to part with their money
for the benefit of any unhappy sufferer who might appeal
to them. Gregory the Great, who succeeded to the Papal
chair A.D. 590, was very earnest in his efforts to put down a
traffic which he regarded as abominable. His letters, addressed
to kings and bishops and others in authority, evince the
warmth of his zeal and the nobility of his nature ; but they
show also that all efforts, up to that time, to eradicate the evil
had proved abortive.

The condition of the Italian Jews at this period seems to
have been unusually prosperous. They were protected by
Theodoric, who several times—at Rome, at Milan, at Genoa—
interfered to chastise those who had wrecked and plundered
Jewish synagogues, and directed that due reparation should
be made. The Bishops of Rome, throughout the century,

and especially Gregory, towards its close, treated them with justice and clemency, and, though filled with an earnest desire for their conversion, repressed all violence or imprudent zeal.

But it was different in other parts of the world about this time. The attempts at proselytizing, which had hitherto erred on the side of holding out worldly inducements to bribe men to embrace the Gospel, were now exchanged for the still worse method of violent compulsion. Chilperic, the youngest son of Clotaire I., a monster of lust and cruelty, appears to have been the first who practised this. Believing, perhaps, that his own misdeeds might be atoned for by what he regarded as zeal in the cause of Christ, he forcibly compelled all the Jews in his dominions to receive baptism on pain of instant death. They appear to have complied—nothing more than the mere performance of the ceremony having been required of them—but to have carried on their own form of worship exactly as before.

Turning now to the Eastern Empire, we find that there is but little mention of the Jews during the fifth century of Christianity. But, whatever changes took place in their condition, we may reasonably infer that they were changes for the worse. Notwithstanding the religious distractions of the reign of the Eutychian Anastasius, the Church continued throughout this century to grow in power, several of the Roman emperors, Theodosius II., Marcian, and Leo, being her devoted adherents. We do not wonder at hearing that in the reign of Justin I., A.D. 518, who was at least as orthodox as any of his predecessors, the Jews were excluded by statute from all offices of state, as well as from holding commissions in the army. His nephew, Justinian, who succeeded him, not only confirmed these laws, but evinced such harshness to both Jews and Samaritans, as provoked a rebellious outbreak among the latter people. One Julian, who (like so many before and after him) professed himself the Messiah, stirred up an insurrection, and was only put down and slain after a bloody battle. Many of the Samaritans, we are told, became converts to the Gospel : but there are shrewd reasons for suspecting that their motive was to escape thereby the consequences of their rebellion.

Encouraged apparently by this success, Justinian proceeded to still harsher measures against the Jews. He no longer allowed their evidence to be taken against Christians. He materially limited their power of making wills and disposing of their property. He enacted that in case of a marriage between a Jew and a Christian—which he strongly discouraged —the control of the children should belong to the Christian parent. Finally, he interdicted the use of the Jewish Mishna, as a production full of absurdity and falsehood, and urged the use of the Greek language by the Jews, instead of the Hebrew. It is hardly necessary to add that these harsh measures had but little effect. The use of the Talmud was not discontinued, and the empire experienced, in the aliena- tion of a wealthy and powerful body, such as the Jews then constituted, a sensible loss of strength.[1] A few years after- wards a new Imperial decree somewhat modified the rigour of these enactments. The Samaritans were allowed to make wills ; but in case of intestacy, if any of their children had embraced the Christian faith, they inherited the father's property to the exclusion of the others ; if a will had been made, unbelievers could inherit one-sixth only of the property under it. About twenty-five years afterwards, the Jews and Samaritans in Cæsarea broke out in insurrection, and were with difficulty put down.

Farther eastward, under the reigns of the Persian sovereigns,

---

[1] What injury they were capable of inflicting on their oppressors, was seen plainly enough at the siege of Naples by Belisarius. Convinced that they would receive no mercy at his hands, the Jews persuaded the citizens to abandon the proposals for capitulation which they were meditating, by promising them supplies of provisions and arms. The siege was in consequence considerably prolonged ; and when the assault took place, the Jews defended one quarter with a desperation which caused great loss of life.

beginning with that of Artaxerxes (the successor, A.D. 384, of Sapor), the Magians, who had obtained the upper hand in the royal counsels, persecuted Jews and Christians with equal severity. Even the observance of the Sabbath by the former is said to have been suppressed. Nevertheless, we are told that the Prince of the Captivity still retained his office, and even his wealth and dignity. The animosities between him and Chanina, the master of the Jewish schools, are related at length by the historians of those times; but are intermingled with wild and fanciful tales, to which it is impossible to attach any credit. It was at some time during this dark period that the Babylonian Talmud, to which reference was made in a recent chapter, first saw the light. It was mainly the work of Rabbi Asa, or Asche, chief of the schools at Sora. But he died before its completion, and the finishing touches were given to it by his pupils. The date of its appearance is a matter of much dispute; but the probability is that it was first published during this period. (See Appendix II.)

Not long after its appearance—early in the sixth century—a fierce persecution was set on foot by Cavades, or Kobad, one of the Persian kings, who desired to oblige all unbelievers in Magianism to embrace its tenets. In his time a Rabbinical impostor, named Meir, who probably pretended to be the Messiah, raised a rebellion, which was prolonged for seven years. Whether the insurrection was due to the persecution or the persecution to the insurrection, does not clearly appear. The impostor pretended, as nearly all his prototypes had done, to work miracles, and, amongst others, to raise up a fiery column, which always accompanied his march, as had been the case with his fathers in the wilderness. He was defeated, and slain by Kobad, and the Prince of the Captivity was involved in his fate.[1]

---

[1] He was hanged, together with the President of the Council. No successor to him was appointed. His son, Zutia II., fled to Judæa, and

The Jews fared no better under Chosroes, or Nushirvan, called 'the Great,'[1] who closed their schools and forbade the propagation of their faith. But, notwithstanding this harshness, the severities of Justinian were felt by the Western Jews to be so intolerable, that they sent a deputation to Chosroes, inciting him to make war on the empire. They roused his cupidity by describing to him the riches which were to be found in Jerusalem, and offered to aid him with 50,000 men. Chosroes listened to their overtures, and twice made preparations for war. But on the first occasion Justinian purchased peace by payment of a large bribe; and on the second the superior generalship of Belisarius obliged him to retreat.

After a reign of nearly fifty years, Chosroes was succeeded by Hormisdas, a weak and vicious ruler, but who nevertheless permitted the Jews to reopen their schools; and a new series of presidents of these, called the Geonim, or the illustrious, assumed authority. Hormisdas was assassinated after a reign of eleven years, and a usurper named Behram (or Varanes, as he is also called) seized the throne, and received considerable support from the Jews. By the help of the Greek Emperor Mauritius, Hormisdas's son, Chosroes II. succeeded in crushing Behram, punishing at the same time with great severity the Jews, who had upheld him. Among others, the Jews of Antioch were put to death, or reduced to slavery.

In A.D. 602, Mauritius was murdered by Phocas, who

---

became President of the Senate there. The office, however, was subsequently revived, and lasted as late as the eleventh century. The Resch Glutha, or Exilarch, as the Prince of the Captivity was called, was, it should be remarked, a distinct person from the Geon. The latter was concerned with religious matters only; the former, with politics.

[1] Of this king many fables are related. A monkish chronicler says that he besieged a fortress defended by evil spirits. Failing to take it by assault, he summoned the ministers of all the religious bodies in his dominions, and ordered them to use their superhuman powers for its capture. The Magi, the Magicians, and the Jews, each in turn essayed the task, but in vain. But, it is added, when the Christian priests employed the sign of the cross, the place was immediately captured.

usurped the throne; and Chosroes, claiming to avenge his old ally, declared war on the assassin and marched on Constantinople. Meanwhile the Jews in Palestine, too eager to wait for the arrival of Carusia, Chosroes's general, rose against Phocas, who had attempted their forcible conversion, and laid siege to Jerusalem. It was defended by the Bishop Zacharias, whose first step was to seize all the Jews in the city. The besiegers gained possession of the suburbs, and began burning the Christian churches. The besieged retaliated by beheading 100 Jewish prisoners for every church destroyed. Neither party would be outdone in barbarity. Twenty churches were demolished, and the heads of 2000 Jews were thrown over the city wall! Unable to reduce the place, the Jews retired to join Carusia, under whose standard they presently entered Jerusalem. They had the insults and wrongs of five centuries to avenge, and they exacted the penalty with no sparing hand, their Persian allies permitting them apparently to do much as they pleased. Every Christian church was destroyed, and the entire Christian population, to the number of 90,000, massacred.

But neither they nor Chosroes reaped much advantage from this success. The war with Phocas was carried on with various fortune until 610, when Heraclius,[1] the son of the Exarch of Africa, attacked Constantinople, overthrew Phocas, and was proclaimed emperor in his place. After a few years of inaction, he roused himself to confront the enemies of the empire. In a campaign, extending over several years, conducted with amazing energy and ability, he recovered the whole of the provinces overrun by Chosroes, who was soon afterwards deposed and slain. Palestine was among the

---

[1] Heraclius is one of the most extraordinary characters in history. Some of his exploits are as grand as any achieved by the most renowned of his predecessors, while sometimes his conduct was unaccountably weak and contemptible. He began by restoring the ancient glory of the Roman empire, but he left it at last weaker than he had found it. The first few years of his reign are the last of Roman glory.

countries reconquered ; and we are told that in 629 Heraclius
went as a pilgrim to Jerusalem, where the cross was replaced
in its ancient position, the Christian bishop restored to his
patriarchal throne, and heavy retribution exacted of the Jews.
Among other severities, the law of Adrian was revived,
forbidding the Jews to approach nearer than three miles'
distance from Jerusalem.

But a new actor now appears on the scene, destined to
exercise the most momentous influence on the fortunes of the
Jews for many generations to come. We must direct our
attention to him.

CHAPTER IX.

A.D. 622–651.

MAHOMET.—CONQUEST OF ARABIA, PERSIA, SYRIA, AND EGYPT.

MAHOMET was born at Mecca, in the April of the year 569. His father Abdallah, and his mother Amina, belonged to the illustrous tribe of the Koreish ; and the guardianship of the Kaaba,[1] the great centre of Arabian worship, was hereditary in his family. Brought up in a priestly household, a man of his intelligent mind would naturally be drawn to examine the received traditions and ceremonial of the national faith ; and, considering how corrupt and degraded this had become in his day, we can well

---

[1] The Kaaba is said to have been built by Ishmael, aided by his father Abraham, in imitation of the shrine which, according to legend, existed in Paradise, and in which Adam worshipped. In one corner of it stands the sacred stone, believed by the Arabs to be the Guardian Angel of Adam and Eve, changed into that shape, in punishment of the neglect which permitted their fall. It was originally of a dazzling white colour, but the kisses of sinful men have reduced it to its present blackness. To this shrine the Arabs make their pilgrimages, performing seven circuits round it, in memory of the seven circuits which the Angels in Paradise had been wont to practise.

understand how an earnest desire to reform and purify it would suggest itself to him. That Mahomet was, in a certain sense, an impostor cannot be denied ; though he cannot fairly be considered such at the outset of his career. But his genuine wish to rescue religion from the grossness of idolatry, and his enthusiastic belief in the sacredness of his mission, became gradually lessened by the admixture of worldly policy, which is ever the besetting danger of reformers. Then pious frauds were resorted to, to ensure the success which zeal and honesty had failed to obtain. When these, too, failed, simple imposture was employed—though, so far as we can judge, his belief in his divine office remained unimpaired to the last. Such has been the history of many a religious zealot before, and since, his time, though none have ventured to put forth claims so daring, or have produced results so vast and enduring.

All sorts of portents are related to have occurred coincidently with his birth. A divine light illuminated Mecca and its vicinity ; the palace of the Persian kings tottered to its foundations ; the sacred fire of the Magi was extinguished in the Gheber temples ; the newborn infant raised his eyes to heaven, and exclaimed, 'God is great.' But notwithstanding these, and many other, divine tokens of the mission he was to accomplish, he continued to lead the life of an ordinary Arab, until at the age of twenty-five a marriage with a wealthy widow, named Kadijah, lifted him to a position of importance amongst his countrymen.

Some fifteen years afterwards the corrupt state of the national religion[1]—which, it is probable, had always more or less engaged his thoughts—seems wholly to have engrossed them. He withdrew from society, passing his days and nights in mountain caverns, visited by continual dreams and

---

[1] The idolatry of the Arabs was, at this time, of the grossest kind. No less than 360 idols had been set up in the Kaaba—many of them gods of neighbouring nations, or of deceased kings and patriarchs.

visions. The idea took possession of his mind that the Deity had sent into the world a succession of Prophets, each of whom was to restore to its pristine purity the faith, which had been gradually declining since the removal of his predecessor. Noah, Abraham, Moses, Jesus Christ, had all in this manner succeeded one another. Now the time had arrived for the appearance of another—that other being himself. This was the revelation which had been vouchsafed to him ; this was the message[1] he was to deliver to men.

He returned home, and began to attempt the conversion of proselytes to this belief ; but his progress was slow, and the opposition he provoked bitter and deadly. He was in his fifty-third year when the crisis of his career arrived, and he had to fly, at the imminent peril of his life, from Mecca to Medina. This is regarded by the disciples of Islam as the first open promulgation of their faith. At Medina he found himself at the head of an armed force, with which he resolved to enter on his mission of converting the world. At the same time he determined that the instrument by which this was to be effected was the sword.

The attempt seemed a wild one. Yet we must remark that the condition of the world at that period was unusually favourable to it. There existed then but two powerful sovereignties—the Eastern Empire, governed by Heraclius, and the Persian kingdom of Chosroes and afterwards of Yezdegird. The two last named were men of very ordinary capacity ; and either indolence or the pressure of external circumstances kept Heraclius inactive. Nor could they com-

---

[1] The Koran claims to be, not the composition of Mahomet, but a divine revelation, which he had to report with the minutest accuracy. It professes to republish what had been already delivered to Abraham, Moses, and Christ, and now more explicitly, to Mahomet. It teaches I. The Unity of God. II. The Ministrations of Angels and Prophets. III. Absolute Predestination, or Fatalism. IV. The Resurrection and Future Judgment. It rejects the Trinity, and Godhead of our Lord, and insists on the divine mission of Mahomet. In this last particular, and in the respect shown to Christ, it differs from Judaism.

mand the services of any great soldier, such as Aetius, or
Narses, or Belisarius, whose military genius might avail in
driving back the invasion of barbarous and fanatic hordes.
They were also greatly weakened by long and desolating
wars. But, however propitious the occasion may have been,
it is obvious that Mahomet, whatever might be his ultimate
views, could not then attempt hostile measures against them.
Necessarily his first task must be to reduce to obedience the
inhabitants of Arabia itself; and the most formidable of these
were the various Jewish communities, with which the land
was at that time overspread.

For many centuries previously to this time, seven or eight
at the least, a Jewish kingdom had been established in that
district of Yemen which was known as Homeritis. During
the long ages when their brethren, in the Holy Land and
elsewhere, were experiencing the most terrible miseries, the
Jews of Homeritis seem to have lived in unbroken peace and
prosperity in the lovely and fertile valleys of Arabia Felix.
The Arians, after a while, had made their way into the
country ; and with them, as seems always to have been the
case, the Jews lived on terms of amity. But when the
Catholic Christians also obtained a domicile in the country,
under the protection of the neighbouring King of Ethiopia,
Dunaan, the Homeritic king, made an effort to exterminate
them. He attacked their principal city, Nagra, with a large
army, induced it to capitulate, and then, breaking faith, slew
and imprisoned the chief men among the Christians. They
were avenged in the ensuing year by the King of Ethiopia,
who marched against Dunaan with 120,000 men, conquered,
dethroned, and slew him. With him the Homeritic kingdom expired; but the subjects of Dunaan formed themselves
into a number of independent tribes, more difficult, probably,
to subdue than any single community would have been.
Mahomet seems to have hoped at first to bring these over
to his views. As has been pointed out, their faith was nearly
the same as that proclaimed by himself, except as regarded

that one article of his own supernatural claims. But the fact
of his descent from Ishmael, instead of Isaac, was an insuper-
able obstacle to any acknowledgment of him by them ; and
he was obliged to resort to the method of conversion which
he had himself proclaimed. The tribes of Kainoka and of
Nadir, the inhabitants of Koraidha, Fadai, and Khaibar were
attacked in turn, and in every instance overpowered and
almost exterminated. The most merciless severity was
shown to the conquered. Seven hundred Koraidhites, who
had surrendered to his mercy, were dragged into the city of
Medina, and slaughtered in cold blood, in the presence of the
Prophet, who himself enjoined and applauded the deed.

In the same spirit, after the capture of the citadel of
Khaibar, Kenana, the gallant Jewish prince, was put by the
conquerors to the severest tortures, to induce him to confess
where he had concealed his treasure ; and when these failed
to accomplish their purpose, his head was struck off with a
sabre. But Mahomet narrowly escaped, at this time, feeling the vengeance of the Jewish people, by the act of a
woman. On his arrival within the citadel, he required that
some food should be served, and a shoulder of lamb was
placed before him and his followers. But the first mouthful
caused him severe internal pain ; and though he instantly
vomited forth what he had eaten, his system had imbibed so
much of the poison which the meat had contained, as to cause
him continual paroxysms of suffering during the remainder of
his life. The Jewish woman by whom the lamb had been
poisoned calmly avowed and justified the deed.[1] Her fate is
uncertain.

Having now attained the position of an independent
potentate, Mahomet despatched letters to Heraclius, Chosroes,
and the Governor of Egypt, inviting them to adopt his faith.
By Chosroes these were received with scorn and anger ; by

---

[1] ' If he is the Messiah,' she said, ' the poison cannot hurt him ; if he
is not, he is an impostor, and deserves death.'

the other two, we are told, with civility and feigned respect. Nevertheless, reports were brought that Heraclius was assembling an army for the purpose of crushing him; and it is probable that Mahomet would now have followed out what had long been his persistent purpose, and entered on the forcible conversion of neighbouring nations, if he had not felt the approaching decay of the powers of life. He did go so far as to assemble an army, and advance across the country to Tabuc; but the tidings brought him that the Syrians had collected large bodies of troops, and the experience of the battle of Muta, in which they had proved themselves formidable enemies, induced him to withdraw to Medina.

But after his death, Abu Beker, the first Caliph, prepared to carry out without delay the programme of his predecessor. An army was sent into Irak, the ancient Chaldæa and Babylonia, under Khaled, called the 'Sword of God,' and one of the most able of the Moslem leaders, with orders to overrun and subdue Hira, Cufa, and Aila, all of them tributary kingdoms owning the suzerainty of Persia.[1] Khaled accomplished his task with astonishing rapidity and completeness; and when he was withdrawn to take the command in Syria, his successors followed up his victories, with but few reverses, into the very heart of Persia, won great battles, captured Modayn, Hamadan, and Istakan (the ancient Ctesiphon, Ecbatana, and Persepolis), and finally hunted down and slew the hapless Yezdegird. With him the Sassanian dynasty came to an end, and the whole of Persia, A.D. 651, submitted to the dominion of the Caliphs.

The like amazing success marked the progress of the warriors of Islam in Syria and Egypt. In the former country, notwithstanding that they were opposed to disci-

---

[1] When Chosroes received Mahomet's letter, inviting him to embrace Islamism, he disdainfully tore it in pieces. When Mahomet heard of this he exclaimed, 'Even so shall his kingdom be torn.' Doubtless Abu Beker had this in mind when he sent out the expedition.

plined troops, who still retained the tradition of ancient Roman warfare, their fiery valour proved everywhere victorious. The light Arab horsemen recoiled indeed from the serried ranks of the Grecian phalanx ; but only to return again and again to the encounter, till their trained antagonists were daunted or wearied out. Whether they fought behind the ramparts of a fortified city or in the open plain, it was the same. Bosra, Damascus, Baalbec, Emesa, after protracted sieges, were compelled to open their gates to the conquerors. At Aizhadin, and on the banks of the Yermouk, military skill and superior numbers were alike of no avail to check the overwhelming tide of conquest.

After allowing themselves a brief repose, the victorious Saracens advanced to besiege Jerusalem, a city regarded by them with a reverence almost as deep as that of the Jews themselves.[1] The reader has already been told how nature and art have combined to render this city almost impregnable to assault. In the present instance its fortifications had been carefully repaired and strengthened, in expectation of a siege; it was well victualled, and garrisoned by a large and disciplined force. Against an enemy so inexperienced in the arts of warfare as the Saracens, it might well have defied even the most persistent blockade. Yet but four months elapsed before an offer of surrender was made and accepted, and the Caliph Omar[2] arrived to arrange the terms. These were, that the lives and property of the inhabitants should be spared, and the free exercise of their religion allowed; but upon conditions to which nothing but the fear of immediate and inevitable death could have induced the Christians to submit. They

---

[1] On the morning of the assault on Jerusalem, the address of Moses to the Israelites in the Koran, 'Enter, O ye people, into the Holy Land, which God hath destined for you,' was shouted aloud after morning prayer, by the whole besieging army.

[2] Omar had succeeded Abu Beker, A.D. 633, less than two years after the death of the Prophet. He was the Caliph who burned the Alexandrian library, and was the first of the Ommiades.

were to build no new churches ; set up no new crosses ; were to make no proselytes to their faith ; nor hinder any Christian from professing Islamism. They were to wear a peculiar dress, carry no arms, possess no Moslem slaves, and salute every Mussulman as a superior ! On the site of the Jewish temple, which had so long lain desolate, a Mahometan mosque was erected : in which, from that day to this, with but a brief intermission, the worship of Islam has been carried on.

If the narratives of the conquests of Persia and Syria appear to us surprising, that of Egypt must be regarded with still greater wonder. The empire of the Pharaohs had indeed greatly deteriorated from its ancient consequence and strength ; but it was still a powerful State, capable of bringing numerous armies into the field. Nevertheless, Amru, who was entrusted with the command of an expedition to overrun and subdue it, had but five thousand men assigned him for the purpose. With these he proceeded to invest Farwah, or Pelusium ; and having captured this city through the treachery of the governor, marched on to Alexandria. That also, after a siege of fourteen months, was surrendered to them, and the submission of all Egypt followed.

In recording this extraordinary career of conquest, our concern of course is, how it affected the Jews ; and everywhere it will be found that—as in the instance of the incursion of the Northern nations—what was ruin and misery to others failed to injure, nay, benefited them. In Persia, Yezdegird had visited them with the most cruel persecutions, had shut up their synagogues and schools, and slain numbers who refused to embrace Magianism. In Palestine they had been subject to harsh laws, unmerited scorn, and exclusion from their ancient capital. In Africa, they had similarly undergone violence at the hands of Arian Vandals and Catholic Christians. All this had now come to an end. Their new masters allowed them equal rights of residence and citizenship, the free exercise of their religion, the secure tenure of their property, equality of imports with their Christian neighbours. Whoever else might have reason to lament the change which had passed over the face of the world, they, at least, had none.

CHAPTER X.

JEWS IN THE EASTERN EMPIRE ; IN SPAIN, IN FRANCE.

RECURRING now to the Jews under the rule of the Eastern emperors, we cannot fail to be struck by the difference of the demeanour exhibited by these latter towards them from what has been recorded of the Moslem conquerors. Mahomet, it is true, would permit the existence of but one faith in Arabia ; but outside the bounds of that sacred land, all who would acknowledge the dominion of the Caliph were secure from insult or wrong. But the Christian emperors of Constantinople—such of them, that is to say, as felt themselves strong enough to invade the rights of any portion of their subjects—made it a matter of conscience to endeavour to require the acceptance of Christianity by the Jews, though at this period they did not proceed to inflict penalties in case of refusal. Even Phocas, whose zeal for the faith could not have been very keen, had sent the Prefect Georgius to Jerusalem, requiring the principal Jews there, on their allegiance, to receive baptism. Heraclius attempted the same, using, it is said, violent and cruel measures to accomplish his purpose, but with very partial success. This emperor had two special causes of dislike to them, one of which appealed to the nobler, the other to the weaker side of his character. The first was the recollection of the barbarities practised by them at the capture of Jerusalem by the Persian troops ; the second, the prediction delivered to him by a soothsayer in whom he trusted, that the Roman empire should be overthrown by a circumcised people.[1] Ignorant altogether of the storm which was gathering in the mountains of Arabia, he naturally presumed the people in question to be the Jews, and therefore sought to avert the evil by converting these to the Gospel. He is said to have been so far influenced by his alarm as to despatch letters to the Kings of Spain and France, urging them to unite with him in the extirpation of the dangerous race.

Whether any of the many feeble successors to the purple who intervened between him and the Isaurian Leo pursued the same policy, we are not informed. But it is unlikely that they would attempt it. The existence of a circumcised and warlike race different from that of the Jews, would in their time have become matter of notoriety ; and alarm would have been directed to a different quarter. Nor would it have been either safe or politic to attack the Jews. Their wealth and intelligence rendered them useful instruments in carrying out the imperial policy, and their numbers and turbulent spirits discouraged interference with them. In the numerous riots which took place between the Orthodox Christians and their adversaries, the Jews were wont to interfere and give the preponderance to the latter.[2] Unless they provoked interference of the authorities by actual sedition, it is likely that they would be left to themselves.

---

[1] One would suspect the genuineness of this story, but that historians accept it apparently without doubt.

[2] The Jews took the opportunity of the popular outbreak against Martina and Heracleonas, to desecrate the church of St. Sophia with every kind of outrage, and apparently with impunity.

But when a powerful ruler in the person of Leo again grasped the sceptre, A.D. 716, the case became different. It was said, indeed, that this emperor had been promised the purple, on condition of his employing the power thus committed to him in the destruction of images in Christian churches ; but the tale rests on no trustworthy evidence, and is disproved by his acts at the very outset of his reign ; for he was no sooner seated on his throne than he required that all his Jewish and Montanist subjects should submit to baptism. The Jews seem to have consented to the ceremony, though they continued the exercise of their own faith without change. What part they took in the subsequent destruction of images,[1] and wrecking of Christian churches, may readily be surmised from what has been already told.

Passing to Spain, we find the Jews, during this century, occupying a different position, and subjected to far heavier penalties. In this country they had long been settled, certainly previously to the Christian era, and, as it would appear, lived in peace and security. Previously to the Council of Elvira, no law is recorded to have been made which restrained their liberty. But it was then decreed that no marriages should take place between Christians and Jews, nor should they sit down to table together. This was the first note, as it were, of the bigotry and intolerance which afterward rang with such hideous discord throughout the length and breadth of Spain. The outburst was checked for a while by the incursion of the Visigoths, who, though Christians, professed the Arian creed. With them, as has been already remarked, the Jews always lived on terms of amity. But towards the end of the sixth century Reccared abjured Arianism, embracing the Catholic faith ; and a new condition of things was soon the result.[2] By the decree of the Council

---

[1] Beyond doubt they were charged with having incited it.

[2] I do not desire to imply that the concord between the Arians and Jews, as contrasted with the disagreements between the Catholics and Jews, is any ground for commending the one or blaming the other. It

of Toledo, held in the fourth year of his reign, Jews were not allowed to have Christian slaves, or to hold public offices, or marry Christian wives, or sing psalms when carrying their dead to the grave.

These decrees were soon followed up by much severer measures. Sisebut, who succeeded to the Gothic kingdom A.D. 612, is supposed to have received an urgent entreaty from the Emperor Heraclius, as has already been intimated, to put down Judaism throughout his dominions.'·· Whether the report be true or not, he certainly acted as though such was his intention. He issued the command that all Jews should offer themselves for baptism, imprisoning many, and putting to death many more, who would not obey his order. Large numbers abandoned their whole possessions, and migrated to various parts of Gaul. Yet the Spanish historians affirm that as many as 90,000 were baptized, not because of any change in their convictions, but through dread of the consequences of refusal. After the death of Sisebut there seems to have been a short lull in the storm of persecution, and many of the pseudo-converts thereupon returned to the profession of their ancient faith.

The fourth Council of Toledo, held A.D. 633, under the presidency of Isidore of Seville, enacted that 'men ought not to be forced into believing, but believe of their own free will.' But although Isidore—to whom in all likelihood this single ray of light in the midst of surrounding darkness must be attributed—could thus give expression to the language of charity and truth, he was not wise enough, or perhaps influential enough, to be consistent; for the decree adds, immediately afterwards, that all who had received baptism—whether willingly or unwillingly—must be compelled to abide by it, 'because otherwise the Holy Name of God would be blas-

may not unreasonably be argued that it is the indifference of the Arians to our Lord's honour, and the zeal of the Catholics for its maintenance, which occasion both the concord and the strife. I only record the fact.

phemed, and the faith disgraced ;' as though there was not
worse blasphemy and deeper disgrace in a false profession
than in an honest renunciation !

The same Council adds decrees against which Isidore's
large and charitable nature must have rebelled. The 60th
canon requires 'that the sons and daughters of Jews should
be separated from their parents, lest they be involved in their
errors ;' the 63rd, that 'Jews who have Christian wives, if they
wish to live with them, must become Christians ; and if they
refuse to obey, they are to be separated ;' the 64th, that 'Jews
who were formerly Christians are not to be admitted as witnesses ;' the 65th, that ' Jews and their descendants are not to
hold public offices, and any one who obtains such office shall
be publicly scourged.' A still more monstrous decree enacts
that any Christian convert who so much as speaks to a Jew
shall become a slave, and the Jew he spoke to be publicly
scourged !

The twelfth Council of Toledo, in 681, repeats these merciless severities, which (it is no wonder to find) could not be
carried into effect, except by direct State interference, and
adds others of a like character. ' The Jews,' it is ordered, ' are
to offer themselves, their children, and their servants for
baptism :' they 'shall not celebrate the Passover, or practise
circumcision :' they 'shall not presume to observe the Sabbath
or any Jewish festival :' they ' shall not dare to defend their
religion to the disparagement of the Christian faith :' and
' they shall not read books abhorred by the Christian faith.'
The penalties for breach of these and the like statutes had
hitherto been death. But the extreme severity of such a
sentence, it is argued, had acted as a preventive to its
being enforced. Therefore new orders were issued, by which
the rigour of the punishments was abated. Henceforth, if a
Jew profaned the name of Christ or of the Holy Trinity, or
rejected the Sacraments, or kept the Jewish feasts, or worked
on the Sunday, he was *only* to receive one hundred lashes
on his naked body, and afterwards be put into chains and

banished from the country, his whole property being confiscated to the State! If a man circumcised his child, he was
to suffer mutilation, or if it were a woman who so offended,
she was to lose her nose. If a Jew presumed to take a public
office under a noble, he was to forfeit half his property, and
suffer scourging ; but if it was under an ecclesiastical superior
that he undertook a situation of trust, he was to lose his whole
estate, or be burned alive! The reader will surely call to mind
Solomon's saying, respecting the 'tender mercies of the
wicked,' as he reads these ordinances.

But the avenger was at hand. For some years past the
tide of Saracen conquest had been rolling along the northern
coast of Africa, until it had reached the kingdom of Morocco;
when it must turn southward into the barren wastes of the
Sahara, or northwards, into the populous and fertile land of
Spain. There could be little doubt which of the two they
would prefer ; and Wamba, one of the wisest and ablest of
the Gothic sovereigns of Spain, in anticipation of such a
catastrophe, collected a fleet, with which he encountered the
Saracens, A.D. 675, and inflicted on them a disastrous defeat,
which deferred the invasion of Spain for nearly forty years.
But in the reign of Egica, and still more in that of his successor, Witiza, the imminent danger of the Spanish monarchy
became so evident, and the fear that the Jews would co-operate
in and accelerate the Mussulman invasion so alarming, that
measures were taken to prevent it which indicate at once
terror, haste, and self-reproach.

At first attempts were made to intimidate the Jews. Egica
declared that he had learned, by their open avowal, that the
Jews had plotted with enemies beyond the sea to effect the
ruin of Christendom. Therefore, to counteract their efforts,
all Jewish children upwards of seven years old were to be
taken from their parents, the males married to Christian girls,
and the girls to Christian men, and the children in all instances brought up in the Christian belief, so that in the next
generation the Jews might cease altogether to exist as a

separate people. This seems to have had no other effect than
that of causing a general flight of Jews from Spain, the very
thing of all others likely to bring about the mischief that was
dreaded. Witiza endeavoured to repair the mistake. He
issued a proclamation permitting all Jews to return to Spain,
and enjoy there the full rights of freedom and citizenship.
But the step was taken too late. If the Jews had concerted
with Muza the invasion of Spain, as their enemies affirmed,
their intrigues could not be annulled. In the year 711, two
years after the accession of a new sovereign, Roderic,[1] to the
throne, the Moors crossed into Spain; a decisive battle was
fought on the banks of the Guadelete, in which the Moslems
were victorious, and the Gothic kingdom of Spain ceased to
exist.

Once more the miseries of fire and sword, which laid waste
the whole of the Spanish peninsula, inflicted no suffering on
the Jews residing within it. Whether any of the accusations
with which the Christians have assailed them—of leaguing
with the Moslem, furnishing them with secret information,
opening the gates of beleaguered cities to them and the like—
contain any admixture of truth, it would be difficult to say.
In some instances the charges are manifestly false; in others
the decision is very doubtful. But even allowing them to be
true, it cannot be matter of wonder that men so persistently
wronged and slandered should turn on their oppressors, when
the opportunity was given them. The settlement of the
Moors in Spain was followed by a long period of prosperity
and peace, during which the Jews became famous throughout

---

[1] The commonly received story—that Count Julian persuaded Muza to
invade Spain, in order to avenge the violation of his daughter Florinda—
is in all likelihood mere fiction. It is not mentioned by any historian for
nearly 500 years after Roderic's death, and then only as a legend. Considering the manners of the time and the unbounded licence of the Gothic
kings, it is most unlikely that such an act, if perpetrated, would have been
so furiously resented : and the invasion of Spain is to be accounted for in
a more simple way, viz., the carrying out of Mahomet's plan of progressive
conquest.

Europe for their wealth, their intelligence, and their learning. A famous Hebrew school was founded at Cordova, to which students from all parts of Europe are said to have resorted.

In France, during this century, something of the same spirit seems to have prevailed, by which the Catholic kings of Spain were actuated. Chilperic, as has been already recorded, towards the end of the previous century had insisted on the compulsory baptism of his Jewish subjects.

Early in the seventh century Clotaire II. issued a decree forbidding Jews to hold any military or civil office. Dagobert, who reigned from 628 to 638, enacted still more sternly, that the whole of his Jewish subjects should forswear their faith or depart from his dominions. It is said that he too acted under the influence of the Emperor Heraclius.[1] But of this there is no evidence, and it has been urged that the royal order, if issued, was but little observed, since the Jews, in the southern parts of his kingdom at least, continued to be a numerous and wealthy body throughout his reign. Wamba, the Gothic king of Languedoc, however, certainly took the step in question, and banished them from his kingdom.

---

[1] Rabbi Joseph, i. p. 2.

CHAPTER XI.

JEWS UNDER THE CALIPHS IN THE EAST.

THE period which ensued after the Conquest of Persia and Syria in the East, and of Spain in the West, is called by Milman the 'Golden Age of Judaism'; but the title does not suit very well with the circumstances of the case. It was not, as the Golden Age of legend is represented to have been, a peaceful and happy beginning, which the crimes of men gradually embittered and corrupted. It rather resembled a succession of cool showers on a burning summer day, when the fierce heat of the morning is tempered during the midday hours, but only to break out with more intolerable oppression as the afternoon comes on. The contrast which this lull in the storm of injustice and cruelty presented to the savage fury of preceding, as well as after times, is indeed most striking. Everywhere the flames of persecution sank down ; and what had been a consuming fire smouldered on, with only a feeble flicker here and there, to show that it was not quite extinct.

In the Byzantine empire we are told singularly little of the condition and actions of the Jews during this period. The emperors who filled the throne were, for the most part, men of very ordinary ability. Nor were there among their subjects men of greater mark. 'On the throne, in the camp, and in the schools,' says the historian Gibbon, 'we search, perhaps with fruitless diligence, for names and characters that deserve to be rescued from oblivion.' This may in itself explain why so little is heard of the Jews. Occupy high positions in Church or State we know they could not, or openly interfere with the direction of public affairs ; and what private influence they might exercise in these would be carefully kept secret. As for attacks upon them, we have already seen that their numbers, their rare intelligence, and their ever increasing wealth, rendered them a dangerous body for any but a powerful ruler to assail ; and assuredly the weak and incompetent occupants of the imperial throne at that era would be but little inclined to make the experiment. What little has been recorded goes to prove that the emperors were anxious to conciliate them. Nicephorus, who received the purple A.D. 793, is said to have shown them particular favour, probably because of their acquiescence in his iconoclastic views ; and Michael the Stammerer, whose reign dates from 821, was reviled by his enemies as being half a Jew.[1] When we remember how Constantinople was at this period distracted at once by civil and religious factions, and that the Jews— however little they might seem to be personally interested in the question at issue—were always ready to throw their weight into the one scale or the other, we shall cease to wonder that they remained wholly unmolested.

In the dominions of the newly established Caliphs they were not only left in peace, but treated with especial honour.[2]

---

[1] Similarly, and for the like reason, Constantine Copronymus was nicknamed ' the Jew.'

[2] The Caliph Almamon, a great patron of learning, caused many of the Rabbinical books to be translated into Arabic, and placed in the Royal Library at Bagdad.

The victorious Arabs were but a rude and uncivilized people, and the aid of the Jews in teaching them the arts and pleasures of a refined state of society was found alike useful and welcome. Their learning, their intelligence, their widespread knowledge of foreign lands, rendered them especially qualified for this office. Omar, the second Caliph, is related to have entrusted the coinage to a Jew, immediately after his accession to the throne. It was a subject with which, as might be expected, he had no acquaintance, nor was there any one among his principal officers who knew more of the matter. Similarly, if an embassy was to be despatched to a foreign sovereign, or a subsidy negotiated, the person selected for the office would in all likelihood be a Jew. When Abu Giafar imposed a heavy fine on the Christians, it was to Hebrew officials that the collection of the impost was committed; and even between sovereigns so potent as Charlemagne and the Caliph Haroun Alraschid, the envoy who was entrusted with the letters and presents was a Jew.

In war they were no less necessary than in peace. The sums required for the equipment of a fleet or the victualling of an army were furnished from Hebrew coffers. Nor were their avocations limited to this. The Jews would accompany the march of the Mussulman armies, and—as their fathers had done in the instance of the Gothic and Hunnite invasions—purchase from the ignorant soldiery the plunder they had amassed, at a price which brought them an enormous profit,[1] or it might be a captive whose family or friends afterwards redeemed him at a price tenfold exceeding what they had given. We learn that at this time they almost entirely abandoned agriculture; partly because of the heavy tax laid on unbelievers, and partly because

---

[1] After the capture of Rhodes, a Jew belonging to Edessa purchased the remains of the celebrated Colossus, which had been lying on the ground since its overthrow by an earthquake. It had been seventy cubits high, and was constructed of brass. The fragments are said to have loaded nine hundred camels. Probably the purchase money was a sum ridiculously small, the profit enormous.

trade had become so much more profitable to them. They
cultivated also astrology and medicine, and became everywhere the most successful professors of both sciences. In
many, if not in most of the royal courts, the chief physicians
and astrologers were Jews. Nor were they less successful in
literature. In the East and West alike, their schools were
crowded with students, and the, names of their learned men of
this era are held in reverence even to the present day.

It is at this date that we first hear of a sect called the
Karaites.[1] They claim, indeed, a far greater antiquity, insisting on their descent from the ten tribes led captive by
Shalmaneser, and putting forward a catalogue of their doctors,
in regular succession from the time of Ezra. But it is believed
that their first founder was one Ananus, a Babylonian Jew of
the race of David, who, together with his son Saul, A.D. 750,
entered a public protest against the extent to which tradition
had corrupted the written word, and insisted on this latter as
the sole rule of faith. We have evidence in the Gospels, of
of the length to which tradition had run even in our Lord's
day, and how He had declared that the Pharisees 'had made
the Word of God of none effect' through it. But after that
time the Cabbalist and Masoric Rabbins, who were the successors of the Pharisees, laid greater stress than ever on the
importance of tradition; and the completion of the Babylonian
Talmud in the sixth century, was, as it were, the keystone of
their work. We cannot wonder that men of sense and reverent
feeling should be shocked at the wild fables and ridiculous
fancies of the Talmudists. It would appear that a strong feeling was widely entertained in secret on the subject; but its
first expression was due to the failure of Ananus to obtain
the dignity of Prince of the Captivity, for which office he was
a candidate. Disgusted at the election of a younger man to
the post, Ananus gathered together the remains of the old

---

[1] Textualists, that is. It was attached to them in the first instance as
a term of reproach.

Sadducean party, or what was so called, and induced them to nominate him as a rival to his successful opponent. Ananus was thrown into prison, but gained the ear of the Caliph sufficiently to obtain his release. He then retired, with his followers, to the neighbourhood of Jerusalem, where they established themselves as a separate sect. They still exist, chiefly in Eastern countries, and in parts of Europe, especially the Crimea.[1]

Notwithstanding the general prosperity enjoyed by the Jews at this period, there were some reverses. Giaffir, called the Great, is said to have issued an edict requiring Christians and Jews alike to embrace Islamism. Al Wathek also, the successor of Mamun, one of the Abbasside Caliphs, residing at Cufa, inflicted heavy fines upon them, partly because they had committed frauds in the management of the finances entrusted to them, and partly because they refused the religion of Mahomet. But the amount of suffering inflicted could not, in either instance, have been great. Motakavel, however, his brother and successor, was still harsher in his dealings with them. He compelled them to wear a leathern girdle, to distinguish them from the Faithful. He prohibited them from using stirrups when they rode on horseback, and afterwards from riding horses at all. A summary of the various badges and

---

[1] The tenets of the Karaites are said to have been :

1. The Creation of the world, as opposed to its eternal existence.
2. That God had no beginning, has no form, and that His unity is absolute.
3. That He sent Moses, and delivered to him the Law.
4. That every believer must derive his belief from the simple interpretation of Holy Scripture, without regard to tradition.
5. That God will raise the dead, and judge men hereafter.
6. That He has not cast away His chosen people.

In recording these opinions, it should be noted that it is quite possible (indeed, likely) that a party existed among the Jews, long previously to the time of Ananus, who held notions identical with or very like them, and who were also called Karaites, *i.e.*, 'Textualists ;' but they did not withdraw themselves into a separate community, under the name of Karaites, until A.D. 780.

marks of degradation imposed on the Jews by European and
Asiatic sovereigns would form a curious study.

To this period also belongs the strange story of the kingdom
of Khozar, which has been regarded by some historians as
being full of misstatement and exaggeration, and by some
as simple fiction. Khozar belonged to the Turcomans, a
heathen people ; and it is reported that, somewhere about
the middle of the eighth century, Bular, its king, a pious and
thoughtful prince, received a revelation through a dream,—or,
according to another version, through the instruction of an
angel,—which showed the hollowness of the religion he professed. Thereupon he began to make inquiry after a purer faith :
and having conversed with learned men professing Christianity,
Islamism, and Judaism, he made his election in favour of the
last-named creed. According to one version of the story, he
came to this resolution in a somewhat singular manner. Con-
versing apart with a Christian, he asked of him whether he
did not consider Judaism preferable to Mahometanism, and
was answered that he did. Then holding a similar discussion
with a Mahometan, he inquired whether *he* did not regard
Judaism as superior to Christianity. Receiving an affirmative
answer here also, he decided in favour of the first-named faith,
as it appeared that it held the first place in the estimation of
the Jew, and the second in that of each of the other two.
Having himself received circumcision, he sent for learned Jews
from neighbouring countries, by whom in time the whole of
his people were brought over to the faith of Israel. A tabernacle was erected, similar to that set up by Moses in the
wilderness, and the Jewish worship regularly carried on.

The authenticity of the story having been disputed some
two centuries and a half afterwards, Rabbi Hosdai, a learned
man, much patronized by Abderraman, the Caliph of Cordova,
resolved to ascertain the truth respecting it, and obtained,
with considerable difficulty, a letter from Joseph, the reigning
sovereign of Khozar. In this the king repeated the history of
his ancestor's conversion, very much as popular rumour had

stated it. The letter of Hosdai is still extant, as well as the reply, and there seems no reason to doubt the authenticity of the former, at all events.

Basnage and others reject the whole story as fable. It is argued that this kingdom of Khozar, when searched for, could no more be found than the Eldorado of the Spaniards, or the dominions of Prester John; even the famous traveller of Hosdai's time, Benjamin of Tudela, though anxious, for the credit of his patron, to discover it, entirely failed to do so. But modern research has proved that such a kingdom did at all events exist; and the most judicious historians, Jost among them, incline to believe that the story may have at all events a groundwork of truth.

In Spain, during this period, all seems to have gone prosperously with the Jews, except that an impostor named Serenus, who professed, as so many before and after his time have done, to be the Messiah, taking advantage of the unsettled state of things between France and Spain, persuaded large numbers of his countrymen to follow him into Palestine, where he proposed to set up his kingdom. He does not seem to have reached the Holy Land, and the greater part of his followers perished in the attempt. Those who survived returned to their homes, but only to find that their possessions had been confiscated to the State.

In the year 750 a revolution took place at Damascus, during which nearly the whole of the Ommiad dynasty (as the descendants of Caliph Omar were called) was cut off, and Abul Abbas succeeded to the Caliphate. Yusef, the Mussulman Emir in Spain, sided with the usurping family; but the Moorish chiefs generally were desirous of establishing their own independence, and finding in Abderachman ben Moasiah a still surviving representative of the Ommiad family, placed him on the throne, under the title of the Caliph of Cordova. His government was wise and powerful, and under him the Jews attained the zenith of their prosperity.

We are now about to transfer our attention to the countries

of Western Europe, where occurred almost every event of importance in which the Jews are concerned for several ensuing centuries. But before doing so, it will be proper to record what is known of the Hebrew communities who dwelt in those countries of the distant East which acknowledged neither the sceptre of Rome nor of Persia. The records of these are very scanty, and rest upon very doubtful authority, but that affords no sufficient reason for not preserving all that can be gleaned from various sources respecting them.

CHAPTER XII

H OW far the bounds of the authority possessed by the Prince of the Captivity extended must always be a matter of uncertainty. Records exist of what occurred in the Roman empire down to the time of its fall, which may be relied on with tolerable certainty. The kingdom of Persia also has its historians, who throw a fair amount of light upon what passed in that country during the centuries with which we have been dealing. But of what took place farther eastward we have no trustworthy knowledge at all. In Arabia, as we have seen, there existed numerous and flourishing Jewish communities—indeed, a Jewish kingdom had endured for many ages there, able to hold its own with neighbouring sovereignties. Again, it is certain that there were not only Jews in Parthia and Media, in Elam (or Persia), Mesopotamia, Cappadocia, Pontus, Phrygia, Pamphylia, and Ionia,[1] as noted

---

[1] 'Asia' in Acts ii. 9, no doubt means the Roman province, over which a pro-consul ruled. It comprised Ionia and Mysia, Ephesus being its capital. It is mentioned also Acts xvi. 6.

in the second chapter of the Acts; but there are grounds for believing that they extended much farther eastward.

The traditions of the Early Church affirm that the Gospel was preached by several of the Apostles—notably by Thomas,[1] Simon Zelotes, and Matthias—in Asiatic Ethiopia, or the Land of Cush; the bounds of which are wholly uncertain, but which extended a long way to the eastward of the two great rivers. It is stated that they encountered opposition from the Jews of those regions.[2] Benjamin of Tudela also affirms that the authority of the Resch Glutha 'extended eastward to the Iron Gates, and as far as India.' This assertion must be regarded as doubtful; but it certainly goes to prove that there were Jewish communities in the districts he names. Nothing, indeed, is more probable than that the Jews should have migrated towards the East, when Chosroes let loose against them the merciless wrath of an Eastern despot. To the West lay the Roman empire, where harsh laws against their nation were in force: to the South the new Arabian impostor was persecuting their countrymen: to the North all was barren and ungenial. But to the East were rich and pleasant regions, where, though they might encounter hostility from neighbouring tribes, they were strong enough to maintain themselves in peace and security. But though there is great likelihood of their having done this, there is no certainty. We must acquiesce in Milman's opinion, that 'the history of the Oriental Jews at this early period is so obscure, so entirely or so nearly fabulous, that it may wisely be dismissed.'

But though authentic history does not record the immigration of the Jews into these countries, there are not wanting incidental evidences to the fact. Take as an example the collection of Eastern tales called the Arabian Nights. The date of these cannot be later than the eighth century, and

---

[1] Matthias is said to have been martyred by the Jews at Sebastople, whichever of the towns of that name may be intended.

[2] See further on what is said of the Jews of Malabar.

they are probably much older. In the various countries to which they relate,—Persia, Turkestan, India, China, etc., the presence of Jews as an integral part of the population is assumed as a matter of course. In Balsora, in Kashgar, and other cities, there is the Jewish merchant, the Jewish physician, the Jewish banker—no strangers evidently, but recognised citizens. In the tale of 'The King of the Black Isles,' described in the story as a part of India, lying to the east of Persia, the people of the country are represented as being changed by enchantment into four different kinds of fishes, the four being the Mahometans, *the Jews*, the Christians, and the Parsees. No writer would have introduced this into his story, if the Jews had not formed a considerable and recognised part of the population.

A fact also is recorded by a Mahometan historian of the ninth century, which shows that even so far east as China, the Jews were to be found in large numbers. He states that when the rebel Bacchoo took Canton, he massacred 120,000 Mahometans, *Jews*, Christians, and Parsees.

The most interesting evidence on this subject is derived from the narrative of the Jesuit Ricci in the sixteenth century.[1] It will be remembered how, 150 years before, Francis Xavier had failed in his earnest efforts to gain access to the Celestial Empire. When Ricci succeeded, and had established himself in Canton, he was visited, soon after his arrival, by a stranger, who professed his satisfaction at the presence of persons of the same faith with himself. Ricci took his visitor into the chapel, where he bowed reverently to the altar-piece representing the Virgin Mary and the pictures of the four Evangelists, whom he assumed to be 'some of the Twelve.' But further conversation elicited the fact that the man was a Jew, and had mistaken the picture of the Madonna for that of Rebekah with Jacob and Esau,

---

[1] For a very complete account of the Jews in China, see Brotier's note, in the third volume of his edition of Tacitus.

and supposed the portraits of the Evangelists to be some of the twelve Patriarchs.

Great curiosity was aroused in Europe by the publication of Ricci's narrative, but further inquiries were checked by his death in 1610. His successors later in the same century, Fathers Gozani, Domenge, and Gaubil, transmitted a good deal of interesting information to their friends in Europe, though they were greatly hampered by their ignorance of Hebrew. Towards the close of the century other missionaries arrived, who were acquainted with the Jewish language; and probably a very complete knowledge of them would have been arrived at, if it had not been that in 1723 the Jesuits were driven out of China, and the country remained closed for nearly 100 years to Christian missionaries.

Nevertheless, much valuable and interesting information was obtained. It appeared, in the first place, that the Chinese Jews were ignorant of our Lord's existence, and did not understand the meaning of the crucifix. When asked if they had heard of Jesus, they replied that there was a holy man so called, who was the Son of Sirach, but they knew of no other. They also had never heard of the Septuagint or Samaritan versions, and their Hebrew text is without the vowel points.[1] Further, they do not call themselves Jews, but Israelites. They are strict observers of the Sabbath, never kindling fires or preparing food on that day. They practise circumcision, and intermarry only with their own people. They keep the Passover, the feasts of Weeks and Tabernacles, and the great Day of Atonement. They believe in a resurrection, in Purgatory and Hell, in Paradise and heaven, in angels and spirits, and in a final judgment.

Their place of worship more nearly resembles the ancient Jewish Temple than the synagogue of later times. It has

---

[1] When questioned as to the absence of these vowels, they are said to have answered, that God delivered the words to Moses with such rapidity that he had no time to insert the vowels.

a Holy Place, and a Holy of Holies, in which are deposited the Books of the Law, and which is entered by the High Priest only. The latter, however, does not wear the Aaronic vestments, a scarf of red silk being his sole distinguishing badge. They still expect the Messiah to come, but their belief on this point is vague.

From some of the particulars recorded of them, the idea was once entertained that they were the descendants, not of the remnants of the Captivity, but of the ten tribes. This, however, is an evident error, as they not only possess the Book of Ezra, for whom they profess profound respect, but those of Esther and Maccabees also.

There is the greatest difficulty in determining when they first arrived in China. According to some authorities, the immigration began several centuries before the birth of Christ. According to others, it was coincident with the persecution of Antiochus Epiphanes, or Pompey's Jewish wars, or the siege of Jerusalem under Titus. Others date it from the period of Chosroes's attempts at forcible proselytism ; and it is certain that there is a mixture of Persian words in their language, which lends some likelihood to this belief.

The most reasonable opinion at which we can arrive is, that although there may have been some connection for commercial purposes in very early times—as early even as those of David and Solomon—there was nothing like a settlement before the 3rd or 4th century preceding the birth of Christ. Then it seems likely that a number of Jews, who may in the first instance have left Palestine under terror of Haman's persecution, established themselves in China. There may have been other immigrations between that time and the destruction of Jerusalem by Titus. But at that period there was a second and a larger influx. From the Jews who then entered China the greater part of the modern Chinese Jews are descended. A third considerable entrance into the country may have taken place in the reign of Chosroes, the likelihood of which has already been pointed out. Supposing these various bodies to have settled in different districts widely removed from one another, the strange variations in their statements respecting their ancestry and date of settlement[1] in China would be accounted for. This theory is in some degree supported by the fact that many of the Chinese Jews report themselves as having sprung from seven tribes, each called after the name of one of the emperors of China. It is not unreasonable to argue that each of these tribes was called after the name of the emperor during whose reign it arrived in the country.

But, whatever may have been the true length of their residence, it is certain that the Taou-kin-keaon (dividers of the sinew, Gen. xxxii. 32), as the Chinese call them, have retained in those far distant lands, and in that extreme isolation, their own habits, sentiments, and religious peculiarities as inflexibly as their countrymen in other lands have always done.

The annals of the Jews of Malabar date their arrival in that country as having occurred A.D. 70, the time of the destruction of Jerusalem by Titus. But others place this event in the fifth century of Christianity, when one of the persecutions occurred in Persia, and caused a numerous exodus of the Jews. The title which the Hebrew leader of the refugees is said to have borne is Rabbana ; and that variation of the title Rabbi is said to belong to that special epoch. In features and colour these Indian Jews very nearly resemble the other inhabitants of the country ; but their religious customs, their prayers, and their reverence for the Talmud, distinguish them clearly enough from all others.

The Jews of Cochin China also claim a very high antiquity. In the latter part of the 17th century a letter was sent by them to the Synagogue of Portuguese Jews at Amsterdam, in which they asserted that their fathers had emigrated to the

---

[1] Thus, Father Alvarez, the Portuguese Jesuit who wrote a history of China, affirms that the Jews had not been settled there for more than 600 years.

Indies when the Romans conquered the Holy Land ; that they had founded an independent kingdom, which had lasted for a thousand years, during which time seventy-two kings had succeeded one another. But a civil war having broken out in consequence of the rivalry of two brothers, a neighbouring sovereign had subdued them. Since that time they had been in subjection to him ; but they were nevertheless well treated and their religion tolerated. How much of this may be true, it would be difficult to say ; but it appears to be beyond a doubt that the Jews of that country have long enjoyed great prosperity, and populate large and important cities.

Mention is also made of another race of Jews dwelling in the neighbourhood of the Mahrattas. They call themselves Beni-Israel, and acknowledge no relationship with the Jews of Malabar, China, or Cochin China ; but we are told that their Jewish physiognomies allow of no doubt of their origin ; nor do they bear any resemblance to their Hindoo or Mahometan neighbours. There are other distinctions also between them and the other Oriental Hebrews. While they resemble them in the invocation of the Supreme God, in the observance of circumcision on the eighth day, in their observance of feasts and fasts, and especially of the great Day of Atonement, they do not celebrate the Feast of Purim and Dedication, do not possess the prophetical writings, have no remembrance of the destruction of the second Temple by Titus—in fine, are unacquainted with the history of their people since the time of the Babylonish captivity. If it were not a subject which past experience warns every prudent man to avoid, one would be tempted to inquire whether here were not to be found some genuine traces of the lost tribes of Israel.

Other fancies have been put forward by one writer or another, intimating the wide dispersion of the Hebrew race, which may be mentioned as curious historical puzzles, though nothing more. Among these is the tale of the Jewish inscription found on a tomb in the island of St. Michael, one of the Azores, which seems to intimate that some Jews once settled there ; who must have subsequently died out. Also the report of the Spaniards who conquered Peru, and who affirmed that they found in that country a large and stately edifice, built after a fashion and by the use of tools unknown to the Peruvians. Tradition affirmed that it was the work of 'bearded men' in very ancient times. It was dedicated to the one Maker of the world, and bore all the appearance of a Jewish synagogue !

THE Mahometan invaders of Spain having accomplished the conquest of that country, again turned their arms northwards, and passed the Pyrenees, but only to encounter, on the plains of Tours, decisive and disastrous defeat.[1] We learn that the Jews were suspected of having invited, or at least encouraged, the attempt. To repeat the remark made in a previous chapter—when we call to mind the treatment they had received at the hands of some of the Frankish kings, and contrast it with the toleration exhibited by the Moslem conquerors of Spain, such an accusation does not seem to us a very improbable one, though no certain evidence of it has been produced. Similarly, some sixty years afterwards,[2] when the Moors again burst into Aquitaine, and were repelled by the Count of Toulouse, the Jews are charged with having betrayed that city into the hands of the invaders.

[1] At the hands of Charles Martel, A.D. 732.

[2] A.D. 793. It is likely that the Jews of Beziers were charged at the same time, or possibly a few years later, with a similar offence. (See p. 27.)

After the retreat of the enemy, and recapture of the town, it is said that the emperor had resolved to punish severely the treachery of the Jewish conspirators, but was persuaded to limit the retribution he exacted to their leaders. Basnage disputes altogether the accuracy of the allegation. But some truth in the story there must be. It is an unquestioned fact that for a considerable period after the Saracen irruption —as late indeed as the twelfth century—it was the custom at Toulouse for a Jew, acting as the representative of the whole of his co-religionists in the city, to appear three times in every year at the gate of one of the churches in Toulouse, and there receive a box (or, as some report, three boxes) on the ear,[1] and at the same time pay over a fine in the shape of thirteen pounds of wax. It would be difficult to understand what could have been the origin of a custom like this,—which reminds us of the penalty imposed on the citizens of Oxford, for their alleged participation in the bloodshed of St. Scholastica's day, and which was exacted up to the commencement of the present century,—unless it was the story of their betrayal of the city, as above related.

But if Charlemagne was cognisant of the disaffection of his Jewish subjects, he took the wisest, and, as the sequel proved, the most effectual mode of curing the evil. A study of this great man's life will convince us that he regarded his sovereignty, not merely as a trust committed to him by the Divine Ruler of the Universe—for that many sovereigns have done—but as a trust held on behalf of the Catholic Church of Christ, which was, in his view, identical with the State.[2] It followed therefore that, in his eyes, whosoever

[1] Hallam ('Middle Ages,' vol. ii. p. 225) quotes from a French historian that it was the custom at Toulouse, at this time, to give *every* Jew a blow on the face on Easter Day, and that this was commuted for a fine some time in the 12th century. This is plainly the same story, with some variations.

[2] The theocracy of the Old Testament, where the religious and civil ruler were one and the same, and which probably was the primitive form of government (Gen. xiv. 18), was the model which Charlemagne considered all rulers ought to follow.

refused obedience to the Church was a rebel to the State ; and the Jews, according to this view of the matter, must be the most inveterate of all rebels.   It is creditable to him, therefore, that he not only abstained from religious persecution, but awarded the most even-handed justice to his Hebrew subjects.   He required of them no more than simple obedience to the laws of the land in matters which did not put any constraint on the conscience.   Thus, in the instance of nuptial contracts, he did not allow them to marry within the degree prohibited to his other subjects, nor to dispose of their property after a manner contrary to his laws.   But these are requirements to which citizens of any country might be reasonably expected to conform.   So again, the edicts which forbade them to keep Christian slaves, or to purchase or keep in pawn the sacerdotal vestments, or the sacred vessels used in churches, were obviously made, not for the injury of the Jews, but for the benefit of the Christian community.   Had such practices indeed been permitted, they could have had no other effect than that of exciting prejudice and disgust against the Jews.   But there was no restriction imposed on their commerce, no special fines levied on their effects.   They dwelt in ease and luxury, in houses as handsome and well furnished as their inclination prompted and their purses would allow.   The most splendid quarter in the rich town of Lyons was that inhabited by the Jews.   In Narbonne, of the two prefects of the city, one was always a Jew.

The same state of things continued through the reign of the son and successor of Charlemagne, Louis le Debonnaire. At his court we are told the Jews possessed so much influence, that nobles and envoys of foreign princes paid court to them, and offered bribes to secure their favour.   An officer known as the 'Master of the Jews,' whose business it was to take special care of their interests, resided in the precincts of the palace.   They were permitted to enjoy, not only all rights possessed by their Christian fellow-subjects, but even more.   The day on which markets were wont to be held, if it chanced to be a Saturday, was sometimes altered for their convenience. Charters are still extant, in which special privileges, such as exemptions from tolls and taxes, or permission to hire Christian slaves, are granted to Jews. In criminal and civil actions, their rights were as much respected, their evidence was accounted as good, as that of the other citizens of the country. Their lives were protected by a heavy penalty imposed on any one who slew them. They were exempted from ordeal by fire or water. Their slaves could not be baptized without their consent. They were free to build their synagogues where they pleased, and carry on their peculiar form of worship within them.

A condition of things like this could hardly fail, sooner or later, to provoke the anger and jealousy of the clergy. Agobard, Bishop of Lyons, saw with indignation the growth of their wealth and importance. It was not only that the ports were crowded with their merchantmen, the quays piled with their bales, the streets thronged with their slaves ; that while Christian men walked afoot, clad in mean apparel, and lodged in humble cottages, the Jew reclined in his chariot arrayed in gorgeous attire, or feasted in a splendid palace. This might be borne. But their synagogues vied in magnificence with the stateliest Christian churches, and their preachers drew away crowds who ought to worship at Catholic altars. It was even said that they sold Christians as slaves to the Moors. Agobard exerted his episcopal power to remedy the mischief, so far as he was able. He forbade under pain of spiritual censure, his flock to sell Christian slaves to the Jews,[1] or to work for them on Sundays or holidays, or to buy wine of them, or deal with them at all during the season of Lent.

It is a marked sign of the times, that the Jews ventured to appeal to the king against this exercise of the bishop's

---

[1] It would appear from this, that the law prevalent in the last reign forbidding Jews to hold Christian slaves, had been relaxed.

authority. Louis sent three commissioners to Lyons to inquire into the matter, who decided against the bishop. Mortified and astonished, he preferred fresh charges against the Jews, and when these also failed of their effect, himself repaired to Paris, and demanded a personal interview with the emperor; it was all in vain. He was refused an audience informed that the emperor had dismissed his appeal, and was ordered to return to his diocese! We can hardly believe that this took place in a country which, two centuries before, had seen Jews forcibly dragged to the font for baptism, and, three centuries afterwards, witnessed their forcible expulsion from the country, for no other offence than that of their national existence.

Under Louis's successor, Charles the Bald, the Jews still continued to enjoy immunity from the persecution; but signs were not wanting that this state of things was not long to endure. Remegius, Bishop of Lyons, following up with more success the efforts of Agobard, caused—we are not told by what means—so many Jewish boys and girls to be brought to baptism, that the parents were fain to send their children to be educated in Arles and other cities. Following up his advantage, Remegius petitioned the emperor that the Bishop of Arles might be admonished to pursue the same course as himself. It would appear that Charles granted this request, for we are informed that great numbers of Jewish children were now baptized. Not long afterwards he is said to have been poisoned by his Jewish physician, Zedekias, who was believed to have been incited to the murder by his country-men. Whether this is true or not must be regarded as a doubtful matter. It was certainly a most fatal as well as a most wicked policy, if it was really adopted. The effect of the death of Charles was to break up the existing authority in France. The strong hand which upheld the law was with-drawn. Disorder and anarchy ensued, from which none suffered so much as the Jews. Popular rumours accused them of secretly abetting the inroads of the Normans, from which the country now began seriously to suffer. It was urged that when the invaders overran districts and sacked cities, the Jews alone escaped injury. This was possibly due to the same causes which had exempted them from suffering during the incursions of the Goths and Huns and other Northern nations, and which have been adverted to in a previous chapter. But, however that may be, it was believed that they were secretly in league with the Northmen, and they became in consequence everywhere the objects of popular execration and attack. At Beziers, in Languedoc, it became the practice every year to drive them about with volleys of stone, from Palm Sunday to Tuesday in Easter Week. During the feeble reigns of Louis II., III., and IV., Lothair, Charles II., and III., scarcely any mention is made of them. But what little is told goes to prove that their position was continually growing worse. As the power of the kings diminished, the protection they were able to extend to the Jews diminished also. The great feudatories dealt with them as they pleased, disregarding the royal authority, or employing it for the oppression of the Jews. During the reign of Charles III., called the Simple, we find the Archbishop of Narbonne demanding (A.D. 897) and obtaining from the king a grant of all the landed property in the possession of the Jews throughout his diocese. Whether this was the effect of an act forbidding the Jews to hold landed property, or mere lawless pillage, makes little difference. Similarly, in 889, the Archbishop of Sens, without any cause assigned or reference to the royal authority, expels the whole of the Jews from the bounds of his episcopate.

In Spain, however, the interval of peace and goodwill lasted long beyond the times of which we are now writing. From the foundation of the Moorish kingdom of Cordova by Abderachman I., A.D. 755, to the close of the tenth century, whatever civilization and learning still existed in Europe found its most congenial home in his dominions. Under him and his successors, the Jews appear to have enjoyed, not only the impartial protection of the laws, but free participation in all public offices and distinctions. They were eminent as ministers of state, ambassadors, and financiers. Under him and his successors, the schools at Toledo, Granada, and Cordova became famous throughout the world, and it was said that there was not a Jew to be found through the whole of Spain who could not read his Bible.

Hitherto the great centres of learning had been in the East, and the most promising scholars, even from Spain itself, had resorted thither. But the Persian Caliphate had, for a century or two, been undergoing a gradual but total change. The sovereigns were enervated by ease and luxury; usurpers rent away large portions of their dominions; and the great Emirs grew ever more independent, grasping at last nearly the whole power of the Crown. It was probably these new rulers who set on foot the persecution of their Jewish fellow-subjects. Indifferent as Omar himself could have been to the high repute which the Oriental Academies had attained, they shut up the Jewish Colleges, exiled their learned doctors, and in fine, A.D. 980, drove the Jews altogether from Babylon. Four of the most renowned of the Rabbins were captured, on their outward voyage, by one of the corsairs belonging to the Caliph of Cordova, whom he had sent to cruise in the Greek Archipelago. These four were Rabbi Shemariah, Rabbi Hoshiel, Rabbi Moses, and his son, Rabbi Hanoch. The fate of these four was remarkable. Utterly ignorant of the high value which men of culture and refinement would set upon his prisoners, the corsair sold Shemariah at Alexandria, and the slave rose to be the chief man among the Alexandrian Jews. Rabbi Hoshiel he similarly disposed of to a purchaser on the coast of Africa; and Hoshiel was thence conveyed to Alkihoran, where he attained the rank of Chief Rabbi. Rabbi Moses and his son he conveyed to Cordova. It chanced that the wife of the former was a beautiful woman, and the brutal corsair, captivated by her charms, assailed her with his importunities. Finding herself wholly in his power, she inquired of her husband whether, at the Day of Judgment, the sea would give up its dead. He answered her from the 68th Psalm, 'The Lord said, Mine own will I bring again from Bashan, I will bring again from the depths of the sea;' on receiving which reply, seeing no other way of escaping violence, she plunged into the sea and was drowned. A similar tale is told of Esther Cohen in the sixteenth century.

On the arrival of the captives at Cordova, the two Rabbins were ransomed by their countrymen, though the latter knew nothing of their ability and learning. Their condition was so miserable that they had no clothes, but only some rags of sackcloth to cover their nakedness. In this sordid guise they entered the schools, over which Rabbi Nathan presided. The discussion in progress was on the subject of the Day of Atonement. Rabbi Moses took part in it, and expounded it with such learning and clearness that Rabbi Nathan rose from his seat and said, 'The stranger in sackcloth is my master, and I am his pupil. Make ye him judge of the Congregation of Cordova.' All present assented. Riches and honours became immediately his portion, and he allied himself with one of the wealthiest families in Cordova. The captain of the vessel, learning the value of the captive, for whom he asked no more than the ordinary price of a slave, wished to cancel the sale; but when the matter was referred to the Caliph, he would not allow it. By one of the disciples of Moses, Rabbi Joseph, the Talmud was translated into Arabic, and gained the translator great repute, though he was afterwards disgraced and driven into exile. Rabbi Hanoch, the fourth of the captives, succeeded to his father's office at his death. By him the fame of the College of Cordova was raised to the highest pitch it attained.

The decay of the Babylonian schools had been in progress throughout the tenth century, learning and ability alike, as the reader has heard, being transferred to the flourishing Rabbinical establishment in Cordova. The quarrels between David ben Zacchai, the Prince of the Captivity, and the

I

celebrated Saadi ben Joseph, the Geon, did much towards bringing this about. There was a temporary rally, when the renowned Scherira, and after him, his scarcely less distinguished son, Hai, held the office of Geon. But the former was deposed and put to death by the Caliph Ahmed Kader; and though Hai escaped and transferred his office to Hiskiah, the great-grandson of David Zacchai, yet the respite was for two years only. At the end of that time the Caliph Abdalla deposed Hiskiah, and finally closed the schools. With Hiskiah, A.D. 1038, the line of the Resch Glutha is generally considered to have become extinct.

CHAPTER XIV.

A.D. 980–1100.

THE JEWS IN SPAIN.—IN ENGLAND.—THE CRUSADES.

WITH the downfall of the Carlovingian dynasty, a period of seven centuries began, during which the Jews underwent the most terrible wrongs and sufferings in almost every European country. In some lands persecution showed itself earlier, in others later; in some it reached a greater height, in others it lasted longer. But several generations passed before it was displayed in all its horrible deformity. During the interval we have now under consideration, A.D. 980 to 1100, though acts of injustice and cruelty were occasionally perpetrated, and a fierce spirit of intolerance manifested— which, it was but too evident, needed only to be roused by some popular tumult, to run to the most fearful heights—yet none of the terrible tragedies were enacted by which the succeeding generations were disgraced.

It is somewhat strange that the first massacre should have occurred among a people heretofore remarkable, not merely for their toleration of the Jews, but for the kindness and consideration uniformly shown them. But in 1068 an insurrection broke out in Granada, during which 1500 families were slaughtered. It had been caused partly by the pride of Rabbi Joseph, the chief minister of the Moorish king. His father, Rabbi Samuel, had gained the royal favour by his knowledge and ability ; and at his death the same high office had been continued to his son. But the latter differed in character from his father, who had ever shown himself humble-minded and forbearing. The hauteur and implacable temper of the son raised him up enemies among the grandees, who were ever on the watch for an occasion to effect his fall. About the same time a fanatical zealot provoked an insurrection by attempting to convert the Moorish people of Granada to the Jewish faith. This is an act forbidden by the laws of every Moslem State, under penalty of death. The indiscretion was taken advantage of by the enemies of Joseph. He was assassinated by the insurgents ; the preacher was hanged, and the mob, not satisfied with this revenge, and doubtless in no way unwilling to despoil the wealthy Jews, attacked and pillaged their houses, massacring them, as the reader has heard, to the number probably of seven or eight thousand persons.

Monstrous and barbarous as this outbreak was, it must be allowed that it was mainly provoked by the Jews themselves ; but in what ensued a few years afterwards at the Court of Ferdinand the First, called the Great, the aggression was wholly unprovoked. This monarch, who united under his sway the crowns of Leon and Castile, had resolved on a religious war for the extirpation of the Moslem power in Spain. But, before entering on this, he was advised by his queen, Donna Sancha, that the surest way to call down the blessing of Heaven upon his enterprise, would be to massacre all the Jews in his dominions ! It is a redeeming feature in the sad history of that time, that the Spanish bishops interfered, and forbade the massacre on pain of spiritual penalties, and the reigning Pope, Alexander II., upheld them in their action. Ferdinand's successor, Alphonso

VI., adopted a totally different policy. He found himself so hardly pressed by the action of the Moors in Africa, that the help of the Jews became a matter of pressing necessity with him.[1] He in consequence not only avoided all persecuting measures, but bestowed on them so many favours and privileges, that Pope Alexander's successor severely censured him for his policy, which he declared to be 'a submission of the Church to the synagogue of Satan.'

At this period we have to mention, as we have not done previously, the position of the Jews in England. It is a popular mistake to suppose that they made their appearance there, for the first time, in the train of William the Norman. Many Jews, no doubt, settled in England at that time ; but others had been resident there, though probably in scanty numbers, before this date. A canon of Egbert of York (made A.D. 740) prohibits Christians from taking part in the Jewish festivals. There is mention of them a hundred years later in a charter granted to the monks of Croyland. The laws of Edward the Confessor (A.D. 1041) declare them to be the property of the sovereign, as was the case at that time in France. But it was not until the reign of William Rufus that they took any part in English history. Then we find that that king, who cared little for religion in any shape, and entertained a bitter dislike to the clergy, permitted the Jews publicly to uphold their religion in any way they pleased. Nay, he proclaimed a formal disputation between the advocates of the rival religions in London, and swore, if the Rabbins got the better of the Bishops, ' by St. Luke, he would turn Jew himself!' The Jews are said to have claimed the victory, though we do not hear of the king keeping his vow. At Rouen, afterwards, he entertained a complaint made by certain Jews, that their children had been beguiled into pro-

---

[1] It was this Alphonso who wrote the singular letter to Yusef, king of the Almoravides, inviting him to fight a pitched battle on the ensuing Monday, 'because,' he said, ' Friday would not suit the Mahometans in his army, or Saturday the Jews, or Sunday the Christians.'

fessing Christianity, offering at the same time to pay a handsome sum if the children returned to their ancient faith. The king took the money, and ordered the converts to abjure their new profession. Failing in one or two instances to effect this, we are told he was very unwilling to refund the money paid him.

These incidents, scandalous as doubtless they are, show nevertheless that the Jews at this time enjoyed immunity from persecution ; unless, indeed, the heavy and lawless exactions made on them by the Norman kings themselves are to be regarded as acts of persecution. The property of the Jews was by no means secure from *them*, but it was secure from all other spoilers. We are told that in London and York they dwelt in splendid mansions, resembling the castles of the barons ; while in Oxford they possessed three halls for the education of their youth,—Lombard Hall, Moses Hall, and Jacob Hall ; nor does their presence seem to have been objected to.[1] They had a cemetery at St. Giles's, Cripplegate.

But it will now be proper to enter on a consideration of the causes which led to the renewal of popular bitterness against the Hebrew race in all the countries of Europe. First among these must be noted the prevalence of the Feudal System. This singular institution was, we must allow, in theory, both comprehensive and consistent. The position and duties of every man were defined, the rights of every man secured and protected. The serf tilled his feudal superior's lands ; the freeman fought his battles. Both received in return maintenance and protection, while from the feudal baron there lay an appeal to the sovereign. But at the same time we must also

---

[1] There appears, indeed, to have been at that time an amount of toleration which may well surprise us. One Mossey, a Jew of Wallingford, was wont, we are told, openly to ridicule the miracles of St. Frideswide. He would crook his fingers as if they were paralysed, and presently straighten them, or limp like a cripple, and then suddenly leap or dance, crying out ' A miracle !' This was a calm on the edge of a storm such as has rarely been seen !—' Rise, Fall, and Future Restoration of Jews,' ch. iii.

allow, as a matter of fact, that under it the very extremity of lawless injustice prevailed—that every feudal castle was practically the stronghold of an arbitrary and irresponsible despot, whose soldiers executed his pleasure, however iniquitous or barbarous, without scruple and without remorse. Still, all classes had nominally the guardians of their rights and interests, with the single exception of the Jews. The latter could not be feudatories. The law of the land and the prejudice of the people would not have suffered that ; nor could they be serfs or vassals. They never practised agriculture, and the noble profession of arms would have been thought disgraced by their admission to it. Consequently, they had no place in society, nor were there any to whom they could appeal for justice or protection, except where they were directly the dependants of the sovereign himself. But even where this was the case, any attempt to obtain justice was precarious and perilous. If one of the robber barons seized a Jew who might be travelling through his domains, and subjected him to agonizing tortures until he had obtained his release by paying a large sum of money—there was practically no remedy. The attempt to obtain it would probably end in twofold loss and suffering to himself. Any sympathy shown him by the peasantry or townsfolk would bring, in all likelihood, the vengeance of the aggressor on them. If they concerned themselves in any way with the sufferer, it would probably be by following the example set them by their superiors, and maltreating and plundering him. In this manner the Jews became the outcasts of society ; and all classes of men were willing enough to adopt the ignorant and rancorous intolerance of the clergy of the day, who (with some noble exceptions) inveighed against them as the enemies of Christ, finding in the odium thus cast on them an excuse for their own lawless rapacity and violence.

Another reason for the general dislike in which they were held was their wealth, and the manner in which it had been amassed. They were, as has been already intimated, the only bankers, almost the only traders, of the day. They had become an absolute necessity of life to many classes of men. If the sovereign wished to negotiate a marriage, or embark in a foreign war, a large sum of money was required, which the Jews alone could supply. The same was the case with the nobles and land-owners of lesser rank ; and even the Christian merchant could sometimes save his credit only by a timely loan, which was to be obtained from none but Hebrew coffers. It was affirmed that the usury exacted for these was inordinate ; that the Jews took advantage of their opportunity to accumulate enormous gains, to the total ruin of their debtors. The rate of interest demanded was, as a general rule, extortionate. Yet it should be borne in mind that the monstrous injustice often shown them, when they were,—on any pretext, or on no pretext at all,—despoiled of their money, if it did not render the exaction of these terms necessary to secure to the lender, in the long run, his fair profit, it did offer a strong temptation for exaction, and gave him a ready excuse for offering only the hardest terms to the borrower.[1] Whatever value, however, this argument may possess, it was utterly disregarded by the enemies of the Jews in those days, who took into account only two facts—one, that the Jews demanded an enormous amount of usury, which brought them immense wealth, and the other, that its payment reduced themselves to poverty.

These influences had been for a long time at work, causing the Jews to be regarded with ever-increasing disfavour. But it may be doubted whether they would ever have burst forth into the furious volcano of persecution which the next generation witnessed, if it had not been that the element of religious fanaticism was now added to those already at work. The cry that Christ was dishonoured through the profanation of the

---

[1] It is plainly intimated by Bernard of Clairvaulx that there were Christians (he probably meant Lombard merchants) who exacted more excessive usury than the Jews themselves.

scenes of His birth and crucifixion by the unhallowed rites of the Infidels, and that it was the bounden duty of all faithful Christians to wrest the holy places from their grasp, now resounded through Christendom, and roused an enthusiasm of which the world had never before beheld the like.

It may surprise us, not that this feeling should have been awakened, but that it should not have been awakened *before*. Three hundred and fifty years had elapsed since the conquest of Jerusalem by the Saracens ; and ever since then it had been in the occupation of the unbelievers. Why was the possession of the Holy City by them a greater outrage on the feelings of Christian men in one generation than in another? Or are we to suppose that men were more zealous for God's honour in the eleventh than they had been in the seventh century? No, not so. The causes which provoked the Crusades were different from these, and they are of importance to us, because they throw a light on the feeling which simultaneously arose against the Jews also.

During the first two centuries of the occupation of the Holy City by the Saracens, the latter had been ruled by the Ommiad or Abasside Caliphs—men who, for the most part, governed equitably, and were courteous and tolerant in their dealings with strangers. The number of pilgrims who visited Palestine was small, and they were uniformly received with friendliness. But in the tenth century, when the idea was widely entertained throughout Western Europe that the world was on the very point of coming to an end, and further, that all who died in the Holy Land would certainly be saved, the number of those who travelled thither was greatly multiplied. Those who returned brought back with them tales of outrage and unprovoked insult, which everywhere roused indignation. Jerusalem had passed into the hands of the Turks, a fierce and uncultured race, who had adopted Islamism in its most fanatic spirit. The murder of men, and the outrages offered to women, were good deeds in their eyes ; and where they abstained from this extremity of violence, it was only to display their hate and scorn under some other form. The resentment which these wrongs called forth had spread through all European countries. The air was, as it were, everywhere charged with inflammable vapour, and it needed only the torch which Peter the Hermit had lighted to cause it to burst forth in one consuming flame. 'Death to the Infidels. It is the will of God!' was the cry that rang throughout Europe. All men hastened to obey the call. From the king on his throne to the journeyman in his workshop, they bound the cross on their shoulders, and went forth to rescue the Holy Land from the profane grasp of the unbelievers.

This is the age of the five celebrated Talmudists, called 'the Five Isaacs,' all of them bearing that name. They are distinguished as Isaac of Cordova, of Lucena, of Barcelona, of Pumbeditha, and of Fez. The Spanish Poet Halevi was born towards the close of this period. From the middle of the eleventh century, Spain was for four hundred years the chief seat of Rabbinical learning. The great schools were at Barcelona, Granada, and Toledo.

To this era also belongs the renowned Solomon Gabriol, poet and philosopher, author of 'The Fountain of Life.' He was born at Malaga, 1021, and died A.D. 1070.

'DEATH to the infidel. It is the will of God!' Such was the cry that rang through Europe—'Death to the Moslem, whose unhallowed shrine overshadows the holy place, in which the Saviour Himself has worshipped, whose blasphemies awake the same echoes which His Divine preaching once called forth!' Yes. But were these the only shrines where false worship was offered? were they in Jerusalem the only ones who blasphemed the Lord? If the slaughter of the unbelieving Turk was acceptable to the Most High, why not that of the unbelieving Jew? It was strange that this peril should not have been dreaded by the Jews dwelling in the lands which the mania called forth by Peter the Hermit overspread. But it does not seem to have done so; they made no attempt to escape from the approaching danger. They even continued the ordinary course of their business, making the same enormous gains out of the Crusaders' necessities, which they had done out of every other political movement for generations past. The great baron, who had vowed to lead his hundreds, or it might be his thousands, of armed followers to the rescue of the Holy Sepulchre, mortgaged his lands, or his jewels, or perhaps sold them outright, to the Jews, on such terms as we can hardly believe that the one could have asked or the other agreed to. Poorer men parted with their all on the like terms. But that there were some shrewd men left among the Christians, who were not carried away by the tide of popular excitement, the whole wealth of the community would have passed into the hands of the Jews. It is needless to add that the bitter feelings towards this isolated race—who were for ever battening on the wants and sufferings of others—were greatly aggravated by these proceedings, and it was not long before this burst out into a flame.

All over Northern France and Germany, the Jews seem to have been numerous at this time ; but in what is now Rhenish Prussia, and along the banks of the Moselle, they were to be found in the greatest abundance. It was near the city of Treves that the first vast multitude of undisciplined fanatics assembled, under the leadership of Walther von Habenicht and Peter the Hermit. As they set forth, under the guidance of a goat and a goose, to find their way to the Holy Land, a cry was suddenly raised, doubtless by some enemy of the Jews, that while they were marching to destroy the enemies of the Lord Jesus in Palestine, they were leaving unassailed at home those who were not only His enemies, but His murderers—the Jews ! The cry was instantly caught up, the frantic crowd rushed into Treves, and began a general pillage of the Jews' houses, and a massacre of their occupants. Taken by surprise, the authorities offered no interference ; indeed, no interference they could have offered would have been of the slightest avail. The unhappy Jews, equally unprepared, could neither resist nor escape. Scenes too shocking for description ensued. Women tied heavy weights round their necks, and threw themselves into the rivers to avoid the last dishonour. Men slew their own children, to

save them from the tortures to which they would be subjected ; their own lives they yielded up in despairing silence.
Some fled to the citadel, hoping to be protected against the
violence of their assailants ; but the Bishop of Treves received
them with threats and reproaches, refusing to interfere in
their behalf, unless they would accept baptism. The same
scenes took place in Cologne, Worms, Spires, and Mayence.
Everywhere the only hope of escape from torture and death
was baptism ; except, indeed, where a heavy bribe had been
paid for episcopal protection, or where, as at Spires, the Jews
armed themselves and sold their lives dearly. The tide of
murder rolled on, sweeping the shores of the Maine and the
Danube, the same scenes being everywhere repeated. In
Bavaria, it is said that as many as 12,000 Jews were
slaughtered. The Emperor Henry IV. seems to have been
the only potentate whom these atrocities struck with horror.
He issued a decree, repairing, so far as was possible, the
wrongs that had been done, and forbidding them for the
future. But, for the most part, the historians of those times
relate the horrors that took place with a *sangfroid* which
speaks volumes as to the light in which they were regarded
by those who witnessed them.

But the three mighty hosts, led by Peter and his two
colleagues, passed on and perished, and the exhaustion
succeeded which such a drain on the population must
necessarily occasion. It was not until half the twelfth century
had passed away that the crusading mania was again roused.
Then a fanatic monk, named Rodolph, commenced a mission
through the German cities, calling on all men, by the watchword ' Hep, Hep ' (the initials of the words *Hierosolyma est
perdita*) to assist in slaying and crushing the enemies of God.
The Jews knew too well, by past experience, that they were
included under this latter term, and many effected a timely
retreat. Nevertheless, a frightful carnage took place in
Strasburg, Mayence, and the other Rhine cities, encouraged,
unhappily, by too many of the clergy. It is like a bright

gleam of sunshine on a dark November day, to read the protest addressed by the saintly Bernard of Clairvaulx, to his brother clergy against the blind and savage spirit by which Rodolph was possessed.[1]

'The Jews,' he writes, 'ought not to be persecuted ; they ought not to be put to death, they ought not to be driven into banishment. What says the Scripture? "Slay them not, lest My people forget." The Jews are living monuments to remind us of the sufferings of the Lord. Therefore it is that they are scattered. . . . Therefore they endure a hard bondage under Christian princes ; yet, in the eventide of the world, they will be converted, and He will remember them. Addressing Rodolph himself, he says, 'You are of another mind from Him who said, " Put up thy sword into the sheath, for he that taketh the sword shall perish with the sword." Does not the Church triumph more gloriously over the Jews when she refutes and converts them, than if she slew them with the edge of the sword?' It is satisfactory also to learn that Pope Eugenius III. advocated the same view, and that Rodolph was ordered back to his convent, though not before he had occasioned the most terrible crimes and sufferings.

But the condition of the Jews grew no better, but rather worse, as the century advanced. The calumny—whether it was the revival of an ancient accusation against the Jews, or one newly invented at this period—of crucifying boys at their Passover, in mockery of the Saviour's passion, was widely diffused and credited. It was reported that, about A.D. 1180, during the youth of Philip Augustus, they had in this manner murdered one Richard, a youth belonging to Pontoise ; and, in confirmation of the truth of the story, the body, when it was conveyed to Paris, worked many miracles. Philip had no sooner ascended his throne than he put forth an edict,

---

[1] Arnold, Archbishop of Cologne, also did his best to discountenance the persecutors. He gave them the fortress of Wolkenstein as a refuge, and they there made an armed and successful defence.

A.D. 1182, whereby all debts due to Jews were annulled, and all pledges held by them were to be restored to the original owners. Not satisfied with this display of somewhat cheap generosity, he made a second proclamation, confiscating all their property which was not removable, and commanding them to sell everything else belonging to them, and depart from his dominions. In vain they appealed for mercy. King and nobles and bishops alike closed their ears. The twofold offence of holding heretical opinions and mortgages on estates was not to be forgiven. It will readily be credited that at the enforced sale of their goods the prices bidden were of the lowest. The unhappy Jews were compelled to depart, amid the execrations of the populace, from the homes in which their whole lives had been passed, carrying with them little but their wives and children. It was not enough that they had been, by the most high-handed injustice, stripped of their possessions ; they were not to be allowed to remain in the land where the wrong had been done, and so remind the doers of their crime !

It will surprise no one to be told that their removal did not increase the wealth or relieve the public burdens of the nation. It was found that the expulsion of the Jews was, as Fouché said of the murder of the Duke d'Enghien, 'more than a crime, for it was a blunder.' Within twenty years Philip found it necessary to issue a new edict, permitting their return. But it *does* occasion our wonder to hear that the Jews consented to the step. It speaks volumes for the depth of the misery to which they had been reduced, that they could be prevailed on to trust themselves again to the justice and mercy of a king who had so flagrantly proved his disregard of both.[1] Not long after their return, we are told that they held

---

[1] They were not readmitted without the enactment of several laws which materially affected their future position. Among others, they were obliged to wear a distinctive badge ; and the persons to whom they might lend money, the articles they might receive in pledge, and the amount of interest they might require, were all settled by statute.

an assembly by permission of the Queen's mother, at a castle on the Seine. Here the old charge of scourging, crucifying, and crowning with thorns a youth whom they had seized was once more alleged against them. Philip repaired in person to the spot, where he condemned eighty of the accused to be burned alive.[1]

In Spain, during this century, the Jews were still equitably dealt with, though there were signs of the change of feeling towards them which was gradually taking possession of the public mind. For this two causes may be assigned. In the first place, the power of the Mahometans, who had always been the protectors of the Jews, was fast waning; and the Christian sovereigns no longer dreaded the enmity of the Jews, who in previous generations might have been dangerous allies to their rivals. In the second, the downfall of the Ommiad Caliphs, who had uniformly been just and generous in their dealings with the Jews, proved most disastrous to them. The Almohades, who, A.D. 1150, superseded them, were fierce and bloody fanatics, inclined to force the faith of Islam on all with whom they came in contact. One of the first edicts of Abdel-Mumen, the founder of the dynasty, required all his subjects, of whatsoever creed, to profess Mahometanism. The usual consequences followed. Many Jews went into voluntary exile; many more made an outward profession of their persecutor's creed, still secretly retaining their own. The happy days of the Spanish Jews were over. Moorish rule was ended.

In the Christian kingdom, however, justice and right still prevailed. The royal authority was uniformly exerted for the protection of peaceable and unoffending men. But there were occasions on which this power proved insufficient to restrain the violence of the people, who had probably learned from their neighbours to regard the Jews with disfavour.

---

[1] See a full discussion of this charge and its probable origin. Appendix V.

Thus, a riot occurred at Toledo, A.D. 1108, instigated, in all likelihood, by the crusaders, who were just on the point of setting out for Palestine. The populace, under the usual pretext of slaying the enemies of Christ, attacked and burned the houses of the Jews, wrecked the synagogues, immolating the Rabbins, as it were, on their own altars, and made a general massacre of the common people. Alphonso tried in vain, first to repress, and then to punish, the offenders.

But this occurrence, shocking as it was, was a mere temporary outburst of popular fury. It was not repeated, not even in the reign of his descendant, Alphonso VIII., in 1171, when, above all other times, a Jewish massacre might have been looked for. This king had become deeply enamoured of a beautiful Jewess, named Rachel Fermosa. For her society he neglected his queen, and withdrew himself from public business. Grave misfortunes ensued: his forces were defeated at Alarcos, and the kingdom menaced by the hostility of the neighbouring states. The people believed that these calamities were due, not to the bad administration of public affairs, but to the indignation of Heaven at the king's unhallowed affection for an unbeliever. Their jealousy was also roused by the favour shown to her countrymen. A rebellion broke out, the rioters burst into the king's palace, and assassinated Fermosa before the eyes of her lover. But they satisfied themselves with her death, and did not molest the Jewish favourites whom she had patronized.

Alphonso IX. showed even greater favour to the Jews than had been bestowed on them by his predecessors. Innocent III. repeated in his instance the charge which Gregory VII. had brought against his ancestor, 'of elevating the Synagogue at the cost of the Church.' He relieved both Jews and Moors, we are told, from the payment of tithes, and allowed them to hold landed property,—a rare privilege in those days. One of his laws—which allowed a Jew, in the event of one of his slaves being converted to Christianity, to claim, at the hands of the person who had converted him whatever indemnity

K

he might think proper—seems to be as unfair to the Christians as the legislation of those times usually was to the Jews.

In Hungary, Germany, and Bohemia, their condition, during the period we have under consideration, appears to have been prosperous. Ladislas, King of Hungary, convened, we are told, a Synod in 1092, in which various regulations relating to the Jews were made. It was ordered that if a Jew bought a Christian slave of either sex, the slave should be set at liberty, and the price paid for him confiscated to the bishop. His son Coloman re-enacted this prohibition against the use of Christian slaves, but permitted the Jews to purchase and cultivate lands, on condition of employing Jewish or pagan labour, and settling in such places only as were under the jurisdiction of a bishop. These laws prove that the Jews must have been both a numerous and wealthy part of the population.

In Germany and Bohemia they had many stately synagogues, particularly in the great towns, and were not interfered with by the government. Nevertheless, they did not escape persecution. A fanatic priest, named Gotesel, incited a band of lawless ruffians, amounting in number to fifteen thousand, to attack the Jews; and he was supported, it is believed, in secret, by persons high in authority. He plundered the property of the Jews, outraged their women, and massacred the men all over Franconia. He then entered Hungary, and commenced perpetrating the like atrocities; when he was attacked and slain, together with the greater part of his followers. Soon afterwards the Landgrave of Leiningen declared in like manner a religious war against the Jews, and having assembled a body of troops, committed great havoc among them, pursuing them at last, like his predecessor, into Hungary; where, like his predecessor again, he was defeated and slain.[1]

---

[1] Rabbi Joseph has given us (vol. i. 30, 35) a long and terrible picture of the barbarous cruelties inflicted at this period on his countrymen,

In Russia, early in the twelfth century (A.D. 1113), there was a savage outbreak in the city of Kief, against the Jews. The same cry seems to have been raised which has so frequently been heard in other lands, their accumulation of wealth, at the cost, it was supposed, of their neighbours. The merciful Vladimir, who succeeded to the throne, tried to protect them, but could only do so by assenting to their expulsion from Russia. This was their first, and their longest, term of banishment from any European country. They were not allowed to return for 600 years.

During this period lived Solomon, called Rashi, or as it is more commonly written, Jarchi. He was the most renowned of the many commentators on the Talmud. It is said that no edition of that work has appeared since his time which had not his commentary appended to it. He was born A.D. 1040, and died A.D. 1105.

---

in consequence of their refusal 'to submit to the proud waters, or enter the House of Error' (*i.e.*, to be baptized, or be admitted to the Church). Comp. Psalm cxxiv. 4.

IT has been noted in a previous chapter that, up to the
end of William Rufus's reign, the chief hardship that
befell the Jews in England was, that the Norman kings
extracted large sums from them, partly as loans—for which,
perhaps, payment was hardly contemplated by either party
—and partly as the price of the protection afforded them.
The same state of things continued during the reigns of
Henry I., Stephen, and Henry II. Throughout this long
period,—not much less than a hundred years,—the Jews
continued to gather in riches without molestation, to an
extent which proved ruinous to themselves in subsequent
generations, little as they anticipated such a result at the
time.[1] There were not wanting signs, however, which might
have indicated the approaching danger. During the reign

---

[1] At a Parliament held at Northampton, when it was proposed to
raise a tax for an expedition to the Holy Land, the Jews were assessed
at £60,000, and the whole of the rest of the population of the country
at £70,000 only.

of Stephen, A.D. 1145, the charge was made against the Jews,—for the first time in England, if not in Europe,—of having kidnapped and crucified a boy at Norwich, in contemptuous parody of the Saviour's passion. The case was brought before the notice of the king, and the accused were adjudged to pay a fine to the Crown—a most suspicious termination of the inquiry. No further outbreak, however, occurred : and during the protracted reign of his successor, Henry II., the same condition of things continued. That able and powerful monarch, whatever might be his difficulties with the clergy, repressed with a strong hand all overt acts of violence against the peculiar people, who looked to him for protection.[1] But he could not prevent their growing unpopularity. Society had become largely influenced by the crusading spirit. The loss of Jerusalem,—which had been wrested by so large an expenditure of blood and treasure from the hold of the Infidel,—roused everywhere a more bitter feeling than ever against the enemies of Christ. It was mainly through the Crusades that the Jews had acquired their wealth ; and the spectacle of unbelievers living in ease and luxury, at the cost of the faithful servants of Christ, whose bones were whitening the plains of Palestine, or who had returned to England to pine in poverty, stirred public indignation to the utmost. The train was already laid for a furious onslaught upon them. It needed but a spark to bring about the explosion.

The crisis came almost immediately after the death of Henry. Anxious at once to show their loyalty and secure the protection of the new sovereign, the Jews sent a deputation, consisting of men of the highest repute among them, to attend the coronation of King Richard, and present him with rich gifts suitable to the occasion. Their presence

---

[1] Two of these, similar to the outbreak in Stephen's time, occurred in 1160 and 1181. It has been shrewdly remarked, that the Jews were always charged with this crime just at the times when the kings wanted money.

was regarded as a profanation of the ceremony, and orders were sent them to stay away. They obeyed, but a few of their number, supposing themselves unknown, or that they would not be noticed, ventured into the Abbey. They were detected and dragged violently out. The popular fury was inflamed. The houses of the Jews were everywhere broken open, plundered, and set on fire. The king endeavoured to put a stop to the riot, but in vain. The pillage and murder went on throughout the entire night. On the following day order was restored, many of the rioters were arrested, and a strict inquiry made. Three were hanged, but it is a curious illustration of the state of the public feeling of the day, that none of these were punished for injuries done to the Jews. Two of the three had robbed a Christian, pretending that he was a Jew, and the third had set on fire the house of a Jew, but, unluckily for the offender, a Christian's house had been burned along with it. It would really seem that, in the existing state of public feeling, the government dared not punish any one for the simple offence of injuring a Jew!

The news of the outbreak ran like wild fire through the country, and everywhere the rabble were roused to the same violence. In Norwich and Stamford, and other large towns, the Jews were attacked, their houses gutted, themselves maltreated and slain. At Lincoln, the humane governor of the castle gave them timely warning. They retired with their valuables within its shelter, and were preserved. At York, a Jew named Benedict, who had declared himself a convert to Christianity to save his life, and had afterwards recanted, became the special object of popular fury. He had died of exhaustion and terror before the commencement of the *émeute;* but the mob, disregarding that circumstance, attacked his house, burned it to the ground, and murdered his wife and children. The other Jews—as many of them, that is, as had heard in time of the danger that was threatening them—took refuge within the walls of York Castle, thinking, probably, to escape as their brethren at Lincoln had done.

Those who were left behind were ruthlessly massacred, man, woman, and child, a few only excepted, who submitted to be baptized.

The Jews within the castle seem to have been received favourably by the governor. But they suspected him of treachery. Unhappily, their Christian brethren had given them but too good reason for their suspicious temper. A rumour was circulated among them that he meant to open the gates to the rioters, conditionally on being rewarded for his treachery by receiving a large portion of the plunder. One day, when he had gone out into the town, they took the desperate step of shutting the gates against him, and, manning the walls, declared they would defend themselves against all who might attack them. The governor's indignation was roused to the utmost at this ingratitude. It chanced that the sheriff of the county was in York, attended by an armed force. The governor appealed to him to recapture the fortress from the traitors who had seized it. The sheriff assented, and, aided by the mob, made an assault on the castle. The besieged defended themselves manfully, and for a long time kept their enemies at bay. At last it became evident that they could resist no further. Then their Rabbi, a man of learning and high character, addressed them, and warned them that there was nothing but death before them—a speedy and honourable death by their own hands, or a death attended by every circumstance of insult and barbarity by the hands of their enemies. Surely it was better to choose the first.

This proposal was agreed to by nearly all present. They collected their valuables. Such as were combustible they burned, the rest they buried. They then set fire to the castle in several places, slew, first of all, their wives and children, and then one another. The Rabbi was the last to die. He stabbed the last survivor of his flock, and then drove the sword into his own heart. The fearful scene which had taken place, a thousand years before, in the Castle of

Masada, was repeated, with scarcely any variation but those caused by the difference of time and place. If any evidence were required of the resolute and unchangeable character of the Jewish people, this story would surely suffice.

In the morning a renewed assault was made, and then came the fearful discovery of what had taken place. The conduct of the victors fully justified the forebodings of the Rabbi ; the few who had shrunk from death at the hands of their countrymen were dragged out of their hiding-places and butchered. Then the work of plunder began. The gold and jewels were carefully secured, but the papers, of which there was a great store, were burned. This was an unhappy mistake for the rioters. The papers were mostly bonds and acknowledgments of debts, the reversion of which, by the law, became the property of the Crown. Consequently, by this act, large sums were forfeited which would have enriched the royal treasury. The reader will not be surprised to hear that a commission of inquiry was straightway sent down to York. But the papers had been hopelessly destroyed, and the ringleaders of the outrage had fled to Scotland. The chief citizens entered into recognizances for the better observance of order ; but it does not appear that any of the perpetrators of this horrible murder of 500, or some say 1500, innocent persons ever underwent any legal penalty.

When Richard returned from his captivity, however, he resolved to place the affairs of the Jews in a more satisfactory condition. He found that during his absence the utmost lawlessness had prevailed. The Norman baron had been in the habit of seizing on any wealthy Jew, carrying him to his castle, and inflicting any amount of torture on him, till he paid the sum demanded of him.[1] He forbade this, declaring the Jews to be the chattels of the Crown, with which it would be treason to meddle. A special court

---

[1] The readers of Sir Walter Scott will remember the graphic scene in 'Ivanhoe,' where Front de Bœuf threatens to roast Isaac of York alive, unless he pays his demand.

in the king's Exchequer was set apart for the management
of Jewish finances. The amount of property belonging to
every Jew was duly registered and assessed. This was no
doubt arbitrary and extortionate, but still it was better
than lawless pillage, and probably did not prevent the
Jews from continuing to amass large fortunes. During the
remainder of his short reign they experienced no further
persecution.

Richard died in the last year of the century, and John, the
cruellest and most detestable of the English kings, succeeded
to the throne. But for a time his usage of the Jews was
milder than that of any of his predecessors. He issued a
charter restoring to them all the privileges they had possessed
in the times of the pure Norman kings. They might dwell
where they pleased ; might hold lands and fees ; their evidence
was to be of equal value with that of Christians ; and, if
charged with an offence, they could be tried only in the
King's Court. With what motive this was done, it is not
easy to say. John may have simply wished to conciliate
their good-will, and so induce them to be as liberal to him
as possible. But the suspicion that he meant to allow them
time and opportunity for accumulating vast riches, and then
seize on them himself, has much to justify it. It is, again,
not unlikely that the countenance which he showed them
rendered them more than ever odious to his subjects ; and
when this became patent, he was in no way inclined to incur
unpopularity on their account.[1] Any way, some ten years
after his accession, there was a sudden and total change in
his demeanour towards them. Without any reason assigned,
the whole of the Jews were arrested, cast into prison, and
their property confiscated to the Crown. Suspecting that

[1] It is said that, deceived probably by the long continuance of their
immunity from ill-usage, the Jews had begun to make display of their
wealth, in a manner which gave great offence to the citizens of London ;
who treated them, in consequence, with many indignities. This had
reached the king's ears, and he wrote a letter to them respecting it.

they had disclosed to the authorities only a portion of their wealth, and that large secret hoards still existed, he caused them to be put to the most cruel tortures, to compel them to give up these also. The well-known tale of the Jew of Bristol, of whom 10,000 marks of silver [1] were demanded, and who, on his refusal, was sentenced to lose a tooth every day until he paid it, is perfectly well authenticated. He allowed, it is related, seven of his teeth to be knocked out of his head, and then, to save the remainder, consented to the payment. The king is said to have obtained as much as 60,000 marks by this pillage of his subjects. Nor did the cruelty and injustice end here. The rebellious barons, regarding the Jews as the property of the Crown, seized upon their treasures and demolished their houses, to repair the breaches in the walls of London.

Before concluding the history of the twelfth century, it will be proper to give some brief account of the various impostors claiming to be the expected Messiah who made their appearance during its continuance, and also to say something of the great doctors and learned men who adorned the period in question.

As regards the first of these subjects—adventurers claiming to be the Messiah of prophecy have put forward their pretensions throughout the whole of Jewish history, from the times of Judas of Galilee to those of which we are now writing; but never in such numbers as at this era. The first of them appeared in France in 1137. He was put to death, many synagogues were destroyed, and their congregations severely punished on his account. Another followed, a few years afterwards, in Spain, where he received the support of a learned Rabbi in Cordova. Notwithstanding this, he seems to have had but few disciples, and soon subsided into insignificance. A third, in Moravia, attracted more attention. He claimed to have the power of rendering

---

[1] Between six and seven thousand pounds, English money.

himself invisible, and several times—it is presumed by the help of some juggling trick—succeeded in escaping from his pursuers. His followers at last, dreading the anger of the king, delivered him up, and he was hanged.

Several more made their appearance in the East, chiefly in Arabia and Persia. One of these, who had been cured, by what he thought a miracle, of his leprosy, drew great multitudes after him. His pretensions were exposed by the Jewish doctors; but nevertheless large numbers of Jews were slain in consequence of the tumults he excited. Another, an Arabian, is chiefly remarkable for the ingenuity by which he escaped torture. He told the king that if his head should be cut off he would rise again from the dead. The king instantly beheaded him with his scimitar, but only to find that the impostor had by this stratagem baffled his tormentors.

But the most famous of all was Eldavid, on whose strange history Disraeli has founded his 'Wondrous Tale of Alroy,'[1] He was born about the middle of the twelfth century, in Amaria, a city tributary to the sovereign of Persia. He was acquainted with Talmudical learning, and had learned, it was said, some strange cabalistic secrets. He raised an insurrection among his countrymen, whom he deluded by several apparent miracles. After some unavailing attempts to get him into their power, the Persians bribed his father-in-law, with a promise of ten thousand crowns, to betray him. His father-in-law invited him to a feast, and there assassinated him.

---

[1] His history is given in detail by the celebrated Benjamin of Tudela.

CHAPTER XVII

IT would be impossible, within the limits of a work like
this, to give even an outline of the great schools of
Jewish learning, which date from an age anterior to the
coming of Christ, and have been continued even to modern
times. The mere enumeration of the names of their
renowned Rabbins, each the author of some profound thesis
or learned commentary, would fill a volume. During the
gloomiest ages of Christendom, when the lamp of learning
was all but extinct, even in the cloister, where alone it
glimmered, the Jews had light in their dwellings, like their
ancestors of old who sojourned in Goshen, while the world
without was wrapped in Egyptian darkness. They are, as
a rule, but little known to ordinary readers, one reason of
which doubtless is, that they concern themselves mainly with
subjects which very nearly affect their own people, and find
exercise for their peculiar mode of thought, but which neither
suit the fancy nor awaken the interest of other races. Their
treatises on the Talmuds and the Cabbala, on cosmogony

and judicial astrology, even their commentaries on the Pentateuch and the Hebrew Prophets, are read with profound attention by their own people; but their learning and ability is lost on other readers. Nevertheless, there are some great names among their literary celebrities, which are familiar to the ears of all students, and with which all ought to be acquainted who would know anything of their history. There are three in particular, belonging nearly to the era with which we are now dealing, which ought not to be passed over. These are Aben Ezra, Moses the son of Maimon, commonly known as Maimonides, and Benjamin of Tudela.

Aben Ezra was born about A.D. 1092 at Toledo, of a family already distinguished for learning and literary ability. He was an eminent commentator and Cabbalist, a writer on grammar, philosophy, mathematics, and astronomy, celebrated also as a physician and a poet. His commentaries include nearly the whole of the Old Testament, the earlier prophets being the only ones on which he has not written. Being a man of substance, he was able to gratify his fancy for travelling, which was a rare taste in those days, but possessed by several others of his brethren also. The places at which his various writings were composed may serve to illustrate the extent of his wanderings. Thus one of his treatises is dated from Mantua, another from Rome, a third from London, and a fourth from some Greek city, and the like. He visited Africa also, as well as Palestine, and conferred with learned men of his own race at Tiberias, where the Patriarch of the West had once fixed his abode. He died on his return from this pilgrimage, in his seventy-fifth year, A.D. 1174. Posterity has bestowed on him the title of 'Hachacham, or the Wise,' and learned men of all races and ages have done justice to his genius and learning.[1]

---

[1] Among his other accomplishments, he was, we are told, a skilful chess-player. The Jews were famous for their passion for and skill at that game. Among Aben Ezra's writings was a poem on chess, which was rendered into Latin, and published at Oxford in 1694.

Still more renowned for the extent and variety of his
knowledge was Moses Maimonides. He was born March
30th, 1135, in Cordova. His father, Maimon, held the office
of Judge of the Jews in his native city, which, indeed, for
generations past had been almost hereditary in his family.
Two different accounts are given us of his early youth; one
says that he showed from the first symptoms of extraordinary
ability, and his father began, almost from his cradle, to instruct
him in the elements of science; the other, that he was
treated by his family generally with contempt, because his
mother had been a woman of inferior birth, and by his
father with harshness, on account of his intellectual dulness.
According to the latter statement, he was sent away from
home to be under the charge of another teacher, but returned
home so greatly improved in learning and manners that the
opinion of his relatives respecting him was altogether changed.
He studied astronomy and medicine under the famous Averroes.
It was in this last-named science that he became especially
excellent, both as a practitioner and a writer. From Averroes,
also, he acquired the knowledge of the writings of Aristotle,
which were unknown in Western Europe at this date.

Intrigues among the Jews of Cordova obliged Maimon to
fly with his family from Spain, and take refuge in Morocco;
but after a short residence in that country he removed to
Egypt, and settled at Cairo. Maimon died soon afterwards,
and his two sons maintained themselves for a while by
trading in jewels; but a revolution having taken place in
Egypt, by reason of the conquest of the country by the
Turks, Maimonides attached himself to Abdebrahim, one of
the Turkish generals, whom he served in the twofold capacity
of counsellor and physician. Though we do not hear of his
having previously practised medicine, it is probable that he
did so, as his knowledge of it appears to have been always
considerable. Through his connection with his Turkish
employer he was not long afterwards brought to the notice
of the famous Saladin, now Soldan of Egypt, who took him

into his employ as his physician. He retained this post at the court not only of Saladin but of his successor, until his death in 1204. There was, however, a very unhappy episode in his life during this period, when he was accused of having attempted to poison the Sultan ; and he was in consequence sent away in disgrace from the court. He is said to have spent the whole time of his exile in a cave, where he studied incessantly, filling many volumes with the fruits of his researches. He was afterwards recalled and replaced in his former office. During what is called the Third Crusade, we are told that he was invited to attend the English King, Richard Cœur de Lion, during his illness, but that he declined the office.

Maimonides had advanced far beyond his contemporaries in knowledge. Instructed in the philosophy of Aristotle, and a devout student of Plato, his mind broke loose from the fetters of Judaical Rabbinism, and sought to base religion on philosophy rather than on revelation. At one period of his life it is known that he did, under strong external pressure, make an outward profession of Mahometanism, or at least conformed to its ritual. Possibly his experience of its rigid stereotyped creed—on account of which Gibbon has bestowed such strange praise upon it—may have made him less tolerant of the fetters of Rabbinical tradition. It is certain that he introduced new lights and strange forms of thought into his teaching, which alarmed and irritated his brother Rabbins. His opinions were attacked by able and learned men ; their supposed errors exposed and condemned. In France, more particularly, the feeling against them became so strong that his works were publicly burned as heretical. A fierce warfare was waged over his writings, which lasted many years, but ended at last in his entire restoration to the respect and admiration of his countrymen. A deputation was sent, in 1232, to his grave in Hebron, to ask pardon of his ashes. If strict justice were done in this life, of how many of its greatest men would not the same entreaty for forgiveness have to be asked ! In Maimonides' instance, at all events, the entreaty

was sincere. He is now acknowledged by the Jews to have
been the greatest man that has arisen among them since the
days of the great Lawgiver who led them out of Egypt.
Their common saying about him is, 'From Moses to Moses
there arose not a Moses!' His writings consist of commentaries and expositions, partly of Scripture, partly of the
Talmuds, treatises on logic, metaphysics, medicine, astrology,
natural history, and other subjects, in such numbers that they
would of themselves form an extensive library.

Here also should be mentioned some others of the chief
writers of that golden age of Jewish literature—the three
Kimchis, Moses, Joseph, and David, born in 1160, 1190, and
1192, all of them Jews of Spanish descent, but natives of
Narbonne, and renowned for their ability and learning.
David, the most distinguished of the three, was the author of
a Hebrew grammar and dictionary of such excellence that
he obtained the title of the 'Prince of Grammarians.' In
the great struggle of those days between the supporters and
opponents of science, he ranged himself on the side of the
former, and travelled into Spain to endeavour to form a league
of those who held his views ; and, though we are told he did
not prosper in his errand, we cannot doubt that his advocacy
had its effect in the ultimate determination of the question.

Nor ought the celebrated Moses ben Nachman, generally
known as Nachmanides, to be passed over, though he belongs
to a generation later than the above. He is chiefly remarkable for the part he took in the public disputation held at
Barcelona in 1263, by order of the King of Spain, between
the Jews and the Christians. Pablo, said to be a converted
Jew, was the disputant on the side of the Christians, and Nachmanides on that of his own people. It lasted four days, and
the reader has already been informed that both sides claimed
the victory. Nachmanides subsequently emigrated to Palestine, where he died.

But the writer of this period with whom we are most deeply
concerned is not a divine or a philosopher, but a traveller, the

well-known Benjamin of Tudela. He is one of the earliest, if not the earliest, of the mediæval travellers—two centuries before Maundeville and Marco Polo. Like the first-named of those authors, he appears anxious to record everything he has seen or heard, of what were in his day the strange and unexplored regions of the East. He cannot match with Sir John Maundeville for monstrous and extravagant fictions; but a very large percentage of his statements must be accepted with doubt and caution. Especially is this the case where the credit of his own people is concerned.

He was born in Tudela, a city of Navarre, somewhere near the beginning of the twelfth century. He left Spain in 1260, and spent about fifteen years in visiting the various Jewish colonies in the East and West. He tells us that in Persia and the contiguous countries he found numerous communities of his countrymen, mostly living at their ease, and enjoying the free exercise of their religion. Thus, at Bassorah, a city situated on an island in the Tigris, he found a colony of four thousand Jews; at Almozal, a city built on the site of ancient Nineveh, out of the *débris* of its ruins, there were as many as seven thousand, ruled over by Zacchæus, a prince claiming descent from David. Journeying thence to Bagdad, he passed Rehoboth, where he found two thousand, and at Elnabar, the ancient Pumbeditha, celebrated of old as the centre of Rabbinical learning, but now fallen from its high estate and sunk to little better than a village, there were still a few doctors and students, and two thousand inhabitants.

Reaching Bagdad, at that time under the rule of Mostanged, a prince who protected and favoured the Jews, he found as many as twenty-eight synagogues, and ten courts, each presided over by one of the chief men of the nation. These ten were called the 'ten idle men,' and were subject to an official whom he styles, after the ancient title, 'the Prince of the Captivity.' He affirms that the authority of this dignitary extended over all the Jews under the dominion of the Caliph of Bagdad, from Syria eastward as far as India. He assures

L

us that he was regarded in the light of a potentate to whom
even the Mahometans were obliged to render reverence, rising
up when he entered their presence, and bowing their heads
as he passed ; and he was escorted wherever he went by a
hundred soldiers.   It is difficult tor cconcile these statements
with what we are told of the entire suppression of the Princes
of the Captivity nearly two centuries before.

Leaving Bagdad, he visited Resen, Hela, Cufa, and Thema,
in each of which he found large and flourishing Jewish populations, and then passed on into Egypt.   Here he found his
countrymen still more numerous.   He mentions a city which
he visited, called Chouts, where there were as many as thirty
thousand.   But no city so called is known to geographers ;
and it is plain, from the errors with which this part of his
narrative is filled, that he either picked up information at
second-hand without inquiry, or was extremely hasty and
superficial in his researches.

He next explored the Holy Land, which, if his account is
to be trusted, had been at this time almost emptied of its
Hebrew inhabitants, those who still dwelt there having been
reduced to a condition of poverty and wretchedness.   In Asca-
lon he found but one hundred and fifty Jews ; in Tiberias,
anciently the central point of Western Rabbinism, there
were but fifty ; in Jerusalem itself, scarcely two hundred.   In
Tyre and Shunem they were more numerous, five hundred in
the one, and three hundred in the other.   But, as a rule, the
cities of Palestine could hardly have contained ten Jews out
of every thousand inhabitants.   The disappearance of the
Hebrew residents was probably owing to the exterminating
swords of the Crusaders.

Leaving Palestine, Benjamin travelled through Greece,
Constantinople, Italy, and Germany, in all of which the
Jewish population was greatly less than we should have
anticipated—due, it is to be feared, in a great measure, to the
cruel and devouring sword of persecution, which had been at
work with fatal effect for several generations past.

CHAPTER XVIII.

JEWS IN FRANCE AND GERMANY.

IN France, during the first quarter of the thirteenth century, no persecutions of the Jews are recorded. In the south their condition appears to have been prosperous. They were protected by Raymond, the heretic but powerful Count of Toulouse. One of the bitterest charges made against him by Innocent III. was, that he employed and favoured Jews ; and when, after his submission, he had to sign the conditions on which his offences would be overlooked, one of them was, that he should no longer employ Jewish officers.

In 1223, Philip Augustus died, and was succeeded by Louis VIII., called, it is to be presumed in mockery, Louis the Lion. During his short reign of three years, we hear that he passed a decree annulling all future interest on debts incurred to Jews, and ordering the payment of the capital, in three separate instalments, each after the interval of a year.

In 1226, Louis VIII. died, and his son, the renowned Louis IX., known to history as St. Louis, succeeded to the throne. He was at the time a minor, and France was under the

Regency of Blanche of Castile for nearly ten years. Louis's first act seems to have been the annulling of one third of all debts due to Jews, and an immunity from arrest or distraint for the two remaining portions. He also called a council at Melun on the Seine, which forbade Christian men, for the future, to borrow money from the Jews on any terms. He is said to have issued this order 'for the good of his soul.' How this could be does not clearly appear. Possibly he felt so strongly the power and the will of the Jews to use their money-lending facilities in an oppressive way that he sought in this way to prevent their injurious influence. Or he may have regarded the scriptural prohibitions addressed to the Jews, against lending their money on usury *to their own countrymen*, as applying to *all* loans on usury, though Scripture expressly asserts otherwise (Deut. xxiii. 20). That this was so seems evident from the fact that Louis's enactment was levelled as much against the Lombards and Caorsini[1] usurers as against the Jews. It would seem that Louis wished to induce them to abandon usury for agriculture or handicraft, as was also the desire of his contemporary Edward I. of England. But both monarchs failed in the attempt.

In the state to which matters had now grown, it would have been next to impossible to abate the dislike of the people to them, so as to induce them to permit the Jews to engage in the work either of the artisan or the peasant. The hatred of the populace was in no way abated by the quiet of the last forty years. In 1239 there were riots in Paris and Orleans, and other great cities, on the old charge of crucifying boys at the Passover, in which property was wrecked and wholesale murders took place. At Ploermel, in Brittany, the duke of that country summoned an assembly of the nobles and bishops, at which it was declared that agriculture was ruined by the

---

[1] Caorsini, Italian usurers who drove a great trade in money-lending.

monstrous exactions of the Jews ; and a series of laws were passed, which for injustice and cruelty exceed any ever put forth in any country. It was decreed that all debts to Jews should be cancelled ; that all Jews should be banished from the country ; that no person who should kill a Jew should be liable to prosecution for it ; and that no judge or magistrate should take cognisance of any such offence. A petition was further addressed to the King of France, requesting him to carry out the same regulations throughout his dominions. The Council of Lyons, held in the ensuing year, required all Christian princes, on pain of excommunication, to force the Jews in their several territories to refund to the Crusaders the sums they had exacted from them. The Jews were forbidden to exact any debt from a Crusader's family, until he himself returned from Palestine, or until satisfactory evidence of his death had been produced. Another Council prohibited them from practising as physicians, 'because, being in direct league with Satan, if they did cure any one, it would probably be by their master's aid !' Whatever evils men experienced, for which they were unable to assign any special cause, were supposed to be due to the secret spells and diabolical influence of the Jews, much as in a succeeding generation the same evils were attributed to witchcraft. The main source and centre of their evil knowledge was supposed to be the mysterious and terrible Talmud. Edicts were issued for its destruction, and it was burned, we are told, by cartloads in the streets of Paris.

A considerable exodus seems to have followed on these measures ; which was taken advantage of by the king, who seized on the goods of those who had taken flight, and thus raised money for the crusade on which he was about to enter. About the same time he ordered them to wear a special badge, called the *rouelle*—a piece of blue cloth worn both on the front and on the back of the Jewish gabardine.

Notwithstanding these severities, it is plain that Louis was actuated more by a desire of converting the Jews to Christ than of venting his horror and hate of them. We read of a solemn conference held in the year 1254 between Rabbi Jechiel and a convert from Judaism, named Nicolas, before Blanche, who acted as regent during her son's absence. Both parties claimed the victory ; neither, consequently, underwent any conversion. It was probably disappointment at this result which induced Louis to send home orders that they should now be banished from the realm, which, we are told, the queen-mother punctually executed.

During Louis's absence occurred also the first 'rising of the shepherds,' as it is called. This was led by an apostate Hungarian monk, who had originally been a Mussulman. The avowed purpose was the rescue of King Louis from the hands of his enemies. They committed pillage and murder wherever they went, but the Jews were the especial objects of their violence. It is probable that if they had confined their outrages to them, they might have escaped punishment. But the massacre of the Christians could not be overlooked, especially of priests and friars ; and the Hungarian and his followers were overpowered and slain.

Philip the Hardy succeeded to the throne in 1270, and one of his first acts was to recall the Jews to France, it having been discovered that, however much the people might complain of their avarice and exactions, they got on considerably worse without them. It is said that during his reign, which lasted for twenty-five years, they continued unmolested, and again gathered in great riches. They were banished, however, from Gascony, in 1288, by Edward I. of England, a preliminary measure, one might think, to his expulsion of them from his English domains. A story is told by Walsingham of his having taken this step in consequence of a miraculous escape which he had from being struck dead by a flash of lightning, which passed directly over his bed and killed two of his chamberlains who were standing close by. As a sign of his gratitude for this deliverance, he is said to have banished the Jews. Edward was a man rather in advance of his day, and it is difficult to believe that he could have thought that the merciless banishment of the Jews would be a fit requital of mercy shown to him. We shall see more of his motives in an ensuing chapter. But it is proper to remark that this age, apparently beyond any other, credited the most extravagant conceptions respecting the Satanic hatred of the Jews for the Christian mysteries. They are continually charged with endeavouring to possess themselves of the sacred wafer, and then offering it the grossest insults, their sacrilege being as often exposed and punished by some special miracle. A woman is persuaded by a Jew to convey to him the consecrated host, which he stabs in several places, whereupon it bleeds profusely ; and some Christian customers, coming in, see it, and indict him for the offence ; or he puts the wafer into his purse, in which are a number of silver pieces, and these are turned into seven wafers, similar to the one he had placed among them. Staggered by the miracle, he becomes a convert to the gospel. Stories like these are continually to be met with. That the mass of the people believed them is beyond dispute ; but whether the more intelligent among the clergy attached any real faith to such tales, or simply used them as a means of accomplishing their own ends, in exciting popular fury against the Jews, is a matter very difficult to determine.

In 1285, Philip IV., called the Fair, the shameless murderer of the Knights Templars, succeeded his father. His first acts were extremely hostile to the Church, but he showed no lenity to the Jews. Six years after his accession, he repeated the act of several of his predecessors, and expelled them from the kingdom. It does not appear that the banishment was rigidly enforced, as we find a second expulsion taking place not many years afterwards. In fact, these repeated sentences of exile and subsequent recall read very much as though they were simply regular stages in a prescribed system of spoliation. After the Jews had been resident in a country a sufficient length of time to have amassed wealth enough to be worth seizing upon, it was discovered that they had been guilty of some terrible wickedness, which rendered it impossible for a Christian sovereign to tolerate them within his dominions. They had seized some Christian boy, perhaps, and indulged their natural hate at once of the Saviour and His worshippers, by subjecting him to death on the cross. The fact that they had done so was made abundantly clear by some astounding miracle, which rendered human testimony needless. The immediate authors of the deed were executed, and their property confiscated to the Crown, and their countrymen were condemned to forfeit all but their movables, and with these to quit the realm. Sometimes the charge was varied, and they were found to have poisoned wells, or leagued with some foreign enemies, or (as we have seen) profaned or insulted the Host. But it always came to the same result. The Jews were driven out of the land, until they were in a condition to pay a large sum for readmission; and then the king, in the midst of his just anger, remembered mercy, and allowed them to return and grow rich, until their renewed wealth brought some fresh wickedness to light.

In Germany, though the virulence of both clergy and people seems to have been very nearly of the same character as in France, the sovereigns of the country were evidently disposed to extend the shield of their protection over this unhappy and persecuted race. Frederick II., a monarch whose character forms a curious and interesting study, dealt with them in a manner which contrasts strangely with the demeanour of contemporary rulers towards them. At Hagenau, in Lower Alsatia, three children had been found dead in the house of a Jew. There was no evidence that the Jew had murdered them; but the tale was instantly conveyed to the emperor with a demand for vengeance. 'Three children found dead! Let them be buried then,' was his answer. He followed up this novel mode of dealing with the matter, by causing a judicial inquiry to be made as to whether it was a regular Jewish custom to sacrifice Christian children at the feast of the Passover. Of course no legal tribunal could give any other decision than that there was no sort of evidence of such a practice.[1]

At the Council of Vienna, held in 1267, restrictions unheard of even in the harshest times were proposed and ordered. The Jews were forbidden to hold even the most ordinary intercourse of every-day life with the Christians. They were not to be allowed to use the public baths, or put up at the public inns, or to accept any public contract, or employ any Christian servant. To the requirements already exacted of them was added that of wearing a high peaked cap, which at once and inevitably declared their nationality. A permit must be purchased, before it could be lawful for any one to buy meat of a Jew.

At Munich, in 1287, an old woman having confessed that she had sold a child to the Jews, whose blood they intended to use for some unholy purpose, the rabble, without further inquiry, slaughtered all the Jews on whom they could lay their hands. The city guard, unable to quell the tumult, advised the Jews to retire for safety into their synagogue, which being a building of solid stone, was likely to be secure against violence. But the populace attacked and destroyed it, and all within it, notwithstanding the efforts of the duke himself to protect them.

To close the horrors of this century, there was another frightful massacre of the Jews at Nuremburg in 1292. A fanatic peasant, named Raind Fleish, gave out, during the war raging between Nassau and Austria, that he had been sent by Almighty God to exterminate the whole race of Israel. The

---

[1] As an instance of the unbounded credulity of the people as to any accusation made against the Jews, it was affirmed that they had entered into a league with the Mongolian Tartars, to enter and overrun Germany. They had loaded a number of waggons, it is said, with arms for their use, and pretended that the casks in which their arms were conveyed contained poisoned wine, which the Mongolians would unsuspectingly drink, and so be destroyed. The story was generally believed.

people, believing him, set upon the Jews in Nuremburg and the other Bavarian cities, and burnt all that fell into their hands. The others, preferring to die by their own act rather than by the swords of their enemies, set their own houses on fire, and perished with their wives and children in the flames.

CHAPTER XIX.

JEWS IN SPAIN.

TURNING now to Spain, we find that the Jews, during
this century, still continued to enjoy, if not the full
measure of justice to which they were entitled, yet nevertheless an amount of it which contrasts favourably with the treatment they underwent in other lands. The wisdom, justice, and
clemency also shown by the Spanish kings on many occasions
are so unlike the spirit manifested in after generations, that
we can hardly believe that we are writing of the same Spain
which approved the barbarities of Torquemada, or the horrors
of the Jewish exodus.

James (or Jayme) I. of Aragon, who began his long reign
early in this century, is said to have granted especial favour to
the Jews, notwithstanding that he showed a very persecuting
spirit in the instance of the Albigenses. He often sought instruction of Jewish Rabbins, and used their books of prayer
in his private devotions, and even, it is said, would not permit
a Spanish translation of the Old Testament to be introduced
into his dominions, because of the value he set on that made

by David Kimchi. His confessor Raimond is believed to
have been in a great measure the cause of his kindly feeling
towards the Jews, being wise enough to know that if the Jews
were to be converted, the best chance of accomplishing it was
by the exercise of mildness and charity.[1] Regulations were
passed in the earlier years of the century,[2] with a view of preventing the excessive usury exacted of Christians by Jews ;
but they are not of a kind to be greatly complained of. The
Jews are not to lend at a higher rate of interest than 20 per
cent., they are not to charge compound interest, and the
interest is never to exceed the sum lent. The Jew, before advancing the loan, is to swear in a public court, on the law of
Moses and the Decalogue, that he will adhere to the law. A
Jew who lends on illegal terms is to lose the amount of the
loan. A decree made by the Cortes at Barcelona, in 1228,
however, deals a more serious blow to the Jews. It enacts
that if there is no documentary evidence of a debt, the oath of
a Jew is not to be held sufficient to establish it. We may not
approve of these regulations, but they cannot be regarded as
grievously oppressive.

It was perhaps through James's influence with Ferdinand of
Castile that the attempt to rouse popular feeling against the
Jews in Saragossa, A.D. 1248, proved a failure. A report was
circulated, that a chorister, named Dominic, belonging to the
cathedral, had been stolen by the Jews and crucified. The
crime was discovered through the appearance of a miraculous
light over the chorister's grave. The body was disinterred
and carried into the cathedral, where it was treated as that
of a martyr and saint. The usual amount of obloquy and
insult to the Jews resulted ; but no steps were taken by the
authorities, and no excesses permitted.

---

[1] Raimond has been supposed by many to have been the author of the
famous *Pugio Fidei*, a severe attack on the Jews. But that book did not
appear till three centuries after his time, and was probably the work of a
Dominican of the same name.

[2] At Tarragona, A.D., 1233 and again 1234.

In 1263, James, who in his later years is said to have been greatly under the influence of the Dominicans, ordered a public disputation upon the relative merits of Judaism and Christianity to be held at Barcelona. The advocate on the side of the Christians was one Pablo, a Jewish convert; on that of the Jews, the renowned Rabbi Nachmanides. The inevitable result followed—both parties claimed the victory. It was at all events so far favourable to the Jews, that it excited the alarm of Pope Clement IV., who urged James to drive the Jews out of his realm, as being dangerous to the faith of the Christians. But the king took no further step than that of levying a tax on them, to defray the expenses of the Christian advocate, Pablo, who was sent on a kind of tour through the great Spanish cities, with authority to hold conferences with the Jews wherever he pleased. Nachmanides, the Jewish champion, possibly dreading Clement's hostility, soon afterwards migrated from Spain to the Holy Land.

The Jews had two other protectors in Ferdinand III. of Castile (already mentioned), commonly known as Saint Ferdinand, and his son Alphonso, called in history 'the Wise.' Ferdinand, who reigned from 1217 to 1252, uniformly treated the Jews with justice and leniency. When his son captured Seville from the Moors in 1248, he set apart, doubtless by his father's direction, three parishes (those of Santa Maria, Saint Bartholomew, and Santa Cruz) for the residence of the Jews, as well as three Mahometan mosques, which they might convert into synagogues. Under these princes the celebrated college at Cordova was transferred to Toledo; which henceforth became the principal school of Jewish learning in Spain.

Alphonso was the author of the code of laws known as *Las Siete Partidas*, which, though it contains much that an after age must needs condemn as unjust,[1] has also many wise

---

[1] There can be little doubt that Alphonso knew how far he could venture in his efforts to uphold reason and justice, and where he must yield to the deeply rooted prejudices of his people. Had he attempted more, he would probably have failed to effect anything.

and equitable enactments, such as we could hardly have
looked for in the legislation of that age. Thus it orders ' that
no force shall be used to make Jews turn Christians, but
rather good example, kindness, and the maxims of the Holy
Scriptures.' Again, 'that synagogues are buildings where
God's name is praised, therefore Christians shall not presume
to destroy or plunder them.' 'No Christians are to cause
molestations to Jews while engaged at their prayers.' Again,
' Saturday is a day whereon Jews observe their Sabbath. As
they are bound by their religion to observe that day, no
person is to summon them, or bring them to judgment thereon. If any sentence should be passed upon them on that day,
it shall be null and void.' No doubt there are, as has been
already remarked, many oppressive and indefensible laws in
the same code, such as those which forbid the Jews to hold
any public post, or eat and drink, or join in merry-makings
with Christians, or use the same baths with them, or administer
to them any medicine, for fear it should be poisoned, and the
like. But these are all in the prevalent temper and spirit of
the day ; and our only surprise is, that the same fountain
should in this manner send forth sweet as well as bitter
water.

A few years afterwards (A.D. 1255) an equally malignant
attempt was made to destroy the Jews. Three persons
belonging to Osuna, in Andalusia, threw a corpse into the
house of a Jew ; then, pretending to find it there by chance,
they brought the usual charge of murder against the owner
of the house. The story was speedily circulated through
the city, and roused the populace to fury. Many Jews were
killed in the streets ; many more took refuge in the houses of
Christian friends. It was the season of the Passover, during
which the Jews refuse to eat any but unleavened bread ; and
not finding this in the houses of their Christian friends, many
were in danger of starvation. At Palma also the same story
was circulated, and caused a similar outbreak. The Jews held
a consultation, and resolved that the only hope of preventing

the mischief from spreading further lay in sending to King
Alphonso a deputation, requesting him to make inquiry into
the matter. But the news of this intention got abroad; the
deputies were pursued by their enemies, and had a narrow
escape of being murdered on their journey. They evaded
their pursuers, but to do so were forced to quit the high road
and take shelter in a wood. The consequence was, that when
they reached the capital they found that their enemies had
already arrived, and had preferred their accusation against
them. They had, however, in King Alphonso not only a just
but an extremely sagacious judge ; and their case was so
strong that it hardly needed the able advocacy of their
delegate, Rabbi Joseph, to ensure success. It was brought to
light that one Juan de Vera had owed money to the owner of
the house in which the corpse had been found, and that he
was extremely anxious to be quit of his debt without the
disagreeable necessity of paying the money. His accomplices
confessed that, at his instigation, they had broken open a
tomb, from which they had abstracted the corpse which had
been found in the Jew's house. The grave was again opened
by the king's order, and found to be empty. The acquittal
of the Jew followed ; and the king sent away the deputies
in friendly sort, yet not without a recommendation to them
to reduce their rate of usury and abate the costliness and
ostentation of their mode of living ; for that these things provoked the enmity of the Christians towards them.

This is a remarkable tale, from the contrast it presents to
the numberless similar occurrences which the history of this
and succeeding centuries records. The calm judicial inquiry,
in which the evidence given on both sides was attentively
listened to and dispassionately sifted, stands out in strong
relief against the incoherent and contradictory charges, the
refusal to listen to explanation or argument, and the invincible prejudice displayed on other occasions. But it may be
doubted whether the most remarkable fact is not the character
of King Alphonso himself. It is wonderful that a man so en-

lightened as he showed himself on many points [1] could have adopted the monstrous bigotry he proclaimed on others. We must, I suppose, conclude that, like the philosopher in Coleridge's 'Friend,' he thought it better to roll in the mire of the common prejudice of his fellow men, than remain isolated from them in solitary cleanliness.

Interesting evidences of the numbers and wealth of the Jews are to be found at this period. An assessment was made in 1286 of the Jews in the three kingdoms of Sancho, the son of Alphonso X., two years after his accession. It appeared that there were in Leon, Castile, and Murcia, 700,000 male Jews above the age of sixteen. The total number, therefore, including women and children, must have exceeded two millions. The annual dues paid by them amounted to 2,310,021 maravedis, nearly one hundred thousand pounds of our money. Considering the enormous difference in value of the precious metals in those times and our own, this proves that the wealth of the Jews must have been extraordinarily great. It is proper, however, to add that both the numbers of the Jews and the amount paid are given somewhat differently by other writers.

In this century two Jewish impostors made their appearance, and obtained great influence over their countrymen, though the falsehoods they palmed off were different from those usually put forward by adventurers of their class. The

---

[1] He was pressed at the trial at Osuna to put the accused Jews to the torture, in order to extract evidence which would satisfactorily prove whether they had done the deed or not. Alphonso refused. He said that he had, two years before, allowed two Jews to be racked in order to discover whether they had stolen two golden goblets. Under the torture they confessed the theft, and were executed for it. Shortly afterwards the goblets were found in the possession of a servant. 'Therefore,' said the king, ' I will have no more examinations by torture. It is evident that the confessions extracted by them are worth nothing.' No conclusion could be more sound. But before another judge it would have been urged and believed that the Jews, or their ally Satan, had hidden the goblets in a servant's chest, in order that a Christian might be unrighteously charged with the crime of a Jew.

first of them, one Zechariah, did not himself claim to be the
Messiah, but to have discovered a new mode of interpreting
prophecy, which showed, beyond dispute, that He was close .
at hand. A belief prevailed among the Jews, that if any man
could attain to a correct pronunciation of the presumedly in-
effable name of God, he would thereby acquire all knowledge
and all power. Zechariah professed to have done this, and
on that ground claimed to declare positively the day of the
Messiah's appearing. The Jews—a large part of them, that is
—credited his pretensions, and went on the appointed day to
their synagogue, clothed in white to receive their Deliverer.[1]
What became of the impostor does not seem to be recorded.

The second pretender professed to have obtained a complete
copy of the book Zohar,[2] of which only fragments were known
to exist. He was a Rabbi, named Moses de Leon, who, being
unable to support himself and his family by the income of his
synagogue, devised this mode of raising money. It seems to
have been a considerable time before it was discovered that
the missing portions of the book were supplied from his own
imagination. The credulity of the Jews, in general so astute,
in this and similar matters, is very surprising.

In A.D. 1291, James II. succeeded to the throne of Aragon.
He was as anxious as his predecessor had been for the conversion of the Jews, and issued several edicts with that design.
He ordered that the Jews should attend the lectures delivered
by Dominican friars on the points of difference between the
Jewish and Christian faith, and further, be required to answer,
if they could, the arguments of their instructors. If they
refused to attend ; probably—though this is not recorded—

---

[1] As these occurrences were nothing in those times without a miracle,
it has been further declared that the Jews, when they entered the synagogue, perceived that their white dresses were covered with red crosses.
This, however, is only the statement of a monk, a convert from Judaism
who wrote two hundred years afterwards.

[2] He is even believed by some to have forged the entire book, as it
now exists.

also if they refused to embark in a controversy, in which success would be more dangerous to them than defeat, they were to suffer such corporal punishment as the friars should adjudge.

This, however, was all that was imposed. The young king refused to repeal the righteous and merciful laws of his great-grandfather and grandfather; and strict justice to the Jews remained the rule in Spain until the thirteenth century came to its close.

CHAPTER XX.

JEWS IN ENGLAND.

H ENRY III. was a minor when the death of his father, A.D. 1216, placed him on the throne. Pembroke and his colleagues, who governed England in his name, began by treating the Jews with greater mildness. They were released from prison ; and twenty-four of the principal men in every town where they resided[1] were appointed to act as the protectors of their persons and possessions. They were declared exempt from spiritual authority, and the property of the sovereign alone ; and the excommunications pronounced by their Rabbins were to be enforced by law. They were ordered, however, to wear the badge previously imposed, two strips of white cloth,[2] sewn on a conspicuous part of their dress, which may, as Milman remarks, have been intended to mark

---

[1] Some towns, as for example Southampton and Newcastle, had petitioned that no Jews might be allowed to reside among them. The request was granted, though it was not found to be any benefit to the towns in question.

[2] This was altered by Edward I. to yellow.

179

them as the royal property, and so save them from injury ; but which was nevertheless far more likely to make them the objects of popular contumely.

In truth, though the kings might pretend to resent affronts and wrongs offered to them, they were, and all men knew that they were, unable to extend any real protection to them, even had they been anxious to do so. All classes of men became, as time went on, more and more determinedly set against them. The barons, on whose estates they held heavy mortgages ; the merchants, who found the trade of the country, in spite of all their own efforts, getting into the hands of the Jews ; the common people, who resented Jewish riches, which contrasted with their own grinding poverty ; above all, the clergy, to whose warnings and threatenings they would not listen—all these bore a bitter grudge against them, which grew more bitter in every succeeding generation. Stephen Langton, Archbishop of Canterbury, together with some of his suffragans, put forth a decree, A.D. 1222, forbidding all Christian men, on pain of excommunication, to sell the necessaries of life to the Jews.[1] The Crown then issued an edict, which commanded all men, as loyal subjects of the king, to refuse obedience to this order ; a needless demonstration, as it would have been impossible to enforce it. But the protection of the king was merely nominal. When the wars in France engaged the public attention in 1230, Henry demanded a third part of their movables to be paid into his exchequer. Two years afterwards he claimed 18,000 marks of them ; and again, four years after that, 10,000 marks. A Jew assured Matthew of Paris that the king had exacted from him alone 30,000 marks of silver and 200 of gold. Other Jews fared no better. Accusations were for ever being trumped up against them. On one occasion they were charged with coining false money, at another, with fraudulently affixing the royal seal to docu-

---

[1] At the same synod he ordered a deacon of the Church, who had turned Jew for the love of a Jewess, to be hanged.

ments, and the like. The Jews seldom took the trouble to defend themselves. Like the aristocrats in France during the Reign of Terror, they knew that they were already condemned when they were brought up for trial. All they could do was to bribe the judges, or the king himself, as the case might be, to pardon their imaginary trespasses.

In 1225, the old charge of stealing children, to crucify them at the ensuing Passover, was again alleged. In this instance the child was recovered before the act of crucifixion had taken place; and some penalty—we are not told what—was inflicted. Some years afterwards, in 1243, the Jews in London were charged with the same offence. Though in this instance the child had not been stolen, but sold, it was averred, by the parents, the murder had been committed, and the corpse was (as usual) discovered by a miracle. A hue and cry was made after the supposed murderers, but they could not be found.

In 1256, the novel spectacle of a Jewish Parliament presented itself, and must have caused, one would think, a good deal of amusement to every one except the unhappy members themselves. Writs were regularly issued by the sheriffs, requiring the Jews in all the larger towns to elect six representatives—it being especially stipulated that they should be the richest men in the place—and two in those towns where they were fewer in number. The speech from the throne at the opening had the merit—not always secured in modern times —of being at all events directly to the purpose. No time was wasted in idle oratory or personal explanations. They were briefly informed that the king required a certain sum of them, which they were to agree to pay, and then they would be straightway prorogued and sent home to fetch it. If it was not forthcoming very speedily, they were assured that their goods would be seized and themselves imprisoned. There is a beautiful simplicity about the entire proceeding, which it is refreshing to read of in these artificial days.

It was not a very politic step, however. The nation began to consider whether it would not be desirable to require that the Jews should be taxed for the benefit, not of the sovereign, but of the nation. If there was all this money to be had, why should it not go to relieve the public burdens, which pressed so heavily on the people, rather than into the pockets of the king only? In the ensuing years, the sum of 8,000 marks was demanded, and taxes were exacted, not of the Jewish men only, but of the women and children. In the three years next following, demands were made to the amount of 60,000 marks,[1] the king being abetted in his rapacity by some traitorous Jews, and especially one Abraham of Wallingford.

But these exactions did exhaust the endurance even of the Jews. An aged Rabbi, named Elias, was deputed to wait on the Earl of Cornwall (to whom the king had made over the Jews for the sum of 5,000 marks), and inform him that it was wholly out of their power to meet any further demands; and if these should be made, they would rather quit the country than submit to them. The earl received them kindly, accepted a very small sum, and dismissed them. Probably he was satisfied that it really was not in their power to pay more. But King Henry next year recommenced his importunities, alleging the enormous amount of his debts as a reason why he must persist.

Probably the condition of his finances explains the excessive severity of his dealings with the Jews, who were accused at this time of their old offence, but with circumstances of additional horror.[2] At Lincoln a child, it was said, had been enticed into the house of a Jew named Copin, where he had been kept on bread and milk for ten days, and then crucified

---

[1] It appears to us that it must have been impossible for any traders, however lucrative their business, to endure such large and continued exactions. The enormous rate of interest levied by the Jews, amounting to 50 per cent. and upwards, goes far to explain it.

[2] It has already been intimated that these charges were always made at times when the kings of England chanced to be in especial need of money. There is no evidence, that I am aware of, to show that the present accusation was due to that cause. But it is impossible to divest one's mind of the suspicion. Henry's extreme severity, at all events, had probably some connection with his urgent need of money.

in the presence of all the Jews in England, who had been
summoned to Lincoln for this purpose ! There had been
apparently a set rehearsal of our Lord's crucifixion, a Jew
sitting in judgment as Pilate. The body had been buried,
but the earth refused to hide so hideous a crime, and cast up
the remains. The Jews thereon were obliged to throw them
into a well, where they were found by the child's mother.[1]

Such was the tale. Copin, when dragged before Lord
Lexington, made a full confession of all that had been alleged,
adding that it was the regular practice of the Jews so to celebrate their Passover, whenever they were able to secure the
necessary victims. So fierce an outcry was raised when this
was made public, that the king revoked the pardon granted
by Lord Lexington, and Copin was hanged in chains. But this
was far from satisfying the popular demand for vengeance.
All the Jews in the land were declared guilty of complicity in
the murder. Ninety-one persons were committed for trial, of
whom eighteen were hanged, and twenty more imprisoned in
the Tower to await the same fate, though it does not appear
that the sentence was carried out. Hugh, as the child was
called, was canonized ; pilgrims from all parts of the world
visited his tomb, where miracles were worked ; and the church
at Lincoln to which his remains were committed was rendered
rich and famous for centuries to come. *The Prioress's Tale,*
written by Chaucer a hundred years afterwards, shows that in
his time the story still retained its hold on the memory of the
English people.

Earlier in Henry's reign, attempts had been made to convert the Jews to Christianity, and a house, called the *Domus*

---

[1] Milman ingeniously suggests, in reference to these continually repeated charges of kidnapping and crucifying children, that the Jews
might have brooded over the horrors imputed to them, until they became
so diseased in mind that they actually executed the acts so persistently
imputed to them. This is an ingenious suggestion, but nothing more.
The confessions wrung by torture from the miserable Jews bear on the
face of them the impress of fiction, and resemble the acknowledgment of
witchcraft obtained by similar means.

Conversorum, was opened for the reception of converts, in Chancery Lane. But it appears that few of these were made. To be sure, the condition annexed to proselytism—that the proselyte should by that act forfeit his whole property[1]— does not seem very well calculated to bring about such a change. After a few years, however, even these efforts seem to have been given up. Harder and harder measure was dealt to the Jews. They were forbidden to have Christian nurses for their children ; they were not allowed to buy or eat meat during Lent ; they could not hold any religious disputations; their very prayers in the synagogue must be uttered in a low tone, for fear that the ears of Christians should be polluted by them ! But, for all their harsh usage, they were regarded as being unduly favoured by the king. When the Barons' War broke out, five hundred of the richest Jews in London were seized, in order to extort a subsidy from them ; the others were pitilessly murdered. Similar scenes occurred in the other large cities. After the battle of Lewes, their condition was in some degree amended ; but to the end of Henry's reign the same system of merciless pillage and cruelty continued with no real abatement.

In 1268 an occurrence took place at Oxford, which might have caused as furious an ebullition of popular feeling as the supposed outrage at Lincoln. As the chancellor and other officers of the University were on their way to the shrine of St. Frideswide, a Jew rushed up, seized the cross that was borne in front of the procession, and trampled it under foot. He escaped before he could be seized. It is wonderful that the act did not provoke a massacre. The presence of Prince Edward, who chanced to be in Oxford, perhaps prevented it. He ordered that the Jews should, as the penalty of their countryman's offence, erect a cross of

---

[1] This extraordinary law, which obtained in France also, is to be explained by the fact that by becoming a Christian a Jew was no longer subject to the exactions of the sovereign. And it was argued that it was not reasonable that his conversion should be at the king's expense.

white marble, with the images of the Virgin and Child, on the spot where Merton College now stands.

The death of Henry followed a few years afterwards. It might have been perhaps expected that Edward, one of the greatest and most humane of our kings, would have reversed the iniquitous policy of his father towards the Jews. But he did not. He passed a law forbidding the Jews to lend money on usury on any pretext whatsoever. His desire seems to have been the same as that of Louis IX. of France, to oblige them to devote themselves to manual labour. But they, it appears, had found a different occupation for themselves—clipping and adulterating the current coin of the realm. Whether this accusation was true or not, cannot be determined with any certainty. There is a *prima facie* likelihood about it. Ground down by exactions, unable to pursue their own trade, or to work at any other, some of them at all events might well be driven to such a mode of obtaining the bare means of living. On the other hand, many were beyond question accused and condemned who were wholly innocent. The king was greatly disturbed at the course things were taking. He could neither conscientiously condemn nor defend the Jews. It is likely that he took his final resolve of expelling them altogether from his dominions, as the most obvious solution of a great and ever-increasing difficulty. When he had once made up his mind on this point, he was determined enough in his mode of carrying it out. He confiscated the whole of their property, except such as they were able to remove, and ordered them to quit England, on pain of death.

It might be thought that, considering what the condition of the Jews in England for the last fifty years had been, the prospect of quitting for ever the scene of their sufferings would have been welcome rather than otherwise.[1] But such

---

[1] Not long previously to their expulsion he had imprisoned every Jew of any note, until they had paid him a subsidy of £12,000.

was not the case. A man's home is his home, after all ; and the effect of hardship and trial is often to endear the scenes of their occurrence more deeply to the sufferers. We are told that the last few days before the departure of the Jews witnessed scenes of the most distressing description ; that they clung to their old haunts with a lingering affection which, one would think, must have moved the compassion of all who beheld it, however deep the prejudices of race and creed.[1] But the stern edict was not revoked. The festival of All Saints—that day sacred beyond all others to mutual goodwill among all the children of the great Father above—witnessed the consummation of the wrongs of the Jewish people. They went forth into penury and exile from the shores of England, and for nearly four hundred years they returned no more.

---

[1] It is remarkable, that although the historians of those times describe the most heartrending sufferings endured by the Jews, there is nowhere any expression of pity or horror in their narratives.

PART II.

FROM THE BEGINNING OF THE FOURTEENTH CENTURY TO THE PRESENT TIME.

THE history of the Jews in France, in the thirteenth century, may be regarded as terminating with their second expulsion from that country by Philip the Fair. That king died in 1314, and was succeeded by Louis X., called in history Hutin, or Mutin (the Turbulent). One of the first acts of the new king was to recall the Jews, who not only consented to return to a land where for generations past they had experienced nothing but harsh and contemptuous usage, but even to pay a heavy price for the privilege. Nothing gives us a stronger idea of the utter helplessness and friendlessness of the Hebrew people at this period than the readiness with which they would accept any conditions whatever that seemed to promise them protection for the moment against violent or lawless outrage. A semblance of justice, indeed, was shown them : their synagogues were restored to them, and their worship again permitted ; they recovered the privilege of burying their dead in their ancient graveyards. Nay, such debts as were still owing to them—the greater portion having been already paid over to the king, who had condescended to make himself their trustee—they were allowed to claim before the public tribunals, conditionally always on their paying two-thirds of it into the royal treasury.[1] In the reign of Philip the Long, a few years afterwards, something like fairness and even mercy seems to have been shown them, possibly as a set-off to the king's exaction of 150,000 livres from them. They were allowed to lend on usury to certain persons and on certain conditions; they might acquire property in houses and land; and they were not required to wear their distinguishing badge while travelling from one town to another.

About this time (A.D. 1319) a novel charge was preferred against them, and which we might believe to have been at least founded on fact, if it did not seem impossible that the Jews of those times could have been guilty of such suicidal rashness. At Lunel they were accused of travestying the Saviour's passion—not (as was the ordinary charge) by the crucifixion of a Christian boy—but by carrying a crucifix in a public procession, reviling it as they went, dragging it through mire and filth, and heaping reproaches upon it.[2] For this offence they were tried, convicted, and punished.

But in 1321 a far more serious calamity befell them. It has been recorded that during the captivity in the East of Louis IX. a multitude of peasants assembled, and declared themselves commissioned from on high to rescue their beloved sovereign from bondage, and they had evidenced their zeal in the cause of Heaven by acts of barbarity towards the Jews. There was no king to be rescued now; but the Holy Land

---

[1] It is noteworthy that this very scant and dubious measure of justice is acknowledged by Rabbi Joshua in terms of great thankfulness. 'He allowed the Jews,' says Joshua, 'to live in his kingdom, for they found favour in his eyes; and he accepted their persons.'

[2] It may be doubted whether this was not a simple attempt to celebrate the Feast of Purim—*the* feast in which they took such special delight. Possibly the supposed crucifix was the figure of Haman on his gallows. See Appendix V.

itself was in bondage, and there were vague prophecies current among them that it could be reconquered only by the mean and lowly. They were headed by a degraded priest and mendicant friar, who affected special sanctity of life, and claimed to work miracles in proof of their sacred mission. They were followed by large multitudes, who ravaged the southern provinces of France, and especially Languedoc, everywhere breaking open the prisons, and swelling their ranks by enlisting the criminals whom they let loose. They spared their Christian fellow-subjects as much as they could, but displayed the most relentless barbarity towards the Jews, whom they everywhere pillaged, outraged, and murdered. The Jews appealed to the Pope and to the king. The former issued an anathema against the insurgents, but it was altogether disregarded ; the latter sent a few horsemen to their aid, who, however, were utterly powerless to help them. They fled in despair to the shelter of any fortified places which would refuse admittance to the Shepherds. Five hundred found a refuge in a castle at Verdun, on the Garonne, which the governor allowed them to occupy. Their enemies followed and besieged them. After a stout and desperate defence, finding themselves unable to hold out any longer, they threw some of their children over the walls, and then (as at Masada and at York) slew each other to a man. When the besiegers broke in, they found no living enemy !

All over Languedoc, at Angouleme, and at Bordeaux, frightful massacres of Jews took place. The excuse alleged for them was, that the plunder of the Jews was necessary to the 'armies of the Lord,' in order to equip them properly for the recovery of Palestine. But, terrible as were their sufferings from the violence of the fanatics, what ensued was even more full of horror. The outbreak was followed, as might have been anticipated, by an epidemic pestilence—the natural result of the scarcity of wholesome food and the corruption of so many human carcases. But the people, possessed as they were by the worst form of religious mania, were easily per-

suaded by their leaders that the malady was caused by the
poisoning of wells and rivers, which again was the work of the
Jews. The Sieur de Parthenay wrote word to the king that
'a great leper, seized on his land, had confessed to him that
he had received from a rich Jew a consignment of drugs, which
were to be enclosed in bags and thrown into the wells.'[1] The
king returned in alarm from Poitou, which he had been
visiting, and ordered that all lepers should be arrested and
put to the question—that is, examined by torture. This
mode of inquiry elicited the usual results. The unhappy
sufferers in their agony confessed everything of which they
had been suspected, however monstrous or incredible it might
be. It appeared that there had been a conspiracy between
the infidel kings of Tunis and Granada, the Jews, and the
lepers, Satan himself presiding at the conference. Woe and
misery were to be wrought on the Christians by the poisoning
of the water which they drank. The lepers were straightway
ordered to be burned, pregnant women alone being spared,
and they only until the time of their delivery. In the instance
of the Jews not even this mercy seems to have been shown :
they were burned without distinction. At Chignon a great
trench was dug, fires were kindled in it, and 160 Jews burned
alive—men and women together. Many women, with their
children in their arms, voluntarily threw themselves into the
flames to escape baptism. In the royal prison at Vitry forty
Jews, who were persuaded that no mercy would be shown
them, resolved to die by their own hands rather than by those
of the uncircumcised. They therefore fixed upon one of their
own number, an aged man greatly honoured and beloved, and
requested him to become their executioner. He consented to
undertake the office, with the help of a youth whom he chose

---

[1] The supposed composition of the drugs in question shows an amount
of ignorance, grossness of thought, and irreverence, which it would be
difficult to match in all history : 'Fiebant de sanguine humano et urinâ
cum tribus herbis. Ponebatur etiam Corpus Christi, et cum essent omnia
desiccata usque ad pulverem terebantur.'

for the purpose. When all but these two had been slain, the old man ordered the youth to kill him also. He was obeyed ; but the young man, lacking the resolution to take his own life, attempted to escape from the prison, when he was taken prisoner, and confessed what had taken place.

In the midst of these horrors Philip V. died (A.D. 1322), and his successor, Charles IV., was pleased to pardon the hapless survivors of this bloody persecution—conditionally, however, on the payment of a large subsidy. When this had been re-ceived, the Jews were permitted to leave their prisons, gather together what they could of their effects, and leave the kingdom. It is evident, however, that the whole Hebrew population could not have quitted the country ; or, if they did, they soon began to return unnoticed to it, for in 1348, when a second visitation of the same terrible disease once more desolated the land, we find that the old calumny was renewed, and with the same merciless result, the sword of the law being let loose to slay those whom the pestilence had spared. Indeed, it is evident that, notwithstanding their multiplied miseries and wrongs, the Jews were still anxious to obtain the permission of their persecutors to reside among them, for we find them in 1360 bargaining with King John (who had been defeated and captured by the Black Prince) to supply him with the means of paying the ransom due from him, condition-ally on their being permitted to dwell in France without molestation for the space of twenty years. A Jew named Manasseh (or Menecier, as he was styled) conducted the bargain on the part of the Jews. The fee for readmission to France was fixed at fourteen florins for each adult ; for children and servants, one florin. Similarly, the annual fee for continued residence was seven florins and one florin. They were to be exempted from all taxes except land-tax. They were to be allowed to hold landed property, build synagogues, and possess cemeteries, and to be exempted from baronial juris-diction, being placed directly under that of the king himself. They were also exempted from what had been always felt

N

by them a heavy burden—the necessity of listening to controversial sermons, preached in the hope of converting them.

It was not without difficulty that the regent, afterwards
Charles V., called the Wise, enforced the observance of these
conditions, as he seems to have done in all good faith. Not
long after his accession the clergy in Languedoc published a
sentence of excommunication against all who should supply
the Jews with fire or water, bread or wine. But, on receiving
an appeal against this severity, the king issued his ordinance
annulling the decree, as being alike unjust to the Jews and
dishonourable to the Church. He twice renewed the compact
with the Jews, once for six and once for ten years, receiving
for the renewal 3000 gold livres. It is evident that during
this interval of repose the wealth of the detested race had
again accumulated. In 1378 they lent Charles 20,000 livres,
and engaged to provide him with 200 more every week. But
the usual result followed : the people began to clamour at
the heavy burdens laid upon them, which they declared were
imposed only for the purpose of ministering to the greed and
luxury of the usurers. In the September of 1380 Charles V.
died, and was succeeded by his son, a minor twelve years
old. Soon after, a tumultuous outbreak took place in consequence of the regent, the Duke of Anjou, having confirmed
the privilege granted to the Jews by the late king. All classes
joined in it. The nobles, who, as usual, were deeply indebted
to the Hebrew usurers, called out for their expulsion from the
country, as the readiest mode of clearing themselves of their
liabilities ; the people, instigated probably by them, pillaged
and destroyed the offices where the registers of debts were
kept, and further gratified their enmity to the hateful race by
plundering their houses of such valuables as they could lay
their hands on, and by tearing their children from them and
carrying them to the churches, where the clergy were always
ready to baptize them. The regent endeavoured to suppress
the disturbance ; he issued a proclamation requiring all
persons, on pain of death, to restore the spoil of which they

had possessed themselves. But we are told that very few obeyed the order.

The regent persisted, however, in the policy he had adopted ; and during the earlier years of Charles VI.'s reign the Jews were treated by the State with equity and mercy. But the evil lay too deep for any legislation to remedy. The distress of the country increased, and with it the difficulty of obtaining money. There was but one class from which money could be obtained, the Jews—and they unwisely abused the power thus put into their hands. Regardless of the angry passions which they were rousing, they continued their ruinous rates of usury until about fourteen years after the accession of Charles VI. Then the storm burst suddenly upon them, and they were once more commanded to quit the country. The step in question was taken in consequence of the condition into which the unfortunate young monarch had now sunk. His melancholy madness rendered him peculiarly liable to the influence of the clergy, who were for ever representing to him the guilt of standing between an accursed people and the vengeance of the God whom they had offended. The queen was won over to side with the persecuting party. The clergy, the nobles, and the people already belonged to it. Nothing for a long time had stood between the Jews and the sentence of banishment but the justice of the king. This barrier was now removed, and the blow fell heavily and suddenly. They were suffered to depart on milder terms than on previous occasions. Leave was given them to recover all debts due to them, and to sell their property as advantageously as they could. But they were allowed only one month in which to wind up their affairs, and then they crossed for the last time the frontiers of France.[1]

---

[1] No formal decree for their restoration was subsequently made, but it is at least doubtful whether the exclusion was rigidly enforced, even in the ages immediately following the decree of banishment. In some places— as for instance Metz—they do not seem to have been meddled with.

THE attentive reader cannot fail to have noticed how scant has been the mention in these pages of the condition of the Jews in Italy. Little has been recorded of them, except that under the rule of the Lombard kings they were uniformly treated with humanity and justice, and that some few of the popes had issued decrees, advising what in these times we should regard as stern measures to be adopted for their conversion, while others forbade any such severities to be employed. But the silence of history respecting them is in itself significant, showing that no social convulsions disturbed the order of their daily lives, no flagrant wrongs and cruelties called out for mention. This is, at first sight at least, surprising. Considering that the clergy throughout what are called the Middle Ages were the persistent adversaries of the Jews, and that Italy was the very centre and source whence the clergy derived their inspiration, we should certainly have expected that the Jews of that country would experience the very extremity of intolerance and harshness. The fact

that they received milder treatment than their neighbours is
due to a variety of causes, which may be briefly touched on.

In the first place, the condition of Italy was different,
during those ages, from that of other European countries.
The feudal system, the source, as we have seen, of so many of
the wrongs and miseries of the Jews, was never so firmly established there as in the other European countries, and it died out
much earlier. The great free cities exercised an authority of
their own, independent of any feudal superior, and in these
the rights of the Jews were maintained almost as inflexibly as
those of the Christians. The continued strife between Pope
and Emperor, Guelf and Ghibelline, so largely engaged the
attention of the Italian nation as to allow them little leisure
to trouble themselves with the affairs of a people who were
contented to live in peace, and whose aid was often found
extremely serviceable by the dominant party. It is certain
again, whatever may have been the reason, that the fanatical
spirit which was so easily roused, and in such fatal excess, in
France and Germany, languished and soon died out on the
Italian side of the Alps. The cry that the Holy Sepulchre
had again fallen into the possession of the infidels found but
a feeble echo in the streets of Naples,[1] Rome, and Florence;
nor do the people seem to have argued, as they did throughout France and Germany, and even occasionally in Spain,
that the outrages charged upon the Mahometans of Palestine were to be expiated by the Jews of Europe.

Again, as a rule, though doubtless with many exceptions,
the popes were more merciful to them than were the sovereigns of any other Christian land. Some pontiffs, as, for
example, Gregory I., Innocents II. and IV., Alexander IV.,
Nicolases III. and V., Martin V., and others, showed them
marked favour; while others, if they evinced no partiality, at

---

[1] In the Norman kingdom of Naples, where the feudal system had a
firmer hold than in any other part of Italy, the Jews were more severely
treated; but even there, as we shall see, persecution was promptly and
firmly checked.

least discouraged persecution, disregarded idle charges, and would allow no violence. Some doubtless issued harsh decrees and curtailed the privileges granted by their predecessors, but such oppression as John of England, Philip Augustus, and Philip the Fair of France exhibited in their dealings with their Hebrew subjects may fairly be said to have been unknown among them. This was in most instances due to the fact that the popes, however low may have been the moral standard of many among them, were as a rule men of cultivation and intelligence, in whose ears the popular charges against the Jews must needs have sounded as idle calumnies.[1] Many among them also were wise enough—if it was only worldly wisdom—to know that conversions effected by force were many degrees worse than unconverted obstinacy, and on that ground forbade such to be attempted.[2]

---

[1] The absurd charges alleged against the Jews were not confined to the crucifying of Christian boys, poisoning of rivers, and insults offered to the consecrated wafer. In Innocent III.'s pontificate they were accused of selling the milk of their women as common milk, in order that Christian children might be brought up on it, and so (it is presumed) imbibe Jewish opinions. It was said that they trampled the grapes in the winepresses in linen stockings, drawing out the best wine for themselves and leaving the refuse for the Christians, in the hope that they would use it in the administration of the Holy Eucharist !

[2] It is a curious fact that the Jews sometimes received the severest treatment from pontiffs whose characters stood high for both justice and mercy, and sometimes were equitably and leniently dealt with by those from whose general character nothing but intolerance and harshness might have been expected. Innocent III. (A.D. 1198) was one of the greatest and best of those who have filled the papal chair—wise and far-sighted, just and merciful. Yet his language respecting the Jews is in the highest degree harsh and intolerant. He repeats the familiar charge that they are guilty of the blood of the Redeemer, and as such are branded with the curse of Cain. He denounces their employment by the State, even as collectors of the taxes, and threatens the severest chastisement to those who show them any favour. On the other hand, Innocent IV. (A.D. 1243), who succeeded to the papacy some fifty years afterwards, an inflexible and haughty bigot, issued a bull in favour of the Jews which is a perfect marvel for its humanity and justice. He denounces the cruelty and lawless violence with which they were treated. He treats

But there was another and a weightier reason for the immunity from persecution enjoyed by the Jews ; and that was, that they were not the sole—in truth, not even the chief—usurers and money-lenders in Italy. The Caorsini, as the Italian bankers were called (presumably from their having first practised their calling in Cahors), were the persons employed by the popes to collect their revenues, an office almost everywhere else entrusted to the Jews. The Caorsini carried on business, though only to a trifling extent, comparatively speaking, in other lands, notably France and England. Henry III. would have expelled them from England if they had not claimed the protection of the Holy Father. It is probably to them that Bernard of Clairvaulx refers when he speaks of usurers more exorbitant in their demands than the Jews themselves. If indeed it is true that their practice was to demand five per cent. per month (after the first month[1]) for their loans, this charge is justifiable enough. These Italian usurers drove a trade in their native land, which, if it did not monopolize the business of the country, at all events threw all competition into the shade. They farmed the tribute and taxes of all kinds levied by the popes on the Christian kingdoms of Europe. They provided subsidies for crowned

with merited scorn the monstrous charges of sacrificing Christian boys in order to use their blood in the Paschal rites, and forbids such charges to be received. Nay, he adds that if the accuser cannot sustain his charge by the evidence of three Christians and three Jews, he must himself undergo the punishment due to a murderer. Sometimes the pontiff and his edicts accord. Martin V.'s acts (A.D. 1417) towards the Jews bear the stamp of his generous character. He orders that all synagogues shall be protected, the Jewish worship permitted, all privileges, customs, and institutions maintained, unless any of these should be found subversive of public morality, or insulting to the Catholic faith. No compulsion is to be used to bring any Jew to baptism. No one is to disturb them in the celebration of their festivals. He repeals the order issued by the Dominicans, requiring them to hear controversial sermons. He gives them full licence to trade. The nineteenth century, in the most enlightened countries, has done little more for them.

[1] They charged no interest for the first month, thinking in that way to escape the odium of usury.

heads, advanced sums on mortgage to the nobles, and loans to merchants and small traders, and were popularly said to be worse Jews than the Hebrews themselves. There were doubtless many Jewish merchants—and wealthy ones—in the great Italian cities, who carried on an extensive and profitable business in money-lending. But they were not, as in neighbouring lands, the universal creditors, and therefore escaped the general detestation entertained for their brethren elsewhere.

Indeed, the mere fact that the grandson of Peter Leonis, a converted Jew, was not only allowed to mix in familiar intercourse with the noblest families in Rome, but was actually raised to the papal chair A.D. 1130, under the title of Anacletus II., sufficiently shows in how widely different a light the Jews were regarded in Italy and other European countries. No doubt his Hebrew origin was continually thrown in his teeth by his adversaries. But his election to the pontificate is a fact beyond dispute.[1]

We may note also the different course pursued in Naples A.D. 1260 by the Italian rulers from that ordinarily adopted on such occasions in other countries. At Trani, in the Neapolitan territory, the Jews had been protected and favoured by Frederick II., to whom they had rendered many signal services. On his death-bed he commended them to the protection of the States, who, however, adopted the opinion, common enough in those times, that the greatest service they could do the Jews was by obliging them to turn Christians. To avoid the persecution which was imminent, they agreed to change their faith, conditionally on being allowed to intermarry with the noblest families in the kingdom. A good deal of indignation was excited by this permission, and this rose to a greater height when several relapses took place. To punish them a monk at Trani buried

---

[1] Bernard of Clairvaux, a zealous partisan of the rival pope, Innocent V., dilates on the outrage offered to Christ through the occupation of the seat of St. Peter by 'Judaica S boles.'—*Bern. Epist.* 124.

a cross in a dunghill, and then accused a Jew belonging to
the city of the sacrilege. A riot was the result, in which not
only the supposed criminal, but all his countrymen in the
town, were murdered. The outbreak extended to Naples,
and similar scenes of bloodshed would have ensued, if the
authorities had not intervened. Alexander IV., the reigning
pope, issued a proclamation requiring the rioters to desist ;
the king and the nobles lent their authority, and the *émeute*
was suppressed before much blood had been shed.

In the fourteenth century, which we have now more especially under consideration, the first thing we have to note is,
the proposal of Pope Clement V., who in 1308, three years
after his accession to office, removed the seat of papal
government to Avignon, where the popes continued to
exercise undisputed authority for a period of seventy years.
Clement V. is a ruler for whom little admiration or respect
can be obtained. Nevertheless, his suggestion—if it did not
amount to an order—that a Hebrew professorship should be
established in every European university, in order that the
Church might gain a complete knowledge of the Hebrew language and literature, and so be enabled the more effectually
to promote the conversion of the Jews, deserves our notice and
respect. The words may have proceeded out of the mouth of
iniquity and falsehood, but they are nevertheless the words
of righteousness and truth.

Clement's successor, John XXII. (A.D. 1316), adopted a
different policy towards the Jews, having been incited to it,
it is said, by his sister, who accused them of having insulted
a cross which was being carried in a procession in which
she herself, in company with some bishops, was taking part.
He straightway published an edict banishing all Jews from
the territories of the Church ; but the edict was revoked
soon afterwards, Robert of Jerusalem having interceded in
their behalf, and a bribe of one hundred thousand florins
paid to the pope's sister.

Clement VI. (A.D. 1342) bears a character in history for

luxury and dissipation which is hardly surpassed by the vilest of the occupants of the papal chair; but his single good point—kindness of heart—was exhibited in his endeavours to suppress the persecution of the Jews, and the friendly shelter which he afforded to such of the unhappy race as sought refuge in his dominions.

The absence from Rome of the popes during the seventy years which elapsed between the settlement of Clement V. at Avignon, and the appointment, in 1378, of an antipope in the person of Urban VI., renders the history of the Jews during this century unusually meagre. But they appear to have lived unmolested in the various Italian towns. They must have been on good terms with the pope's legate at Bologna, where they presented him with a copy of the Old Testament Scriptures, said to have been written by Ezra himself. This is still preserved, we are told, in the library of the Dominicans in that city. They were protected also by the Venetian government, which allowed them to settle as bankers in their city. They were careful, however, to maintain a strict supervision over them, and in 1385 obliged them to live within the Ghetto, as the Jewish quarter in an Italian city is usually styled.

Learning flourished in Italy among the Jews during this century. The recently founded universities were thronged with Jewish students, and classical literature was especially studied. There were several scholars among them of great repute. Pre-eminently conspicuous are Immanuel ben Solomon and Moses Rieti. The former of these, regarded by the Jews as the greatest of their poets, and said to have been the friend of Dante, wrote a work on Paradise and Hell which is an imitation of the *Divina Commedia* of the great Italian. He wrote also religious poetry and several commentaries on the Old Testament Scriptures.

CHAPTER XXIII.

A.D. 1300–1400.

GERMANY, THE LOW COUNTRIES, ETC.

THE history of the Jews in Germany throughout the fourteenth century is one long series of wrongs and barbarities. Almost immediately after its commencement, the disturbances at Nuremberg, which had been suppressed by Duke Albert some ten or twelve years previously, broke out afresh. In the course of these the mob, seizing on Mordecai, a Rabbi of learning and high repute, publicly hanged him. In the next generation, a man named Armleder, a publican by trade, incited an outbreak among the peasants of Alsatia with such fatal effect that more than 1500 Jews were slaughtered. In Swabia also great numbers were murdered; while at Deckendorf we are informed that the whole of the Hebrew inhabitants of the town were massacred, and their property pillaged or destroyed. There appear to have been no special grounds for these enormities. The whole atmosphere was, as it were, charged with deadly vapours, and the slightest spark of discontent was enough to cause a disastrous explosion. The authorities in some cases sided with the rioters; in others they stood aloof, and allowed them to work their pleasure; while in some few they interfered to stay the mischief if they could, generally with but little success. Great injury was also done to the Jews all over Germany, by the censure passed on them by Pope Clement V. for their excessive usury. Numberless lawsuits, we are told, were in consequence instituted against them, in which their right to recover money lent on interest by them was challenged. A few years subsequently the whole of the Hebrew population of Hungary was expelled from the country by Louis I., who displayed his intemperate zeal, not by that act only, but by his attempts, in concert with Casimir of Poland, to force the profession of Christianity on the Lithuanians.

But all those troubles, trying as they must have proved to the unfortunate Jews, were as nothing when compared with the terrible afflictions which that people were called upon to endure, in consequence of the outbreak of the fearful pestilence known in history by the name of the 'Black Death.' This appeared in Germany 1348, and was so fatal that the country was almost depopulated by it. It was sudden and rapid in its effects. Tumours, mostly of a black colour, made their appearance in the groin and axilla, accompanied by spitting of blood. In three days, at longest, the crisis was reached, and few survived it. The science of the day could not explain its origin, any more than it could cure, or even palliate, its virulence. In the absence of any reasonable explanation of the causes of the outbreak, the terrified multitude caught at whatever was suggested to them. It was first attributed to the indignation of Heaven at the outrageous wickedness of the age; and large bodies of men banded themselves together to make atonement for this by fasting and penitential discipline. They formed into companies, men and women, of all ranks and ages, naked to the waist, and marked with a red cross; and in this state marched in procession through the chief cities, scourging themselves as they went, and calling on all to follow them.

But a new and much more welcome theory was presently
started—that the pestilence which was slaying its thousands and tens of thousands was due to the Jews. It is
said that the Flagellants first suggested this ; but there is
little reason for supposing so. The first idea in the minds
of uneducated men, when attacked by some malady of
which they have had no previous experience, is that they
have been poisoned or bewitched ; the next, to fasten upon
the person by whom the drug has been administered or the
spell wrought. Now, it was argued, if this wickedness had
been devised by any one, it must have been by some inveterate enemy of Christian men ; and who were such inveterate enemies of Christian men as the Jews? They, in
truth, and they only, were capable of malice so subtle and
deadly! Again, it was clear that these operations had been
carried on in some wholesale manner. The criminals must
have infected the air or poisoned the water. The idea, once
conceived, spread like wild fire. No inquiry was made ; no
proofs were called for. What need of them? It was clear
as the day that the Jews had poisoned the wells and foun-
tains ! The supposed murderers were everywhere pursued
with the most merciless barbarity. Some were dragged
before the tribunals, where a form of trial was gone through.
Some were slaughtered by the mob without any investigation
at all. It mattered little which course was pursued. The
result was invariably the same.

The persecution seems to have commenced in the autumn
of 1348, at Chillon, in Geneva, where criminal proceedings
were taken against them, on the specific charge of having
poisoned the wells. The same inquiries took place in other
towns, as Berne and Freiburg. Some poison had been
found in a well at Zoffingen—though by whom put in
there was no evidence to determine. But the usual mode
of eliciting evidence in those ages was resorted to, and with
the customary result. Balavignus, a Jewish physician resident at Thonon, having been put on the rack, confessed

that Rabbi Jacob, of Toledo, had sent him, by a Jewish boy, some poison in the mummy of an egg. The poison consisted of a powder, sewn up in a thin leathern pouch, and it was accompanied by a letter commanding him, on penalty of excommunication, to throw the powder into the principal wells of Thonon, in order to destroy the people who lived there. In obedience to this injunction he had distributed the poison in various places, and more particularly had thrown it into a spring on the shore near Thonon. He swore by the Law and the five Books of Moses that this confession was true, and also implicated several other Jews as accomplices. Another Jew, of Neustadt, named Banditono, was similarly put to the torture, and confessed to having thrown a packet of poison, given him by one of his brethren, into a well at Carulet, and denounced other Jews, whom he named, as having done the same. Eight others underwent the same treatment, and made confessions, all nearly resembling the two above quoted, with the difference that some admitted that the whole Jewish people, except those under seven years of age, were privy to and articipators in the plot. It is wonderful that they did not implicate the infants in arms!

The persecution soon spread to neighbouring lands. At Basle the populace obliged their magistrates to take an oath that they would burn all the Jews in the town, and forbid any of their countrymen to settle in their country for two hundred years to come. In compliance with the order, all the Jews in the place were shut up in a wooden building and burnt alive. At Bennefeld, in Alsace, a diet was held, at which a similar decree was made. At Spires the Jews, driven to despair, shut themselves up, together with their wives and children, in their houses, which they then set on fire, and all perished in the flames. In Mentz and Eslingen similar tragedies were enacted. In the first-named city, when the Flagellants made their entrance, the Jews began by repelling the violence offered them; but, perceiving the impossibility

of making any effectual resistance, they too fired their dwellings and destroyed themselves and all belonging to them.
In Eslingen it was the synagogue, with the entire Hebrew
population of the place, that was consumed; and it is related
that mothers were seen to fling their children into the burning
pile, to prevent their undergoing compulsory baptism. At
Strasburg two thousand Jews were burned on a scaffold
erected in their own burial-ground. For months the same
cruelties were perpetrated along the Rhine and the contiguous
cities. The history of these times is one unvaried repetition
of horrors, which it wearies the pen to describe and sickens
the heart to peruse. Everywhere there are the same groundless and monstrous charges, the same blind and fanatic fury,
the same merciless and exterminating hate. And, worst of
all, these atrocities are committed in the name of Christ and
His Gospel! If we could conceive that the gates of hell
had been broken open, and its inmates had overrun the earth,
the deeds we might have expected of them were just what
the rabble of these German cities actually performed. They
did not, however, wholly escape the consequences of their
own lawless cruelty. In many places the Jews, before inflicting death upon themselves, turned their swords against their
persecutors, and inflicted severe retribution on them; while
in Frankfort their despairing rage caused the destruction
of the town-hall and cathedral and a large portion of the
city.

It would not be just to omit the fact that several among
the European sovereigns condemned these proceedings, and
did their best to check them. Clement VI., a self-indulgent
and easy-tempered man, whose reign was a continued scene
of slack and voluptuous living, was nevertheless roused by
the enormities of the wrongs which he saw perpetrated on
the helpless Jews, to exert himself to the best of his power
in arresting the popular frenzy and punishing the offenders
Charles of Moravia, also, Duke Albert of Austria, and others,
would fain have saved them if they could. But the fury

of the people would not be restrained, and Albert was obliged
to condemn five hundred of them to the flames. In Lithuania
alone were they permitted any respite. Here they were
protected by Casimir III., King of Poland, known in history
as the Great. He confirmed the privileges granted them by
his predecessor Boleslaus, and bestowed additional favours
on them. It is popularly believed that he was induced to
show them this consideration by his attachment to a beautiful
Jewess named Estherka.[1] It is at least certain that throughout his reign the Jews in Poland escaped persecution, and
large numbers of Jews migrated to that country.

The history of the Jews in the Netherlands during the
fourteenth century very nearly resembles that of their German
brethren. They had settled long before in the Low Countries,
where the trade had fallen almost entirely into their hands.
Their numbers were swelled by fugitives from England and
France, from which countries, as we have seen, they had
been forcibly expelled. They were treated sometimes kindly,.
sometimes harshly, according to the caprice of the rulers
and the people. They were expelled from the duchy of
Brabant in 1370, on account of a charge of sacrilege, which
was very frequently made in mediæval times. It was said
that they had stolen and then stabbed the holy wafer at
Brussels, which bled profusely. A banker of Enghien,
named Jonathan, was charged as the chief offender, on the
evidence of a woman, who confessed to having been an accom-

---

[1] i.e., Little Esther. Some historians have doubted this story. They
point out that Casimir's demeanour towards the Jews was only of a piece
with his conduct towards the lower classes of his subjects generally. He
showed so great a regard for the rights of the despised serfs that he
was called 'the Peasant King.' Again, it is certain that Casimir's edict
is dated 1343, and his connection with Estherka did not begin till 1350.
On the other hand, Casimir's one weakness was his passion for women,
and the Polish historians say distinctly that Estherka gained great
privileges from him for her people. Probably both explanations are
correct. He granted the edict of 1343 from a sense of justice, and the
monopolies of the Jews, later in his reign, at Estherka's entreaty.

plice. All the Jews suspected were put to torture, and afterwards torn with red-hot pincers, and then burned.[1]

Such Jews as had taken refuge in Bohemia do not appear to have fared much better than their brethren in other European countries. The Emperor Wenceslaus, son of Charles IV., a lavish and dissipated sovereign, anxious to recover the goodwill of his subjects, whom he had alienated by his excesses, issued a decree discharging all his nobles from any liabilities they might have incurred to the Jews. The people thereupon, who had been afraid to meddle with them, because they regarded them as living under royal protection, considering that they had now lost the emperor's favour, broke out into a riot at Gotha, where they massacred large numbers of them. They were presently joined by the peasants, and the outbreak extended to other cities. At Spires the whole of the Jewish residents, with the exception of some few small children, who were reserved for the font, were put to the sword.

Soon afterwards the cry was raised again that the springs and rivers had been poisoned; and the Jews were subjected to a second persecution all over Germany, and in parts of Italy and France. We are informed that the emperor was fully convinced of the falsehood of the accusation—which, indeed, it is difficult to believe that any person of sense and education could ever have credited. But it was in vain to attempt to reason with the multitude ; and, despairing of obtaining peace or quiet in his kingdom so long as the Jews were allowed to reside in it, he issued an order requiring them either to accept Christianity or depart from the empire. The observation, already made in the instance of other lands, naturally recurs to us when we read his sentence. What punishment could it be to them to leave a country where

---

[1] In 1820 a commemoration of this miracle took place in St. Gudule, when eighteen pictures were painted for the church, describing the entire action of the story, the tortures of the Jews being minutely depicted.

they had been so persistently and so remorselessly wronged? Nevertheless, it is evident that it *was* a punishment, and a severe one to them. It is to their honour that few of them accepted the alternative offered them, but went forth into exile, with all its sorrows and privations, rather than forsake their ancient faith.

The reader will not wonder that in an age of such un-exampled misery, few German Jews were distinguished for their literary success. Isaac of Düren, Alexander Cohen of Cologne, Halevi of Mentz, Isserlein of Marburg, and Lipman of Mulhouse, were among the most celebrated writers of these unhappy times.

UP to this time, as has been already remarked, the Spanish Jews had enjoyed a freedom from persecution which presents a favourable contrast to the monstrous wrongs and cruelties which they underwent in other lands. The fourteenth century witnessed the gathering of the storm which, in that which ensued, was to burst with such deadly fury on the devoted race ; nor were they even now exempt from occasional foretastes of its visitation. At its outset Ferdinand IV., known in Spanish history as 'the Summoned,'[1] a youth at that time under age, occupied the throne, but the administration of affairs was in the hands of his mother, the queen regent. It should be noted that, although the Jews still

---

[1] Ferdinand had condemned to death two cavaliers named Carvajal, on a charge of murder, refusing to hear their defence. Immediately before their execution they summoned Ferdinand to answer for his unjust sentence before the tribunal of God within a month. He died exactly a month afterwards.

retained the rights and privileges accorded them by previous generations, they were fast becoming odious in the eyes of all classes. The *haute noblesse* were jealous of the court favour which the Jews had so long enjoyed, and were seeking for an opportunity to oust them from it; the lesser nobles were deeply in their debt, and looked to a popular outbreak as the readiest mode of ridding themselves of their encumbrances; the priesthood were, as a rule, though with some noble exceptions, their bitter enemies, continually denouncing them to the people, as the causes of every national misfortune that befell them. This was partly due to religious bigotry, partly to their jealousy of the greater wealth and the superior medical skill of the Jews, which prevented them from acquiring the money and the influence over the people which a successful exercise of that profession would have ensured. As for the people, they were largely under the influence of the clergy, and readily believed the stories poured into their ears. Besides, the spectacle of the riches and luxury in which the Jews lived provoked at once their indignation and their rapacity. The train had been laid, and it needed nothing but the application of the spark to fire it.

Ferdinand's favourite minister was a Jew named Samuel, a man of great ability, and, it is said, of a haughty, imperious temper. His death was mysterious. An assassin, who was never discovered, entered his house, A.D. 1305, at Seville, and stabbed him to the heart. It was not difficult to guess at the motives or the instigators of the deed; but nothing was brought to light. His successor seems also to have been a Jew, for a league was formed among the grandees against him. They presented a petition to the Cortes, assembled at Medina del Campo, requesting that measures might be taken to restrain the insolence of the Jews. An order was passed, accordingly, that they should not in future be collectors of taxes.

This was soon followed up by other like attacks. In 1313, Rodrigo, Bishop of St. Jago, held a provincial council at

Zamora, at which manifestoes were presented, which showed but too plainly how fast the animosity against the Jews was ripening. Several of the constitutions of the council breathe the same spirit. It was enacted that Jews, henceforth, shall hold no post or dignity ; and any Jews who hold them shall resign such within thirty days. They shall not be admitted as witnesses against Christians, nor claim, as hitherto, the benefit of the laws. No Christian women shall be nurses to Jewish children. Jews shall not attend Christians as physicians. They are prohibited from inviting Christians to their feasts. They shall not associate with Christians, lest they teach them their errors.

Some of these decrees were re-enacted at the Councils of Burgos and Salamanca, in 1315 and 1322, where it was also ordered that any Christians should be excommunicated who were present at Jewish marriages ; and any Jews who called themselves by Christian names should be punishable as heretics !

In 1325, Alphonso XI., son of Ferdinand IV., was declared to be of age. His first acts showed that, whatever might be the sentiments of the nobles, the clergy, or the people, he was resolved to uphold the Jews. He chose as his minister of finance, Joseph of Ecija, a Jew of great administrative ability ; and one of his first acts was to declare null and void various bulls and prelates' letters, which had been obtained by persons owing debts to Jews, by which those debts were cancelled. He also granted the Jews licence to acquire landed property, though he limited the amount which they might hold. But he could not overcome the popular animosity against them. Don Joseph was presently accused of having, in concert with Count Alvar Osorio, bewitched the king by giving him magical potions. Osorio was sacrificed to these machinations ; and Don Joseph, though he escaped on that occasion, was not long afterwards charged with keeping fraudulent accounts, and dismissed from his office. Probably, however, the king deprived him of his situation as the only mode of saving him from the malice of his enemies, for we find that he did not withdraw his friendship from him.[1]

In 1348, the king was induced to sign an order for the banishment of all Jews from his dominions, on account of an insult which they had offered to the Host, as it was being carried in procession through the streets. The order was cancelled, however, on the discovery being made that the supposed insult was a mere accident, and the person by whom it was thought to have been offered was a Christian. The revocation provoked a riot, which was with difficulty put down by a determined exercise of the royal authority.

This disturbance had hardly been quelled, when one more furious still broke out, caused by the spread of the plague, which had originated in Germany, into the Spanish peninsula. The cry was raised here, too, that the Jews had poisoned the waters of the Tagus—a crime impossible of commission! Nevertheless, on that indictment massacres were perpetrated in several of the cities, especially in Toledo, and 15,000 Jews are said to have been murdered.

During the reign of Pedro, called the Cruel, who succeeded in A.D. 1350, the Jews recovered all, and more than all, their former ascendency. Notwithstanding the prohibition of the law, Samuel Levi, a Jew, became the royal treasurer. He it was who built the famous synagogue at Toledo, which in its own peculiar style has no rival. He was a man of rare ability, and his administrative genius soon filled King Pedro's coffers ; but, unhappily for himself, it filled his own also. A charge

---

[1] A strange, almost incredible story is told of the fate of Joseph Gonzales, master of Calatrava, offered to pay 800 lbs. of silver into the king's treasury, conditionally on his making over to him eight of the principal Jews of the kingdom, to be dealt with as he pleased. The king consented. Gonzales seized Joseph, and Samuel, the king's physician, and put them to the torture, to compel them to surrender the whole of their wealth. They died under the infliction ; but he obtained enormous sums from them and his other prisoners. Gonzales was raised to great honour, and made Bishop of Alcantara. He afterwards forfeited the king's favour, was arrested as a traitor, and beheaded.

was brought against him of mal-administration of the revenues ; and, though it does not appear that this was proved, it brought to light another and far more grievous offence—that of being too wealthy. He was sent to prison where he was racked, to oblige him to disclose the full extent of his riches, and he expired under the torture.

But though the king sacrificed his favourite minister to his own avarice, he did not withdraw his countenance from the Jews. They continued, to all outward appearance, to prosper ; but the public hatred of them was ever on the increase, and the time approaching nearer and nearer when a heavy reckoning would have to be paid. Lopes de Ayala, the chancellor of the Count of Trastamara, afterwards king, under the title of Henry II., expresses the general sentiment of the Spanish people respecting them. He describes them as ' the blood-suckers of the afflicted people, as men who exact fifty per cent., eighty, a hundred—. . . Through them,' he writes, ' the land is desolate ; . . . tears and groans affect not their hard hearts ; their ears are deaf to petitions for delay.' Much of Pedro's unpopularity was due to the favour he showed to this people. He was himself stigmatized as a Jew. It was affirmed that he was the child of a Hebrew mother, who had been substituted for the true Infant of Spain. The Jews stood bravely by him, and suffered heavily in consequence. Many were slain for espousing his cause at Toledo, many more at Nejara ; and at Monteil, where the final struggle between Pedro and Henry took place, the slaughter of Jews was enormous.

But Henry, when once seated on the throne (A.D. 1369), was too politic a ruler to alienate such useful servants of the crown as the Jews had proved themselves to be. He pursued the traditionary policy towards them, interposing the shield of his protection between them and the hostile people. To the remonstrances addressed to him by the Cortes against their occupation of posts of dignity and importance, or possessing the same rights and advantages enjoyed by Christians, he simply replied that he considered it right that their ancient status should continue.

Henry died A.D. 1379, and was succeeded by John I., who pursued the policy of his father and grandfather, so far as the Jews were concerned, refusing to listen to the angry remonstrances continually addressed to him by the Cortes respecting them. Early in his reign occurred the strange but successful plot of the Jews against their countryman, Joseph Pichon, a man of wealth and influence, holding the office of Crown Treasurer. They had apparently become jealous of his favour with the king, and resolved on compassing his death. They applied accordingly to John for a warrant to punish a convicted unbeliever,[1] though without revealing his name. The king having unsuspiciously signed it, they bribed the executioner to put the sentence immediately into effect, and Pichon was seized and beheaded, without having even been informed for what crime he was arraigned. The king, when he discovered the trick that had been played on him, was extremely indignant. He punished the immediate authors of the crime with death, and deprived the Jews of the right of determining their own causes.

The king's influence was to some extent successful in restraining the popular hatred of the Jews. But when he died, A.D. 1390, and was succeeded by his son, Henry III., a lad eleven years old, there was another popular outbreak. Ferdinand Martinez, Archdeacon of Ecija, had, during the reign of John, been continually in the habit of reviling the Jews, and stirring up the populace to attack them. The late king had discountenanced his proceedings; but he was no sooner removed than Martinez threw aside all restraint, and by his harangues roused the smouldering hatred towards the Jews, which had long possessed the people, into a fierce and destructive flame. The Jews' quarter was attacked. Pillage,

---

[1] The probable explanation is, that they knew Pichon was meditating a change of religion, the scandal of which they were anxious to prevent.

murder, violation, followed ; four thousand were slaughtered, the archdeacon heading the mob, and urging them on to still greater atrocities. No steps were taken to punish the perpetrators of this violence. The contagion soon spread to other cities. In Cordova, in Valencia, in Burgos, in Toledo, in Barcelona, in Pampeluna, and other towns of Aragon and Navarre, there were similar massacres. As many as two hundred thousand Jews are said to have been forced to receive baptism. Such as escaped with their lives were stripped of all their possessions, and their houses plundered and burned.

King Henry III., who, like many other sovereigns, was largely dependent on the Jews for the maintenance of his revenues, was reduced to great straits to support his household expenses. An anecdote is related of him which, if true, curiously illustrates the history of those times. He is said to have found his exchequer so low one day as to be obliged to pawn his cloak to pay for his supper. He was informed that in the palace of the archbishop an entertainment was in progress, at which every delicacy was provided in profuse abundance. He repaired thither in disguise, and learned not only that the wealth of the revellers had been truly reported, but that it had been amassed by fraud and peculation. The next day he sent for the grandees of the court, and among them the archbishop, and inquired of him, ' How many kings have you known in Spain ? ' The archbishop answered, 'Three—your grandfather, your father, and yourself.' ' Nay,' rejoined Henry ; ' young as I am, I can remember at least twenty, though there ought to have been only one. But it is time that I put my rivals down, and reign alone.' At the same moment a band of soldiers, accompanied by an executioner, and carrying ropes and gibbets, entered the apartment. The grandees threw themselves at his feet, and entreated his mercy. He spared their lives, but required a strict account of their management of his affairs, obliging them to refund large sums which they had embezzled.

Many Spanish Jews were eminent in literature during this

century. Rabbi Abner, the physician, known as a Jewish
writer previously to his conversion, wrote afterwards an able
refutation of Kimchi's work against Christianity. Solomon
Levi, also a convert to the Gospel, is known in history as the
Bishop of Burgos, a learned and successful writer. This also
is the age of Don Santo de Cañon, the celebrated troubadour,
who, like the two before mentioned, renounced Judaism for
Christianity.

CHAPTER XXV.

THE records of the Jews in Central Europe during this century are unusually scanty. They had been—nominally, at all events—expelled from various parts of it ; and, though it is very probable that they were permitted, through contempt or compassion, to linger on in their old homes, yet they would be careful, as far as possible, to avoid notice. In Poland alone they seem to have flourished in prosperity and peace, and to have received large accessions of members from less kindly disposed countries.

But we hear something, nevertheless, of them. In Guelderland they were numerous, and lived securely under the protection of its rulers, particularly in the cities of Zutphen, Doesborg, and Arnheim. In the last-named city a Jew was even appointed the physician to the town; and decrees were issued prohibiting, on severe penalties, any ill-treatment of Jews in public or private. On the other hand, a singular fact occurred during this century, which seems to manifest the very opposite state of feeling. A noble lady of Guelder-

land having married a Jew, was regarded as an adulteress
for having so done, and was burnt alive at Cologne for the
offence. The Jews also were driven out of the neighbouring
city of Utrecht in 1444; nor were they allowed to return
to Holland until after the revolution of 1795. Commercial
jealousy was probably the cause of this expulsion.

In 1453 there were Jewish riots in various parts of Silesia,
and particularly in Breslau, where more than forty Jews were
burnt. In the following year Ladislaus, King of Hungary,
allowed his subjects to drive the Jews out of his dominions,
seize on their houses and lands, and cancel all debts due to
them. The only conditions he required of them, in return
for this permission, was their making good to him the tribute
which had been paid by the Jews. These outbreaks appear
to have been caused (as was so frequently the case, both in
previous and subsequent generations) by the influence of
fanatical monks, who made the tour of Central Europe,
denouncing the Jews as the enemies of God and man, and
calling on all Christian men to avert the displeasure of
Heaven by slaying and expelling them. A preacher named
Capistran in this manner raised commotions in Silesia, and
in Southern Germany Bernard produced the same disastrous
effects. In Styria, late in the century, the people petitioned
Maximilian to be permitted to drive the Jews out, as their
Hungarian neighbours had done in the previous generation.
They alleged the old charge of kidnapping and murdering
children, and offered him 30,000 florins as a compensation
for the loss of the Jewish tribute. We read that they were
expelled accordingly in 1496. Similar expulsions took place
in Mentz, Nuremberg, and Trent. In the latter place the
accidental death of a child—attributed, as usual, to the Jews
—was the cause of their banishment. But the mania for
the removal of the Jews from all the countries of Europe—
either because their presence was held to be like that of
leeches fastening on the human frame and draining its life-
blood, or because it was feared that the vengeance of Heaven

would visit all those who offered shelter or kindness to its
enemies—seems now to have taken the place of the thirst
for their blood which distinguished the ages immediately
preceding. The idea was quite as unreasonable and unjust,
but a shade less horrible and revolting.

In Italy, as in previous generations, the Jews, if they did
not receive the full rights of humanity, were at least treated
with toleration, and even some degree of kindness. The
demeanour of the popes towards them was, as before, very
capricious—varying, in fact, with the religious convictions or
state policy of each succeeding pontiff. In 1417, when the
schism of the double papacy came to an end through the
unanimous election of Martin V., the Jews marched, according
to ancient custom, in the papal procession, with lighted
torches, chanting Hebrew Psalms, and presenting to the
newly-made Pope a copy of the Pentateuch. Martin V.
received it with a benediction, and a prayer that the veil
might be removed from their eyes, so that they might rightly
understand the Law. He then issued a proclamation, in
which they were dealt with mercifully and justly. Their synagogues, their form of worship, their privileges, usages, and
institutions were to be respected, so only that they offered
no affront to the Christian faith. No forcible attempts were
to be made to baptize their children, and no one was to
interrupt their festivals. With Pope Eugenius IV., who
succeeded in 1431, the condition of things was changed. The
stern and inflexible character, so forcibly exhibited in his
dealings with the Council of Basle and the Eastern Church,
was evinced also in his treatment of the Jews. By a bull,
issued in 1442, he deprived them of most of the privileges
which his predecessor had bestowed on them. He excluded
them from almost every profession, forbade them to eat and
drink with Christians, or to attend them medically in sick-
ness, compelled them to wear their distinguishing badge, and
declared void any bequests which Christians might make
to them. His successor, the beneficent Nicolas V., who was

elected A.D. 1447, pursued a wiser course. He published a decree forbidding compulsory baptisms, and warning all persons to abstain from offering insults or injuries to the Jews. During the rule of the remaining popes of the century, Calixtus III., Pius II., Paul II., Sixtus IV., Innocent VIII., and Alexander VI., the Jews seem to have been little interfered with. Odious as is the character of the last-named pope, it must be recorded to his credit that he afforded shelter to the wretched exiles whom the cruelty of Ferdinand and the Inquisition had driven out of Spain, as we shall presently record.

In the chief Italian cities also the Jews were, on the whole, well treated. The Venetians, as we have seen, allowed them to open a bank in their city; and they appear to have been the first who did so. But it may be doubted whether any large amount of gratitude was due to them on that account. It is tolerably clear that the Caorsini, Lombards, and Florentines (as the native money-lenders were called), who had hitherto engrossed the trade, exacted such enormous profits that the change to the Jews must of necessity have been a commercial advantage. It was doubtless on this account that their establishment at Venice was speedily followed by their admission to Genoa, Florence, Mantua, Verona, and Leghorn—in fact, into all the leading Italian cities—their central seat of business being fixed at Rome.

But if the amount of interest they demanded was not so exorbitant as that of the Caorsini, it was still enough to be a heavy burden on all classes.[1] Towards the end of the century the celebrated Bernardino di Feltre was stirred up to preach publicly against their exactions, and the terms on which Christians stood with them, at Piacenza. It is curious to read the language he employs, which is a strange mixture of the most truly Christian and the most utterly unchristian

---

[1] It is stated that the Jewish money-lenders demanded thirty-two and a-half per cent. on their loans, together with compound interest !

sentiment. He regards the Jews simply as if they had been wicked men, towards whom Christian charity must be felt and shown, but whom it is the duty of all Christian men to shun and condemn. No Christian, he says, ought to employ a Jewish physician ; no Christian ought to be a guest at a Jewish feast—the risk of moral contamination is too great! 'Yet,' he adds, 'in defiance of these obstacles, which the law, no less than duty, enjoins, Christians had recently resorted in crowds to a Jewish marriage feast which lasted eight days ; and it was notorious that whenever Christians were attacked by illness they resorted to a Jewish physician!' The mob, as might be expected, understood very little of his refined distinctions. They interpreted his words as an exhortation to make an attack on the Jews. They rose accordingly, and hanged and tore in pieces all they met with.[1]

He employed, however, more reasonable means of rescuing his countrymen from the clutches of the Hebrew usurer than these. He set up banks, at which a lower rate of interest was required than that demanded by the Jews, but at the same time sufficiently remunerative, provided the debts contracted were faithfully discharged. These he called Monte della Pieta. They met at first with very decided success in the chief Italian cities, and particularly in Mantua, Brescia, and Padua. In the last-named place they so engrossed the money-lending business that the Jews were obliged to close their own bank. There can be no doubt that the scheme was both commercially and philanthropically wise. Yet, after all, it did not prosper. Possibly the publicity of the dealings with Bernardino's banks was not acceptable to borrowers, who might wish the fact of their having been obliged to borrow to be kept secret. Possibly those who would fain have been customers were too deeply involved in debt to the Jews to be able to break loose from them.

---

[1] The Jews were actually driven out of Ravenna in 1484, in consequence of the agitation he stirred up against them.

Possibly it was the effect of long habit, which men are ever unwilling to depart from. But, whatever may have been the cause, the scheme, after a brief period of success, began to languish, and in some places altogether failed.

It was revived later still in the century by the celebrated Girolamo Savonarola, who professed his object to be the same as that of Bernardino—rescuing his countrymen, and especially the poor, from the ruinous exactions of the Jew money-lenders, whom he denounces in the most unmeasured terms, as that 'most wicked set, the enemies of God.' Not contented with this harsh language, he obtained a decree of the State, ordering them to quit Florence within the year.

It may not be amiss, at this point of history, to inquire how far the severe language and harsh treatment with which even really good men among the Christians of the Middle Ages were wont to assail the Jews, had any reasonable justification or excuse. There were some men, as we have seen, with whom the prejudices of their brother Christians had little or no weight; who were capable of regarding the Jews as the children of their Father in heaven, and as such their brethren, though, doubtless, their erring brethren. They might rightly, in such men's eyes, be the subjects of entreaty, warning, perhaps punishment, but never of hate or contempt. But they who were thus raised above the convictions of their age were very few. And there were others—men of the highest character, whose devotion to God's service and love for their fellow-men cannot be questioned—men like Louis IX. of France, Peter of Clugny, Savonarola, Martin Luther, Cardinal Borromeo—who regarded the Jews with horror and detestation, as persons beyond the pale of charity, who were simply to be crushed and trampled out.[1] How are we to

---

[1] Peter of Clugny wrote : 'If the Saracens are justly to be detested, how much more are the Jews to be execrated and regarded with hate !' Louis IX. charged them with being in league with evil spirits to injure and destroy men. It has been affirmed that Luther treated the Jews with lenity and toleration. But, if he ever really did evince this spirit

account for men like these so viewing them? Was the character of the Jews in the Middle Ages such as really to merit a condemnation so unqualified? Is the portraiture of the Jew given by our great dramatist [1] a true one? Shylock is depicted as sordid, vindictive, without mercy and without natural affection. Is he the genuine Hebrew of the sixteenth century, or the mere embodiment of blind and inveterate prejudice?

What do travellers answer when asked whether the soil of the Holy Land is waste and barren, unable to support even its sparse population? They will tell us that it is naturally rich and fertile, but has become unproductive by long neglect and abuse.[2] As it has been with the land of the Jews, so it has been with themselves. Their true national character is among the noblest—if it is not the very noblest—that the world has seen. Whatever great qualities humanity may possess, it is by men of this race that they have been exhibited in their highest development. If we ask from what nation has arisen the ablest legislator, the most far-seeing statesman, the wisest philosopher, the most chivalrous warrior, the greatest monarch, the most Heaven-inspired poet, we must answer, in every instance, From the nation of the Jews.

---

towards them, it was only at the outset of his career. Later on he was stern and merciless in his tone towards them. 'Burn their synagogues and schools,' were his words ; 'break into and destroy their houses. Forbid their Rabbins, on pain of death, to teach,' etc.

[1] Shylock, it should be noted, whether a fair picture or not, of the Jews of Shakspeare's time, is at least a genuine character—a real man. But the Barabbas of Marlowe's *Jew of Malta* and the Fagin of Dickens's *Oliver Twist* are simply coarse and gross caricatures, pandering to the vulgar taste of the day.

[2] Palestine is a land 'rich in its soil, boundless in its capabilities of production, glowing in the sunshine of an almost perpetual summer—this enchanting land was indeed (what the patriarch had described it) a field which the Lord had blessed. . . . But Mohammedan sloth and despotism have converted it into a waste rock and desert, with the exception of some few spots, which remain to attest the veracity of the accounts formerly given of it.'—Bannister's *Holy Land*, pp. 37, 38.

Nor is it to individuals alone that this applies. What struggle for national independence was ever more gallant than that of the Maccabees? Which among all the countless nations, overthrown by the military genius of Rome, ever resisted so long, or with such fatal effect, her illimitable power, as the defenders of Jerusalem? But, no doubt, centuries of oppression had their effect in deteriorating the nobler, and developing the meaner, features of the Jewish character, until the Jews became at last almost—though not quite—what their persecutors believed them to be.[1] Shut out from every nobler pursuit, forbidden the career of the statesman, the soldier, the artist, the author, or the physician, except within the narrow bounds of their own despised race—they were driven to the one sordid trade of money-getting, and compelled even in that to practise the extremity of exaction and rigour, or else—subject as they were to continual lawless plunder—they could not have lived. If they were at any time disposed to show mercy, no one believed it to be anything but a subtle scheme for securing some worldly end. Treated systematically as the outcasts of humanity, what wonder if they often really became so?

[1] Every reader will remember the noble passage in *Ivanhoe*, where Bois Guilbert taunts Rebecca with the degraded character of her countrymen, and she answers him by appealing to their former greatness. 'Thou hast spoken of the Jew,' she says, 'as the persecution of such as thou has made him. Read the ancient history of the people of God, and tell me if those by whom Jehovah wrought such marvels among the nations were then a people of misers and usurers!'—*Ivanhoe*, chap. xvi.

THE scenes of violence and bloodshed which had been provoked by the fanatic zeal of the Archdeacon of Ecija were a foretaste of the fearful tragedy which was to take place in Spain in the ensuing century. But it can hardly be said that he occasioned it. The evil had long been gathering, and must have broken out, sooner or later, in Spain. He may have precipitated it, but nothing more.

The main cause of the mischief was, beyond doubt, the improvidence and want of steady industry among the people. In all business transactions they were continually applying to the Jews, unable, as it seemed, to buy or sell, to sow or reap, without resorting to them. The result was the pauperizing of all classes of the community except the Jews, who continued to heap up enormous wealth.[1] The people would not believe that this was the result of their own improvidence, and that there could be no remedy for it except in persistent industry

---

[1] A similar state of things exists in South Russia to-day.

and prudence. They made repeated complaints of having been overreached and defrauded ; but, when the cases were inquired into in a court of law, it was found that nothing could be proved against the alleged offenders. This only fomented the growing discontent. To all thoughtful observers it was evident that a popular convulsion could not be far distant.

Henry III. died in 1406, and was succeeded by his son John II., an infant not two years old. Early in his reign Vincentius Ferrer, a Dominican, made his appearance as an itinerant preacher in Castile and Aragon, calling on the Jews to renounce their ancient faith, and accept that of Christ. He was a man of the most ardent zeal, indefatigable energy, and burning eloquence ; and the stern asceticism of his life caused him to be regarded as a saint. His fierce invectives against the impiety and obstinacy of the Jews exasperated the people against them ; and it very soon became evident that there were for them two alternatives only—conversion or destruction. Vincent went from town to town, carrying a crucifix in one hand and a copy of the Mosaic Law in the other, followed everywhere by an armed rabble, who maltreated and murdered all who refused to hearken. Many of the Jews embraced, or pretended to embrace, Christianity. Many more abandoned all their worldly possessions, and fled to Barbary ; some also to Portugal,[1] and other Christian States Some would neither abjure their faith nor fly, and their descendants underwent the terrible consequences of their parents' constancy. Ferrer is said to have converted 35,000, or, according to others, 50,000 Jews. Even a Hebrew authority places it at 20,000. How many of these converts were real believers in Christ we shall have occasion subsequently to inquire.

---

[1] Hearing, it may be, of this, Ferrer besought permission of the King of Portugal to enter his dominions, as the messenger of Heaven. The king replied, he was welcome to come, but he must first prove his mission by putting on a crown of red-hot iron ! Ferrer declined to avail himself of this offer !

In 1406 the old charge of insulting the Host was revived, though with some variation in the circumstances. Some Jews were accused of having bought the consecrated wafer from the sacristan of the cathedral at Segovia. They threw it into a caldron of boiling water, when it rose to the surface. Alarmed at the sight, they wrapped it in a cloth, and gave it to a Dominican friar, who informed the bishop of the occurrence. The bishop caused the Jews to be arrested and tortured. Among them was Don Meir, the king's physician. The torture not only elicited a confession of the particular crime charged on the sufferers, but of the murder of the late king by poison. Don Meir and the others were drawn and quartered at Segovia; soon after which it was discovered that the whole charge was a fabrication.

Another similar story is related about the same time. A nobleman, who bore a bitter dislike to a bishop, bribed his cook to poison him. The conspiracy was discovered, and the cook put on the rack; but he would not confess the name of his suborner. By the advice of the latter, the next time he was racked he declared it was the Jews who had bribed him. This was instantly credited ; and, as he had named no particular persons as his accomplices, a great many Jews were put to death on suspicion.

In 1412 the queen-regent Catherine promulgated a series of ordinances against the Jews, equalling in severity anything that had been issued before. They were not to be physicians or surgeons ; they were not to sell bread, wine, or any other provisions ; they were to keep no Christian servants ; were not to eat and drink with Christians, or attend Christian marriages or funerals ; they were to live in the Jewries or ghettoes only, and these were to be surrounded with a high wall, having only one entrance-gate ; they were to wear a carefully prescribed dress of very common material ; and any Jew or Jewess who ventured to put on costly attire was liable to have the whole stripped off their backs. They were not permitted to change their place of residence, and were allowed neither to shave their beards nor cut their hair! No Christian woman was to enter the Jewish quarter, on pain of a heavy fine, if her character was respectable, or of being whipped out of it, if it was not! Finally, they were not to be smiths, carpenters, tailors, shoemakers, curriers, clothiers, or to sell any of the goods made by these, except to Jews.

In 1413 the Antipope, Benedict XIII., convened an assembly at Tortosa, for the purpose of presiding at a disputation between certain chosen advocates of Judaism on one side, and of Christianity on the other—the subjects of discussion being, whether the Messiah had already come, and what was the value of the Jewish Talmud. Considering who were to be the judges, it is no great wonder that the Jews were anxious to decline the discussion. But this they were not suffered to do. The Christian champions were Jerome of Santa Fe, Beltran, Bishop of Barcelona, and Garcia Alvares —all of them able men and converts from Judaism. Sixteen learned Talmudists appeared for the Jews. Sixty-nine meetings were held ; and it is almost unnecessary once more to add that both parties claimed the victory. A bull was issued by the Pope, commanding the burning of the Talmud, and imposing fresh penalties on such Jews as remained unconverted. It appears, however, that large numbers submitted to baptism.

In 1420 the young king assumed the regal authority, and held it till 1454. During his reign the Jews seem to have been, comparatively speaking, unmolested ; and, as was always the case under such circumstances, to have regained both their wealth and their political influence. In 1435 the Jews at Palma were charged with the old stock offence of crucifying children, though this time the victim was a Moor. They confessed, as usual, under torture, and, having agreed to accept baptism, were pardoned. In Toledo, in 1441, the Infante Henry, who was in rebellion against his father, being greatly in want of money to pay his troops, was advised to plunder the houses of the Jews—both those who adhered to

their old creed and those who had recently been converted—
as the surest and most popular mode of raising funds. He
greatly approved of the counsel, and proceeded straightway
to follow it, notwithstanding the opposition of the principal
citizens and the clergy. The populace, we are told, followed
his example. In 1445 the Jews of the same city were accused
of having undermined the streets through which the procession of the Host was to pass ; and one of the customary
massacres would have taken place, if the authorities had not
made inquiry and ascertained that the charge was wholly
without foundation. Again, at Tavora, some youths, after one
of their feasts, sallied forth into the streets, and slew several
Jews whom they met, their excuse being that they thought
the Jews were on the point of making an attack upon *them.*
A similar story to that propagated at Palma was also fabri-
cated at Valladolid of some Jews at Savona. But in no case
did any of the wholesale massacres take place by which the
Spanish cities were disgraced both in previous and after
times.

In 1454 Henry IV. succeeded his father. His action at
Toledo, thirteen years before, in plundering the Jews, caused
the idea to be entertained that he would be unfavourable to
them ; but his conduct, when he came to the throne, did not
bear out the notion. A riot having occurred in 1461 at
Medina del Campo, in consequence of the preaching of an
enthusiastic monk; and a number of Jews having been slain
and their property pillaged, Henry put the outbreak down,
and executed due justice on the rioters. He also appointed
a Jew, Gaon by name, as his finance minister, and sent him
to levy the taxes in the Basque provinces. But this was
regarded by the Basques as an infringement of their con-
stitutional rights. The Jew was assassinated in the streets
of Tolosa ; and when the king sent to require the surrender
of the murderers, he received a defiant refusal, nor did he
venture to take any measures against them.

It was evident that the feeling against the Jews was once

more growing to the fatal height it had attained in other lands. In 1468 the Jews of Sepulveda, a town near Segovia, had, it was averred, seized on a Christian infant, carried it to a sequestered spot, and there, after barbarous ill-usage, crucified it. Their Rabbi, Solomon Picho, was declared to have been the instigator of the deed. The Bishop of Avila put the accused, sixteen in number, to the torture, and having elicited the usual confession, caused some to be burned and some hanged. But these severities did not satisfy the people of Sepulveda, who required the extermination of the Jews. They rose accordingly, and massacred all who did not save themselves by flight. Similar insurrections took place in Cordova, Jaen, Toledo, Segovia, and other cities.

The spirit thus evoked was allayed for a time—probably because Henry not only lent it no help, but was in his heart favourably inclined to the Jews. A deputation, composed of converts to Christianity and those who still professed their ancient faith, residing in Valladolid, waited on him, to ask his protection against the oppression and injustice of the partisans of his sister Donna Isabella, and were kindly received. Though no satisfaction was given them for the wrongs they had undergone, injustice for the future was restrained. When at a Cortes, held in 1469, a petition was presented to him, praying him to forbid the Jews thenceforward to farm or collect tithes, he paid no heed to it. But the spirit of persecution was checked for a time only. In 1473 it broke out again, and deluged all Andalusia with blood. A new feature was now manifested, likely to produce the gravest consequences. The storm of persecution had hitherto fallen on those only who persisted in refusing to adopt the Christian faith. But persons were now included in it who had lately become converts to the Church, and who were known by the title of the 'New Christians.' Their fidelity to their new belief was greatly suspected ; and, it cannot be denied, with a good deal of reason. And, besides, these New Christians were, after all, guilty of that gravest of all Jewish offences—acquiring wealth at the expense of the old Christians. The mobs in the Andalusian cities attacked old and new Jews alike. In Jaen, the constable of the town, Franza by name, who interfered to protect them, was assassinated while hearing mass in the cathedral itself, and the pillage and murder went on unchecked. The example was soon followed in Castile. In Segovia, in 1474, Don Juan de Pachecho, wishing to provoke a rising for the execution of a political intrigue, thought the most likely mode of succeeding was by exciting an armed attack on the converted Jews, it being easy then to divert the rabble to his purpose. The insurrection was put down by the royal forces, but not before great numbers of the Jews had been slain.

Henry died in the same year, 1474, and was succeeded by his sister Isabella. Her title to the crown was doubtful, as there was a daughter of Henry's second queen, named Juana, who, if legitimate, was the rightful heir. But the whole nation seemed to have concurred in rejecting Juana's claim; and, though her cause was taken up by the King of Portugal, to whom she had given her hand, his complete defeat at Toro extinguished her hopes for ever. Five years afterwards Ferdinand succeeded to the crown of Aragon, and his union with Isabella may be said to have created anew the long extinct monarchy of Spain.

In the following year a Cortes was held at Toledo, and many laws were enacted for the government of the now united kingdoms. Among these was an ordinance, that not only should the Jews be compelled to reside within the bounds of their own Jewry or ghetto, but also that any Jew who should presume to live elsewhere should forfeit all his property, and his person be at the disposal of the king. In other respects the regulations passed were neither oppressive nor unreasonable. Within the bounds of their ghetto, all privileges which of late years they had been permitted to enjoy were allowed them. But shortly after Ferdinand's accession to the united throne of Castile and Aragon, he introduced into his dominions a new engine for the oppression of the Jews, the infamous Inquisition, the working of which produced more momentous and terrible consequences than he himself, in all likelihood, foresaw ; which culminated, indeed, not only in the misery and ruin of the Jews, but in the decay and degradation of Spain herself.

This was the era of the famous Isaac Abarbanel, the favourite minister of Alphonso V., of Ferdinand and Isabella of Spain, and of Ferdinand, King of Naples. He was distinguished, not only as a statesman, but as an author. He wrote valuable commentaries on the Pentateuch and the Prophets, as well as many other works. Jacob Mantenu also, physician to Paul III., and the Latin translator of Maimonides, belongs to this century.

THE Inquisition, introduced into Spain by Ferdinand, with
the consent of Isabella,[1] was not a new institution. It
had been established in France early in the thirteenth century,
the object then being to compel the return of the Albigenses
to the orthodox faith. It had worked terrible woe to that
unhappy people ; but two hundred and fifty years afterwards
the heresy had so nearly died out, that the Inquisition would
have died along with it, if it had not been that the outcry
respecting the New Christians, as they were called—that is
the recent converts to Christianity—once more set the hateful
machinery in operation. The height to which the persecution
of the Jews had risen in the fifteenth century had left them no
alternative but apostasy or death. It is no wonder that large

---

[1] It was with great difficulty that this was obtained. Isabella, though
a dutiful daughter of the Church, had a superior intellect and a tender
heart ; and both revolted against the proposed measure. Torquemada,
who had been her confessor, was obliged to appeal to a promise she had
made him, years before, to extirpate heresy, if she ever could. Even then,
her assent was most reluctantly given.

numbers of the Jews preferred the former. It is said that no less than thirty-five thousand persons had been induced to accept baptism by the preaching of Vincent Ferrer alone. For a time the clergy felt overwhelmed with joy at this signal triumph ; but after a while grave suspicions of the sincerity of these new converts began to be felt. Outwardly, no doubt, they conformed to the requirements of the Church; but it was suspected that they still continued to observe in secret the Jewish ritual.

Three inquisitors were appointed, Torquemada, Juglar, and D'Avila; and their first act was to put forth an edict, in which they declared it to be the duty of all faithful Christians, without paying any regard to rank or condition, to accuse to the tribunal any whom they knew to be open professors but secret enemies of Christ. Any who did not do so became themselves amenable to the law for their criminal silence. To facilitate such accusations, a manifesto was issued, in which various proofs were mentioned by which a 'secret Jew' might be detected. We learn from it that a man might be accounted as a concealed Jew if, among many similar evidences, he—

1. Put on clean clothes, or had a clean table-cloth on the Saturday, or dispensed with a fire on the Friday night.

2. If he washed the blood from meat, or examined the knife before slaying an animal.

3. If, on the Day of Atonement, he asked forgiveness of those whom he had offended, or put his hands on his children's heads to bless them, without making the sign of the cross.

4. If he gave his children Jewish names.[1]

5. If he ate the same meat as Jews, or sat down to table with them. If, when dying, he turned his face to the wall, or let any one else turn it. If he washed a corpse with warm water. If he spoke approvingly of the dead (such person

---

[1] By a previous law of Henry II., he had become punishable if he gave his children *Christian* names. It must have been a hard matter to know what to call them.

being a Jew), or made lamentation for him, or caused a body to be buried in virgin soil, etc.

If it were not that these enactments were followed up by the most barbarous and insatiable cruelties, it would be difficult to read this extraordinary catalogue of offences without a smile. But all disposition to mirth vanishes when we remember what ensued. Great numbers of arrests, we are told, were made—the practice of keeping the accuser's name a profound secret rendering it easy to indulge malevolence without the risk of exposure. The accused, not being told the exact nature or details of the charges against them, were unable to disprove them ; and, not being confronted with the witnesses, could not expose their falsehood. Both witnesses and accused, again, were frequently put to the severest tortures, under the pressure of which they made confessions which they were not allowed to retract. In short, it was wholly impossible for any one to escape condemnation when it was the wish or the interest of the inquisitors to condemn him ; and it is no wonder that the list of their victims should have extended to a length so fearful.

Fearful indeed it is to read. During the eighteen years of Torquemada's inquisitorship, more than ten thousand persons were burned alive ; more than six thousand corpses, of persons found guilty after their deaths, were dragged from their graves and fastened to the stakes, along with the living victims; while nearly one hundred thousand were stripped of all their possessions, and sentenced to life-long imprisonment.[1]

All classes of men were shocked and alarmed at these dreadful scenes.. The Cortes appealed to the Pope, who made a feeble attempt to interfere, but soon desisted ; while, in

---

[1] The wholesale butchery of the Autos da Fé, as these executions were called, is one of their most shocking features. On the 4th of November, 1481, three hundred Jews were burned in Seville, and in other parts of the same province two thousand more. In Saragossa the two surviving inquisitors avenged the assassination of their colleague by two hundred deaths at the stake.

Saragossa, a conspiracy was organized, and Arbues d'Avila, one of the three inquisitors, was assassinated in the cathedral. But this did not benefit the unhappy Jews. Whether guilty or not of the act, all men considered them so, and left them to what they regarded as the just penalty of their crime.

Thus far the persecution had been directed entirely to the *conversos*, or New Christians. Such of the Jews as had refused to abandon their faith had been left uninjured ; nor is it unlikely that they considered this as being the just reward of their constancy. But their turn was now to come. Ferdinand and Isabella, who had at last succeeded in reducing the whole of Spain to their sovereignty, resolved that thenceforth none should breathe the air of that land who denied the Christian faith. In 1492 they issued the memorable decree, commanding all Jews to renounce their creed or depart from Spain. It was dated March 30th, and allowed them four months in which to prepare for their departure. Any Jews who presumed to linger in the country after the expiration of that date, or to return to it at any future time, were to be liable to the penalty of death, and the forfeiture of all their goods. Any persons who publicly or privately sheltered or protected any of the proscribed race, after the 31st of July, were to be punished by the confiscation of their entire property.

The blow fell like a thunderbolt on the unhappy people. It has been several times remarked that, considering the irreconcileable enmity entertained towards them, and the incessant wrongs they underwent, it could have been no great privation to be exiled from lands which contained none but bitter and merciless enemies. But they do not understand human nature who would so argue. Man is like a creeping plant, which puts out its tendrils to clasp the objects nearest to it ; and, though these may be rough bark or barren rock, it cannot be torn away from them without resistance and pain. And if this was applicable to the Jews in all countries, it was especially true as regarded Spain. There, for centuries, they had dwelt, peaceful, prosperous, and happy. While

their brethren in other lands underwent cruel insult and
wrong, they had been protected against violence by wise and
just rulers. Only recently had the hand of violence been
raised against them ; and they might surely hope that it
might be withdrawn ere long, when calmer reason again bore
sway.

An attempt was made to induce the king to forego his
purpose. The celebrated Isaac Abarbanel [1] was at the time
high in his confidence and favour. He threw himself at
Ferdinand's feet, and offered, in the name of his people, no
less than 30,000 ducats, as the price of their continuance in
Spain. So large a sum tempted Ferdinand, who was at all
times avaricious, and was at that moment greatly in need of
money. He wavered, and might perhaps have revoked his
edict, if Torquemada, who had heard of the offer, had not
burst into the presence-chamber, holding a crucifix in his
hand. 'Behold,' he cried, ' Him whom Judas sold for thirty
pieces of silver! Sell Him again, if you will, and render an
account of the bargain to God!' Isabella also took part
against the Jews. It may well be, that the notion of being
bribed to forego her duty roused an indignation which she
would not otherwise have felt. Any way, the offer was
rejected, and the miserable Jews had to set about making the
best provision they could against the approaching day of
exile. They were allowed to sell their landed property and
houses, but only, of course, at an enormous disadvantage.
Bernaldes states that he saw Jews give a house in exchange
for an ass, and a vineyard for a small bale of cloth, purchasers
continually holding off from completing a bargain, which they

---

[1] Don Isaac Abarbanel was born at Lisbon in 1437, and early gained
the notice of Alphonso V. He was obliged to leave Portugal suddenly in
1482, having been suspected of taking part in Bragazza's conspiracy
against John II. He was kindly welcomed by Ferdinand and Isabella,
who made him their Minister of Finance. In 1492, he was obliged to
quit Spain along with his countrymen. He found refuge at Naples,
where he was employed by Ferdinand and Alphonso II. He shared the
exile of the latter monarch, and removed to Venice, where he died.

knew they must ultimately get on their own terms. They were forbidden to carry away with them gold or silver ; but we are told that they contrived to secrete large quantities of it in the saddles and halters of their horses. Some even swallowed it, and it is said, in some instances, to the amount of thirty ducats ! The rich Jews paid the expenses of their poorer brethren,[1] practising towards each other the greatest charity.

At the beginning of July, they set out on their mournful journey to the seaports, old and young, rich and poor, a long and melancholy *cortège*. The Rabbins, we are told, encouraged them, and engaged musicians to play, and bade the boys and girls sing, so as to keep up the spirits of the wayfarers. But the mirth must have been forced and hollow. Their fathers could not sing the Lord's song while compelled to dwell in a strange land—how should they sing it when forced to leave their own ?

There is considerable difference in the estimate made by historians of the numbers that went into exile. Mariana reckoned it at 800,000. Others place it much lower ; but at the least calculation it must have reached some hundreds of thousands. An immense concourse assembled at Barcelona, Valencia, Carthagena, Port Maria, and Gibraltar. Vessels had been provided at all those ports, whence they were transported to Italy, or various places on the coast of Africa. The miseries endured during the voyage, and after the landing had been

---

[1] The charge of sordid indifference to the sufferings of others has always been made against the mediæval Jews ; nor can it be denied that there is truth in the allegation. But it was only towards the Christians that this was displayed. To their own countrymen they have in all ages been generous and charitable in the extreme. Be it remembered what kind of charity had been shown *them* by their Christian brethren, and that *they* had not been taught ' to do good unto them that persecute you.' When the Jews at Rome were unwilling to receive their exiled brethren of Spain, Alexander VI. expressed the utmost surprise. ' This is the first time,' he said, ' that I ever heard of a Jew not having compassion for a Jew.'

effected, exceed all power of description. Some of the vessels took fire; others were so overloaded that they sank. Many were wrecked on barren places along the African shore, and died of cold and hunger. Some captains purposely prolonged their voyages, in order that the provisions might run short, and their passengers be obliged to purchase water and food of them at any price they might choose to exact. On board one vessel, a pestilential disease broke out. The captain landed all the emigrants on a desert island, where many perished of famine. Another party was forced to go ashore at an uninhabited spot, where a large portion of them were devoured by wild beasts. Those who reached Fez, in Morocco, were not allowed to enter the town, but were compelled to encamp on the sands, suffering the most grievous privations, and exposed to the brutal insults of the natives.[1] A Sallee pirate allured a number of boys on board his vessel, promising to bestow some provisions on them, and then carried them off before the faces of their parents, who stood imploring and shrieking for mercy on the shore, to sell them as slaves at a distant port.

Those that were conveyed to Italy were somewhat less harshly treated. The captain of a vessel bound for Genoa, passing along the African coast, saw a number of naked wretches, who apparently had been cast by the sea upon it. On inquiry he found that these were a number of Jewish exiles, who had been barbarously compelled to land there. He took them on board, made them some clothes out of sailcloth, and conveyed them to Genoa. There they were permitted to land; but were met by priests carrying bread in one hand and a crucifix in the other, nor would they bestow the former on them until they had consented to accept the latter also. Nine crowded vessels reached the Bay of Naples;

---

[1] Some of the stories related of the atrocities perpetrated on these miserable wretches are too shocking for repetition. They are related by several historians, but I think it better, for the credit of human nature, to suppress them.

but disease, caused by the hardships and privations of the voyage, was raging amongst the passengers. The infection was speedily communicated to the city, and 20,000 persons are reported to have died in consequence. In Rome, even the selfish nature of Alexander VI. was moved at the recital of their sufferings. He not only gave them shelter in his own dominions, but wrote to all the Italian States, desiring them to extend to the Jewish exiles the same privileges which had been enjoyed by their resident brethren.[1]

---

[1] It must be noted, however, that, although Alexander showed compassion to the fugitives, he made them pay a heavy price for his protection of them, and also bestowed on Ferdinand the title of 'the Most Catholic,' in requital of the banishment of the Jews from his dominions.

NO mention has hitherto been made of the Jews dwelling
in Portugal. Little is said respecting them by historians;
and the idea has in consequence been entertained that they
were few in number, and had little influence in the affairs of
the country. But that is a mistake. They settled early in
various parts of Portugal, and under the rule of the first
Portuguese kings bore an important part in its concerns. In
the reign of Sancho I., in 1190, a Jew, Don Solomon Jachia, was
made a field-marshal, and commanded the Portuguese army.
In 1248, Sancho II. appointed so many Jews to public offices
that the Pope of the day, Gregory IX., remonstrated with
him on the subject, and requested that Christians might be
chosen for the various posts of receivers and farmers of the
revenue, which then were generally occupied by Jews, to
the oppression and injury of Christian men. We are told
that, in requital of the royal protection granted them, the
Jews furnished an anchor and a cable of sixty fathoms' length
to every king's vessel which left port.

The same favour was continued by subsequent monarchs. In 1289, the clergy laid a complaint before Pope Nicolas IV. against King Dennis, that he appointed Jews to the highest offices in the State; the Chief Rabbi Judah being his High Treasurer and Minister of Finance. The consequence was they stated, that he permitted his countrymen to dispense with the payment of tithe due from them, and also to lay aside their distinguishing badge. But the complaint seems to have been without foundation. When, at Evora, in 1325 sumptuary laws were enacted respecting dress, no exceptions were made in favour of the Jews; and, unless a composition entered into with the Jews of Braganza, accepting a fixed sum in lieu of the annual taxes, can be regarded as such, no special favour was shown them.

Alphonso IV., in 1340, remitted the extraordinary impositions which, from time to time, had been exacted of them, commuting them for a sum which, though *per se* large, was a great relief to them. His successor, Ferdinand, in 1371 ordered that all the privileges which had been granted by his predecessors to the Jews should be confirmed. He had a Jew, Don Judah, for his treasurer. In 1389, John I., at the suit of Moses, his physician, gave his sanction to the bull of Clement VI., which had been confirmed by the newly elected Pope, Boniface IX., granting the Jews licence to celebrate their feasts, and practise the rites of their religion without interruption from any. In short, up to the date of the accession of John II., in 1481, though laws were passed from time to time, imposing penalties and restrictions on the Jews, which we in the present day should consider harsh and unfair, there was nothing which amounted to persecution.[1]

---

[1] Thus, the Jews were compelled to live in their Jewry; they could not have Christian servants; they were prohibited from entering the houses of Christians, unless they were accompanied by two Christians; they were not allowed to wear silk dresses; they were not allowed to collect the revenue of the Church. But no one could do them wrong without their obtaining redress; there was no hint of confiscating their wealth; and they were free to practise any trade or profession.

On the accession of John II., in 1481, he held a Cortes at Evora, when great complaints were made of the luxury in which the Jews indulged, and the display they made of their riches. They rode splendidly caparisoned horses, wore silk doublets, carried jewel-hilted swords, entered churches, where they made a mock of the worship in progress ; above all, refused to wear the badge by which they were distinguished. Jewish artisans, too—cobblers, tinkers, and the like—roamed about the country, making their way into houses, while the men were engaged at work in the fields, and perverting the women. The king replied to these various complaints, promising to restrain the indulgence in splendid apparel, and to oblige the Jews to wear their badge ; but adding that, as regards other offences, if it could be proved that they had committed them, the law would punish them.

In 1491, when the expulsion from Spain took place, large numbers of the exiles found a refuge in Portugal. It was the most likely spot for them to select. There was no long and perilous sea-voyage to be encountered, and the similarity of language and customs of the two countries made the change less harsh and painful. But though John permitted the fugitives to find a shelter in his dominions, it was only for a brief interval, and upon very stern conditions. He required that all persons, excepting children at the breast, should pay the sum of eight crusadoes (19s. 4d.) each, in return for which they received a certificate, entitling them to reside eight months in the kingdom. At the expiration of that time, the king engaged to provide vessels, on reasonable terms, to convey them to any land they might select. Those who could not pay the crusadoes, or lingered in Portugal after the prescribed time, were to become the slaves of the king.[1] Upon these terms as many as 20,000 families, amounting probably to more than 100,000 persons, crossed into Portugal, with the

---

[1] Except smiths and armourers, who were permitted to remain in the country if they chose.

intention probably of quitting its inhospitable shores as
speedily as possible. But the eight months passed, and large
numbers still lingered. Some were doubtless too poor to pay
for a passage, for which exorbitant prices were charged. The
king had, indeed, ordered that no more than a reasonable sum
should be asked, but his commands were slackly and carelessly
carried out, and complaint would have been worse than use-
less. Many were terrified by the tales of barbarities practised
on their countrymen by the savage inhabitants of the African
coast, and many had been enfeebled by the pestilence which
had broken out among them. No sooner had the eight
months expired than the penalty was enforced, and the whole
of the loiterers became the slaves of the king. Those who
were young and able-bodied were forcibly baptized, and then
carried off to colonize the island of St. Thomas, in the
Gulf of Guinea, which had recently become a Portuguese
possession.

In 1495, John was succeeded by Emmanuel, known in
history as ' the Fortunate.' His succession appeared at first to
promise the miserable Jews some respite from their sufferings.
He revoked the edict under which such as had remained in
the kingdom became slaves. He refused a large sum of
money which had been presented to him by some wealthy
Jews, and professed his determination of treating them with
equity and mercy.

Unhappily, the gleam of sunshine soon passed away, and
was succeeded by a fiercer tempest than any that had yet
darkened their skies. In an unhappy hour Emmanuel sued
for the hand of the Infanta Isabella, daughter of the Catholic
sovereigns of Spain ; and they would not consent to the
marriage, except on the condition that their son-in-law should
banish the Jews from Portugal, as they had banished them
from Spain. We may believe that there was a struggle in
his mind, for he was evidently inclined to be compassionate
towards the unfortunate race, which he had already be-
friended. But what, after all, were a few thousands of

wretched Jews, when compared with the fulfilment of his
hopes? Nay, he would win the approval of his lady-love by
doing even more than had been required of him. He would
win her favour at once, and that of Heaven also, by his fulfilment of their wishes. He issued a proclamation from Muja,
ordering all the Jews still within his dominions to embrace the
Christian faith within the space of three months, or to depart
from Portugal. Three ports were at first named—Lisbon
Oporto, and Setubal—from any of which the Jews might
embark; but subsequently this order was revoked, and Lisbon
was named as the only place of embarkation. It is probable
that Emmanuel expected, after the great reluctance which
the Jews had manifested, on a recent occasion, to quit their
present place of abode for unknown and unfriendly regions,
that the greater part, at all events, would choose baptism
rather than deportation. When he found that this was not
the case, but that great numbers were resolute to depart, and
were making the needful preparations for their voyage, he was
greatly disconcerted. The glory of making converts to the
Church would be denied him, and he would lose a vast number
of wealthy and valuable subjects. He resolved not to forego
these advantages without at least making another effort to
secure them. He despatched a secret order that all children
under fourteen should be separated from their parents, and
brought up in the Christian faith. This was not to be carried
into effect until the day of embarkation came, so that there
would be no time left for disputing or evading the decrees.
But the king's intention was by some error divulged; and, lest
the Jews should contrive to defeat it, it was put into immediate execution. Such scenes of horror ensued as imagination
cannot picture. It was the repetition, on a larger scale, of the
massacre at Bethlehem. Children were dragged forcibly from
the grasp of their parents; infants torn from their mothers'
breasts, to undergo what they regarded as worse then death.
Many, in the distraction of their agony, flung their children
into the wells and rivers, or slew themselves with their own

hands.[1]   One miserable mother threw herself at the feet of the
king, as he was riding to church—to *church!*   Great God of
Mercy, that men should dare to bring such deeds into Thy
very house, for Thine approval!   She cried out that six of
her seven children had already been taken from her—would
he not spare her youngest to her?   The courtiers mocked at
her misery.   The king bade his attendants remove her from
his path—'the poor bitch,' as he expressed it, 'robbed of her
whelps!'—whether with her petition granted or not, we are not
told.   But the people were not so deaf to the common instincts
of humanity as their monarch.   They assisted the Jews to
conceal their children, and the inhuman command was only
partially carried out.   Nevertheless, this last deadly blow had
gone further to break the hearts of the Jews than all their
previous sufferings.   On condition of receiving back their
children, and that the Inquisition should not be introduced
into Portugal for twenty years to come,[2] many of those who
had hitherto resisted all attempts to proselytize them consented to receive baptism.   The more steadfast spirits, whom
no amount of suffering could subdue, were either shipped off
to foreign lands or remained behind after the appointed day,
and became the slaves of Emmanuel.

   It must not be supposed that these acts of bigotry and
pitiless cruelty were done with the universal consent of the
Portuguese people.   The rabble, indeed, in every land can at
all times be stirred up to hunt down and oppress those who
differ from themselves on almost any subject, without reflection and without remorse; yet, even among them, as we have
seen, the natural feelings of compassion could not be wholly
stifled.   But among the more educated and thoughtful classes

----

[1] The corpses of these were publicly burnt, as a token of the anger of
Heaven against *their* wickedness!

[2] The converts also stipulated that, when the Inquisition was set up, its
judicial proceedings should be so far modified that accused persons should
be confronted with the witnesses against them; and, in case of condemnation, their entire property should not be taken from their families.

there were many who not only disapproved the act of their
sovereign, but openly expressed their dissatisfaction. Bishop
Osorio has plainly recorded the view which he and others
took of it. 'Some of the king's counsellors,' he says, 'were of
opinion that the Jews ought not to be driven away, since it
was notorious that the Pope himself permitted them to reside
in his dominions. Other Christian princes in Italy, following
his example—as well as some in Germany, Hungary, and
other European States,—granted them the same liberty, and
allowed them to practise various trades and professions. As
for converting them to the Church, banishment would be less
likely than any other step to bring that about. The Jews
would carry with them their perverse dispositions. *Cælum
non animum mutant qui trans mare currunt*—a change of
residence would have no effect in producing a change of conviction. Nay, to send them over to Africa would be to destroy
what hope at present existed of their conversion. Living
among Christians, they might be influenced by the Christian
example set them [alas! what kind of Christian example *had*
been set them?] and adopt the true faith. But, mingling with
blind and superstitious Mahometans, how could they learn
any good? Again, to put the matter on wholly different
grounds, it would be most injurious to the State to send out of
the land a people possessed of abundant wealth, which would
then enrich their enemies.' But the words of Divine and
human wisdom alike failed to produce any effect on the
infatuated king and his advisers, and the fatal policy was
persisted in.

During this century many learned and able writers belonging to the Hebrew race have transmitted their names to
posterity. Mention has been made in the previous chapter of
Isaac Abarbanel, divine, philosopher, and historian, the most
celebrated Jew of his age. Contemporary with him were
Isaac Aboab, author of commentaries, essays, and sermons;
David ben Solomon Jachia, grammarian, poet, and Tal-
mudist; Judah, Joseph, and Samuel Abarbanel, sons of the

renowned Isaac, the first-named also an author of repute ;
Solomon ben Virga, the historian ; David ben Joseph Jachia,
philosopher, grammarian, and poet ; and many others.

During this century printing-presses were introduced into
Portugal by two Jews, Eliezer and Izarba, by whom some
beautiful editions of the Pentateuch and the Targum of
Onkelos were produced. Hebrew presses were also set up
about the same time in many of the great Italian cities.

THE Jews had now been expelled from England, France, parts of Germany and Central Europe, Russia, Spain, and Portugal.[1] They were also shut out from Holland and the Low Countries, these being subject to the control of the Empire. It does not appear that they had ever established themselves in Sweden, Denmark, or Scotland, to any great extent. In fact, the only European countries in which they continued to reside in any considerable numbers, at this period, were Italy, Poland, and Turkey. It was chiefly in the East and in Northern Africa, under the rule of Mahometan princes, that they found a refuge. We shall speak first of the residents in Europe during this century,

---

[1] It would, however, be a mistake to suppose that they were not to be met with in those countries. Even in England, though the law forbade any settlement, Jews were occasionally to be found, whose presence was tolerated. This was still more the case in France and Germany ; while in Spain and Portugal great numbers remained, whose profession of Christianity was very widely known to be a mere pretence. Of them we shall speak in the next chapter.

and then proceed to record the fortunes of their brethren who had migrated to the East.

They were received, as we have seen, with more kindness than might have been expected in Italy. Many of the Popes were far-sighted enough to perceive that, by expelling the Jews from their dominions, they were simply transferring capital and intelligence to other countries.[1] Leo X., in 1513, checked the zeal of certain preachers, who were inveighing against the Jewish usurers in Rome. He had no mind to have popular tumults excited, which might oblige him to drive out men whose residence in the city was so advantageous to him. His successor, Clement VII., adopted a similar policy. When he heard of the persecution in Portugal, A.D. 1523, undergone by the New Christians (as those Jews were called who were recent converts to the Church), he not only sent an invitation to them to come and live in his dominions, but intimated that he should not inquire what had happened to them previously in Portugal. It need not be said that great numbers availed themselves of his offer. Paul III., 1539, espoused their cause still more openly. He would not permit the Inquisition to continue its persecuting and bloody work within the Papal States. Whatever offences might have been charged against the Jews in their own land, when they crossed the confines of his, a full amnesty was granted them. Especially this was the case in the rising city of Ancona. Entire freedom of trade was permitted, no inquiries being made as to any man's creed. There was complete equality of taxation. No one was compelled to wear any distinguishing badge. We are told that, in consequence of these measures, Ancona grew rapidly in population and wealth. It was doubtless in consequence of this special favour that Cardinal Sadolet complained, at Avignon, of the extraordinary favour shown

---

[1] Sultan Bajazet was shrewd enough to apprehend this. When he heard of the banishment of the Jews by Ferdinand, he exclaimed: 'A wise king this, who impoverishes his own kingdom to enrich mine!'

to the Israelites; and we learn that, later in his reign, Paul issued a bull, annulling the decrees he had made in their favour, and requiring that converts to the Church should be separated from their relatives.

Ten years afterwards Julius III. confirmed the privileges which his predecessors had granted; indeed, he went further. Considering that the Reformation was making dangerous progress in Italy, he thought it necessary to set up the Inquisition in Rome. But he especially exempted the Jews of Ancona from its supervision. And, as regards the other Jews in his dominions, he gave the most stringent directions to his legates and cardinals to show the most complete toleration to their religious opinions and observances. They were to make no inquiry as to what they professed, or what they might formerly have professed—this last promise being obviously intended to meet the case of those Jewish exiles who, in their native country, had been induced to make a nominal profession of Christianity, which they had now laid aside.

His tolerant treatment of them, however, was subjected to a severe trial. A Franciscan friar, one Corneglio of Montalcino, had become a convert to Judaism, and forthwith was possessed with a spirit of proselytism, which drove him openly to preach the falsehood of Christianity in the very streets of Rome! He was seized, and inquiry made as to the cause of his apostasy. Fortunately for the Jews, this was alleged to be the study of the Talmud, not the personal influence of any Jew. Of the Talmud, accordingly, the penalty was exacted. It was ordered to be publicly burned in Rome and other Italian cities. The Jews, who had lived in terror of a furious popular outbreak or a stern papal decree, were allowed to escape scot free—an act of mercy which is gratefully recorded by one of their Rabbins.

But it was different when Paul IV. succeeded to the pontificate, a man of arrogant and impetuous character, who carried intolerance, it might be said, to the highest

pitch of which it is capable.[1]   He was as stern in his demeanour to the Jews as he was to the Reformers.   He renewed all the hostile edicts that had been in force against
them in the time of his predecessors.   He prohibited them
from holding real property, and compelled them to sell
what they were possessed of within six months,—of course
at a ruinous loss.   He debarred them from trading in corn,
or any of the necessaries of life, though he allowed them
the privilege of dealing in old clothes, with which traffic
they have been so generally associated in the popular fancy.
He ordered all their synagogues but one to be destroyed.
He was the first to shut them up in the Ghetto, where, for
centuries afterwards, they were forced to live.   He obliged
them again to wear a distinctive dress—the men yellow
hats, the women yellow hoods—to abstain from work on
the Sunday, to keep from all intercourse with Christians,
and especially from attending them as physicians, and to
pay a tax for the instruction in the Christian faith of any
Jews who were inclined to embrace it.

His rule, however, only lasted for four years, and Pius
IV., who succeeded him in 1559, somewhat, though not very
greatly, relaxed the sternness of his predecessor's policy.   He
maintained the enforced residence within the Ghetto, but he
enlarged and improved it, and forbade the exorbitant rents
which the owners of houses had hitherto exacted.   He removed several restrictions on their trade, and permitted
them to hold real property up to the value of 1500 ducats.
He allowed friendly intercourse between them and their
Christian fellow-subjects, and, though he would not dispense with the cap, which was one of their distinguishing
badges, he changed its colour from yellow to the less remarkable one of black.

Pius V., 1566, a man of austere and sombre character,

---

[1] Paul IV. was the Pope whose overbearing dealings with Queen
Elizabeth precipitated the rupture with the English Church.   He was
also the author of the well-known *Index* of prohibited books.

revived in a great measure the harshness of Paul IV. He banished the Jews from all the cities in his domains, except Rome and Ancona, and revived most of the severities with which Pius IV. had dispensed. He seems to have tolerated the presence of the Jews at all, only because by that time it had come to be generally understood that to expel them from any country was to destroy its commercial prosperity. There was little change in their treatment when Gregory XIII. followed, A.D. 1572. He promulgated a bull, which he caused to be fixed at the entrance of the Ghetto, which prohibited the reading of the Talmud, and required all Jews who were more than twelve years of age to appear periodically, for the purpose of listening to sermons preached for their special conversion. What effect these had in producing the desired result, we are not informed.

In 1585, however, Sixtus V. assumed the pontificate—a man of far higher character and more commanding mind than any of his predecessors during the present century. His mode of dealing with the Jews was at once humane and statesmanlike. He swept away with a stroke of his pen the vexatious and frivolous restrictions which had been imposed on them ; he gave them free access to, and unrestrained residence in, all the cities of his dominions ; he allowed them to carry on whatever trade they might prefer ; he ordered the full toleration of their religion ; subjected them to the same civil tribunals and the same taxes as their Christian fellow-subjects. He also limited the amount of usury which they were permitted to exact to eighteen per cent.

After his death, in 1590, there was a succession of Popes who vacated the papal chair almost immediately after occupying it.[1] Clement VIII., who was elected in 1592, confirmed the bull of Pius V., by which they were banished out of all the papal cities except Rome and Ancona ; but to these he added Avignon, where they have since resided, with full liberty of

---

[1] Urban VIII., Gregory XIV., and Innocent IX.

holding their religious belief and maintaining their form of worship.

In the other Italian States their condition during this century appears to have been quite as good—somewhat better, indeed, than it was at Rome. In Florence they were kindly received, and so well protected by the laws, that we are told it was a favourite saying in that city, that 'a man might as well insult the Grand Duke himself as a Jew.'[1] In Venice they were equally in favour. They had already, in the previous century, obtained permission to set up a bank in the city, the Senate being aware of the commercial advantages obtained by the residence of the Jews among them. They disapproved the step taken by the Spanish and Portuguese kings, and themselves employed Jews on missions of importance, as for instance Abarbanel, to negotiate a treaty with Portugal ; and in 1589, another Jew, Daniel Rodriguez, to put down some troubles in Dalmatia, which he successfully accomplished. In Livorno (Leghorn), which the Medici in the latter part of this century took under their special protection, designing it to become a great mart of European trade, a quarter was especially assigned to the Spanish and Portuguese exiles, who flocked thither in great numbers. It was, indeed, declared to be a Jewish colony, and it has continued to flourish from that day to the present time. The Spanish language is still spoken by the Hebrew population, and the Mosaic ritual is maintained, says a modern writer, in great splendour.

At Ferrara, the Spanish and Portuguese emigrants were received with the same favour, and the like privileges, which had been accorded by other Italian princes. Their numbers were so great, that the duke was induced, probably by popular

---

[1] A remarkable instance of the esteem in which they were held in Florence is to be found in the quarrel between Florence and Milan in 1414. The Florentines, considering that they had cause of complaint against the Duke of Milan, sent a Jewish banker, named Valori, as an ambassador to him. The duke refused to receive a Jew as an envoy. which the Florentines so highly resented that they declared war against him.

clamour, to revive an old law, requiring them to wear a small
yellow circle on the breast. From the same cause, popular
pressure, he was obliged in 1551 to dismiss the whole of the
Hebrew population from his realm, in consequence of a widespread, though it would seem unfounded, belief that they had
brought the plague into Ferrara. They were, however, soon
permitted to return. Many Jews also settled at Bologna,
Cremona, Modena, Mantua, Padua, and other large towns,
where they were kindly received.

At Naples only of the Italian cities they were not permitted
to find a home. In the first instance, as the reader has learned,
a considerable number of the Spanish exiles had found
refuge in that city, where they had been received in a friendly
manner. But the invasion of Charles VIII. of France exposed
them to fresh persecution. Wearied out by their endless trials,
they lost heart at last, and consented to embrace the Christian
faith. But, as in the other instances, the conversion was only
nominal, and the danger had no sooner passed than the pseudo-
converts returned to their former profession. A few years
subsequently Gonsalvo de Cordova took possession of Naples
in the name of the King of Spain. He raised the question as
to whether they ought not to be driven out of the country,
which had now become part of the Spanish dominions. But
the idea had now got possession of most people's minds, that
to expel the Jews from any country was to do it serious injury.
He therefore proposed to introduce the Inquisition, which
would retain the Jews in the land, but compel them to keep
to their newly made profession. This, however, did not please
the Neapolitans, who rose in insurrection, and the government
were fain to compromise the matter by expelling the Jews;
though it is affirmed by some of the Jewish writers (as, for
example, Orobio de Castro) that these stern measures were
adopted only so far as the Sephardim (or Spanish Jews) were
concerned.

In this century great numbers of Hebrew printing-presses
were set up in Italy, which were under the management of

R

learned Jews. Among these was the celebrated Abraham
Usque, by whom the well-known Bible of Ferrara, a Spanish
version of the Old Testament, was printed. Hebrew presses
were also erected at Cremona, Leghorn, Padua, Genoa, Rimini,
and Verona, as well as the central city of Rome. The renowned Daniel Bomberg of Antwerp established himself at
Venice in 1516, and his works attained great celebrity. He
also published the first complete edition of the Talmud, and
the first Rabbinical Bible. To this age also belongs Rabbi
Joseph, the historian of the French Crusades and the sufferings of the Jews in Castile, Asarja de Rossi, and Abraham
Portaleone.

CHAPTER XXX.

A.D. 1500–1600.

THE JEWS IN PORTUGAL, SPAIN, AND HOLLAND.

THE Jews having been publicly expelled from Portugal and Spain, it might be thought that there was an end of their history, so far as those two countries are concerned. So, doubtless, there would have been, had the expulsion been a complete one. But it was notorious that, though they had been nominally driven out, great numbers remained, who, though they called themselves Christians, were in reality Jews, and nothing but Jews. Miserable as was the condition of those whose sufferings have been described in the previous chapters, it may be doubted whether those who stayed behind were not more wretched still. True, they had escaped the dreaded severance from home and country ; they might still dwell among the familiar scenes of youth and manhood ; they had not undergone the horrors of the outward voyage, and the landing among barbarous and inhospitable strangers. But there was the self-reproach and shame of a false profession of faith ; there was the necessity of complying with forms and observances which in their heart they hated ; there was the continued dread of detection and ruin. They knew themselves to be the objects of continual suspicion, that keen and merciless eyes were ever upon them, and that on the slightest evidence of any open recurrence to the worship which they still secretly rendered, the fearful scenes, still fresh in their memory, would be renewed.

It was not long before these anticipations were fulfilled. On Easter Day, 1506, a fierce and sanguinary outbreak occurred in Lisbon, which illustrates only too faithfully the state of public feeling in that day towards the New Christians—which had now become the customary designation of the Jews. Its immediate cause was an insult offered to a famous miraculous crucifix, which had been brought out of the cathedral into the great square. The plague had broken out in the town, the season was unusually dry, and the pestilence was aggravated by the want of water. It was hoped that through the aid of the image some help might be sent from above. On a sudden, while the eyes of all were anxiously fixed on it, the features of the sculptured Christ were seen to smile. The people all broke out into expressions of admiring thankfulness, except one man, who declared that the smile had been caused by a stream of light let in by a lamp through the back of the figure. He was one of the New Christians, and the hollowness of his profession had already been suspected. The Dominicans denounced him as an apostate, and he was instantly struck down and slain. The mob followed up this deed of violence by attacking and slaying all the countrymen of the offender whom they encountered. The monks incited them to further excesses, promising (it is said by a Jewish historian) that whoever should murder a Jew would not have to pass more than one hundred days in purgatory, let his offences be what they might. The rabble, thus incited, assailed, gutted, and burned the houses of all the Jews in the town ; men, women, and children were everywhere massacred ; those who had fled into the churches for sanctuary were torn from the altars, dragged out, and burned. For three days the carnage went on unchecked. At the end of that time King Emmanuel, who had been absent at Abrantes, returned to Lisbon. He sent a body of troops into the town sufficient to quell the disturbance; the ringleaders of the outbreak were arrested and hanged; and the magistrates, who had shown their incompetency to deal with the emergency, removed from office. Such of the New Christians as had escaped the murderous hands of the mob again passed under the protection of the law. Yet they could not but have felt like men dwelling near the crater of some volcanic mountain, which might at any moment burst forth in torrents of burning lava, and overwhelm them utterly; and it is worthy of notice that, although the rioters were sternly punished for their lawless violence, no reparation was made to the Jews—not even an expression of regret was uttered for the unprovoked and cruel wrongs they had undergone. It is passing strange that they should have still clung to a land so unkindly, and still more strange that those who had quitted it for other countries, where at least life and property were secure, should have been anxious to return to it.

Yet this did occur. When Charles V., the grandson of Ferdinand and Isabella, succeeded in 1519 to the throne of Spain, some of the Jewish exiles sent a deputation to him, requesting permission to reoccupy their ancient homes, free from the perpetual and pitiless interference of the Inquisition. In requital of this service, if he should be inclined to render it to them, they offered no less a sum than 800,000 crowns of gold. Charles received them favourably, and his council advised the acceptance of their offer. But Cardinal Ximenes, who had succeeded Torquemada as Inquisitor General, interfered, and sternly warned Charles that he could not comply with the request without unfaithfulness to Christ. Charles yielded, as his grandfather had yielded to Torquemada, and the petition of the Jews was rejected. Under the same influence he refused the Portuguese refugees permission to continue in Holland, whither many of them had fled. All who had not resided for six years in that country were obliged to quit it.

In 1521 John III. succeeded Emmanuel as King of Portugal. The latter had promised the New Christians, on their consenting to receive baptism, that the Inquisition should not be introduced into Portugal.[1] But some of John's advisers persuaded him that this promise was not binding, for two reasons —first, because the New Christians were notoriously unfaithful to their engagements; and secondly, because he had no power to make such an agreement without the consent of the Pope. To the Pope therefore John appealed for leave to set up the Holy Tribunal. But Clement VII. and his cardinals at once refused the petition, and ordered that all the New Christians whom John had arrested should be set at liberty. When, in 1534, Paul III. succeeded Clement, John renewed his petition. But Paul rejected it as resolutely as his predecessor had done, pointing out that Emmanuel's promises ought in honour and good faith to be respected.

John, however, was not to be discouraged. Learning that the Emperor Charles V. was on his way homeward, after his military success at Tunis, he resolved to avail himself of the opportunity. Charles would be entitled by the exploits he had performed to a triumph, at which custom allowed him to ask any favour he pleased from the Pope. He besought Charles therefore to make the establishment of the Inquisition in Portugal the privileged request. Charles assented,[2] and the Pope, though sorely unwilling, was obliged to grant it. At

---

[1] In the account given at the time of their conversion (1497), it is said that the Inquisition was not to be introduced 'for twenty years,' viz., till 1517. But it is plain that there must have been another promise for a longer period, though no record has been preserved of it. The Pope, indeed, Paul III., plainly said as much.

[2] Charles, throughout his reign, was harsh and stern in his dealings with the Jews. His private secretary, Solomon Malcho, who had been an enforced convert to Christianity, afterwards returned to his old belief, and tried to convert the Emperor to it. The latter handed him over to the secular arm at Mantua, and he was burned at the stake.

the same time, however, he stipulated that all the Portuguese Jews who had been imprisoned up to that time should be released from prison, and receive a free pardon. This condition the king refused to comply with ; and the Pope had to exercise his personal authority, placarding the pardons on the doors of the churches, and sending his own officers to release the prisoners. The Inquisition, however, was set up in Portugal ; and the same results attended the measure as had followed from it elsewhere, on all other occasions. Many of the secret Jews, foreseeing these, fled to other lands ; where, if not actually safe from persecution, they would be at all events less liable to it.

Not many years afterwards, Jews and New Christians were to be met with in considerable numbers in various parts of the newly discovered regions of America, both in the countries which had been taken possession of by Spain and those which had fallen to the share of Portugal. In Africa also, and all over Asia, they settled—sometimes a scattered few, sometimes in larger communities. So numerous, indeed, were the emigrants, and so injurious to the national welfare was their departure found to be, that repeated edicts were issued by the kings of Portugal, forbidding it on the severest penalties. The simple method of detaining them, by making their residence in the country agreeable, or even endurable, to them, does not seem to have been thought of.

In Europe their chief place of retreat was Holland. While this was under the government of Spain, they were as sternly excluded from it as from every other portion of his Catholic Majesty's dominions. But when the long struggle for independence ended in the emancipation of the Seven United Provinces, the Spanish and Portuguese emigrants were favourably received there. In 1590, three Portuguese Jews, the advanced guard, so to speak, of a numerous host which was to follow, were hospitably entertained. From Embden in 1594 came ten more, who had borne the Portuguese names of Lopes Homen and Pereira, but who, as soon as they had settled in the Dutch capital, resumed their original designation of Aben-dana. The first synagogue was built there, in 1598. Notwith-standing the flight, however, of so many of the so-called New Christians from Portugal, enough of them remained be-hind to form a powerful party in the capital, which more than once, during the latter part of the century, interfered with considerable effect in the affairs of the State.

It remains that we say somewhat more respecting those Jews who still continued, as we have said, to reside in Spain and Portugal. A stranger, and at the same time a more instructive, history is not to be found in the annals of the world. Bigotry has never been so blind, so determined, so unscrupulous, as it was in Spain under the iron rule of the Inquisition. Arbitrary power has never been exercised more freely, more persistently, more pitilessly, than by Torquemada and his successors. The eyes of the Inquisition were every-where—spying out men's ways, not only in their discharge of public duties, but following them, Argus-like, into the privacy of their family intercourse—nay, into the solitude of their closets and bedchambers. Their ears drank in men's secret whispers, uttered only in the hearing of their nearest intimates—their wives or their children. They did not hesitate to inflict the most dreadful tortures in order to elicit the information they desired. They spared, in the prosecu-tion of their task, neither the weakness of womanhood, the tenderness of infancy, nor the infirmities of age. Yet they could not penetrate the mystery of secret Judaism. Men obtained the highest rank in the State, and filled the most important offices, honoured and dreaded by all men, who nevertheless belonged to this despised and proscribed race. The blood which was supposed so to degrade the man in whose veins it ran was owned by the greatest and noblest of the land—the marquis, the duke, and the prince, with their high-sounding titles and their lengthy pedigrees. Towards the end of the eighteenth century, it is related of the cele-brated Portuguese minister, Pombal, that the king, having proposed at a meeting of the council that all who were of Jewish descent should be obliged thenceforth to appear in yellow caps, attended at the next council with three yellow caps in his hand. The king having inquired the meaning of this procedure, he replied that it was intended to carry out the proposition the king had made. 'One cap,' he observed, 'is for your majesty, one for the Grand Inquisitor, and the third for myself.'

Stranger still, but equally certain, is the fact that secret Jews held posts of dignity, not in the State only, but the Church also. There were convents full of Jewish monks and Jewish nuns. Priests said mass at the altars, and received confessions, and pronounced absolution, who regarded all these rites as false and impious. Nay, secret Jews wielded the powers of the Holy Office itself. They saw men dragged before them, and tortured and condemned them to the stake, for holding precisely the same faith as themselves—pronounced, it may be, the sentence with their own lips, and then went to their homes to take part in the proscribed rites themselves. If anything could prove more clearly than has been already proved, the folly, no less than wickedness, of religious persecution, it would surely be this strange and startling history.[1]

Nor ought we to quit this subject without remarking on the just and stern retribution with which the nation has been visited that did these things. At the beginning of the sixteenth century Spain was the leading power in Europe, containing forty millions of inhabitants, for which its rich and productive soil afforded ample subsistence. The empire of the New World, which was, as it were, committed to her care, poured wealth without limit into her lap. What is she now? Abroad, her name carries little respect; she has sunk to a

---

[1] For a vivid picture of the strange condition of society in Spain at this period, the reader should study Miss Grace D'Aguilar's beautiful little tale, entitled *The Vale of Cedars*. See also some striking details in Borrow's *Bible in Spain*.

secondary rank among the nations. Her voice is never heard in the settlement of European interests. At home, her population has diminished to little more than one-third of what it was four centuries before ; her commerce is paralysed ; her government unsettled. The poverty and ignorance of her people seem to be ever on the increase, and strife and anarchy continually distract the land. Who can doubt that her double sin—against the Indians of the New World, and the Jews of the Old—has brought down this heavy judgment on her?

THE condition of the Jews during the sixteenth century in those parts of Germany and Central Europe where their presence was still tolerated, does not materially differ from what it had been for many previous generations. We hear of fewer outbreaks of lawless violence, and the atrocities committed on them seem a shade less barbarous. But the history is in the main such as the Christian chronicler must record, and the Christian reader peruse, with feelings of shame and sorrow. At Mecklenberg, just at the end of the previous century, the oft-repeated, though never proved, accusation had been revived of bribing a Christian priest to sell the consecrated Host; which the Jews who purchased it immediately proceeded to stab, drawing forth (it was alleged) the very blood of the Lord Jesus, whose body it was. A grave and minute inquiry was set on foot. Thirty Jews, together with the priest, were condemned to be burned at the stake for the offence. Some Jewish women and children were implicated in the charge. One of the former is related to have put two of her daughters to death, in order to save them from the horrors that awaited them, and to have been on the point of killing a third, when she was snatched from her. Two years afterwards, another charge was brought against some Hungarian Jews, or rather another form of the same charge: this time the offence being murdering a Christian in order to drink his blood.[1] The accused were put to the torture—not so much, we learn, to elicit the fact whether *they* were guilty, as whether the whole Jewish people of Hungary were not implicated in the crime. Monstrous as this may seem, it was not the first time, by any means, that such a belief had been entertained.[2] Possibly, indeed, it was hoped that under the pressure of their agony the sufferers would confess that, or anything else that they were required to admit, and so give a pretext for a general massacre. If so, the attempt failed, for we find that only those who had been accused of the crime suffered for it.

A few years afterwards, at Nuremberg, and again at Cologne, expulsions of the Jews took place. In both cities, though a number of charges were alleged against them, the real offence seems to have been their commercial success, and the heavy load of debt contracted to them by the citizens of the two towns. The shortest mode of paying off the liabilities, it was found, lay in finding their creditors guilty of some offence for which they were punishable by the confiscation of their property, including, of course, all debts owing to them. But these expulsions, however unjust, do not appear to have been stained by the additional guilt of bloodshed.

In 1509, a Jew who had been converted to Christianity, Pfeffercorn by name, filled with the zeal for which proselytes

---

[1] See Appendix V.

[2] In the reign of Henry III. in England, at the inquest held on Hugh of Lincoln, A.D. 1255, it was declared that the whole of the Jews in England were privy to, and guilty of, the crime.

are always remarkable, suggested to the Emperor Maximilian that all books which upheld or set forth Jewish doctrine, and especially the Talmud, the great repository of Jewish fable, should be everywhere destroyed. He had already written more than one book, in which he charged his country-men not only with denying the truth of the New Testament, but with departing from the commandments of the Old. He accused them also of using imprecations against Christians, both in public and private. These had so much effect upon Maximilian, that he is reported to have been half inclined to grant his request. He resolved, however, to appoint a commission of learned men to examine and report on the matter. At the head of this was placed Reuchlin[1] (otherwise Capnio), the most famous Hebrew scholar of his day, and a man of large and liberal views. He advised the Emperor that such of the Jewish books as contained blasphemies against our Lord (as undoubtedly some of them did) had better be destroyed ; but those which simply treated of the tenets and ritual of the Jews ought to be retained. He pointed out how impossible it was to suppress books which a certain number of readers were resolved to preserve. This would have been at any time difficult, but since the invention of printing it had become morally impossible, as the Jews had now begun to make free use of the printing-press.[2] We cannot wonder much

---

[1] Johann Reuchlin was born at Pforzheim, December 28, 1455, of poor parents. The sweetness of his voice attracted attention to him, and he was sent to be educated at Paris. He began his career as a teacher of classics at Basle, but soon abandoned this for the profession of the law. In 1482 he had become known as a Hebrew scholar, and he was noticed by the Emperor Frederick III. In 1498 he returned to Stuttgard, where his fame continued to increase ; in consequence of which Pfeffercorn's proposals were submitted to him by Maximilian. The most celebrated satire of the day, the *Epistola Obscurorum Virorum*, was written to uphold his views, and had the effect of completely crushing his adversaries. Reuchlin died at Stuttgard, December, 1521.

[2] Some of the Jewish books were no doubt extremely offensive to

that a man of Pfeffercorn's temper would not acquiesce in a decision like this. He attacked Reuchlin in an angry pamphlet, to which Reuchlin replied. The dispute was referred to the Pope, and Hochstraten, a Dutch Inquisitor who had espoused Pfeffercorn's quarrel, repaired to Rome to advocate it ; but the papal decision was in favour of Reuchlin. The Jewish books were spared. Nevertheless, it may be doubted whether the affair was favourable to them. The result was to attract the attention of Christian scholars to these Jewish attacks on Christianity, and replies were in consequence written, which were probably more damaging to Judaism than any burning of their books could have been.

Out of this controversy a number of sects seem to have arisen—at least, they are first noticed by writers about this time, and they disappear from history soon afterwards. Among these Seidelius of Silesia, George de Novara, and Francis David are the most remarkable.[1] They held opinions culled, some from Judaism, some from Christianity, and differed widely from one another. They had the usual fate of eclectics, being rejected and despised by both parties.

In 1516 the Jews had a narrow escape of being expelled from Frankfort. An assembly, consisting of deputies from various sovereigns and free towns, was held in that city, for the purpose of organizing measures for their banishment. Fortunately for them, the deputies could not agree among

---

Christians, as, for example, the *Chisuk Emunah* of Isaac ben Abraham, a Polish Jew. The Portuguese Jews translated it into their own language, and diffused it widely. The *Nitzachon* again, ascribed to Rabbi Lipman, of Mulhouse, was equally, if not more virulent. It could hardly be expected that even the wisest and most far-seeing men of the sixteenth century would tolerate these.

[1] Seidelius taught that Messiah, when He came, would come to the Jews only, the Gentiles having neither part nor lot in Him. Francis David acknowledged Jesus Christ, but held that it was sinful to pray to Him. George de Novara claimed to believe Christian doctrine, but denied that Messiah had come. He was burnt at the stake.

themselves. The Jews were, however, driven out of Branden-
burg. Lippold, physician to the elector of that country,
was charged with having poisoned his employer. He made a
confession under torture, and was executed ; after which all
his countrymen were driven into exile.

Towards the middle of this century the Jews were for the
first time expelled from Prague. They had dwelt unmolested
in that city from time immemorial. No one knew when
they had first settled there ; but tradition said it was in times
when Bohemia was yet heathen ; and inscriptions on some
of the older graves in their moss-grown cemetery are quoted
in proof of the fact. The very latest date assigned for
their arrival is the tenth century of Christianity. They had
built a noble synagogue, and had opened an academy, over
which a renowned Jewish doctor presided. But in the
troubled times which followed the burning of Huss and
Jerome of Prague they continually fell under the suspicion
of one, or, it might be said, both parties, the Jews being
too cautious to ally themselves with either. This feeling
grew stronger when the Reformation itself had fairly engaged men's minds. Among the mutual jealousies and
suspicions which had taken possession of men's minds, that
of the secret plottings of the Jews in favour of their
antagonists, was one of constant occurrence. It chanced
that terrible conflagrations broke out in some of the larger
cities, and among others, in Prague. The Jews were instantly suspected of having caused it. Being suspected was
in those times very nearly the same thing as being convicted
of it. All those that escaped the flames were banished from
the city, with the exception of ten families, who obtained
permission to remain. The Emperor was not convinced of
their guilt, but the feeling that had been provoked was too
strong for him to cope with. He saw plainly that nothing
but the death or the banishment of Jews would satisfy the
people, and he chose the more merciful of the alternatives
offered him. Towards the latter end of the year the real

incendiaries were discovered, and the Jews were then permitted to return.

About eight years afterwards another outcry was raised, this time it being affirmed that the Jews had been praying that disaster and ruin might befall the Christians. Their books were seized as a punishment, and carried off to Vienna, so that the Rabbins had to officiate in the synagogues as well as they were able, reciting everything from memory. We must suppose that this charge was disproved, as the other had been, for the books were soon afterwards restored. Even this was not the end of their troubles. Before the year was out, there came another peremptory order for all the Jews, except the ten privileged families, once more to leave the city and settle elsewhere in Bohemia; and this time it does not appear that they were allowed to return.

Merseburg again—the capital now of one of the regencies of the Prussian States, which consists almost entirely of cessions made by Saxony in 1815—was another of the cities in which the Jews claimed to have resided without interruption for nearly fourteen centuries. Yet, so widespread had the feeling against them become, that they were forced, in 1559, to quit this city also, notwithstanding that the Emperor Ferdinand was willing to help them to the utmost of his ability. He not only protected them, indeed, but granted them a privilege which had been accorded to their ancestors in the East, many centuries before—that of having their own special ruler, who was known by the same title as that borne in the earliest Christian times by the Patriarch of the East, viz., the 'Prince of the Captivity.'

In Moravia, in 1574, a similar flame of persecution broke out. We are not informed what were the precise charges, but no doubt they were much the same that were alleged against almost all Jewish congregations in Central Europe about this time. Many Jews, we learn, were burnt at the stake, and many more put to death in other ways. They appealed to the Emperor Ferdinand, who appears always to have been willing to assist his Jewish subjects to the best of his ability. He did interfere, and stopped the executions, but not before many victims had been sacrificed.

In Franconia, six years afterwards, there was something of a similar outbreak. In this instance the Jews were accused, as they were in many other places, of having set on fire the town of Bamberg. But here they escaped without undergoing any further severity than having to make good the loss which those had suffered whose property had been destroyed.

In Poland and the Ukraine a more merciful state of things prevailed. In both these the Jews enjoyed entire freedom alike from pillage and persecution. In the first-named country they were chiefly engaged in trade, which they almost monopolized; in the latter, almost exclusively in agriculture.

But in Russia proper the race of Israel continued to be, as tradition declares it always to have been, harshly treated— such Israelites, that is to say, as were still permitted to dwell in the country, the Jews generally having been expelled from it, as the reader has learned (A.D. 1113). Late, however, in the previous, and early in the present century, during the last years of the long reign of Ivan III., a most singular apostasy to Judaism is recorded to have taken place, the truth of which we should certainly be inclined to doubt, if it had not been so respectably attested. A Jew named Zacharias, about A.D. 1490, began to attempt the conversion of certain Russian priests to Judaism, and succeeded to an extraordinary extent in the design. The converts adopted all the Jewish rites, except that of circumcision; which they dispensed with, because, in event of discovery, it would be a certain proof against them. The apostasy spread rapidly and widely. Ecclesiastics occupying the highest positions in the Church, even the Patriarch Zosimus himself, became perverts. The conspiracy, if it may be so called, was at last discovered, and a great number of these 'secret Jews' summoned before the council and convicted. They were punished after a more merciful manner than that adopted towards their brethren in Spain. They were set on horseback, with their faces towards the tails of their steeds, dressed after a bizarre fashion to resemble devils, and paraded through the streets amid the jeers of the rabble. Zosimus was sent back to the monastery of which he had been archimandrite. But, though the evil was detected, it is doubtful whether it was extirpated. It is said to have lingered in the Russian Church long afterwards.

Rabbi Joseph ben Meir is the great Jewish historian of this period. He was born at Avignon in 1496, and wrote a *Universal History*, and a *History of his own Times*. The latter, though its statements must be taken with reserve, is regarded generally as a valuable book. David Gans also, born 1541, was a renowned scholar and author. He died in Prague, A.D. 1613.

WE have now recorded the fortunes of the Jews, during the sixteenth century, in all the countries of Europe where a domicile was allowed them, as well as in Spain and Portugal, where, though banished by law, they were still, under a nominal profession of Christianity, permitted to linger. We have now once again to transfer our attention to eastern and southern lands, in which, under Mahometan rule, they found a more merciful refuge. Before doing so, however, it is proper to repeat the remark already made, that, although legally forbidden, during those centuries, to enter several of the European kingdoms, it is far from certain that they were not to be found in them, and that in no inconsiderable numbers, though doubtless they were careful to keep out of sight as much as possible. Reference has been made to a Spanish historian, who says that 'many of the Spanish exiles fled to England, establishing themselves in three of the largest towns—Dover, York, and London—and that they built synagogues in the last-named city, where

they afterwards carried on a thriving trade.' 'From 1291
to 1655,' writes a pamphleteer in 1753, 'the Jews have run
the hazard, as they do in another country [doubtless Spain],
where so many of them have expired, and annually still
expire in the flames ; but meeting all along with lenitives
[merciful usage], they have made true one of our English
proverbs of claiming an ell's longitude for an inch's allow-
ance.' [1]

In France it is certain that they were tolerated, so long,
probably, as they did not make themselves conspicuous.
Rabbi Joseph relates that Henry II. allowed certain Jews
from Mauritius to reside in the French cities, and in 1550
granted them his protection and various privileges. His
father and his queen, Catherine de Medici, had Jewish
physicians, who were high in favour with their employers.
We are told that the Parliament of Paris condemned in
severe terms the inhuman conduct of the sovereigns of
Spain and Portugal ; and that many of the Portuguese
emigrants were suffered to establish themselves at Bordeaux and Bayonne, where they have since resided without
molestation. The same, no doubt, was the case among the

---

[1] *Some Observations of a London Merchant about the Bill for the
Naturalization of the Jews*, A.D. 1753. The writer had probably conversed with persons who remembered the state of things in England
before the readmission of the Jews. As regards the assertion of the
Spanish historian, therefore, there is very reasonable likelihood of the
Jews having been allowed to live without molestation in England during
the reigns of the Tudors. Indeed, as Disraeli has remarked, if there
had been no Jews in England, Sir E. Coke would hardly have insisted
so forcibly on their not being admissible as witnesses. But the
statement respecting the building and public use of synagogues must
be taken with reservation. The expulsion from Spain occurred a little
before the close of the fifteenth century. Scarcely more than fifty years
afterwards we find Cromwell's divines declaring that 'for the Jews
to have synagogues, or any public meetings for worship, was not only
evil, but scandalous to Christian churches.' Surely they could not have
said this, if synagogues had so recently existed in London, and worship
been celebrated in them !

German States; where, if the Jews were persecuted in one city, it was comparatively easy to fly for shelter to another.

So likewise in Russia. The Jews have never been re-admitted to the provinces from which they were originally driven out. But Russia has in modern times acquired by conquest extensive territories in which there was a large Hebrew population. She did not carry her dislike so far as to expel them from her new dominions, and has as many as two millions of Jewish subjects. But her feelings towards them have undergone but little change.

Doubtless many of the Spanish and Portuguese fugitives betook themselves to one or other of the above-named countries. But it is tolerably certain that the great mass chose the Mussulman kingdoms in Asia and Africa as their future abiding-places. Whether it was due to the scorn, the calm indifference, or the compassion, with which the Mahometan princes regarded them, it is certain that they permitted them the free exercise of their religion, and the full possession of civil rights. In Persia and Media, even before the Spanish exodus, they seem to have been very numerous, though the particulars recorded respecting them are extremely scanty. During Timour's wars, they naturally suffered, among all the other inhabitants of Persia, from the inroads of his savage soldiery, which took little account of the difference of creed among those whom they attacked and conquered. We are informed that their synagogues were wrecked, their schools destroyed, and great numbers of them slain in the capture of cities. These troubles had hardly subsided when the irruption of the fierce Shah Ismail Sofi once more threw everything into disorder. His rapid and signal success is said to have produced such an effect upon them, that they were persuaded he must be the Messiah who was to come. The idea was encouraged by the fact that Ismail had declared himself to be a prophet sent from God to reform the corruptions of Islamism. But he received their homage very coldly[1]—indeed, is said to have treated them with less consideration than any others of his new subjects.

One of his successors, Shah Abbas, a generation or two afterwards, brought about a severe persecution of the Jews in his dominions, though in a very singular manner. He had issued a proclamation granting great privileges to such strangers as should settle in his dominions. The Jews immediately availed themselves of this, and crowded in such numbers into the country that they speedily engrossed the trade. This was no more than was their ordinary wont; but Shah Abbas's subjects were greatly aggrieved, and made bitter complaints to the king. Thereupon he made a very minute inquiry into their peculiar habits and opinions, possibly in order to find some excuse for banishing them from the land. Learning that they had long expected the arrival of their Messiah, and were still waiting for Him, he insisted on it that they should name some time by which, if He had not made His appearance, they should admit their belief to be unfounded, and conform to Mahometanism. After long consultation among themselves, they told Shah Abbas that they would agree to fix seventy years as the prescribed limit—doubtless arguing that most probably all concerned, but certainly Shah Abbas, would be dead before the arrival of that day. The king received the reply with gravity, and caused it to be formally registered, and deposited in the

---

[1] This king seems to have had a dislike to excessive homage, which was a rare feature in an Eastern prince. It is recorded of him that on one occasion, after one of his great victories, his soldiers saluted him with Oriental adulation, some declaring him to be a prophet, others an angel, and others God Himself. Finding that he could not dissuade them from their impiety, he ordered a deep pit to be dug, and then, throwing one of his shoes into it, gave out that the man who honoured him most was to fetch it out. Numbers instantly threw themselves into the pit. He then gave orders to have the earth thrown back again, burying the whole of his worshippers alive! Doubtless none ever offered him adoration again.

archives of the kingdom. It is probable that the memory of it died out even before the end of Shah Abbas's reign. At all events, when the appointed period approached, wars and commotions of one kind or another occupied men's minds, and no attention was paid to the subject. But, more than a hundred years afterwards, Shah Abbas II., in an unlucky hour, chanced to light upon his ancestor's decree. It was of course found that, although the seventy years had long expired, and the expected Messiah had not made His appearance, the Jews had not adopted the Moslem faith, nor were they disposed to do so now. Here was a clear proof of their treachery and falsehood ; and the consequence was a massacre which is said to have lasted for three years, those only escaping who abjured their religion, or fled into Turkey on one side, or India on the other. After a while, however, it was found that the supposed converts, though nominally Mahometans, as their brethren in Spain had professed to be Christians, were in reality Jews at heart. Wiser than Ferdinand and his successors, Shah Abbas recalled his decree, and allowed the pretended Mussulmans to return to their real creed.

But little is known of the Jews in the Eastern Empire during the period preceding the capture of Constantinople by the Turks, in 1453. But, a generation or two after that event, large numbers were to be found both in Constantinople itself and other parts of the Sultan's European dominions. The Spanish exiles who resorted thither found a large number of synagogues already in existence, served by a priesthood in no way inferior to what their own had been at home. They did not, however, amalgamate with these, but built new synagogues in Constantinople, Jerusalem, Damascus, Saloniki, and other great cities, each of which long afterwards retained the name of the original builders, one being called the synagogue of Toledo, another of Lisbon, another of Aragon, and the like. The Turkish government treated them with great liberality, allowing them unrestricted

freedom in establishing manufactures and transacting commerce, permitting them also to hold landed property.
Whatever amount of their wealth had been stripped from
them by their Spanish persecutors, we may be sure, was
now speedily recovered. Nor does it appear that they
were subjected to any excessive exactions. They paid a
certain amount of taxes, no doubt, and were occasionally
liable to arbitrary demands, from which no one in the East
is secure; but, on the whole, they were mercifully dealt
with. Here too, as in all other lands where they have
resided, their great financial and diplomatic ability was
utilized by the Turkish rulers. Selim I. (A.D. 1512) trusted
much to his Jewish physician, Joseph Hamon. His son,
Solyman II., called 'the Magnificent' (A.D. 1520), similarly
employed Moses Hamon, the son of Joseph, who, by his
influence with his royal master, on one occasion saved the
whole of his people from massacre.[1] Solomon Ashkenasi
was selected as the Sultan's agent to conduct a negotiation
with the Venetian Republic. Joseph Nasi obtained such
favour with Selim II. (A.D. 1566) that he was made Duke
of Naxos, and was even designated King of Cyprus, though
that intention was never carried out. After the disastrous
battle of Lepanto, another Jew, Solomon Rophé, was sent
to arrange a treaty of peace with the Venetians.

The Spanish Jews, among their other effects, brought their
printing-presses into Turkey, where, by the favour of the
Sultans, they were set up. At Constantinople and at Saloniki
they were soon in active employment. The Old Testament
Scriptures in Hebrew and Spanish were printed and largely
circulated, as well as many Jewish writings which had hitherto

---

[1] A Turk, having reason to suspect one of his neighbours of an attempt
to seduce his wife, assassinated him, and to escape suspicion threw the
corpse into the Jewish quarter. It was found there, and occasioned a
popular insurrection, in which the Jews would have been murdered to
a man, if Moses Hamon had not prevailed on Solyman to order an
inquiry, by which the truth was elicited.

remained in manuscript. At Saloniki a famous college was established, at which there were said to be as many as 5000 students. There was also a valuable library, which unfortunately was destroyed by fire in 1545.

The Holy Land is another country to which, as we might naturally expect, refugees from other lands resorted. It had always been regarded as a befitting thing for Jews of an advanced age to make a pilgrimage thither, and die among the hallowed scenes of their cherished traditions. With every persecution in European countries the number of these increased; and at the beginning of the sixteenth century Palestine was filled with swarms of Israelites, who, as a rule, were poor and destitute, and suffered greatly from the rapacity of Turkish officials. The Jewish communities in other parts of the world regarded it as their duty to support these needy brethren, and in larger cities collections were regularly made in the synagogues for this purpose. As no attempt apparently was made to provide them with the means of supporting themselves,—and possibly none could have been made with success,—the distress was always considerable, and after the Spanish exodus rose to a still greater height.

Another quarter to which large numbers of the expelled Jews migrated was the northern coast of Africa. This was a region already familiar to them. Egypt had, for a great length of time, been a favourite place of abode with them, and this had more particularly been the case since the time of Maimonides. Schools had been established in Cairo, Damietta, and other Egyptian towns, to which great numbers of students resorted. In the kingdom of Morocco, again, the banished Jews settled in great numbers. This was, indeed, the nearest country to Spain, Portugal excepted, and communications had for a long time been kept up between the inhabitants of the two kingdoms. In Tripoli also, Oran, Fez, Tunis, and Algiers, many Jewish families established themselves. But they did not receive the same friendly welcome which their brethren experienced in the East. They were allowed liberty of conscience, no doubt, and the protection of the law; but that was all the favour accorded them. The authorities laid heavy burdens on them, and at times exacted large sums as subsidies, after a fashion which greatly resembled the dealings of the English and French sovereigns several centuries before. The lower orders looked on them with fanatical prejudice, and they were obliged to wear black turbans, and boots of a different colour from those of the natives of the country. Yet their position, on the whole, was not unhappy. They were largely employed in the iron-works among the mountains of Morocco, as well as in building and agriculture.

One feature in their history deserves especial mention. In 1578, when the ill-fated expedition of Sebastian of Portugal took place, large numbers of Portuguese nobles and gentlemen were made prisoners, and sold as slaves in the market-places of the chief towns of Morocco. Many of these were bought by Portuguese Jews, who must have been sorely tempted to requite the injuries themselves and their fathers had received on these captives, who were wholly at their mercy. But they took a nobler revenge. They not only exacted no ransom of them, but allowed them to return to their homes, requiring of them no other condition than that of passing their word of honour that they would, on arriving in Portugal, remit to their former masters the sums that had been paid for their redemption from slavery. History has recorded few nobler actions.

CHAPTER XXXIII

A T the commencement of the seventeenth century the
Reformation may be regarded as an accomplished fact.
The great flood of controversy which had broken up the
Church had begun to subside, and whatever countries had
been gained by the new opinions, or had been retained by the
old ones, remained in both instances firm to their allegiance.
It might have been expected that the great changes which
had been worked would largely affect the condition of the
Jews, and ultimately, no doubt, they did so ; but for the time
the effects were scarcely discernible.   No doubt, in Protestant
countries the clergy could no longer put in force the terrible
engines of persecution which had hitherto been ready to their
hand ; and this was in itself an immense relief.   Again, in
lands which still owned the supremacy of Rome, much of the
virulence of the priesthood against the Jews was of necessity
abated.   They had graver and more absorbing occupation for
their thoughts.   In the momentous struggle which was in
progress the Jews were more or less overlooked.   But the

bitterness of feeling towards them was scarcely, if at all, diminished. The leaders of the Reformed movement themselves regarded the Jews with but little favour. They could not, indeed, but abhor the barbarities which had been employed against them by the rulers of the Church; but they had little idea, so far as themselves were concerned, of showing consideration towards the obstinate and rebellious race which persisted in rejecting Christ.[1] This, however, was not universally the case. Frank du Jon (Franciscus Junius), the well-known Dutch Reformer, urged on his countrymen, in earnest and emphatic language, the duty owing by all Christian nations to their brethren the Jews, who were to be won by the spirit of love to the fold of Christ. So did Isaac Vossius, Professor at Amsterdam, who addressed a letter to the Jews, strongly indicative of this temper. The Arminians of Holland again, and their allies, evinced a most brotherly kindness towards such Jews as had taken refuge in their country. The celebrated Hugo Grotius was especially remarkable for the respect he entertained for the Rabbins and their opinions. Indeed, though some of the leading Reformers occasionally expressed themselves in a manner which was inconsistent with the wise principles they professed, yet the general effect of their teaching grew and strengthened as generations went on, and resulted at last in a widespread and enlightened toleration.

---

[1] It has already been observed that Martin Luther, though sometimes he speaks of the Jews rather with considerate compassion than anger, at other times, and especially later in his career, uses the very bitterest language respecting them, as, for instance, in his tract (published in 1543) on *The Jews and their Lies*, the title of which, it may be remarked, is quite in accordance with its contents. And again, in his exposition of Psalm xxii., written many years earlier, he thus writes : 'Doubt not, beloved in Christ, that after the devil, you have no more bitter, venomous, violent enemy than the Jew.' He also enjoins the sternest and most violent measures to be used against them. The great founder of Calvinism, again, though he is less fiery and vehement in his denunciation of them, cannot be said to regard them with any greater favour. He sees in them nothing but the virulent, determined enemies of Christ, whom it would be weakness, if not sin, to treat with any favour.

It must also be remembered that the Jews themselves—for
a long time, at all events—showed no more inclination to
embrace Gospel truth, as set forth by the Reformers, than
they had been in previous generations to accept the tenets of
the Romish Church. It was not, indeed, to be expected that
the deep mutual rancour which had been the growth of so
many generations—of savage cruelty on the one hand, and
sullen, inflexible hate on the other, could be removed by any
sudden change, even if its results had been far more beneficent.
It is far easier to provoke international animosities than to
compose them again. Let us remember how long, in this
country, the bitter dislike and contempt of the French nation,
which Nelson and his school did their best to encourage as the
best safeguard of England against successful invasion—let us
remember, I say, how long it lasted, after all possible danger
of the dreaded results had passed away. It cannot, indeed,
be said to be dead even now, though three generations have
passed away since it was called forth. Remember also that
the mutual antipathy of the Englishman and the Frenchman
could not for a moment be compared, in respect of its
bitterness, with that which existed in those dark and miserable times between the Jew and the Christian. Let us be
thankful that a spirit of toleration and mercy has been
growing, however slowly, and still continues to grow, and pray
that our children may behold the ripe perfection of that
glorious harvest.

Not much is recorded of the Jews in Germany and the
other countries of Central Europe during the earlier portion
of the seventeenth century. There was a disturbance at
Frankfort in 1614, which proved disastrous to them, though
it does not seem to have arisen from religious bitterness. It
will be remembered that, as nearly as possible one hundred
years before, there had been a proposal to exile all the Jews
in the town. That originated in commercial animosity, and
nothing but the mutual jealousies of the deputies present at
the meeting had prevented its being carried out. On the

present occasion a revolt of the trade guilds against the town authorities had been successful, and the first act of the guilds was to expel the Hebrew traders, of whose prosperity they were jealous. But two years afterwards the sedition was suppressed, and the leader of the *émeute* put to death, whereupon the Jews were permitted to return. A similar expulsion took place in Worms, when the fugitives found a protector in the Elector Frederick.

In the year 1619 began the terrible 'Thirty Years' War,' from which all classes of men suffered heavily, and the Jews as much as any. During the celebrated siege of Prague they rendered great service to the Emperor. Rabbi Leo has written a history of the incidents of that eventful period; in which he praises highly the conduct of his countrymen, their zeal and courage throughout the siege, and especially their piety, in assembling in their synagogues to implore Heaven to grant their countrymen victory, and reciting a litany composed expressly for the occasion by one of their Rabbins. He is persuaded, indeed, that the preservation of the city was entirely owing to their intercession.

If such was the case, it is to be feared that the Emperors Ferdinand II. and III. did not evince the gratitude which would be due from them. We learn that in 1630 the first-named took from them their privilege of farming the revenues of the Hungarian kingdom. His reason for doing so does not flatter them. He says it was because 'they had neither conscience nor honesty, and were therefore unworthy to enjoy it.' They must, however, have regained it, since we find that they were again deprived of it, in 1647, by his successors.

In 1650 a great meeting of Jews, at which three hundred Rabbins were present, is said to have been held on the plain of Ageda, thirty miles from Buda, to determine a question which, it appeared, was agitating the minds of many—whether the Messiah had not already come. The sole authority for the occurrence appears to be one Samuel Brett, who published an account of it in London, A.D. 1655, five years after the supposed assembly. Most historians reject the story as a mere invention, designed partly to facilitate the conversion of the Jews, partly to throw obloquy on the Church of Rome. Among those who refuse it credit, is the celebrated Menasseh ben Israel, whose authority carries great weight. Further, in the narrative itself, the imputing by the Pharisees of the miracles of our Lord to the agency of magic, reads like a plagiarism from Matt. xii. 24 ; as also their objections to His mean origin, to a similar extract from Mark vi. 3.[1]

On the other hand, some authorities accept Brett's statement as genuine ; and there are circumstances in it not easy to reconcile with the notion of imposture. Thus, the author gives his name and the particulars of his own life and career, which it would have been easy to disprove, if they were fictitious ; and, as the publication of the story must have provoked a good deal of angry feeling, it is at least strange that this was not done. But when Nathaniel Holmes republished the history, as he did eleven years afterwards, he added no hint that its authenticity had been so much as suspected. Nor again, still later, did the compiler of the *Harleian Miscellany*, who also reproduced it. Further, Brett states that the Jews, when they broke up their meeting, resolved to hold another in three years from that time—two years, that is, after the date of Brett's publication. An impostor, one would think, would not have inserted this perfectly needless addition to his narrative, which could only lead to his detection. The idea which the entire story gives is rather exaggeration than imposture. Such a meeting as he describes might really have taken place ; but the numbers, the character of the speakers, and the interest felt by the Jews generally in the proceedings, have been greatly overstated. It will be better to give Brett's story with this caution appended to it.

He states that the first meeting took place at the time and

---

[1] It may be added that the very existence of the Sadducees, as a sect, at this period of history, is an anachronism.

for the purpose already stated, the King of Hungary having first granted permission. A vast number of learned Jews from all nations repaired to the spot, and encamped in tents round a central pavilion, where the council sat.

The first day was employed in examining the credentials of the various Rabbins. On the second, Rabbi Zechariah, who had been chosen president, proposed the main question, 'Whether the Messiah had already come, or were they still to await His advent?' Some, we are told, argued that He must have come. They had now suffered, they said, for 1600 years the heaviest woes, nor did there seem any prospect of these coming to an end. But why should God thus delay the coming of the Deliverer? Neither they, nor their fathers for many generations, had been guilty of idolatry, which alone would be an adequate cause for withholding Him. But the sense of the assembly was against this view. It was affirmed that He had not come, and that the sins of the people had delayed His advent.

Next it was debated in what manner He would come; and here there was no lack of unanimity. It was agreed that He would appear, according to the old belief, as a conqueror, who would restore the kingdom to Israel; that He would uphold the Mosaic law in all its integrity, and that He would be born of a virgin. Some of those present then raised the question whether Jesus the crucified might not be the Messiah. But the Pharisees objected that Jesus had been a person of low birth and condition, whereas the Messiah would appear surrounded by all the accessories of earthly grandeur. A Rabbi named Abraham rejoined that it was difficult to account for the miracles wrought by Jesus, unless He was the Messiah. But Zebedee, a chief Pharisee, rejoined that these miracles had been effected by magic. In this the Sadducees present concurred, though they had hitherto opposed nearly all that the Pharisees advanced.

The congress had lasted for six days, when some priests made their appearance, who, at the request of the King of Hungary, had been despatched from Rome. These at first only attempted to prove that Jesus was the Messiah, and, while discoursing on this topic, seem to have been heard with patience. But when, digressing from this, they began to insist on the authority of the Church, and demand the submission of the Jews to the Pope, the whole assembly broke out into a tumultuous cry of 'No Christ!' 'No God-man!' 'No intercession of saints!' 'No worship of images!' 'No prayers to the Virgin!' The meeting broke up in disorder, coming to no conclusion. But it was alleged that many Jews were shaken in their belief.

In another part of Europe—the part, indeed, in which the Jews had hitherto enjoyed the most entire immunity from suffering—great troubles befell them about this time, in consequence of the rebellion of the Cossacks against the rule of the Poles. In the spring of 1648 massacres of Jews took place in the countries which lie to the east of the Dnieper, in which thousands perished. Still larger numbers were carried off as prisoners, and sold in Turkey. During the interregnum following on the death of King Ladislaus, hordes of barbarians overran the Ukraine, committing great havoc, from which all the inhabitants suffered, but none, we are told, so much as the Jews.

In 1670 the Jews were banished from the Austrian dominions by the Emperor Leopold, a weak and narrow-minded prince, who was easily persuaded to adopt measures which he was as speedily obliged to modify or reverse. He had granted, only a short time before, Rabbi Zachariah permission to build a magnificent synagogue and schools for the revival of learning. But the synagogue had hardly been finished when it was turned into a Christian church by the Emperor, and the whole of the Jews exiled from his dominions. The reason of this is said to have been that the Empress attributed her barrenness to the displeasure of Heaven at the toleration shown to the Jews. But her death in her confinement, shortly afterwards, doubtless had a counter-effect on the mind of

T

the Emperor ; and we are not surprised to hear that the Jews were recalled, and re-established in their possessions.[1] It was upon this occasion that the Jews expelled from Vienna found a refuge in Berlin, where a thriving community grew up.

In this century many learned Jews and Christian Hebrew scholars appeared, whose names are well known, even at the present day. Among these the most distinguished were Rabbi Menasseh, of whom we shall have occasion to speak presently, and the Christian writers Pocock, Surenhusius, and Vitringa. But the most renowned Christian Hebraists of this century were the two Buxtorfs. The elder, Johann, born at Westphalia in 1564, and dying in Basle in 1629, is the author of the famous Hebrew dictionary and grammar continually quoted by Hebrew scholars. His son, also called Johann, born 1599, and dying in 1664, finished the concordance which his father had commenced.

---

[1] A different explanation has been given of Leopold's strange changes in his treatment of the Jews. He is said to have shown them favour at first, on account of his attachment to a beautiful Jewess. But she was assassinated ; and Leopold, at first believing the deed to have been done by the Jews, banished them. Afterwards, being convinced of his mistake, he allowed them to return.

CHAPTER XXXIV.

THE JEWS IN HOLLAND.—DA COSTA, SPINOZA.

THE reader has already learned that, towards the close of the last century, many of the Portuguese exiles found a refuge from persecution in Holland. In truth, of all the countries of Europe, at this period of their history, none showed them such kindness as the republic of the Low Countries. If the Reformation had done the race of Israel no other service than that of opening to them this place of shelter, they would still have been largely indebted to it. No dream of the imagination could exceed the wretchedness of the Jews in Spain and Portugal at the outset of the seventeenth century. They had to choose between ruin, torture, and death on the one hand,—not for themselves only, but for their wives and children also,—or the surrender of their cherished faith, which was, in their eyes, the surrender of all hope, here and hereafter. Their only escape from these stern alternatives lay in a lifelong duplicity and imposture, which must needs degrade them in their own eyes to the very dust. Of the three terrible issues thus offered them, we have seen that many

of them did choose this last ; but our contempt is disarmed,
and only our pity is awakened, as we peruse their melancholy
history. The toleration, however, that prevailed in Holland
afforded a means of escape alike from the humiliation and
the danger in which they were living. As the century advanced,
increasing numbers of New Christians made their escape to
the Low Countries, where they renounced the false profession
they had made, and returned openly to their ancient worship.
It has been already mentioned that in 1598 the first Jewish
synagogue was built in Amsterdam. Ten or twelve years
afterwards the numbers had so increased that a second
became necessary, and in 1618 a third.

But it was not only the exiles from Spain and Portugal who
crowded into Holland as a harbour of refuge. From many
parts of Germany and the contiguous countries, whenever the
flame of persecution broke out, as it was ever apt to do on the
slightest provocation, the Jews, who had heard of the justice
and favour shown to their countrymen by the Dutch, came
to partake of it themselves. From Poland and Lithuania,
again, thousands of Jews emigrated, driven from their homes
by the ravages committed by the Cossacks, who, under
Chelmnicki, had risen against their Polish masters. A large
proportion of these settled in the United Provinces. One
company, which consisted of three thousand, landed at Texel,
and there were many others almost as numerous. After
some inquiry they were received at Amsterdam, and permission given them to build a synagogue.

Thus the Jews of Holland were divided into two societies
which might be called the Spanish and the German
synagogues.[1] Their religious tenets were doubtless in complete harmony. But they had different usages and historical
traditions, and they are said to have entertained mutual
jealousies and enmities. Possibly the imposture of Rabbi
Zeigler, one of the numberless adventurers who have claimed

---

[1] The Sephardim and the Ashkenazim, as indeed is the case in other
countries also.

to be the Messiah, or His forerunner, may have done something
to create this severance. Zeigler professed to have seen the
promised deliverer at Strasburg, and assured his countrymen
that, as soon as they had declared their readiness to accept
him, he would appear, destroy the kingdom of Christ (as he
called the supremacy of the Gentiles), and extend his own
from one end of the world to the other. The Messiah was
also to hold a council at Constance, which would last for
twelve years, and all religious difficulties would be composed
at it. As the Messiah did not appear, Zeigler's followers were
so far undeceived; but the mischief which his imposture had
occasioned lasted long afterwards.

This epoch is remarkable for a demonstration of intolerant
bigotry—not, as heretofore, evinced by the Christians against
the Jews, but by the Jews against some of their own brethren.
One would certainly have thought that they had had such
convincing proof of the folly, to use no harsher term, of endeavouring to compel men by the infliction of disgrace and
suffering to adopt or renounce a religious belief, that they
would have abstained from such a course themselves. et
their dealings with the two celebrities of this age, Uriel da
Costa and Baruch Spinoza, exhibit an amount of harshness
and injustice which their own persecutors could hardly have
exceeded.

Both these men were of Portuguese extraction, and belonged
to families which went by the name of New Christians. Both
were remarkable for great mental activity and an unusually
speculative turn of mind. This natural tendency was doubtless fostered by their own early experience—the truth or
falsehood of every dogma of their belief having been, as it
were, forced upon them as a matter of logical inquiry. It
required little knowledge of human nature to understand that
the opinions entertained by men like these could be influenced
only by calm reasoning and reflection. Yet a course was
pursued towards them which could only have been successful
in the instance of the weakest or the most timid of men.

Uriel da Costa had belonged to a family of Maranaos, or New Christians, in Spain, where he had not only professed Christianity, but had been ordained a priest. Like so many of his countrymen, he had fled from Spain, and at Amsterdam threw off his pretended belief. But his early experiences had taught him distrust ; and he was not disposed to acquiesce implicitly in the Rabbinical interpretation of the Scriptures. After a protracted controversy he composed a work, which he entitled *An Examination of Pharisaical Tradition*. The book does not appear to have been published, or even printed, but was circulated in manuscript among the members of the Jewish community. An eminent Rabbi, Samuel da Silva, took up the controversy, and published a reply to Da Costa's work, which he called *A Treatise on the Immortality of the Soul*. To this Uriel replied by a review of his own essay, enlarged by a refutation of Da Silva's argument. This gave great offence, and severe measures were taken. He was thrown into prison, on the charge of having denied the immortality of the soul. He was with difficulty released, on condition of paying a heavy fine, and suppressing the obnoxious writings. The effect of this harshness was, not to silence, but rather to provoke him to more determined antagonism. He was soon publicly excommunicated, and became, both in opinion and practice, a pronounced Deist. But, after fifteen years of suffering, wearied out by a controversy in which he found himself forsaken by all his friends, he twice sought a reconciliation with his synagogue. Now was the time when he might have been won from his errors. Tenderness and mercy would probably have had their effect on a nature which had much that was noble and generous intermingled with its pride and virulence. But unhappily a different course was pursued. On the second occasion he only obtained readmission to communion by consenting to undergo a public scourging in the synagogue,[1] the shame and

---

[1] It is added that he was afterwards compelled to lie on the ground, while the whole of the congregation walked over him.

degradation of which so affected him that a few days afterwards he destroyed himself.

Da Costa's history has doubtless its moral lesson and its
melancholy interest. But in neither particular can it compare
with that of Spinoza. In a work like this, neither a lengthened
biography of this man nor an analysis of his philosophy can
be inserted. Nevertheless, considering the vast influence
which his peculiar opinions have had on modern thought,[1]
he cannot be dismissed without some notice.

He was born at Amsterdam in 1632. His father had
emigrated from Lisbon some years previously, driven thence
by religious persecution. Young Spinoza was instructed in
Hebrew literature by Mosteira, Chief Rabbi of his synagogue,
and in Latin by Van Ende, a physician, for whom he conceived a warm affection. He soon grew dissatisfied with
his teachers ; and, his revolt from Rabbinical authority at-
tracting notice, remonstrances and threats followed. These
failing of effect, he was publicly excommunicated,[2] and his
life attempted. Thereupon he retired to Rhynsburg, where
he supported himself by grinding optical glasses. Afterwards
he removed to Voorburg, and again to the Hague. At all

---

[1] All the great modern thinkers speak with reverence of Spinoza, with
the single exception, perhaps, of Leibnitz. Lessing was one of the first
to recognise his profound ability. S. T. Coleridge and Goethe express
the greatest admiration for him, the latter affirming that he was one of
his three great teachers. Later, Herder, Schleiermacher, Hegel, and
others have spoken to the same effect. But though his opinions have
exercised a wide and most important influence on the minds of others,
he has established no school of adherents to his own peculiar philosophy.
It may be doubted whether he ever made one genuine convert.

[2] The sentence of excommunication against him ran thus : 'Cursed
be he by day, and cursed be he by night ; cursed in going out, and cursed
in coming in. And we warn you, that none may speak with him by word
of mouth, nor by writing, nor show any favour to him, nor be under one
roof with him, nor come within four cubits of him, nor read anything
written or composed by him.' And this sentence was pronounced by
men who had themselves experienced the enormities of religious persecution !

these places he led a quiet, studious, very pure and beautiful
life, keeping up a correspondence with some of the greatest
philosophers of the day, and more than once refusing offers
of advancement. No man was more highminded or unselfish.
His favourite pupil, De Vries, who knew that his own hours
were numbered, proposed to make Spinoza his heir. But
De Vries had a brother living, and Spinoza insisted that
the money should be left to him. At his father's death
his sisters claimed the whole property, on the ground of
Spinoza's excommunication. Spinoza vindicated his right in
a court of law, but voluntarily gave up the property in
dispute. He died, as calmly as he had lived, of consumption,
A.D. 1677, in the forty-fifth year of his age.

No man has ever been more fiercely assailed or more
enthusiastically defended. He has been denounced as an
Atheist, a Pantheist, a blasphemer, and a fatalist. He has
been upheld as a man eminently holy, a devout lover of God
and of Christ.[1] Strange as it may seem, all these statements
may be said to be true, though of course in different senses
of the terms employed. For his Atheism—he seems to have
been repelled, from the first, by the anthropomorphism of the
Scriptures. It was not merely that God was there represented
as possessed of an eye, a hand, etc., but as performing human
actions, and influenced by human feelings. This was, in his
view, absolute falsehood,[2] and the result was that he entirely

---

[1] Some have declared him to have been actually a Christian. But
though certain passages in his writings may seem to favour that idea,
his unhesitating rejection of the doctrine of the Incarnation renders it
impossible.

[2] It should be here observed that the Scriptures do not teach anthropomorphism of any kind as actually true, but as the only mode by which
man, in the bounded and darkened condition of his intellect, during his
present state of being, can apprehend God at all. The Scriptures contain
the most distinct denials of anthropomorphism, considered otherwise
than as metaphor. Thus, Exod. xxxiii. 20: 'Thou canst not see My
face, for there shall no man see Me, and live,' i.e., 'He must be wholly
out of the body, in order to apprehend Me'—apprehend Me, that is,

rejected the God of revelation, and with Him, of course, the whole scheme of salvation as propounded in the Bible. Thus, then, he may be styled an Atheist. But, on the other hand, he constructed a system in which he affirmed that there exists but one substance, though with infinite attributes, and that this substance is God, who is either absolutely or in some modified form everything. The man who holds this cannot, it may be said, be an Atheist.[1] He is, again, no Pantheist, for he distinguishes between God and the universe ;[2] yet the Christian Pantheists, as they may be called, claim him as their own, if not their founder. For the other charges, he no doubt affirms that, as nothing can be done, either directly or indirectly, except by God, all human acts, however wicked, may be said to be done by Him. This, according to our ideas, is both blasphemy and fatalism. Yet Spinoza attributes the *act* only, not its moral wickedness, to God. When pressed to say whether the atrocious murder of Agrippina by Nero was due to God, he answered that it must be so due, so far as the act was concerned. But no act is good or evil in itself, and it was Nero's evil mind, not God's, that made the crime.[3] So with his fatalism. When he denies that man can act otherwise than as God wills, he appears to enunciate

with the eye of the spirit, not of the body. See the use of the two words expressing bodily and spiritual vision (John i. 18 ; John xvi. 16 ; Rev. iv. 2, etc.). Again, 'God is not a man, that He should lie,' or 'that He should repent' (Num. xxiii. 19). In the anthropomorphic images of Scripture, 'God is seen only through a glass, *darkly*,' as St. Paul says.

[1] We have in more than one of his writings a distinct denial of his Atheism. 'His critics,' he says, 'do not know him, or they would not so easily have persuaded themselves that he taught Atheism.' See also his Treatise, *De Deo et Homine.*

[2] 'Those,' he says also in the same epistle, 'who would identify matter with God *totâ errant viâ.*'

[3] It is again proper to remark that this theory is wholly untenable. The operations of the human will are as much acts, as the operations of the human hand. Nero, if Spinoza's view were correct, could be no more free mentally to conceive wickedness, contrary to God's will, than he was free manually to perpetrate it.

the plainest fatalism ;[1] nor do I see how any other conclusion can logically be drawn from his premisses. But then Spinoza also teaches the beauty, the happiness, the necessity of holiness, of moral culture and self-discipline—things not merely inconsistent, but irreconcilable, with fatalism. He holds language which an apostle might endorse. ' Justice and charity,' he writes, ' are the one infallible sign of the catholic faith, the genuine fruits of the Holy Spirit. Where they are found, there is Christ. Where they are wanting, Christ is not. For by the Spirit of Christ are we led to justice and charity.' We are *led*—so, too, the Scriptures teach—*led*, if we will follow ; not blindly driven, as the fatalist must believe.

On the whole, a wise man will hardly speak otherwise than with respect and tenderness of Spinoza. No doubt, notwithstanding the depth and acuteness of his intellect, in which respects he has never probably been exceeded by any of human kind, his system is full of inconsistencies, and has little practical value. How could it be otherwise, when he has attempted that which Revelation itself has with difficulty effected ? But he was honest, patient, humble, beneficent, as few men have been ; and his desire to attain to truth was earnest and unselfish. As in the case of pious heathens, like Aurelius, we cannot be sure that Christianity was ever put before him in its true aspect. The frivolities of the Talmud, the traditions of the Inquisition, the Church of Roderic Borgia and his successors—were none of them likely to lead him to Christ, as revealed in His blessed Word. Let our sentence on him be, what every good man says of those whom he respects, and yet from whom he is constrained to differ : ' Cum talis sis, utinam noster esses.'[2]

---

[1] There are, indeed, passages in his works where he denies, or seems to deny, the free will of God Himself.

[2] ' In Spinoza,' says an eminent historian of the Jews, ' were to be found the seeds of a Pascal, if he could only have received Christianity, of which, indeed, he always spoke with respect.' But he had no faith in it, and is only one more illustration of St. Paul's saying : ' Without faith it is impossible to please God.'

Besides the eminent writers of this century already mentioned, Da Costa, Spinoza, Orobio da Castro, Thomas—or,
as he is called by his countrymen, Isaac—de Pinedo, one of
the most eminent Greek scholars of the day, deserves mention
not only for his classical learning, but for the unusually mild
and charitable tone he uniformly employs when speaking of
the religion of Christ. To this date also belong David Lara, the
lexicographer ; Benjamin Musafia, the naturalist ; and Isaac
Uziel, Emanuel Gomez, and Enrique Enriquez, the poets.

In the earlier part of the century considerable numbers
of Jews sailed for the Brazils from the various ports of
Holland, under the leadership of two Rabbins, to found a
Jewish colony. It throve and attained a considerable amount
of prosperity until, in 1654, the Portuguese obtained possession of Brazil. Under these new masters, free exercise of
their religion was not allowed the Jews. They therefore
quitted the country, some returning to Holland, others settling
in Cayenne or Surinam.

FEW words will suffice to relate what befell the Spanish and Portuguese Jews during this century. Beyond the fact, already rcorded, of their oft-recurring migration from both countries to the friendly shelter offered by Holland, there is little to tell. Those who lingered behind, unable or unwilling to quit the land of their birth, continued to practise the old deception, and, when discovered or suspected, to undergo the same merciless severities as their fathers had endured. There is no need to repeat the hideous and monotonous tale of their sufferings. The awe and terror with which the Inquisition was regarded were ever on the increase; until notoriously not the common people, not the grandees and nobles only, but the sovereigns themselves, became little better than its instruments. Early in the century Philip III. is related to have been present at the burning of a Jewish girl, and to have been unable to repress some token of natural horror at the sight. This was noticed by the Grand Inquisitor, who, not satisfied with reproving the monarch for his weakness, ordered some of

the coward blood to be drawn from his veins, and burned by
the public executioner! Later in the century, in 1680, M.
Villars, Louis XIV.'s ambassador at the Court of Spain, describes an Auto da Fé which he witnessed at Madrid, where
twenty Jews were publicly burned, with attendant circumstances of revolting barbarity. He relates how the king,
Charles II., was present, but occupied a lower seat than that
assigned to the Grand Inquisitor.

If we are curious to know what were the sufferings inflicted
at the examinations held in the dungeons of the Inquisition,
we may learn them from the narrative of Orobio, an eminent
Portuguese philosopher and physician. He was suspected of
Judaism, and thrown into prison. After some preliminary
inquiries, having refused to confess, he was carried, he tells us,
into a subterranean vault, dimly lighted, where two officials
were seated—the judge and secretary of the Holy Office. He
was stripped, strong cords were tied to his hands and feet, the
other ends being passed through iron rings in the walls.
These were then drawn tight, so that he remained suspended
by the cords, which the executioner kept drawing tighter and
tighter, until the surgeon certified that further pressure would
destroy life. The cords cut into the flesh and made the blood
burst from under the nails. He was then told that this was
only the beginning of his sufferings, which would be increased
in intensity until he confessed. This scene was frequently
repeated during three years, at the end of which time, perceiving that his resolution was invincible, they healed his
wounds, and permitted him to depart. He fled to Toulouse,
and afterwards to Amsterdam, where he threw off his mask,
and professed himself a Jew.

Manasseh Ben Israel was another celebrated Portuguese Jew,
who was mainly instrumental in the restoration of the Jews to
England, from which they had been banished for more than
three hundred and fifty years. His father had escaped from
the dungeons of the Inquisition at Lisbon, and settled with
his family at Amsterdam. He was distinguished as a poet, a

philosopher, a physician, and a theologian. His high reputation doubtless was the reason why he was chosen by the Jews at Amsterdam to proceed to England and endeavour to obtain from Oliver Cromwell,—who at that time (A.D. 1656 swayed the destinies of England,—permission for the Jews to return thither. Manasseh presented an address, skilfully drawn, in which he argued that, as regarded both the spiritual and temporal interests of England, it would be to their advantage to grant re-admission to the Jews. He asserted that the restoration of Israel was close at hand, and that they who showed kindness to the people of God would be surely rewarded for it in that day. In a secular point of view also, those nations had always been found to flourish most in their undertakings who had sheltered the Jews. He also exploded the calumnies, so often raised against his nation, of crucifying children, and using Christian blood for ritual purposes.[1]

Cromwell received him favourably ; but, aware probably of the difficulties with which the question was beset, referred the matter to an assembly of twenty-three persons, whom he appointed to consider the question. Of these, seven were merchants, two lawyers, and the remaining fourteen divines. He himself presided, and opened the debate with an address which those who heard it declared to be one of the ablest and most eloquent he had ever delivered. They had first to consider, he said, whether the admission of the Jews would be legal, and secondly, whether it would be expedient. The lawyers present having at once decided that there would be no illegality, he proceeded to the other question. But here there was much difference of opinion. The citizens were divided as to the alleged commercial advantages, while the theologians disputed so long and so hotly as to the religious aspect of the question, that Cromwell grew weary, and adjourned the consideration of the matter, so far as the council was concerned, *sine die*. Meanwhile he connived at their resettlement,

---

[1] Manass. *Vindiciæ Judaicæ*. See Appendix V.

granting them a kind of special protection. Nearly at the
same time a piece of land was granted them as a burial-
ground, on a nominal lease of 999 years. Whether this
action on the part of the Protector gave offence, or whether it
was the effect of mere gossip, the wildest and most ridiculous
rumours were circulated on the subject. It was said that the
Jews had sent a deputation to England to ascertain whether
Cromwell was not himself the Messiah, and that they went to
Huntingdon to search out his pedigree; also, that they had
made an offer of £500,000, to purchase St. Paul's Cathedral
for their synagogue, Henry Martin and Hugh Peters being
the persons who were to conduct this negotiation. It may be
mentioned, in connection with these strange rumours, that
Harrington, in his *Oceana* (A.D. 1656), gravely proposes to
relieve the Government of the difficulties which the management of Ireland caused them by selling that island to the
Jews.

It does not appear that any public measures were taken respecting the Jews during the remainder of Cromwell's government. We have seen that, though their residence in England
was a breach of a law still in force, it was not likely that it would
be very rigidly insisted on, unless where persons were obnoxious on other grounds; and Cromwell's friendly feeling towards
them would of course render their position more secure. It is
likely that they came back singly or in small numbers, and
were allowed to establish themselves without molestation
during the next few years. Then, in the sixth year after the
Restoration, some agitation having been raised respecting
their presence in England, formal permission was given them
by Charles II. to reside in Great Britain, together with liberty
of commerce and worship. It is not unlikely that this concession was made to gratify Antonio Mendez, physician to the
King of Spain, and his brother Andrea, chamberlain to the
Infanta Catherine of Portugal, Charles's queen. It is certain
that the brothers about this time came to England, where they
settled, resuming their real name of De Costa. Some years

afterwards, during the reign of James II., the Jews obtained a remission of the alien duty, which had been imposed on their traffic. This was, however, again exacted in the ensuing reign.

At the accession of William III., when money was wanted for the prosecution of the war in Ireland, it was proposed to require a subsidy of one hundred thousand pounds from the Jews, taking a leaf out of the book of the old Norman kings. But the times were changed. The Jews protested, with an eye, doubtless, to similar exactions to follow, that they would rather leave the country than comply ; and they could not now be shut up in prison, and put on the rack, and suffer the daily extraction of their teeth until they paid it. The statesmen of the day perceived that it was simple pillage, and withdrew the proposal.

The days of barbarous and cruel violence had indeed passed away, and happily for ever. It is perhaps a fortunate circumstance,—grave as were the injuries resulting to both parties from it,—that the Jews were absent from England for so long a period. The tradition of persecution had, in consequence, long been broken off. In Spain, in Portugal, in Germany, even in Holland and Italy, people still living had themselves witnessed,—or had heard from their fathers,—the imprisonments, the expulsions, and the massacres of the Jews on the occasion of some religious excitement. But the fires of persecution had been cold for centuries in England, and no one was inclined to rekindle them now, even had it been possible to do so.[1]

In Italy, throughout the seventeenth century, the condition of the Jews seems to have been fairly prosperous. Little is related of them, and that is the best evidence that they were exempt from injustice and persecution. Of the ten occupants of the papal chair during this century, the only one who

---

[1] Manasseh did not live to see the success of his efforts on behalf of his countrymen. He died on his journey back to Holland, in 1657.

seems to have interfered much in their affairs was Innocent XI.,
and his dealings with them, as we shall presently see, were
lenient and friendly. It is said that at the outset of the century there were more than a hundred synagogues of the Jews
in the Italian cities. In those situated on the sea-coast the
commerce was, to a great extent, in the hands of the Hebrews,
and their wealth was continually on the increase. Jews also
continued to be employed in diplomatic missions by the Italian
governments—by the Republic of Venice, the Dukes of Ferrara, and even by the Emperor. The same, indeed, was the
case all over Europe. The kings of Denmark, Sweden, and
Prussia,—nay, even of Spain and Portugal, notwithstanding
their implacable persecution of the Jewish nation,—were in
the habit of employing Jews as their emissaries. Sir William
Temple, who was English ambassador at the Hague in 1668,
expresses his astonishment at this fact. The Baron de Bel-
mont was the Spanish minister in Holland during the whole
of the latter half of the seventeenth century, and Nunez da
Costa held a similar office under the crown of Portugal, though
both these were notoriously Jews.

In literary eminence the Italian Jews of this century are
said to be inferior both to the generations which preceded
and those which followed them. This is attributed to the severe censorship of the press, which is always unfavourable to
literature. The famous Leo of Modena, head of the synagogue of Venice, and author of many works, both in Italian
and Hebrew, on antiquities and theology, is an instance of
this. He was on the point, we are told, of making a translation of the Hebrew Scriptures into Italian, which would have
been beyond doubt a valuable work, but the Inquisition commanded him to desist.

But if their writings were handled with severity, the same
cannot be said of their persons. It is mentioned, indeed, that
in Rome, during the pontificate of Innocent XI., they were in
such favour with the people that their synagogues were fre-
quented by the latter, and in such numbers that the Pope was

obliged to threaten his subjects with excommunication, and a fine of twenty crowns every time they resorted to a place of Jewish worship.

The same pontiff was very earnest for their conversion. He built seminaries where Jews might receive instruction in the Christian faith, and houses where such as had become converts might be maintained. He caused sermons to be preached, in which it was proved from the Hebrew Scriptures that Jesus Christ was the Messiah whom they expected. In order to encourage still further proselytes to the Christian faith, some person of high rank, a nobleman or a cardinal, stood godfather to them on the occasion of their baptism. A handsome present in money also was made them : they were dressed in white satin, and carried about Rome in fine coaches for a fortnight afterwards, receiving everywhere the congratulations of the spectators. At the same time it was very plainly intimated to them, that if they relapsed into Judaism they would straightway be burnt alive.[1]

It is certainly strange that under such circumstances conversions were not effected. Innocent evinced not only the controversial zeal which many before and after him have shown, but also an amount of real charity and goodwill which must, one would have thought, have had a very potent influence with the Jews of that day. When the Venetians, in 1685, after their successful war in the Morea, brought back a

---

[1] Throughout this and the succeeding century, and, indeed, for fully half of the present century, however much the stern rigour of previous ages of persecution may have been relaxed, the condition of the Jews was miserable in the extreme. They were strictly confined to their Ghetto, the gates of which were closed regularly every evening at eight o'clock, and such Jews as had not returned by that time were obliged to remain outside all night. In front of a small church standing near the entrance of the Ghetto was fixed a large wooden crucifix, highly coloured and gilded, with the inscription, ' All day long have I stretched forth Mine hands to a disobedient and gainsaying people.' Into this church the Jews at one time were driven with scourges, by order of the popes, to listen to sermons preached against their obstinacy and rebellion.

large number both of Christian and Jewish captives, they gave the former their freedom, but retained the latter in servitude. Innocent, however, interfered, and insisted on their liberating the Jews also. But we learn that, notwithstanding all his generous exertions on their behalf, he failed in making any considerable number of real converts. Cardinal Barberini who had spent large sums and used great exertions in endeavouring to accomplish this work, was compelled to own that the conversions had been for the most part insincere. It is not, indeed, by such means as those employed that converts can be made.

As regards the distinguished literary men of this period, it has already been remarked that there were fewer of these than in previous and subsequent generations ; and, in the majority of European nations, such as there were do not contrast favourably with either their predecessors or successors. There were, however, writers of genius and learning ; among them Solomon Norzi, of Mantua, is the author of a celebrated Massoretic work which, though it was not published till a century after his death, has attained a great reputation The two Aboabs, both residents in Venice, were celebrated for their writings : the former, Emmanuel by name, being the author of an able work on tradition ; the latter chiefly remarkable for his exposure of the impious impostures of the pretended prophet, Sabbathai Sevi. Judah da Modena produced many greatly admired works, and, in particular, a Hebrew lexicon, and a *System of Artificial Memory.* Solomon Medigo, physician to Prince Radziwill at Wilna, and Moses Luzzato, of Venice, should also be mentioned.

CHAPTER XXXVI.

JEWS IN THE EAST.—SABBATHAI SEVI.

THE condition of the Jews in the East during this century does not call for much remark ; indeed, little has been recorded respecting it. The treatment they received at the hands of the Mussulmans, both princes and people, was curiously different from that which they experienced from the Christian populations of Europe. The first named did not regard the Jews with any particular favour or respect,—in fact, the disdain they evinced for them was even greater than that entertained by their Christian contemporaries,—but there was no *active* enmity. They looked on with scornful indifference while the Israelites plied their busy trade, aware though they might be that the wealth they accumulated was in a great measure drawn from their own coffers. They would spit in contempt as they passed a Jewish synagogue, but they would not raise a finger to cause its demolition or prevent any number of worshippers from crowding into it. All over Turkey, Arabia, and Persia, some Jews were to be found in every town, where they were allowed to live and thrive, unless they broke some law or offended some faithful Islamite. But if they did either of these things, they were apt to experience scant ceremony and sharp punishment.

The reader has heard, in a previous chapter, of the massacre perpetrated by Shah Abbas II., which appears to have occurred about A.D. 1666. It is said to have lasted three years, and to have almost exterminated the Jews in his dominions. It is, however, involved in great obscurity, the dates given by different writers varying considerably. But in this year, 1666, not the Jews of the East only, but all over the world, were greatly excited by the appearance of the most persistent and successful impostor that had arisen among them from the time of Barchochebas. Sabbathai Sevi, a native of Smyrna, and son of a poulterer in that city, was born in 1625. He was sent to school, where he made such rapid progress that he was appointed a Rabbi when he was only eighteen years of age. He early attracted attention and had many followers, who believed in the pretensions which, even then, he put forward, of being the expected Messiah. At the age of twenty he married a woman of great beauty and rank; but the marriage was only a nominal one, as he lived entirely apart from her. He was compelled to give a divorce, and soon afterwards made a second similar marriage, with the same result. He practised strict asceticism, fasting six days in every week, and bathing continually in the sea at midnight. At twenty-four, his reputation had increased so greatly, that he ventured to put forth publicly his pretensions to be thought the Messiah, and, in proof of these, ventured to pronounce publicly the name of Jehovah, which is absolutely forbidden to the Jews. The Rabbins were horror-struck at his impiety, and declared him to be worthy of death. He was compelled to fly from Smyrna, and took refuge in one city after another, until in Gaza he made an important proselyte, the celebrated Nathan Benjamin. This man, a person of position and influence, professed to have seen in a vision the

Lord Himself; who informed him that the promised Deliverer had come in the person of Sabbathai Sevi, and that he, Nathan Benjamin, was the Elias who was to herald his coming. The reader will remember that this is the exact repetition of the imposture of Barchochebas and Rabbi Akiba, fifteen hundred years before. Aided by this ally, Sabbathai preached in Jerusalem, and resided for thirteen years in that city, continuing to gain proselytes and bearing down all opposition.

The imposture was aided by the remarkable fact that, according to the interpretation of some eminent Cabalists of a passage in the book of the prophet Daniel, the Messiah would make His appearance about the year 1675. One of Nathan Benjamin's first steps, when he felt himself strong enough to take it, was to assemble the Jews resident in Jerusalem, and inform them that, by virtue of the authority committed to him from on high, he abrogated the fast which would otherwise be observed in the ensuing June, because the time of the coming of the Messiah was a festal one, inconsistent with mourning of any kind. He then brought Sabbathai out to them, who, he said, in the ensuing November would go forth in power and destroy the Ottoman empire. He encountered determined opposition from the wiser among his countrymen, who perceived that his pretensions were not only without foundation, but were likely to bring the gravest calamities on the Jews everywhere throughout the Sultan's dominions. They even went so far as to try him as a rebel and an impostor, and condemn him to death. His adherents, however, were too many and too powerful to permit of this sentence being carried into effect, and he continued to reside without molestation in the city.

After a period of thirteen years from the date of this announcement of his pretensions, he made an expedition into Egypt, where he married, for the third time, the daughter of a Polish Jew, who professed to have received a revelation that she was the destined bride of the Messiah. But the marriage, like the two former ones, was only a marriage in name; and Sabbathai returned to Jerusalem, where he resided for three years more, and then publicly proclaimed himself in one of the synagogues as the Messiah. This once more roused the indignation of the Rabbins, who pronounced against him the sentence of excommunication. This sentence he found too strong for him to struggle against, and he fled to his native city, Smyrna.

The report of his condemnation had preceded him; but he was nevertheless welcomed in his native city with almost regal honour. Every evening he paraded the streets, accompanied by a train of followers, carrying banners, and singing hymns in his praise. All resistance offered to him proved vain. A Jew of high rank, named Anakia, attacked him in the market-place, branding him as an impostor. But his fate did not encourage others to pursue the same course. He returned to his home, and had scarcely entered it, when he suddenly fell from his chair a corpse. The reader will not require to be told that Sabbathai's friends declared this to be God's judgment on the blasphemer!

His pretensions now rose higher.[1] He assumed the state of a monarch. He divided the kingdoms of the earth among his partisans. He named his two brothers sovereigns of Judah and Israel, while he himself took the title of 'the King of the Kings of the Earth.' He ordered the name of the Sultan to be removed from the prayer offered up for the sovereign in the Jewish liturgy, and his own to be inserted in its place. Embassies arrived from foreign communities charged with rich presents and assurances of devoted loyalty. These were sometimes kept waiting two or three weeks for an

---

[1] He is said to have quoted Isaiah xiv. 14: 'I will ascend above the heights of the clouds,' and to have appealed to his followers to say whether they had not seen him so ascend ; to which they made answer that they had ! It must be added, however, that, if he did quote the passage in question as applicable to himself, he could hardly have studied its context.

audience. His picture was exhibited in public, surmounted by a golden crown ; and multitudes of prophets of both sexes thronged the streets, declaring in the name of Heaven his approaching triumph. Some of these are said to have acquired in a moment a miraculous knowledge of Hebrew !

It was not in Smyrna only, or in its vicinity, that the madness prevailed. In those European cities in which the largest number of Jews were to be found,—Hamburg, and Frankfort, and Amsterdam,—all other topics of interest were postponed, and business was broken off to discuss the doings of the newly risen Prophet of Israel. The excitement was not less in the East, where the husbandmen are related to have refused to do their ordinary work in the fields, because the Deliverer of Israel had come. If Sabbathai had been really a man of ability and courage, there is no saying what he might not have effected. It is probable, however, that the extraordinary amount of success to which he had attained now embarrassed, rather than gratified, him. He felt that he could neither recede nor stand still. His partisans insisted on his passing over to Constantinople, and advancing his pretensions in the face of the Sultan himself. He made the voyage accordingly, attended by a vast number of his adherents, and was received by the Jews of Constantinople with the utmost enthusiasm. The Sultan was at the time of his arrival absent, but Sabbathai demanded an audience of the grand vizier. The latter sent immediately to his master for instructions, and delayed giving any reply until he received them. The Sultan's reply was, that Sabbathai was to be arrested and kept in safe custody until his return. First one, and then a second officer of janissaries were accordingly sent ; but in the presence of Sabbathai they were so overpowered by awe that they dared not execute their office. Once more, if Sabbathai had had boldness equal to the occasion, he might have made himself master of Constantinople. But he surrendered himself of his own accord, and was kept in a kind of honourable captivity in the castle of Sestos, where, however, his followers were freely permitted to visit him. He put out a manifesto ordering that the fast which was always strictly observed on the anniversary of the destruction of Jerusalem should be suspended, and the day celebrated as a festival, it being the birthday of the Messiah. At this juncture there arrived a learned Cabalist, Rabbi Nehemiah, the head of one of the synagogues in Poland, who took up his abode in the castle as Sabbathai's guest. A few days' intercourse satisfied him that Sabbathai was simply an impostor, and as such he denounced him to his followers. Roused to fury, the partisans of the prophet would have killed him on the spot; but Nehemiah snatched a turban from the head of one of the Turks, and declared himself a Mussulman. The janissaries instantly interfered to protect him, and he was conveyed to Adrianople where he had an interview with the Sultan. The latter now returned to the capital, and summoned Sabbathai to his presence. The impostor in the hour of trial entirely lost the hardihood which he had hitherto displayed, and, when the Sultan demanded of him whether he was the Messiah, could not summon courage to reply. The Sultan proposed to test his pretensions by shooting three poisoned arrows at him. If these failed to wound or injure him, his title should be at once acknowledged ; if the result should be different, death or the profession of Mahometanism must be his sentence. Sabbathai did not hesitate. Following the example of Nehemiah, he placed a turban on his head and exclaimed—' There is but one God, and Mahomet is His Prophet ! '

It is most extraordinary that this apostasy, evidently the result of mere cowardice and imposture, did not provoke the contempt alike of the Turks and the Jews. But by the Sultan he was loaded with honours, and the Jews did not withdraw their belief in his miraculous pretensions. With unabated impudence he put out a declaration to the effect that God had changed him from an Israelite to an Ishmaelite. He quoted the example of Moses, who dwelt for a time among the Ethiopians, and the fifty-third chapter of Isaiah, where it is

said that the Messiah was numbered among the transgressors
For a long time he continued to maintain his double character
of the deliverer of the Jews and the devoted believer in
Mahomet. Some even declared, after the fashion of the
Gnostics in the early Church, that the true Sabbathai had been
taken up into heaven, and it was only his likeness or phan-
tom that had undergone degradation and apostasy. Great
numbers of Jews, indeed, were induced, by his example, to
become Mahometans; and at length the injury to the
Jewish community became so great, that they exerted all the
influence they could command with the grand vizier, who
caused Sabbathai to be arrested and banished into Bosnia·
There, in 1676, ten years after his apostasy to Mahometanism, and in the fifty-first year of his age, he expired in a
castle near Belgrade. According to some, he died a natural
death; according to others, he was beheaded in prison. The
latter is the more likely supposition. Though he endeavoured
to persuade the Jews that, notwithstanding his profession of
another faith, he was at heart a Jew, they entirely distrusted
him; and it is likely that the assurances to which they would
lend no credit nevertheless caused suspicion and uneasiness
among true followers of Mahomet. Thus it would be the
interest of both parties to cut short his career.

In the long catalogue of impostors who have succeeded for
a time in blinding the eyes of those to whom they pretended
a mission, the case of Sabbathai Sevi seems the most extraordinary.

There have been innumerable false Messiahs, from the days
of Judas of Galilee almost to our own time; and to each of
these in turn the Jews of their day accorded, for the time at
least, a ready welcome, which, in almost every instance,
ultimately gave place to a total disbelief in their pretensions.
In the instance of this man alone, the faith placed in him
was not exchanged for contempt and distrust. Yet he was
certainly the one among all the pretenders to a Divine mission

who most deserved such ignominy. Judas,[1] Barchochebas, David Alroy—however unfounded their claims to be the Messiah—at all events persisted resolutely to the last, and died with the same watchword on their lips that they had uttered during life. But though Sabbathai openly avowed his own imposture, his followers continued to believe in him. More than one prophet arose after his death, and obtained credence by affirming that Sabbathai had been translated into heaven, as Enoch and Elijah before him, and would, after a stated interval, reappear on earth. Sabbathaism, as it was called, became the creed of a powerful and numerous sect, of which we shall hear in the ensuing century. It is said that even now it is not extinct. This example is one proof out of many that human credulity exceeds all bounds of calculation.

Among those who continued to uphold Sabbathai after this fashion long after his death, the most noted were Nehemiah Chajon and Abraham Michael Cardoso. The plea urged by the latter in behalf of his principal may safely be pronounced the most extravagant that has ever been advanced. It was doubtless great wickedness, he said, to apostatize to Islamism; but then it should be remembered that the Messiah was not to come until mankind were all good or all bad. There was no prospect of their all becoming good. So Sabbathai, by his wickedness in accepting Mahomet, was helping on, like a true prophet, the coming of the Messiah !

---

[1] Whether Judas himself ever claimed to be the Messiah is doubtful. But a considerable section of his followers certainly believed him to be such.

CHAPTER XXXVII.

JEWS IN SPAIN, ITALY, AND FRANCE.

W E enter now on the eighteenth century, and are, as it were, in sight of the history of our own times. The position in which we find the Jews is in the main the same which they at present occupy. In Romish countries they were still liable to sharp persecution, sometimes from mob violence, sometimes from the action of the Church. The lands in which the severest measures were enforced continued to be Spain and Portugal, where the Inquisition was dominant throughout the entire century, though its power gradually but very evidently diminished as the years passed on. In the reign of Philip V., who succeeded to the Spanish throne A.D. 1700, and held it till 1746, the first direct blow was given to its authority. In the War of Succession, which began at the outset of his reign, his French allies treated the Inquisition with very scant respect. They broke open the prisons of the Holy Office, released the prisoners, and even seized the silver images in the Dominican chapels, melting them down to pay the expenses of the campaign. The king took no part in the spoliation; but when the Inquisitors appealed to him against the sacrilegious violence of the French, he replied that he could not interfere with the measures taken by his allies. He was a weak and sombre-tempered young man, though not, it would seem, a religious bigot, and allowed the clergy in the main to have their way. One *Auto da Fé* was held every year throughout his reign; and the number of victims is said to have amounted to 14,000. There can be little doubt that the greater part of these were 'secret Jews.' It is beyond dispute that throughout this century, and long afterwards— even, it is said, to our own times—secret Judaism continued to maintain its hold; and from time to time discoveries were made, and executions followed.

In 1713 the English were confirmed in the possession of Gibraltar, which had been wrested from Spain some ten years before. But it is a singular fact that the Spaniards, even when yielding up their stronghold to Great Britain, could not endure that the Jews should be allowed to live in peace there ; and one clause of the treaty stipulated that ' no Jew should be tolerated in that city.' [1]

Ferdinand VI. succeeded his father in 1746, and reigned till 1759. He bears the character of a good and wise prince, and no public *Auto da Fé* took place in his time, though there appear to have been a considerable number of petty local executions. Probably these took place without his sanction, or even knowledge. He died without issue, and was succeeded by his brother, Charles III. He again was an able and vigorous sovereign, and the power of the Inquisition still further diminished during his reign. Three years after his accession he took the decided step of banishing the Grand Inquisitor for encroaching on the privileges of the Crown. In 1770, and again in 1784, he ordered that any procedure against offenders must be approved by the king, and sufficient

---

[1] This was soon set aside, being contrary to the spirit of English law. The Jews established themselves in Gibraltar, and are now a thriving population, with four synagogues.

evidence adduced to justify imprisonment. He was succeeded by his son, Charles IV., the weak and miserable victim of Napoleon's ambition. The Inquisition was upheld during his reign, though it does not appear that any *Auto da Fé* took place. Very much the same is the history of the Jewish persecution in Portugal, the power of the Inquisition, though greatly limited, still subsisting to the very end of the century.

In Italy very nearly the same state of things continued as has been described under the history of the previous century. On the separation of the kingdom of the Two Sicilies from that of Spain, Charles, who succeeded to the sovereignty, reversed the policy which had been pursued by his predecessors, and invited the Jews to settle for sixty years in his kingdom. He offered to confer upon them rights and privileges which would have left them little ground of complaint. They were to be allowed to hold lands, except such as conferred feudal rights on their possessors. They were to be permitted to trade with all parts of the world, exempt from any special impost—on the same terms, in fact, as his Christian subjects. They might practise all professions, that of the physician included, and have Christian patients, if the latter desired it. They might also follow any handicraft; they might serve in the army; they might freely print and circulate their literature; they might have Christians in their service. They were to be free also to build synagogues and celebrate their religious rites; and the authority of their clergy was to be upheld by the State. All men, in fine, were forbidden, under severe penalties, to insult or wrong them; and all attempts to proselytize their children were to be discouraged. We do not wonder at hearing that Jews in great numbers, from all parts of Europe, accepted King Charles's invitation; neither can it move our surprise to hear that his subjects were not inclined to acquiesce in their sovereign's enlightened views. The Pope of the day, Clement XII., and his confessor, a man of great influence in the Church, denounced the concessions made to the Jews; the clergy preached inflammatory sermons from their pulpits, a Capuchin friar publicly warned the king that, as the punishment of his guilty act, he would die childless. The Jews could not face the storm. They knew that any attempt to open shops, or bring their merchandise into Naples, would be the signal for a riot, not improbably for a massacre. After a brief sojourn in the city, they withdrew from it.

In 1775, Pius VI., the Pope whom Napoleon imprisoned and deposed, revived some of the harsh laws against the Jews, whose condition, for a long time past, had been growing more peaceful and assured. He issued an edict by which Rabbinical literature was suppressed; no Hebrew book, or even manuscript, might remain in the possession of a Jew. He was required to keep himself rigidly within the limits of his Ghetto; he was obliged again to wear his yellow badge; when a corpse was buried, no funeral procession was allowed; no Jew might employ a Christian midwife or wet-nurse; and, *vice versâ*, a Christian might not employ Jews. The old enactment requiring Jews to attend controversial sermons was again enforced; and the Rabbins were obliged to draw up lists of their disciples, who were required to be present. This seems to have been at the outset of Pius's long reign. The outbreak of the French Revolution, and the troubles which it brought upon him, probably gave a new direction to his thoughts.

Turning to France, we find that the condition of the Jews during the eighteenth century was very peculiar. It has been mentioned in a previous chapter that, although nominally excluded from France, they had long been suffered to dwell there under protections granted to them by Henry II. and others. There were, indeed, three different sections of Jews resident in France at this time—the Portuguese Jews, to whom charters were granted by the French Parliament A.D. 1550. These were chiefly to be found in Bayonne, Bordeaux, and its vicinity. They appear at first to have passed under the name of New Christians, and as such, no doubt, were obliged to submit themselves to the ordinances of the Church;

but in the fierce strife which ensued between the Catholics
and Huguenots they escaped notice. It is said that they
contracted marriages according to their own rites, and evaded
the baptism of their children. There were, again, the Jews of
Avignon, who were either Italians or native Frenchmen.
These had been tolerated by the Popes during their residence
there, and probably no great notice had been taken of them
since the removal of the papal court. Again, after the
conquest of Metz and Alsace, a considerable number of
German Jews became subjects of France. It is likely
that they by no means regretted the change of masters; for
only a few years before, the Parliament at Metz had burnt
a number of Jews on the old charge of murdering infants.
Louis XIV. granted the Jews of Alsace the same privileges
possessed by Bordeaux and other cities—that of free commerce, on condition of paying a certain poll-tax, subsequently
compounded for a lump sum. Nevertheless, all over Lorraine
and Alsace the Jews, during this century, were harshly dealt
with. Their usurious exactions rendered them odious to the
people, as indeed had been the case with their ancestors for
many generations. In Strasburg only a few Jewish families
were allowed to reside. In Lorraine the laws of Duke
Leopold, made in 1724, continued long in force. By these
only 180 families were permitted to reside and to carry on
trade; and even these were required to live within the Jewish
quarters.

When the Edict of Nantes was revoked, and all the subjects
of the King of France were required to accept the ordinances
of the Catholic Church, the Jews in France were in some
danger of persecution. But the act seems never to have been
carried out so far as they were concerned. As before, the
clergy were too busy in enforcing the law against Huguenots
to trouble themselves about a handful of Jews. But, though
they were kindly treated, it would be a mistake to suppose
that they were naturalized, as some writers have affirmed. It
is said that they offered the Regent Orleans two million livres

in exchange for the privilege of naturalization—a sum which
that impecunious potentate would have been well pleased to
lay his hands on. But he was afraid of the unpopularity he
would incur by the act, and refused the offer. The writer of
the pamphlet respecting the Naturalization Bill of 1753,
quoted in a previous chapter, says : ‘ It is a vulgar error to
suppose that the Jews in France were naturalized subjects ;
and any Frenchman of whom you asked the question would
laugh in your face.’ It appears to have been only in certain
cities that the Jews were allowed to reside permanently. In
Lyons they could only reside three months consecutively. In
Paris it is said their residence was altogether prohibited.

Louis XV. appears to have treated them with kindness, and
to have discouraged a step which was made to abridge their
privileges. He also showed much favour to the celebrated
Samuel Bernard, the famous banker of his day, who afterwards
became a convert to the Church. As the century advanced,
and Voltaire and the Encyclopædists began to exercise a
wide influence in France, it might have been expected that
they would have exerted it in favour of the Jews ; who,
although they were no longer exposed to the terrible sufferings
they had undergone in previous generations, were still subject
to a more modified religious persecution—a thing utterly
abhorrent to the writers in question. But the Encyclopædists
disliked the Jews almost as much as the Christians. The
Hebrew race had suffered cruelly in previous ages, as being
the enemies of the Gospel. But in the eyes of the infidel
writers they were almost as objectionable, as being the living
witnesses of its truth. No Dominican persecutor of the
fifteenth century would have viewed the Jews with more
contempt and hatred than does Voltaire, the advocate of
religious tolerance.

In fact, it is obvious that the Jews had to undergo many
hardships in France during the reigns of Louis XIV. and XV.
A few years after the accession of Louis XVI., the mildness
of whose temper had become generally known, a petition was

X

presented by the Jews to the king and council, complaining of the heavy burdens laid upon them. Besides the fees exacted for the royal protection, a capitation tax was imposed upon them by the feudal superior on whose estate they resided. The right of residence was only personal, and a fresh sum had to be paid for every child that was born to them. Further, a toll was paid by every Jew at the gate of every city which he entered, as though he had been a horse or a sheep. There were besides restrictions on their commerce, which weighed heavily upon them.

The appeal to Louis XVI. was not in vain. The obnoxious capitation tax was abolished in 1784 ; and in 1788 a commission was appointed, of which Malesherbes was the president, and the first act of the latter was to put an end to the toll at the city gates.[1] Malesherbes also set on foot measures for ameliorating generally the condition of the Jews. He proposed to give a prize for the best essay on the subject. This was gained by the celebrated Abbé Grégoire, whose essay was very generally approved. Steps were taken to carry out some of the improvements suggested. But before this could be done the Revolution had begun, and liberty, equality, and fraternity for all men had become the general cry in France. The Jews were not slow to avail themselves of their opportunity, and sent in their petition to the General Assembly to be admitted to the rights of equal citizenship. The question was discussed in the National Assembly, and was affirmed, though not until after considerable debate. On the 17th of September, 1791, the decree was passed by which Jews, without exception or distinction, were admitted to the rights of French citizenship. It was ratified also by the Constitution of 1795.

---

[1] The tariff of tolls has been preserved, and has a curious sound. For a Jew 12 deniers (about 1d.), a Jewess and child 9 deniers, a Jewess 6 deniers ; for a dead Jew 5 sous, a dead Jewess 30 deniers.

THE condition of the Jews in Germany, Prussia, and Austria, at the outset of the eighteenth century, was, if we may believe the historians of the time, an unusually wretched one. The accounts given by the eminent German Jew, J. M. Jost, of the sufferings of his countrymen at that period, cannot fail to move the reader's compassion.[1] 'They were,' to use his own phrase, 'a heap of suffering.' Insult and wrong had, indeed, for many an age, been their portion—a fact to which every history of them that has been written bears

---

[1] J. M. Jost, a German Jew, born A.D. 1793, died 1860, a professor first at Berlin, and afterwards at Frankfort-on-the-Maine. He is the author of the *History of the Israelites*, in nine volumes, published in 1820–28, and of the *History of Judaism*, in three volumes, which appeared later. Up to the time of the appearance of H. Graetz's great work, *The History of the Jews*, Jost's was the most trustworthy authority. 'It is the mature work,' writes Milman, 'of an indefatigable and eminently fair writer. Of course, as a Jew, he presents the doctrines and usages of his race in a favourable light, but he always fully deserves a respectful and candid hearing' (Milm. *Hist. Jews*, vol. ii. p. 476 n.).

323

melancholy witness. In many countries of Europe, however, the period succeeding the Reformation had brought some amelioration of their condition. But in the countries which we have now under consideration, the Jews had sunk, if it was possible, to a lower position than they had occupied before. Their miseries had, in truth, endured so long, that they had become almost insensible to them. The favourite German proverb, which was current for many centuries, may by itself serve to show the light in which they were regarded. 'Happy is that town,' was the saying, ' in which there is neither a Jew, a tyrant, nor a leper.'

To begin with Prussia. We have seen how, in 1670, the Jews had been driven by Leopold I. out of Vienna, and had found a refuge in Prussia ; which the humanity of Frederick William, who, on account of his wisdom and piety, obtained the popular title of ' the Great Elector,' had accorded them. His son, Frederick I., lay under obligations to Gompertz and Elias, two Jews who had been of great service to him in providing him with resources in carrying on the war in which he was engaged. When the Jews had been driven out of Austria, they employed these two men to plead their cause ; and the result was, that a certain number of Jewish families were allowed to establish themselves in Berlin, Potsdam, and other cities of the Electoral State. From this permission the whole history of the Prussian Jews may be said to date. The action of the Elector produced considerable discontent among his subjects; but the Elector was firm, and a few years afterwards a special body of rules for the Jews of the electorate was drawn up and put in force. It was, on the whole, extremely favourable to them, though they were still excluded from all public offices, and freedom to worship according to their own creed was not allowed them. But soon afterwards, some Jews, who were the court jewellers, obtained permission to hold religious services in their own private houses. This was a step towards allowing a synagogue to be built, in which public worship was offered ; but the ritual, we are told, underwent the strictest examination, to make sure that it did not contain anything insulting to Christianity. In 1712, the king prohibited, under severe penalties, the influx of wandering Jews into the country—a measure which, though it might seem to be unfriendly to the Jewish people, was in reality of the greatest benefit to the respectable portion of them. During Frederick William's reign also, a splendid synagogue— the finest, it was said, in that day in all Germany—was built and opened under the royal sanction, notwithstanding the outcry that the concession provoked.

In 1717, King Frederick died, and was succeeded by Frederick William, the father and predecessor of Frederick the Great. He was a sovereign of the most despotic character, though neither cruel nor unjust. His characteristic qualities were displayed in his dealings with the Jews. He continued the privileges granted to them by his father—indeed, added some others. But, on the other hand, he imposed upon them some rather arbitrary burdens, which, however, savour more of eccentricity than harshness. Thus, if the king at his hunting parties killed more wild boars or stags than he could consume at his own table, the Jews were obliged to purchase what remained. It is said that the Jews, unable to eat up the venison themselves, made a present of it to the public hospitals. Again, on the occasion of any event of importance in a family, such as succession to an inheritance, the birth of an heir, the marriage of a son, etc., every Jew was obliged to make purchases to the amount of three hundred thalers at the royal porcelain factory. Towards the end of the century, during the reign of Frederick William II., they were released from this obligation on paying down the lump sum of four thousand thalers.

In 1740, Frederick William died, and his son, who bears in history the name of ' the Great,' succeeded to the throne. His dealings with the Jews were very peculiar. He had no predilection for them ; indeed, whatever personal feeling he entertained for them was of an opposite character. The friend and pupil of Voltaire, he shared that philosopher's prejudice against them. They were no friends of Christianity, to be sure ; but they were the religious ancestors of the Christians, the strongest witnesses of the truth of the Gospel, and as such odious in his eyes. On the other hand, there was a grim sense of justice discernible even in his strange legislation respecting them ; and, independently of this, he was shrewd enough to see that persecution of them was by no means a profitable policy. ' No one ever got any good by injuring that nation,' was his observation on one occasion. Indeed, his legislation seems to have been designed more for the purpose of preventing the increase of their numbers, than for exacting severe imposts or restricting their civil privileges. Thus, in 1750, the edict he issued for the regulation of the Jews in his dominions draws a strict distinction between the Jews that are tolerated by inheritance and those that are personally tolerated—where the toleration, that is to say, does not descend to the children of the person to whom it is granted. To the latter class belonged all those who were not directly engaged in trade, or did not hold any post or office in a synagogue. Among those who were tolerated by inheritance, the privilege of domicile descended to one child only. Subsequently, in consideration of the payment of seventy thousand thalers, the privilege was extended to a second child, though he could only enjoy it on producing evidence that he was in possession of a property of one thousand thalers. A foreign Jew could not settle in Prussia, unless he paid an exorbitant price for his admission. If the widow of a protected Jew married one who was not so protected, she was obliged to leave the country. Besides these burdens, and of course the ordinary taxes paid by all the king's subjects, there were several imposts. There was a patent of protection whenever a child was born, a tax upon every marriage, and upon the election of every elder of a synagogue. The Jew was also excluded from all civil offices, from agriculture, from keeping an inn, a brewery, or a distillery, from setting up a manufactory of any kind, or from practising the profession of a physician or a surgeon. All Jewish servants who wished to marry were obliged to leave the country. Finally, the Jews were interdicted from acquiring house property, unless they had the express permission of the king. In no case could a Jew possess more than forty houses.

In 1786, Frederick William II., the nephew of Frederick the Great, succeeded to his uncle's throne. He was a wise and merciful sovereign, and he endeavoured to ameliorate the condition of the Jews, partly by mitigating the rigour of existing laws, partly by enacting new ones. Since his time, the state of things has gradually but surely improved. But the legislation of those times, as an intelligent writer has remarked, ' bears the stamp of the fearfully degraded state of the Jewish population, and of the oppressive, exclusive, and repressive measures which were thought needful to the interests of that portion of the community.' [1]

The position of the Jews in the Austrian dominions, in the early part of the eighteenth century, was no better than in Prussia. The Emperor Charles VII. entertained a dislike to them, which induced him to listen readily to any enemy who traduced them. The same was the case to perhaps a greater extent with the Empress Maria Theresa, his daughter. A few years after her accession she decreed the banishment of all the Jews in her dominions, amounting, it is believed, to two hundred thousand persons. A considerable number did take their departure; and the rest would have had to follow, if the intercession of the English and Dutch Governments had not induced her to forego her purpose. Subsequently she relaxed the severity of her dealings with them. She not only permitted their residence, but allowed them to follow certain trades, as, for example, dealing in jewels, or opening shops as money-changers or manufacturers. They were

---

[1] *Israel and the Gentiles* (Da Costa, p. 519), a work I have often consulted with profit.

permitted to carry on their services in their synagogues, though they were strictly confined to their houses on Sundays, especially during the hours when Christian worship was going on.

When Joseph II. came into full possession of the imperial power, by the death of his mother in 1780, one of his first acts was to publish an edict of toleration, by which the status of the Jews was greatly improved. All the old prohibitive regulations were annulled. The Jews were at liberty to take up their abode in any town throughout the Austrian dominions, and in the country also—though, in that case, they were required to seek the Emperor's permission. He also opened to them the schools and universities throughout the empire, allowing them to take degrees as doctors in medicine, civil law, and moral philosophy; but he obliged them to open elementary schools of their own for the preparation of their children to enter those belonging to the State. He allowed them to follow any trade they fancied, with the single exception of the manufacture of gunpowder. They were free also to attend the public markets and fairs throughout the country, to wear what apparel they pleased, to occupy any house in any quarter of the towns, and use the public promenades as freely as the other inhabitants. They might also enter the army—indeed, after a while, they became liable to the conscription—and might be made non-commissioned officers; but as, according to the military code of Austria, none can hold commissions who are not of noble blood, they could rise no higher. Lastly, their children were protected against proselytism, it being unlawful to attempt inducing them to change their religion until they had passed their fourteenth year. This edict may be regarded as marking a new era in Jewish history; and whatever amelioration may have taken place in European legislation, so far as they are concerned, in reality dates from it.

In 1781 Councillor Dohm published his famous treatise ‘on the amendment of the political position of the Jews.’ This

writer upholds the principle of bestowing liberty and equality
of rights on the Jews, of their free admission to schools and
colleges belonging to the State, of their unfettered practice of
trades and professions, and even of their participation in public
offices of trust. But he contends that the authority of the
Rabbins over their congregations, their infliction of discipline,
and, under some circumstances, of excommunication, must
be upheld by the State. The publication of the work excited
a good deal of angry feeling among the German Jews. The
renowned Moses Mendelssohn, of whom we shall speak in the
next chapter, published a letter respecting it, in which he
denounced the spiritual tyranny of the Rabbins in indignant
language, which had a very wide and important effect on his
countrymen.

In Russia, during this century, the position of the Jews was
fully as miserable as in any European country. It has been
already pointed out, that by the strict law of the land their
presence was not permitted at all. And in Muscovy proper
the exclusion was enforced with stern inflexibility. Under
Peter the Great a few Jews were admitted into other portions
of his dominions, the Czar having declared—so at least popular
rumour affirms—that 'he did not fear the presence of any
Jews, for his Russians were a match for the craftiest among
them.' But during the reign of Elizabeth (A.D. 1545) their
residence in Russia was again proscribed. They had contrived to secure the property of certain Siberian exiles, and
invested it in foreign countries. Later in the century the
policy of the emperors towards the Jews seems to have been
to drive them out of the towns into the rural districts, with
the idea, so often entertained by one theorist or another, of
inducing them to discard commerce for agriculture. In the
Ukraine, and there only, apparently, they have adopted that
mode of life.[1]

---

[1] The readiness of the Jews of the Ukraine to employ themselves in
agriculture may be accounted for by the extreme fertility of the soil. In
natural productiveness no portion of Europe surpasses, and few can be

Of the Jews in Poland, which for many ages has been the country in all Europe where the Hebrew race has found the most secure home and the most hospitable treatment, we have not yet spoken. Their history, during the eighteenth century, is mainly the history of religious adventurers and rival sects. It will be better to consider these in a separate chapter.

found to equal it. Wheat, oats, and barley are raised with scarcely any exertion of labour, and the pasture-land is rich and luxuriant. This may account for the singular difference of habits which the Jews of these countries exhibit, as compared with their countrymen everywhere else. It should be added that, as there is little trade and few manufactures, many of them, at all events, must live by agriculture or not at all.

F ROM the times of the Maccabees, if not earlier, to those of the impostor Sabbathai Sevi, Rabbinism had prevailed in the Jewish Church. The only opposition had come from the Karaites, of whom we have already spoken, and they were but a small sect, commanding little influence. Eminent Jews, again, such as Solomon Ben Abraham of Montpellier, in the thirteenth century, or Nathanael Tribotti of Rome, or the more renowned Maimonides, might put forward opinions which the Rabbins condemned, proceeding sometimes to the excommunication of the offending writers. But either the latter submitted, or modified their opinions, or their judges reconsidered their decisions ; and Rabbinical theology continued in the main unaltered. But the followers of Sabbathai Sevi formed themselves into a distinct sect, calling themselves Jews indeed, and professing the principal doctrines of the Jewish faith, but differing from it, at the same time, in the most essential particulars.

His followers, as we have seen, were not alienated by his

apostasy or undeceived by his death. One prophet rose after another, who formed his own theological system, resembling Sabbathaism in its general outline, but having peculiar and distinctive features of its own. Most of these secured, during their lifetime, at all events, a large and enthusiastic following, while, in some instances, their teaching was adopted as a rule of faith long after they had passed away from earth. Among these prophets two of the most remarkable were Malach and Hajun. These men were two Rabbins belonging, the one to a Polish, the other to a German, synagogue, who, A.D. 1700, had made a pilgrimage to Jerusalem, there to announce the immediate coming of the Messiah. Most of their companions died of want or fatigue on the journey ; and nearly all the survivors, following the example of Sabbathai, went over to Islamism. But the two leaders, and especially Hajun, zealously propagated their opinions, notwithstanding the most determined opposition of the Rabbins of Jerusalem and Constantinople. Among the doctrines preached by Hajun was that of a Trinity of Gods, though the Three were perfect in their unity. This dogma—very nearly coinciding, if not identical, with the Catholic doctrine of the Trinity—he professed to find in the Book of Zohar.[1]

It is scarcely necessary to add that such teaching provoked the animosity of the Rabbins to the utmost. In A.D. 1722 Hajun and his followers were publicly excommunicated by all the synagogues, and his influence in the East was almost entirely destroyed. In Central Europe, however, he obtained some support. He ingratiated himself with the Emperor Charles VI. by his denunciation of the Jews, and many congregations in Bohemia and Moravia attached themselves to him. Attempts were made to extend his influence into Holland, Hungary, and other European countries, but with

---

[1] 'There be Three Lights in God : the Ancient Light, the Pure Light, the Purified Light. These three make one God.' For Book of Zohar, see Appendix.

little success. A similar movement was initiated shortly afterwards by Moses Luzzato ; who, in concert with a physician
named Jethukiel, collected a congregation at Wilna. He was
excommunicated by the Rabbins, and repeatedly obliged to
retract his statements. He led a wandering, unsettled life, and
at last travelled to Jerusalem, where he ended his days in 1747.

Another and more important sect, appearing at least to
derive its origin from Sabbathaism, is that of the Chasidim,
which established itself chiefly in Poland, Galicia, and Russia.
This is, according to a well-known writer of the present day,
the religion of nearly all the Jews in Galicia, Hungary, Southern Russia, and Wallachia. Its founder was one Israel Baal
Schem, who first appeared in Podolia in 1740. He claimed to
be the representative of God on earth, and as such, his commands were to be obeyed with implicit submission. His early
history is full of fable, wild, extravagant tales being told of it,
which are unworthy of repetition. The orthodox Rabbins say
he was a man of mean rank and extraction, possessed of no
real ability, and who affected sanctity and mystery in order
to impress his followers. A certain supernatural power was
invariably claimed by the students of Cabbalism, but those
assumed by Israel had apparently no limit. He could absolve
from all sin ; he could cure all diseases by his simple command ; he could work the most stupendous miracles ; he was
endowed with all knowledge, not only of the past, but of the
future also. The main drift of his teaching, which entirely
rejected the Talmud as a Rabbinical tradition, was the necessity of learning, by continual contemplation and self-mortifica-
tion, the true nature of God, and also of entire submission to
the Tzaddikhim, or priesthood. We are told by Dr. M'Caul
that they are in the habit of spending every Sabbath with
their Tzaddik, coming in for the purpose from many miles
round, bringing with them provisions for the meals of the
day, as well as presents for the Tzaddik. They consult him in
all difficulties, accepting his replies as inspired by Heaven ;
arrange their private affairs, and compose their quarrels at his

bidding. At Israel Baal Schem's death, his disciples insist that he was taken up to heaven, there to dwell with the holy angels, and make effectual intercession with Almighty God in behalf of every Jew who brings up his children in accordance with the teaching of Chasidism, and obeys the Tzaddik. He was succeeded in his authority by his three grandsons, who were his chief disciples. But this of necessity broke up the community into three distinct bodies, and further divisions have since taken place, though the various synagogues of Chasidists spread over the countries of Eastern Europe are on the whole at unity with one another.

A few years later another strange development of Cabbalistic Sabbathaism made its appearance, under the name of Zoharism. Jacob Frank, its founder, is said to have been born in Poland, *circ.* A.D. 1722. In his youth he was a distiller of brandy, and he first appeared as a religious teacher in Turkey, A.D. 1760. He was then approaching his fortieth year. He followed the Chasidists in his attacks on the Talmud and his devotion to the Book of Zohar. Such fierce dissensions ensued that the Polish Government,—for it was in Poland that he first put forth his theological dogmas,— found it necessary to interfere. But Frank found a protector in the Bishop of Kaminiek, who perceived, or thought he perceived, in Frank's system the elements of Catholic Christianity. Frank himself encouraged this by submitting to Christian baptism, and publicly burning the Talmud. He also declared his belief that God had appeared in human form for the expiation of man's transgression, and that He will hereafter appear again, also in human form, for the final deliverance from the power of evil. This sounded orthodox enough ; but Frank was careful not to say in whose person God had thus appeared on earth, and whether, in fact, he accepted Jesus Christ, or Sabbathai Sevi, as the Messiah.

But neither the Jews nor the Christians were content to leave matters in this condition. The Rabbins, who regarded Frank with a mixture of alarm and dislike, denounced him

to the Polish Government as an apostate to their community
(and so legally liable to their censure), and to the papal
nuncio as an heretical Christian. Neither of the parties
appealed to were disposed to overlook the accusation ; and
the Zoharites found themselves on the brink of a twofold
persecution. Frank himself was thrown into prison, and his
followers were scattered in all directions, most of them endeavouring to seek a refuge in Turkey. On their way, while
passing through Moldavia, they received harsh usage from
both the authorities and the populace. Those that remained
behind were obliged to profess Christianity. Frank himself
remained in prison, until the fortress in which he was confined
was captured, in 1777, by the Russians, who set him at liberty.
He then travelled through Poland, Moravia, and Bohemia,
everywhere levying large sums on the synagogues which still
continued to support him, until he reached Vienna, where
he resided for several years, under the protection of Maria
Theresa. From thence he journeyed to Brunn, in Moravia,
and finally established himself at Offenbach, in Hesse, where
he resided until his death, in 1791.

A strange mystery attended his daily life, upon which no
light has ever been thrown. He was apparently without
pecuniary resources, yet he lived for many years—ten or
twelve at the least—in a style which could only have been
maintained by the most lavish expenditure. He had a re-
tinue which might have vied with that of an Eastern prince,
of several hundred beautiful Jewish boys and girls ; carts,
said to contain gold and silver, were continually brought to
his place of residence ; when he went to perform his devotions,
he was conveyed in a chariot drawn by the finest horses that
could be procured, and a guard of ten or twelve Uhlans, wearing a splendid uniform of green, scarlet, and gold, rode on
either side of it. The service was performed with a great
display of magnificence, accompanied by various strange
ceremonies, the meaning of which has never been explained.
When he died, as he did some three years after his settlement

at Offenbach, he was buried with the utmost pomp and splendour, as many as eight hundred persons attending his funeral ; and a costly cross was set up over his grave. But the secret of his unbounded riches was interred with him. His family, it was found, had been left entirely destitute. They appealed to his followers, who had shown such devotion, but wholly in vain ; and they relapsed into absolute beggary. Such of his followers as survived him joined the Roman Catholic Church of Poland. It is believed, however, that they still cherish in secret some of their founder's peculiar tenets.

Nearly about the same time another Jew appeared, very different in character and opinions from Jacob Frank, but destined to exercise a far wider and more permanent influence. Moses Mendelssohn was born of humble parents in Dessau, A.D. 1729. His thirst for learning showed itself from his childhood, and his early application to study is said to have permanently injured his health. At the age of thirteen he followed his favourite teacher, Rabbi Frankels, to Berlin, where, after many years of labour, he obtained a tutorship in the family of Herr Bernhardt, a silk manufacturer. Soon after he formed an acquaintance with the philosopher Lessing,[1] and became known in the literary world by the publication of his philosophical works, and especially of *Phædon, or the Immortality of the Soul,* in imitation of Plato. Other works followed, which increased his celebrity. Having obtained the prize of the Berlin Academy for an essay on the Evidence of Metaphysical Science, he was elected a member of that society; but Frederick the Great struck his name off the list, considering that a Jew was not worthy to belong to so august a body. His writings nevertheless continued to attract popular admiration; and the entire emancipation from the fetters of Rabbinism which they displayed encouraged many of his friends to hope that he was already a Christian in

---

[1] Nathan the Jew, the hero of Lessing's famous play, *Nathan der Weiss,* was designed as a portrait of Mendelssohn.

principle, and was on the high road to adopting it as his profession. The celebrated Lavater addressed a letter to him, urgently entreating him to take this step. But Mendelssohn courteously but firmly refused, remaining nominally a member of the Jewish synagogue to the day of his death, though he absolutely refused to allow his spiritual pastors to impose any restrictions on his private judgment. It seems to have been his principle to minimize the differences between Christianity and Judaism, and, while remaining a Jew in name, to be a Christian in spirit.

Mendelssohn's name is greatly honoured and admired, but it may be gravely questioned whether the course he pursued was either defensible in itself or beneficial in its results. None of his followers have been able to maintain the position he took up. Some have adopted the genuine faith of Christ, some have renounced distinctive religion altogether. It was remarkable that all Mendelssohn's descendants, including the famous Mendelssohn-Bartholdy, the composer, became Christians. So did Louis Borne, and Neander, the historian and the renowned poet, Heinrich Heine.

We must not pass over Mendelssohn's three celebrated friends—Wessely, the father of modern Hebrew poetry, David Friedlander, the founder of the Jews' Free School at Berlin, and Isaac Euchel, the translator of the Jewish prayer-book. These men, though less distinguished than their great contemporary, have exercised so large an influence on their countrymen and co-religionists that they may be said to have almost entirely changed the tone of Jewish thought and feeling.[1] The synagogue service has also undergone considerable alteration. The prayers and sacred poems have been abridged, and preaching very generally introduced.

---

[1] There were other distinguished men belonging to this age, which, indeed, was unusually rife in literary talent. Joel Lowe, professor at Breslau, Herr Homberg, superintendent of Jewish education in Galicia ; Aaron Wolfsohn, also professor at Breslau ; and Solomon Maimon, author of several philosophical works and his own autobiography.

Even the use of organs is not unusual. Indeed, the old stereotyped service seems to have been exchanged for a ritual according in minor matters with the sentiments and inclination of each congregation.

In Russia, during this century, the condition of the Jews seems to have varied according to the caprices alike of the rulers and the people. They were admitted within the Muscovite kingdom by Peter the Great; but in the reign of Elizabeth, A.D. 1745, their residence was again forbidden, on the ground that they had been maintaining a treasonable correspondence with some Siberian exiles. The expulsion could not have been general, since only a few years later, in 1753, the old charge of sacrificing children was again alleged against them ; an appeal was made to the reigning pope, Benedict XIV., and his successor (Clement XIII.) undertook to make an investigation. He accordingly commissioned Count Bruhl to inquire into the matter, adding, to his honour, that he was to disregard all hearsay evidence, and be satisfied with nothing short of proof. It needs not to add that he did not obtain that. But the popular fury rose to such a height that an imperial ukase was found necessary to control it. The same charge has been repeated since, with the same total absence of evidence, even in our time.

DURING this century no marked change of any kind took place in the position of the English Jews, though their affairs several times came before the notice of the legislature. They had obtained under the Stuarts liberty to carry on their public worship, to practise all trades and professions, and hold all property, except such as was not permitted to aliens. None of these privileges were withdrawn or modified during the eighteenth century. On the other hand, the Jews were not naturalized, could not possess land, could not hold any public office of whatsoever kind—were not, in any real sense, English citizens. Yet it was evident they regarded themselves as permanent settlers in the country. They began to build synagogues, and to establish schools, hospitals, and other charitable foundations for the benefit of their community. It should be noted that, as in Holland, so in England also, there were two classes of Jews—the German and Polish (called the Ashkenazim), and the Spanish and Portuguese (the Sephardim).[1] These agree in their religious opinions, but in other matters differ considerably from each other, and it is said that intermarriages between them were for a long time rare. The last-named were the first to erect a synagogue, which was, opened in 1662, in King Street, Aldgate. In 1676, a larger synagogue had to be provided, and a third was built three years later. This stands in Bevis Marks, and remains to this day, but little changed in appearance. In 1703 the Jews' Hospital was opened, which now stands in Mile End Road. In 1730 a girls' school was built by Isaac da Costa, and called after his name ; and in 1735 another school for general education was set up and endowed by Ruez Lamego.

The German and Polish Jews did not settle in England for a generation later. They were, on the whole, inferior in respect of culture and education, as well as less wealthy, than their Spanish brethren. They provided themselves with a place of worship about the beginning of the last century. It was enlarged in 1722. The present Hamburg synagogue was erected in 1726 ; and the Great Synagogue, in Duke Street, in 1763.

The first legislation of the century respecting the Jews was in 1703, when an Act was carried obliging the Jews to make provision for any members of their family who might become converts to Christianity. This was passed in consequence of the action of a wealthy Jew, whose daughter had been baptized ; immediately after which he turned her out of doors in a state of entire destitution. Not long afterwards, the question of their naturalization began for the first time to be agitated. A proposal was made to the Treasurer Godolphin, in Queen Anne's time, to purchase the town of Brentford for their

---

[1] Ashkenaz, the son of Gomer (Gen. x. 3), is traditionally reported to have settled in Germany. Zarephath and Sephared (Obad. 20) in France and Spain. Hence the German and Spanish Jews have been styled Ashkenazim and Sephardim. These being at one time the principal countries in which the European Jews were found, have caused the whole of the nation to be classed under one head or the other.

occupation, the purchase carrying with it the full rights of citizenship. Godolphin was urged by influential persons to accept it. But he foresaw the opposition which both the merchants and the clergy would offer to it, and declined the proposal. A few years afterwards a pamphlet was issued by the notorious John Toland,[1] who has very generally been branded as an infidel, but who appears to have been really guilty of nothing worse than eccentricity. He urged the wisdom and justice of naturalizing the Jews. But John Toland, one of whose works had been ordered to be burnt by the public hangman, was not a very likely person to be listened to on such a subject. It appears to have drawn forth a pamphlet, written in 1715, deprecating in strong language the proposed naturalization. It is curious to read this pamphlet, which may be seen at the British Museum. The writer repeats with unabated acrimony the charges which had been made for centuries against the Jews, but which the English people had now happily ceased to act upon. It says the reasons why Edward I. expelled them from England were, first, their crucifying and torturing Christian children ; secondly, their betraying the secrets of the State to foreign enemies ; thirdly, their tampering with and debasing the coinage ; fourthly, the hatred which they bore to Christian men ; and, lastly, their extortionate usuries. Of these, the first two could hardly be expected to obtain any credit, and must have been repeated merely for form's sake, like the preamble of a deed. The fourth, too, almost all men at that day would reject

---

[1] John Toland, as he was called, though his true baptismal names were James Julius, was born in Londonderry in 1669. His parents were Roman Catholics, but he seems early to have rejected Romish teaching. He studied successively at Glasgow, Leyden, and Oxford. At the last-named university he seems to have obtained the reputation of a free-thinker; and his book, *Christianity not Mysterious*, excited a ferment which there is little or nothing to justify. It was condemned by the Irish Parliament, and burnt by the hangman. Leland ranks him among Deistical writers ; but he hardly seems to deserve, and is certainly not worth, Leland's censures.

as absurd in itself; because, if the Jews really entertained
this bitter hate against Englishmen, why should they be so
anxious to dwell among them? The third and fifth undoubtedly have some truth, though the charge of debasing
the coinage was never satisfactorily proved, and at all events
could not reasonably be charged on the Jews of the eighteenth
century. With the last we have more than once dealt in this
history. The idea, again, that the Jews are the enemies of
Heaven, and that showing favour to them is disloyalty to
Almighty God, already belonged only to the past. The
writer's real ground for objecting is, no doubt, the injury supposed to be done to English trade by the competition of the
Jews, whose presence in England he is anxious to prove does
not increase the wealth of the community. No Naturalization
Bill was introduced, but in 1723 another step was taken
towards improving their condition. It was then enacted that
when any one of His Majesty's subjects professing the Jewish
religion shall present himself to take the customary oath of
abjuration of the Pretender's supposed rights in England, he
shall be permitted to omit the words ' On the true faith of a
Christian.' This is the first time that any regard for a Jew's
conscience or feelings was manifested in any public document.
In 1740 another Act of Parliament conceded to foreign Jews
who had served for two years on board a British man-of-war
the privilege of British citizenship.

In 1753 Mr. Pelham, at that time Premier, brought forward
his famous Act for the naturalization of the Jews. One reason
for it is said to have been the loyal services rendered by the
Jews to the Crown during the attempt of Charles Edward,
in 1745, to regain the throne.[1] The Bill was introduced into

---

[1] The Jews had given the Government valuable help. They lent a
large sum on very liberal terms, and agreed to take the Government
paper as long as gold continued to be scarce. Two Jews fitted out vessels
at their own cost, which they placed at the service of the king. Great
numbers of Jews also enrolled themselves in the volunteer troops hastily
raised by the ministry.

the House of Lords early in the session, and passed without opposition,[1] almost without remark. It provided for the naturalization of all Jews who had resided in England for three years consecutively. But it should be noted that it did not permit them to hold any public offices, not even of the most petty character. They could not even be excisemen or custom-house officers. Nevertheless, notwithstanding the extreme moderation of the Bill, when it was brought into the Commons, an angry debate ensued. Some members declared that to admit Jews to the privilege of citizenship was an insult to the Christian faith. The inspired Word, it was said, had declared that they should be scattered over the face of the earth, having nowhere any fixed abode ; to give them a permanent home, therefore, was to fly in the face of God and of prophecy. It would deluge the kingdom with Jew usurers, brokers, and beggars. The Jews would buy up advowsons, and so ruin the Church ! Pelham answered, that the fears expressed were idle and chimerical, that the Jews were too few and uninfluential to work any of the mischief that had been predicted ; and, as they could not take any part in our religious services, or even enter our churches, it was impossible they could injure the Church. As for any supposed opposition to the will of God, if there had been any such Divine decree as was represented, it would be impossible for man to overthrow or even to modify it. The Bill passed by a majority of ninety-five, only sixteen being found to vote against it. But the Bill, though accepted by Parliament, excited out of doors a perfect storm of indignation. The peers, and especially the bishops,[2] were pursued by mobs with insult and rancour. The

[1] Lord Lyttelton, the author of the *Life of Henry II.*, is said to have declared on this occasion that ' the man who hated another because he was not a Christian, was no Christian himself'—a sentiment worthy of him.

[2] It is a singular fact that, although the bishops had nothing to do with the promotion of this Bill, the principal odium of it was cast upon them. It was held that they were bound in conscience to prevent its passing, or at all events to do their best to prevent it. William Romaine affirmed, in

common people filled the streets with cries of 'No Jews—no wooden shoes!' 'The wooden shoes' were typical of the French peasants, who ordinarily wore them. The popular *brocard* 'No wooden shoes' thus meant 'Nothing French.' There was no kind of connection between the Jews and the French, but the rhyme between 'Jews' and 'shoes' hit the popular fancy, and so the two cries were combined in one.

The members of the House of Commons were threatened with the loss of their seats; and, as Parliament was near its last session, this was no idle menace. As the autumn advanced, the agitation increased. A clergyman named Tucker, who had written a pamphlet in defence of the measure, was attacked and maltreated by the mob. The Bishop of Norwich, Thomas Gooch, also an advocate of the measure, when he went down to his diocese on his confirmation circuit, was everywhere insulted. At Ipswich the boys whom he was about to confirm shouted out to him that they wished to be circumcised; and on the door of one of the churches a paper was found, announcing that the bishop would confirm the Jews on the Saturday, and the Christians on the Sunday next ensuing.

It was not by the mob only that these clamours were raised. The Lord Mayor and Corporation of London, actuated, it is to be feared, by commercial jealousy, publicly denounced the measure as an inroad on the Constitution and an insult to the Christian religion, and the country clergy everywhere preached the same from their pulpits.

The ministry found that they could not withstand the popular fury. On the very first day of the ensuing session, immediately after the Peers had agreed to the usual address

a pamphlet which attracted much attention, that 'the set of bishops then on the bench were the only ones from the time of Christ who would have countenanced so anti-Christian a measure.' The general charge made against bishops is that of intolerance. It is curious to observe that, if they ever are in advance of the laity in tolerance, it is at once made the subject of bitter reproach to them.

to the Crown, the Duke of Newcastle made an harangue, declaring that disaffected persons had made use of the Act passed last session in favour of the Jews to raise discontent among His Majesty's subjects. As the Act itself was of little importance, it had better be repealed. As little opposition was offered to this proposal as to the original Bill. Some few did indeed protest against this concession to mob clamour ; amongst them the Bishop of St. Asaph and Lord Temple. But in the Lower House both parties seemed to vie with each other in expressing their aversion to this unfortunate measure

Even this ready compliance with the popular will did not allay the ferment that had been excited. There was, it appeared, an Act in existence, by virtue of which any Jew who had resided for seven years in any of His Majesty's American plantations might become a free denizen of Great Britain. It was discovered that this was fraught with almost as much danger to the interests of the English people as the obnoxious measure which had just been removed from the statute book. A member of the Lower House moved that a list of the Jews who had availed themselves of the benefit of this Act since 1740 should be laid on the table for the perusal of the members of the House. It was found that, as claiming the privilege in question was attended by a good deal of expense and trouble, very few Jews had availed themselves of it. Nevertheless, as the *possibility* still remained that Jews in great numbers would at some future time take advantage of the Act in question, and so deluge England with Jews, whose presence would be in the highest degree prejudicial to the interests and even the safety of Great Britain, Lord Harley asked for leave to bring in a Bill to strike out of the Act its obnoxious clauses. But at this point Government refused to concede any further to out-door clamour. Lord Harley's motion was seconded by Sir James Dashwood, and supported by other influential persons. But Mr. Pitt made one of his great speeches against it, and it was rejected by a decisive majority. The whole affair is a curious instance of how easily the English people may be stirred up to loud and clamorous indignation upon the most trivial subjects, in which neither their safety nor their convenience are in any way concerned ;[1] though they cannot, like their Continental neighbours, be induced to proceed to acts of violence, unless where some real danger threatens them or some important interest is at stake.

During the remainder of the century, and indeed for a large part of that which followed, no new attempt was made to accomplish the naturalization of the Jews. It was probably felt by their friends that the angry and unreasonable prejudice which had been roused by the proposed measure of 1753 would in all likelihood break out as virulent as ever,[2] if a similar Bill should be brought into Parliament. It is also a singular fact that many of the Jews themselves were not anxious for the measure to pass, as they feared that the conversion of many of their communion to the Christian faith might follow from it.

But there were not wanting signs that the feeling towards the Jews was gradually growing more considerate and kindly. In 1781, when the island of St. Eustatia was captured by Rodney, a complaint was made in Parliament that undue

---

[1] It is a most curious illustration of this that, up to the middle of the present century, although all bequests made by Jews to their countrymen for charitable purposes, such as building hospitals, endowing almshouses, etc., were held valid, and would be enforced, if necessary, by the Court of Chancery, any provision for the education of their children in their own faith was accounted void. A bequest made about the middle of the century, by a Jew named De Pass, of £1,200 for the purpose of building a college for Jews, was similarly declared void by the Law Courts, because it tended to propagate a false belief, and the money was given to the Foundling Hospital.

[2] During the No Popery riots of 1780, the Jews in Houndsditch, fearing that the violence of the mob would be attracted to them, as it had so often been on occasions of popular tumult, wrote up each on his door front : 'This is the house of a true Protestant.' The father of Grimaldi, the clown, is said to have exercised a still more comprehensive caution, and to have inscribed on *his* door, not 'No Popery,' but 'No Religion.' Lord George Gordon, the leader of the riots, consummated his erratic career by professing the Jewish faith, in which he died.

severity had been shown the Jews in seizing their property, and transporting them from the island. General Vaughan, who commanded the land forces, represented that he had shown the Jews the greatest consideration, had caused their persons to be respected, and, on finding that their property had been seized by mistake, had immediately ordered it to be restored to them. No more had been done for them than justice required ; but the tone of both parties, when speaking of the Jews, was strikingly different from what it probably would have been had the occurrence taken place some generations earlier.

Towards the close of the century, a body known as the Board of Deputies was formed, which gave the Jews the means of expressing in an official manner the wants and sentiments of the Jewish residents in Great Britain. It was originally appointed for the purpose of conveying to George III. the congratulations of the Jews in England on his accession to the throne. Once established, it renewed its meeting when occasion required, and has frequently played an important part in Jewish affairs

THE JEWS IN ENGLAND—*continued.*

I T does not surprise us, as was remarked in the last chapter, that no step was taken to amend the position of the Jews during the latter half of the eighteenth or the first quarter of the nineteenth century. For many years after the struggle of 1753 its memory was fresh in men's minds ; and to have attempted its renewal would only have called forth a more bitter expression of hostility. Then the struggle with America, the horrors of the French Revolution, the excitement of Napoleon's wars, the trade riots and domestic disturbances of the later years of the Regency engrossed men's minds, and they had neither leisure nor inclination to attend to the grievances of the Jews. Even when, in George the Fourth's reign, questions of internal policy again became the topic of the day, the disabilities of the Roman Catholics, a numerous and influential portion of the nation, naturally took precedence of those of the Jews. But when these had been removed, and the Test and Corporation Act had, in 1829, been repealed, the Board of Deputies, already referred to, felt that their opportunity had arrived. They applied to the leading states-men of the day, and among others to the Duke of Wellington, pointing out that, as he had recently carried through Parliament a Bill for the relief of the Roman Catholics, he was in consistency bound to do the like for the relief of the Jews. But the duke answered that such an attempt would raise so angry an outcry as to render the success of the measure hopeless.

Nevertheless, something was done. The first step was taken in 1828, when the restrictions were removed which had been imposed on the admission of the Jews to the Stock Exchange. Up to that time only twelve Jewish brokers had been allowed there, and the privilege of entry had to be purchased by the payment of a large sum to the Lord Mayor.[1] This was now abolished ; and in 1830 Mr. Robert Grant, afterwards Lord Advocate in the Grey Ministry, introduced into the House of Commons a Bill for the removal of Jewish Disabilities. It was rejected by the large majority of 163. The Reformed House of Commons passed it three years afterwards, but it was thrown out in the House of Lords.

Still the cause of the Jews progressed. In 1830 an Act was passed, legalizing Jewish marriages, which the law, up to that time, had not recognised. In 1832 they were admitted to the franchise, and became free of the City. They were now allowed to open shops there, which they had hitherto been prohibited from doing. In 1833 a Jew, Mr. Goldsmid, was admitted as a barrister by the Society of Lincoln's Inn. In 1835 Mr. Salomons, also a Jew, was made Sheriff of Middlesex. In 1837 Mr. Montefiore was knighted by the Queen ; and in 1844 the Jews were declared eligible to all municipal offices. Mr. Salomons was made an Alderman in 1847, and Lord Mayor in 1856.

About this time a movement was set on foot in London for

---

[1] Sir Moses Montefiore paid £1,200 for his admission to the Stock Exchange.

the reformation of the Jewish Church ... It is stated that during the first half of the present century the services in the synagogues were ill-conducted and ... ly attended. Attempts were made by some ... ranks of the community to bring about an improvement, ... for a long time with little success ... until, in 18..., matters ... The reformers among whom Sir Isaac ... was conspicuous, withdrew from the ... brethren, and built what was called the Reformist Synagogue ... situated in Upper Berkeley Street. The object of the ... chiefly to improve the existing liturgy, partly by ... and partly by the removal of certain expressions ... ... which do not harmonise with the feelings of educated Jews in the present day. ... great deal of ... feeling was called forth on the occasion, and the ... of the ... seceders were freely pronounced. ... a few years ... the ..., all to ... and has now ... Both the Sephardim and Ashkenazim, indeed, ... made considerable alteration in their liturgies in the ... of the present century.

In 18.. an important step was taken for ... of the Jewish emancipation. At the general ... in that year Baron Lionel Rothschild offered himself as a candidate for the city of London, and was returned ... the session of 18.. opened, Lord John Russell, then ... brought in

¹ In the twelfth prayer, used by the Jews ... in their public worship, occurred the words 'Let there be no ... ... who apostatize from the true religion, and ... heretics ... ... they be perished in a moment. And let the kingdom ... the Roman empire be speedily rooted out and broken ... ... In the liturgy of the Ashkenazim this prayer which tradition ascribes to Gamaliel) now stands thus: 'Let the slanderers have no hope and all the wicked be annihilated speedily, and all tyrants be cut off ...' but that of the Sephardim the prayer runs: 'Let slanderers have no hope, and let all presumptuous apostates perish in a moment. My ... enemies and those that hate Thee be suddenly cut off, and all ... that work wickedly be suddenly consumed, broken, and rooted out; and ... Thou ... speedily in our days.'—Horne's *Introduction*, iii. 47.

a Bill to om from the Parliamentary oath the words, 'on the true faith a Christian,' which rendered it impossible for a Jew to tal t. The Bill was carried by a majority of 66. It was t o introduced into the House of Lords by the Earl of Carli ho urged that the Jews were now the only persons exc ed from Parliament on account of their religious opinions. s uniformity of belief on religious subjects had ceased to c required as the condition of admission to the legislatur was obviously unjust to exclude Jews on that ground. I e Bill was opposed by the Archbishop of Canterbury, o argued that the measure was inconsistent with the natio profession of Christianity; also by the Bishop of Exet ho declared it to be a breach of the contract made b en the sovereign and the nation—that 'the Crown nd maintain the laws of God, and the true profession the Gospel.' On the other side, Archbishop Whately rued that the spirit of Christianity forbids us to require nposition of civil penalties on those who differ from it. I a division the Bill was lost by a majority of 25.

An a cpt of a different character was now made to obtain t bject desired. On the 26th of July, 1850, Baron Rothscl resented himself before the Speaker to take the necessar ath; and when the Clerk presented the New Testament, h id, 'I desire to be sworn on the Old Testament.' Sir R. is rose to oppose this suggestion; the baron was ordered ithdraw, and a long debate ensued. The opinion of the officers of the Crown having been taken, the House solved that Baron Rothschild could not take the oath, ex t in the ordinary manner prescribed by the law. It was ed, however, that another Bill should be introduced for the ef of the Jews in the ensuing session.

This s accordingly done. The Bill was brought in and carried, ough by a reduced majority, and was then sent up to the rds, by whom it was, as before, thrown out. Its rejectio as followed by a second attempt, similar to that of Baro Rothschild in the preceding year. Alderman

Salomons, who had been returned for the borough of Green-wich, presented himself at the table, and demanded to be sworn on the Old Testament. He was ordered to withdraw, but refused to do so, until given into the custody of the Serjeant-at-Arms. He also voted in two or three divisions, although he had not taken the oath. The House declared this procedure to be illegal, and an action was brought against Alderman Salomons in the Court of Exchequer to recover of him the penalty of £500, which he was said to have incurred by voting in the House of Commons without having previously taken the oath. Judgment was given for the plaintiff. Mr. Salomons appealed, and the case was again heard before six of the judges, but they confirmed the decision of the previous court.

From that time until 1858 Bills were repeatedly brought into the Lower House, and passed by majorities, sometimes larger and sometimes smaller, until the year above named, when, under a Conservative Government, the Commons admitted the Jews by a resolution setting aside the standing order of the House, and Baron Rothschild took his seat as the first Jewish member. In 1860 a Bill was passed through both Houses, allowing the Jews to omit from the Parliamentary oath the words, 'on the true faith of a Christian.' To complete the history of Jewish emancipation, it should here be added that in 1873 Sir George Jessel was made Master of the Rolls, being the first Jew admitted to the English Bench ; and in 1885 Sir N. Rothschild was created a peer, the first who has entered the English House of Lords. No Jew has as yet been a Cabinet Minister ; but it is obvious that, whenever it shall serve the interest of the party which has for the time a predominance in the country to make a Jew Lord Chancellor, or one of the Secretaries of State, or even Premier, there will be no legal obstacle, and probably no opposition offered to such a measure. The struggle, in fact, is over. The Jews are fully emancipated.

The history of this protracted strife is full of interest to the student of Jewish history, because it illustrates in the most forcible manner the difference of opinion in men's minds respecting the Jews, which has existed from the earliest ages of the Church—which, indeed, still exists, notwithstanding the great change in their condition which this present century has brought about. Many sincere Christians still think that the nation, in admitting Jews to the legislature, has been guilty of a breach of its duty in the sight of God. There is, first of all, the belief that the Jews are a people lying under the curse of God, and that to show any favour to them is to rebel against this decree. We have seen what revolting barbarities this idea led to during the Dark and Middle Ages. Its nineteenth-century form—of standing aloof, and withholding civil rights from them—is less shocking in its results, but equally false in principle. God has doubtless His own purposes towards them, and they are a standing miracle, an enduring evidence of the truth of His prophetic word. But He has not commanded us to be the instruments of what we may suppose to be His pleasure, and can do His work without our help. Every faithful follower of St. Paul will regard the Jews in the same light in which he regards them.[1] Every sincere believer in the Lord will echo the same prayer [2] that He offered for them. Again, there are those who, though they would repudiate the notion above suggested, still think, with Archbishop Sumner, that the admission of the Jew to the legislature is a repudiation of our national Christianity ; or, with Bishop Philpotts, that it is a breach of the sovereign's coronation oath. If this were so, no faithful believer, no loyal citizen could uphold the measure. But let us consider what this 'admission to the legislature' really amounts to.. A Jew who enters Parliament cannot, in consequence of his entry, himself make or alter laws. He has only one voice out of a thousand in any legislative enactment. It will be said that he ought not to have any voice at all. But if so, he must not

---

[1] Romans x. 1.   [2] Luke xxiii. 34.

have the elective suffrage ; or he may help to return a member who represents his opinions. Nay, even if he has not the suffrage, he may, by the use of his money, his station, his personal character, his tongue as a public speaker, his pen as a writer, exercise a powerful influence in the settlement of public affairs, which is, in fact, legislation. The only mode of preventing him from doing this would be to do as our fore-fathers did in England, as Torquemada did in Spain—to forbid him to dwell in the land at all. They were at least consistent, and could be so in no other way.

Again, does the sovereign, by giving the royal assent to a Bill for the removal of Jewish disabilities, violate the under-taking of the coronation oath, ' to maintain the laws of God, and the true profession of the Gospel ' ? By the ' laws of God ' we must, I presume, understand ' the *commandments* of God ' to be meant. The phrase occurs continually in Scrip-ture in that, and no other, sense. But how is the maintenance of these impaired by the admission to the legislature of the Jew, who acknowledges these commandments as religiously as does the Christian ? Again, there is ' the true profession of the Gospel '—that is, I conclude, the profession of the Gospel, untainted by heresy or falsehood. But the Jew would have no power of tainting this, though he *were* to become a member of Parliament. Parliament does not determine theo-logical controversies, sit in judgment on heresies, does not admit candidates for orders, does not ordain or consecrate. If the Jew were to be allowed, through his election to the House of Commons, to meddle with any of these things, that would, no doubt, be a very different matter, which all loyal Church-men would resist to the utmost. But notoriously the Jewish member of Parliament neither possesses nor desires anything of the kind.[1]

---

[1] Sir G. Jessel would not present to a living, which was in his patron-age as Master of the Rolls, on the very grounds here alleged—that he had nothing to do, and ought to have nothing to do, with the Christian

There is, in truth, a confusion in some men's minds between 'God's laws' and Christian dogmas, which misleads them. As Head of the State, the sovereign upholds the ' laws of God '—of public morality, that is to say—which are rightly so called, because they are primarily of God's ordering. These, all men, whatever be their distinctive creed, are bound to support. As the Head of the Church, again, the sovereign maintains Christian dogmas through the ministrations of those who hold offices in that Church, and takes cognisance of denials and perversions of the Faith. To these offices there never has been any proposal to admit the Jews, nor is there the least likelihood that such ever will be made.

Church. No doubt, in the present anomalous state of things, questions relative to the Church might be brought before Parliament with which no Jew could with any propriety interfere. But if he is to be excluded on that ground, then all but genuine members of the Church ought to be excluded also.

CHAPTER XLII.

A.D. 1800–1885.

JEWS IN FRANCE, ITALY, AND GERMANY.

WE hear no more of the Jews in France, after the relief granted them by the Republican Government, until 1806 ; when Napoleon, who by his victory at Austerlitz had obtained almost undisputed supremacy in Europe, was arranging his schemes for carrying out that darling dream of his imagination, the Continental system. Few men were keener or more far-sighted than Napoleon. It cannot be doubted that he saw the great value which the cordial co-operation of the Jews would be to him, if he could only obtain it. Their secret but widespread system of mutual intercommunication,[1] their wealth, their intelligence, their perfect mastery of the principles of commerce, would greatly facilitate the designs he contemplated. It is probable that even then he meditated the resuscitation of the Kingdom of Poland, as a formidable opponent to Russia ; and the vast number of Jews to be

---

[1] Baron Rothschild, by his private agencies, was enabled to inform the British Government of the escape of Napoleon from Elba, and Wellington's victory at Waterloo.

found in those countries rendered their goodwill of the utmost importance to the success of such a scheme. He convoked a meeting of Jews in Paris, which, to gratify their national sentiment, he called a Sanhedrin, and submitted to it twelve questions,[1] mainly relating to their social life and position in France. It had the effect, as he doubtless had anticipated, of drawing forth an assurance of their appreciation of the privileges of French citizenship, and their warm affection for their native land, as they designated France. The Imperial Government professed itself satisfied with the reply. A second Sanhedrin was summoned, at which foreign Jews were invited to attend, and a kind of constitution framed, by which it was hoped that the Jews everywhere throughout Europe would be bound. It was ratified by an imperial edict, and was, on the whole, extremely favourable to them. It took effect in France and all countries to which Napoleon's authority extended, though in some parts, as Alsace, concessions were made to popular prejudice, and the privileges of the Jews curtailed. The effect was soon seen in the purchase of estates by Jewish proprietors, the employment of Jewish capital in manufactures, and the participation of the Jews generally in national schemes of foreign and domestic policy.[2]

---

[1] These questions were: 1, 2, 3. Are polygamy, divorce, and intermarriage with Christians allowed by Jewish law? 4, 5, 6. In what light are Frenchmen regarded by Jews, and do the Jews feel themselves bound by the laws of France? 7, 8, 9. In what manner, and by whom, are the Rabbins elected, and what are their powers? 10, 11, 12. Are there any professions forbidden to Jews? Is usury, with their own people, and with strangers, permissible? The Jews answered: that polygamy was forbidden; divorce allowed, if in accordance with the law of the land; intermarriage legal, but not celebrated by any religious rite; that the Jews regarded Frenchmen as their brethren, and acknowledged French law; that any profession was lawful; that the Rabbins were elected according to custom, and had no judicial authority; that legal interest was permitted, but usury forbidden.

[2] In a return made in 1808, scarcely more that a year after Napoleon's edict, it is declared that there were then 80,000 Jews in France, of whom 1,232 were landed proprietors, 250 were manufacturers, and 797 military men, among whom were officers of all ranks, up to field-marshals.

At the Revolution of 1830 the most complete equality of citizenship was granted them; and since that time there has been no alteration in the laws of France, so far as they are concerned.

In Italy the condition of the Jews has varied very little during this century, though public attention has been once or twice directed to them. In most of the large cities, though they are regarded with a species of tacit dislike, no open wrong is done them. In some, as, for example, Florence, they are treated with strict justice, indeed, it might be said with favour. Their rights are protected, and they are allowed to pursue all trades and professions, except that of the physician. At Rome, on the accession of Pio Nono, among the various liberal measures adopted by him was one in favour of the Jews. At that time they were strictly confined within the precincts of their Ghetto; they were obliged every year to send a deputation of four elders to ask permission to reside during that year at Rome, and they were required to attend periodically to listen to sermons preached for their conversion. All these obligations were annulled by the new pontiff. On the 17th April, 1847, he went in solemn procession to the Ghetto, and ordered the wall of partition between it and the rest of the city to be thrown down.[1] He rescinded the regulations whereby the Jews were compelled to sue for permission to dwell in Rome, and to attend controversial sermons. He even substituted a star for a cross, in an order of merit which he instituted, that he might not offend their feelings. After the Revolution of 1848, however, the old regulations were again enforced.

In the summer of the year 1858 public attention was again drawn to the condition of the Jews in the Papal States. On the 23rd of June in that year Signor Mortara, a cloth merchant of Bologna, received a visit from the police; who, it appeared,

---

[1] The Ghetto had been thrown open during the French possession of Rome; but in 1815, when Italy returned to its old masters, the former state of things was resumed.

had been sent by Padre Felletti, Chief Inquisitor of Bologna. It was night, and Signor Mortara's seven children were all in bed. They were awakened ; an inquiry was made as to the names and ages of each ; and the parents were then informed that a maid-servant, who had been in their service, had given evidence to the effect that six years before, when one of their children, Edgar by name, had been dangerously ill, she had secretly baptized him. The child was therefore a Christian, and must be given up to the Catholic Church, to be bred up in that faith. The mother screamed and fainted. The father appealed to the Archbishop of Bologna and the Governor, but without effect. The child was forcibly seized by the Carabineers, and sent to Rome.

Signor Mortara followed, and had an interview with Cardinal Antonelli. The line he took does not seem to have been the one which would naturally have suggested itself to an Englishman. He did not represent that, even assuming the girl's statement to be correct, it would be a most monstrous perversion, alike of natural right and Christian doctrine, to suppose that her act could be any sufficient ground for removing a child from the care of its parents, to which the Providence of God had entrusted it. Probably he knew, however, that any such plea would be urged in vain, and that his only chance of success lay in disproving that any such baptism as the servant alleged had ever taken place. He therefore brought forward evidence that the child had not had the dangerous illness which she declared it to have had, and further, that the servant girl's character was so bad that her evidence was of no value. Antonelli was not to be convinced. He did, indeed, so far relent as to allow the parents occasionally to see their son ; but the priests continually interfered ; and at last, finding probably that they made no progress in reconciling the child to his new life as long as the father and mother had access to him, they conveyed him away altogether.

The story excited a profound sensation throughout Europe. Several of the Great Powers remonstrated with the Vatican, urging that the boy ought to be restored to his parents. Their representations failing, Sir Moses Montefiore, the well-known champion of Jewish rights, undertook a journey to Rome, where he had an interview with Cardinal Antonelli, and asked to be allowed to plead his suit personally with the pope. His efforts were zealously seconded by Mr. Odo Russell, the British Agent, but they proved futile nevertheless. Sir Moses was informed that Pio Nono regarded the affair as one which had been finally settled, and which he declined to reopen. The boy's mother is said to have died of grief. However that may be, it is certain that no more shameful tale of persecution ever disgraced the annals of the Papacy. It is a consolation to know that the establishment of the Italian monarchy brought freedom and civil equality at last to the Jewish people.[1]

In Germany, their history during this century is full of interest, partly on account of the remarkable variations of policy exhibited from time to time in the dealings of the German Government with them, and partly from the conflict of opinion between the ancient Rabbinical schools and what may be called the neology of modern Judaism, which, originating as we have seen with Mendelssohn and his contemporaries, derived afterwards much of its inspiration from Strauss and other kindred writers.

After the fall of Napoleon, when Germany was reconstructed professedly as nearly as possible on its ancient basis, one article of the Federal Act of the Germanic States, promulgated in June, 1815, secured to the Jews the possession of equal rights of citizenship throughout Germany, conditionally

---

[1] Since the complete consolidation of the Italian kingdom under Victor Emmanuel, the Jews in all parts of Italy have enjoyed the rights of citizenship without any restriction. They are free to live wherever they like, follow any trades or professions, and are entitled to hold the same offices and perform the same duties as all other Italian citizens. The Ghettoes are everywhere abolished—that is, every one who chooses is permitted to live in them, and no one who does not choose is required to reside there.

only on their compliance with the laws of the State in which they resided. But it is always easier to frame a law than to ensure its observance, and this was especially the case in Germany, which consisted of a great number of federal States, in which there was a great difference of opinion on many subjects, and especially as regarded the status of the Jews. The principle of Jewish equality, social and political, with the Christian inhabitants of every country, did make its way, but very slowly, and several generations passed before it came to be fully acknowledged.

Nor was it only the *vis inertiæ*, so to speak, of public opinion that had to be overcome. In some countries, at all events, there was a positive reaction against the favour which had been shown by Diets and Governments to the Jews. Even as early as 1815, Frankfort, Lubeck, and Bremen made several enactments, revoking the civil privileges which had been granted to the Jews. Commercial jealousy does not seem to have been the main, or at all events the sole, occasion of this change of policy. The Jews were attacked by men of learning and ability, whom we might have expected to be superior to the prejudices they displayed. The faults of their national character were alleged against them—their exclusiveness, their inveterate obstinacy, their greed of gain, and especially the bigotry of their religious belief. This was no doubt offensive to the rationalizing school, which was rising into eminence. Some of the German professors insisted on their being regarded as always and everywhere aliens, who could not be made to amalgamate with any other nation— who might exist in great numbers *in* any land, but would never be of it. The effect of this agitation was, for the time, at all events, to throw back the question of Jewish emancipation. They were excluded from holding magisterial offices, professorships in the Universities, commissions in the army. In some States the question of their expatriation was mooted ; it was even carried out at Lubeck, so far as the city itself was concerned. In other places something of the old mediæval

outrages were renewed. At Hamburg and other towns the
houses of the Jews were pillaged and demolished. It is even
said that in some places the old cry of the monk Rodolph,
' Hep, Hep,' was again heard.

The revolutionary outbreak of 1830 in France spread into
Germany; but the extreme Liberal party did not now advocate,
as before, the entire social and political equality of the Jews
with their fellow-citizens. Hatred of dogmatic teaching seems
to have overpowered every other consideration ; and as the
dogmatism of the Jews has always been one of their most
marked characteristics, the Rationalist leaders, among whom
Bruno Bauer was conspicuous, clamoured for their suppression
as a religious community, and the withdrawal of civil rights
and privileges from them. The orthodox Jews did not lack
able and zealous champions ; but, as has been already intimated, it was not from Christians only that they encountered
opposition. As some nominal Christians in Germany, and
certain others who could hardly claim the title of Christian
at all, had dealt with the historical records and theological
dogmas of the Gospel, so did nominal Jews deal with those
of Judaism. ' In the Synagogue, as in the Church,' says Da
Costa,[1] ' everything that was national and Israelitish, all that
was supernatural and beyond the reach of unassisted human
reason, was furiously attacked and rejected.' It was not
merely that novelties were introduced into the ancient Hebrew
liturgy and synagogue service, that organs and music were
imported, and sermons preached in the German language, and
new prayers interpolated, and old prayers excluded, but the
fundamental doctrines of their faith were questioned and dis-
credited. One party proposed to abolish the Jewish Sabbath,
substituting the Christian Sunday for it. Another openly
declared that they looked for and desired no Messiah to
come. Another more insidiously averred that they did indeed
believe in the future advent of the Hope of Israel, but He was

---

[1] *Israel and the Gentiles*, p. 597.

not a Person, but simply the representative of ever-advancing
enlightenment and benediction—one who always had been
and ever would be coming, but who would never come until
the perfection of humanity had been reached. But a theory
like this would be more embarrassing to the Jew than its
counterpart was to the Christian. Rationalists might declare
the Incarnate God to have been a personified myth, an ideal
Being, in whose reputed words and acts Christian ideology
found embodiment. But there were His words, which no
man could have spoken ; and there were His acts, which no
man could have performed ; there were His predictions, which
the history of the world since His day had made good, and
which nothing but Divine Wisdom could have uttered. The
Jews had nothing of this to sustain them, and it cannot surprise
us that many among them found no shelter in such a sea of
doubt, except in embracing the Christian creed. Hence, in all
likelihood, the number of conversions which are reported to
have taken place in Germany at this period. Da Costa reports
them as having amounted to five thousand in twenty years.

But orthodox Judaism made a resolute stand against the
evil. Schools and colleges were established in the great
German cities, presided over by learned and zealous teachers :
nor is there any lack of distinguished writers and able
preachers among them. Among scholars, Raport and Leopold
Zunz were pre-eminent ;[1] among historians, Geiger and Graetz,
the last-named the author of the most copious and learned
History of the Jews which has yet appeared. The German
Jews have also distinguished themselves in every department
of science and literature—in politics, in music, in metaphysics,
in medicine, in the *belles lettres.* Their free admission to all
public offices, and the full rights of citzenship, dates only from
the reconstruction of the German empire ; but it is now fully,
and we may hope finally, secured.

---

[1] Zunz is the author of a masterly review of Jewish ethics, and two works
on the poetry of the mediæval Jews. He also wrote a notice of the celebrated Rashi, and other works.

CHAPTER XLIII

IN Spain, until quite within the last few years, there was no material change in the condition of the Jews from what it had been during the eighteenth century. In 1808, when Spain fell under the authority of Napoleon, the Inquisition was suppressed. It was revived again when the country returned, in 1814, to the dominion of its native sovereigns, but only to last for a few years, being finally put down by the Cortes in 1820. The old intolerance, however, the iron legislation of Ferdinand and Isabella, still continued virtually in force. Jews, as such, could not reside with any safety in Spain, until—as it has been before observed—quite recently, when the example shown everywhere in civilized Europe has at last had its effect, and the Jews have been permitted to return to a country for which, notwithstanding the persecutions of many generations, they have ever cherished a warm attachment. In 1881, the Spanish Ambassador at Constantinople so far reversed the traditional policy of his country, as to offer a shelter in Spain for some Jewish fugitives from Russia; and in some of the principal Spanish towns Jewish worship is now publicly celebrated.

The same is the case in Portugal. In 1821 the Cortes abolished the Inquisition, restored the ancient rights possessed by the Jews previously to the reign of King Emmanuel, and decreed that Jews might everywhere settle in Portugal.

In Holland and Belgium there is perfect freedom and equality. This dates from 1796, when the French gained possession of the country, and introduced the same regulations which existed among themselves. These were not at first entirely acceptable to the Jewish residents, because, while on the one hand they removed many restrictions hitherto imposed upon them, they also restrained the power of the Rabbins, and required Jews to take part in all public duties and burdens. But the rights of citizenship were found to be a boon more than compensating these drawbacks; and there is now no distinction between them and the native inhabitants of the countries in question.

In Denmark, Sweden, and Norway, the number of Jews is insignificant, and but little attention appears to be paid to them. In Switzerland they were long treated with extreme harshness. French influence, so efficient in other contiguous countries, did very little for them. It is only within the last ten years that religious freedom has been conceded to them by the State.

To pass to a more important country, Austria, the Jews, early in this century, were somewhat severely dealt with. The successors of their great patron and friend, Joseph II., annulled many of the privileges he had granted them. Indeed, for the greater part of the present century they have been subject to what must be regarded as unreasonable restrictions. They were not allowed to rent or purchase land, nor could they remove from one place to another without the special permission of the Government, and a heavy capitation tax was exacted of them. This, however, was reduced in 1848, and twenty years afterwards they obtained from the Govern-

ment the entire freedom which they now enjoy. Several
Jews, we are told, are now members of the legislature.

These regulations have the force of law in Hungary as
well as in Austria proper ; but neither the Government nor
the people accord them the perfect liberty and equality which
the law professes to secure. The antipathy to them all over
Central Europe is well known. In Hungary, within the last
few years, this has been painfully illustrated by the trial at
Nyireghyaza, which for many weeks attracted the attention
of all Europe. As it illustrates, more forcibly than any comment could do, the true status of the Hungarian Jews, it will
be proper to give an outline of the occurrence here.

. In March, 1882, a young girl named Esther Solymosi suddenly disappeared. She was discontented with her situation,
and had quarrelled with her mistress. A few weeks afterwards, a Jew named Scharf, together with one or two other
of his countrymen, was charged with having murdered her,
in order to use her blood for ritual purposes. At first, the
sole evidence was a Jewish child, five years old, who said
that he had seen his father and brother cut the girl's throat,
and catch her blood in a basin. The brother, a boy of
fourteen, at first denied any knowledge of the transaction,
but afterwards retracted the denial. He now said that he
had not been present when the deed was done, but he had
seen it through the key-hole of the door of the tabernacle.
There was no corroborative evidence of his tale, and, in
addition to the fact that it was in the teeth of his first
evidence, it was proved that it was impossible to see through
the key-hole of the door in the way he had described.

Six weeks afterwards a body, which was sworn to be that
of Esther Solymosi, was found in the river Theiss. It was
dressed in her clothes, and identified by means of a peculiar
scar. It was pretended that the body of another person had
been dressed in Esther's clothes, in order to frustrate inquiry.
But the case broke down, and the Jews were fully acquitted.
The verdict was accompanied by an official declaration that

the oft-repeated charge made against the Jews, of using Christian blood in their services, is a baseless calumny. But the popular outcry with which the acquittal was received shows how deeply seated the prejudice of the Hungarian people on this subject still is. The inquiry, in fact, revealed a mass of ignorance, prejudice, and uncharity which would have been bad enough in the twelfth century, but which in the nineteenth is almost incredible. The lower classes, indeed, are, in most European countries, still steeped in ignorance. But what are we to think of men of education—mayors, commissioners of police, lawyers holding high offices—who could believe that the Jews made use of Christian blood in the performance of their religious rites? What are we to think of a public prosecutor who could declare that the Jews wanted Christian blood, and could not have wanted it except or ritual purposes? It is an astonishing instance of how far inveterate prejudice can influence the minds of even educated men.[1]

In Russia, as has been before remarked, the number of the Jews is greater, and the treatment they experience more harsh, than in any other country in the world. From Russia proper—'Holy Russia,' as it is styled—they have been for many generations excluded, nor are they by the law allowed to remain there now. The law is often evaded, and great misery frequently results from it. Some idle or malicious story gains currency, and stirs the populace to a fierce fanatical outbreak, in which pillage, outrage, and massacre are perpetrated on a large scale; or else the authorities are suddenly stirred up to a real or pretended zeal for the vindication of the law, and thousands of Jewish families are all at a moment required to emigrate from the country. In 1846, the Czar Nicholas issued a new ukase, requiring all Jews who dwelt within five-and-thirty miles of the German and Austrian frontier to remove into the interior. The ground alleged for

---

[1] See Appendix V., Blood Accusation.

this edict was, that large quantities of goods had been smuggled across the frontier. The English Board of Deputies, among whom were Montefiore and Rothschild, laid a statement before Lord Aberdeen, then Foreign Minister, pointing out the terrible suffering and ruin which this measure would occasion. Lord Aberdeen pleaded their cause with the emperor, who was induced to suspend his ukase, at first for three years, and after that again for four more. Finding that he could not succeed in obtaining its entire revocation, Montefiore made a personal expedition to St. Petersburg, where he was kindly received by the Czar, and succeeded in inducing him to cancel the edict. Under Alexander II. the grievances were in some degree alleviated. A few have been allowed to leave the old over-crowded settlements, and establish new commercial centres in other provinces of the empire. But their condition is still extremely miserable. They are loaded with special imposts, and subject to all manner of restrictions : they are excluded from many professions, or are only enabled to follow them by paying bribes to officials, who have them completely at their mercy. Fanatical risings against them also are frequent, being connived at, if not actually encouraged, by the authorities.

In Servia, their condition is somewhat better. Forcible emigrations have occasionally occurred, but not to the same extent as in neighbouring countries. Much the same is the case in Moldavia, where they were allowed to follow most handicrafts. It is said that the roofs and pinnacles and churches throughout the country are the work of Jews, and almost every inn has a Jewish landlord. Of late years, however, their privileges have been abridged, and they have been subjected to a good deal of harsh usage.

In Roumania their treatment has been even worse. It may be doubted whether even in Russia the Jews have undergone so many and such undeserved wrongs. It will be remembered that Roumania is the most recently established of all the European kingdoms, having been recognised as an independent State by the Treaty of Berlin in 1878. One of the conditions of their admission to the list of European sovereignties was embodied in Article 44 of the Treaty :—

'In Roumania the difference of religious creeds shall not be alleged against any person as a ground of exclusion from civil and political rights, admission to public employments, and the exercise of professions and industries in any locality whatsoever.'

But the congress had hardly been broken up, when the Roumanians endeavoured to escape from the obligation thus laid upon them. Instead of conferring the privilege of naturalization on the whole of the Jews throughout the country by one sweeping measure, they granted it only to such individuals as applied for it, and required of those certain conditions with which it would be difficult for many Jews, and impossible for many more, to comply.[1] The consequence has been that although there are said to be more than two hundred and fifty thousand Jews in Roumania, who have been for many generations past resident in that country,[2] little more than a thousand have been naturalized ; and even in the instance of these, the naturalization is only personal, the children of such persons being reckoned as aliens. In 1884 no single Jew obtained the privilege. In short, the condition on which Roumania was admitted by the Congress of Berlin to rank as a sovereign State has been deliberately and systematically evaded. This has, indeed, been pointed out to the Roumanian Government by some of the Signatory Powers, but without effect.

---

[1] They were required to present petitions, in which the applicant stated the amount of the capital he possessed, and the profession or calling which he followed. After the presentation, he was obliged to reside for *ten years* in the country, during which he must prove himself a useful member of society. It is obvious that in these stipulations there is ample opportunity for refusing naturalization to any Jew whom the Government might dislike.

[2] They are chiefly Sephardim fugitives from Spain in the fifteenth and sixteenth centuries.

It must not be supposed that the withholding of naturalization is merely a sentimental grievance. It entails disabilities of the gravest character, debarring them from most professions and trades, and hampering the Jews seriously in such as they are allowed to follow. No Jew can be a government, a railway, or a sanitary official, a director of a bank, a broker, a clerk, or a chemist. They are excluded from all places of public education; in many places the right of keeping inns has been withdrawn from them; there is a continual agitation in progress to deprive them of the power of carrying on the few trades still allowed them. Only in the year 1884 what was called the ' Hawking Law ' was passed, by which hawkers were liable to prosecution if they traded without a licence, and this licence is invariably refused to Jews. Nor does the tale of their wrongs end with their exclusion from all privileges of citizenship. They are exposed to insults and wrongs of all kinds, for which there is practically no redress ; no court of law would venture to give an impartial judgment in any suit between a Christian and a Jew.[1] Any attempts to bring the question of their rights before the Senate inevitably fail, permission even to discuss the question being refused. The press, in most countries the advocate of toleration and freedom, is here the bitterest and loudest supporter of injustice and oppression. In fact, the worst intolerance of the worst periods in France, Spain, and Germany is displayed in the Roumania of the present day. It is sur-

---

[1] At Botouschani, in 1885, five Roumanians were charged with murdering a Jew. The evidence was clear, but the defence was, that a Christian could not be punished for killing a Jew ; and a verdict of acquittal was given, but coupled with an order to pay a thousand francs to the Jew's family for the murder. Quite recently an illustrated newspaper issued a large engraving, of which the murder of a Christian child by Jews— the old, shameless, worn-out, a thousand-times-disproved, calumny—was the subject. It is impossible to believe that the proprietors of the paper knew perfectly the falsehood and calumny which they were circulating ; but they knew that the bitter hate entertained towards the Jews would ensure them a remunerative sale.

prising that the European Powers who imposed their conditions on the Roumanian Government at the Berlin Congress have not felt themselves bound in honour to see them loyally carried out. It may surely be hoped that they will before long awake so far to a sense of their responsibility as to do so.

THE position of the Jews in Morocco is less secure than in most Mahometan countries. They suffer from the fanaticism of the Mahometans, who are a less humanized race than their Asiatic brethren. Robbery and murder are perpetrated almost with impunity, the protection of the law being almost a dead letter, so far as they are concerned. As an evidence of their abject condition, it is said that they are compelled to go bare-foot in most of the principal cities. Beyond the bounds of Morocco large numbers of Jews lead a nomad life, dwelling in tents, keeping flocks and herds, and cultivating the land in their vicinity. Their condition in Cairo and Alexandria is somewhat better, and there are many wealthy Jews in these cities. But everywhere they are liable to the outbreaks of blind fanatical fury to which reference has so often been made. An instance of this occurred in 1863, which it is important to notice, as showing only too plainly the condition of things in those countries. A Spaniard had died suddenly at Saffi, and the Spanish authorities required an examination into the circumstances of his death. To avert suspicion from themselves, the Moors accused a Jewish boy, who was in the dead man's service, of poisoning him. He denied the crime, but was scourged until he confessed it, and implicated several other persons. A popular outbreak would have ensued if the Morocco Jews had not appealed to Sir Moses Montefiore. He requested the intervention of our Government, and made an expedition to Morocco, where he not only succeeded in releasing several Jews, who had been detained in prison on charges which could not be proved, but obtained an audience of the Sultan of Morocco, who received him with great distinction. He pointed out to the Sultan that the Jews of Morocco were without any legal protection, and were in consequence frequently subject to outrages for which they could obtain no redress ; and he entreated that equal justice might be secured to them as to other inhabitants of the country. In a few days an edict was issued, commanding that in future Jews, Christians, and Mahometans should be treated with equal justice throughout the Sultan's dominions. Experience has shown that it is more easy to obtain these concessions from Moslem sovereigns than to ensure their due observance by subordinate officers. Still, there can be no doubt that this is a great advance in the social condition of the Jews of Morocco.

There are a good many Jews in Brazil and in the United States of America. In the last-named country it needs not to be said that they enjoy the most entire toleration. Jewish hospitals, Jewish orphanages, free schools, alms-houses, benevolent institutions of all kinds, exist in the principal cities, in which also magnificent synagogues are to be found. The authority of the Rabbins, however, is not so great, as a rule, as it is in European countries. It is said that there is great laxity in their ritual—some discarding Hebrew altogether in their liturgies, some making the Sunday instead of the Saturday their day of religious observance. Their increase of population during the last few generations has been extraordinarily rapid. Jews are found scattered in Mexico and in the great South American cities, but not in any great numbers.

In the dominions of the Sultan, both the European and the Asiatic, the position of the Jews during the present century has varied little from what it was in those which preceded it. As has been already remarked, they are more kindly and fairly treated than in other Mahometan countries—the result, probably, of freer communication with Europe. But here, too, they are liable to sudden outbursts of religious fanaticism or commercial jealousy, and on these occasions they suffer great injustice and cruelty. Two signal instances of this occurred A.D. 1840.

In that year, a Greek boy in the island of Rhodes having suddenly disappeared, a woman affirmed that she had seen him, shortly before, in company with a Jew. It chanced to be near the time of the Passover, and, strange as it may seem, some of the European consuls, on no better evidence than this, raised the old slander that the boy had been murdered, in order that his blood might be used for ritual purposes. The Jew was arrested, and denied any knowledge of the boy. He was thereupon put to the torture, under which his reason gave way, and he uttered the names of several Jews, who were at once assumed to be his accomplices. They were seized, and in their turn put on the rack ; the Jewish quarter was closed, and no food allowed to enter it ; and it is even said that an attempt was made to convey a dead body into one of the houses, in order that it might be found there. The story spread in all directions, and popular risings and outrages on the Jews ensued.

The affair at Damascus was even more serious. Father Tomaso, a monk, who for many years had practised medicine, suddenly disappeared. A report was spread that he had been last seen in the Jewish quarter, which was instantly invaded by a mob of Christians, who denounced the Jews as his murderers. Count Menton, the French Consul, actuated, it is believed, by political motives, took up the matter and insisted on the punishment of the offenders, as he chose to consider the Jews. He produced persons who swore that the monk had been seen to enter the shop of a Jewish barber, from which he had never issued forth again. The barber was seized and bastinadoed, until in his agony he accused several of the richest Jews in the city as having been concerned in the murder. They were subjected in their turn to tortures, under which two of them died, and several more confessed their complicity in the crime. A young Jew, who swore that he had seen Father Tomaso enter the house of a Turkish merchant, on the evening of his disappearance, was bastinadoed to death, in order to induce him to retract his statement. The French Consul now laid the confessions which had been extracted from the prisoners before the Turkish Pacha, and insisted on their being immediately put to death.

Fortunately the Pacha thought it his safer course to apply to head quarters for instructions, and thus sufficient time was given for the report of what had occurred to reach England. There it created a profound sensation. A large meeting of influential Jews was held in London, at the house of Sir Moses Montefiore, who was deputed to seek an interview with Lord Palmerston, at that time Foreign Secretary. From him Sir Moses received all possible help; but it was thought advisable that a special mission should be sent to the East to represent the matter in its true light to the Turkish authorities. Sir Moses himself undertook the office, and proceeded to Syria, accompanied by M. Cremieux, a Jewish member of the French Chamber, and several others. They learned that at Rhodes the prisoners had been liberated, and the governor who had sanctioned the proceedings dismissed from his office ; but the Damascus affair was still undetermined. Sir Moses obtained an interview with the Pacha of Egypt, who endeavoured to compromise the matter by offering to pardon all the prisoners who had been accused. But he was answered that it was not justice to pardon innocent men. What was demanded was a complete and honourable acquittal of the accused. This was presently granted, and the prisoners discharged from custody. Subsequently Sir Moses had an interview with the Sultan himself, on the 6th of November in the same year, 1840, when he obtained from him—as he had formerly done from the Sultan of Morocco—the celebrated firman, which granted to the Jews, everywhere throughout the Turkish dominions, the most complete protection.

In Persia, Bokhara, Yemen, and Central Asia, numerous colonies of Jews exist, engaged as a rule in trade, but also occasionally employed in agriculture. They are not as wealthy, apparently, as their Western brethren. Many of them, indeed, are extremely poor, earning their subsistence as day labourers. They speak and write their own language only, though able to converse with the inhabitants of the country. They live very much among themselves, never intermarrying with strangers, and carry their differences to the Rabbi of their synagogue, who, indeed, is the judge authorized by the law for the settlement of their disputes. One cause of their isolation is their fear of allowing their children to study secular subjects, which they think would be likely to undermine the foundations of their faith.

In the Holy Land, it was reported in 1881 that there were about 15,000 Jews in Jerusalem, about half its population. Whether that is correct or not, it is certain that the number of Jews in that city is steadily, though not rapidly, increasing, and has been on the increase ever since the Crimean War. Whatever may be thought about that war, one of its consequences was to open Palestine to European settlers ; and, as might have been expected, the Jews availed themselves of the opportunity of obtaining for themselves a home in the ancient land of their fathers. But very few of those who have attempted this possessed the means of comfortably establishing themselves. It has been remarked by one who knows the Jews well, that they are contented to live elsewhere so long as life goes prosperously with them. It is the poor, the unfortunate, the persecuted, who seek a refuge there. Old people

again, whose children are out in the world, come to spend the
remainder of their days in religious exercises. A few Rabbins
also devote themselves to the work of looking after the various
communities thus established. The Montefiore Testimonial
Committee has done something to assist this immigration. It
has established agricultural communities in various places,
notably beyond the western walls of Jerusalem, where four
thousand Jews are lodged in comfortable houses, especially
built for them. The population has trebled itself, according
to trustworthy information, since 1860.

But there are great drawbacks. The Jews are not naturally
disposed to manual labour, preferring, as they themselves say,
to work with their brains rather than their hands. There is
also the temptation—which always besets those who live, to
some extent, on the charity of others—to abuse the generosity of their benefactors, by doing no work at all themselves.
There is also the competition of the native labourer, the
fellah, who is used to the climate, and hard labour and poor
food, and who can live at about one-third of what is necessary
for the Jew. On the whole, it cannot be said that the lower
classes of Jews are prospering in the Holy Land.

There are, however, many synagogues both of Ashkenazim
and Sephardim Jews in Jerusalem, and Talmudical schools
supported by large contributions levied on Jews throughout
the world. Schools also exist at Hebron, Tiberias, Safed,
Jaffa, and other towns. There are also three Jewish hospitals
in Jerusalem, as well as numerous almshouses. All sects of
Jews are represented in Jerusalem, Chasidim and Karaites,
as well as the orthodox adherents of the Rabbins. On the
whole, though there is no doubt that the condition of the
Palestinian Jews has been ameliorated of late years, it is still
doubtful whether any permanent improvement can be effected
while the country continues to be subject to Turkish misrule.

Here, then, we bring to an end this strangely varied, yet
still more strangely monotonous, narrative—not, as in the case
of any other ancient people, because its national history has

come to an end, but simply because we cannot read the future. Eighteen centuries have, in all other instances, effected so vast a change in the condition of a nation, that it is difficult to trace any identity between its earlier and its later generations. Eighteen centuries ago our own ancestors were savage tribes, living in wattled huts, staining their naked bodies with woad, and practising barbarous and bloody rites. In language, in religion, in mental and moral culture, in social organization, they were so wholly different from ourselves that it is difficult to discover any point of resemblance between the two. But in all these respects, the Jew of the first century differs but little from his descendant eighteen hundred years afterwards. He speaks the same tongue, he holds the same creed, he observes the same habits, or nearly the same habits, of life as his forefathers did all that long period ago. And yet that long period is not half the life of the Jewish people. It began in an age when the tradition of the Flood was still fresh on earth ; it is still in the fulness of its life, when the eye of faith can distinguish, not very far off, the dawning of the Judgment Day. How is this strange tale to end ? What is to be the last act of this amazing drama ? Jerusalem has been long trodden down of the Gentiles ; the times of the Gentiles are nearly fulfilled. What is to follow ? Are the Jews to be restored, as a distinct people, to the Land of Promise, and there accept Him whom their fathers rejected as their King? There is no subject on which speculation is more busy, or on which more confident judgments are pronounced. But it is the voice of man that speaks, not of God. One thing alone is sure. God has not cast away His people. Who can read their history, and doubt that ? But when, where, or how, He may be pleased to take them again into favour, no man can foretell. Our children will behold the solution of the riddle, and bless God for His mercy. Let us, too, bless God, and wait in faith.

THE END.

STATISTICS OF JEWISH POPULATION.

I T is always difficult to determine the number of Jews resident either in the Holy Land or in any other country of the world. The remark applies to ancient, even more than modern, times. It is not only that the information afforded by writers is scanty, but that the statements made by some historians differ greatly from those supplied by others; while a good deal must be rejected as wholly incredible. To take an instance, we are informed by the author of the Book of Samuel,[1] that the military population of David's kingdom was 1,300,000. But in the parallel passage in the Book of Chronicles[2] the number is stated to be nearly 300,000 more. 'To attempt reconciling these discrepancies,' says an intelligent writer,[3] 'would be wasted labour.' During the reign of Rehoboam, B.C. 975, the number of the men of Judah who drew the sword is rated at 180,000.[4] But at the accession of his son, not twenty years afterwards, it is 400,000.[5] Whether we are to attribute these contradictions to corruptions of the text or to different modes of calculation, signifies little to us. The two statements are quite irreconcilable with one another. Josephus's numbers, again, are wholly untrustworthy. He reckons the sum of those who returned with Zorobabel from Babylon, at the enormous figure of 4,628,000 and

---

[1] 2 Sam. xxiv. 9.   [2] 1 Chron. xxi. 5.   [3] Adam Clarke.
[4] 1 Kings xii. 21.   [5] 2 Chron. xiii. 3.

47,000 women.[1] This is, of course, an absolute impossibility ; and
we know, from the books of Ezra and Nehemiah, that the real
amount was 42,000.[2] It has been suggested that Josephus's text is
corrupt in this passage. But if so, it may well be assumed to be
corrupt in other similar places also. Thus he affirms that the
numbers shut up in Jerusalem during the siege by Titus was
2,700,000,[3] while the estimate of Tacitus is 600,000.[4] Here again,
though the reckoning of the Roman historian is probably below the
mark, he having omitted to allow for the unusual number of residents
at the time of the siege, yet that of Josephus must be rejected as
incredible.[5] The circumference of the walls of Jerusalem is generally
admitted to have been about four miles. The space thus enclosed
within the walls would be about equal to that part of the area of
London which extends from Tyburn Gate to the British Museum
in one direction, and from the Regent's Park to Whitehall in the
other, drawing an imaginary circle, of which the Regent's Circus
would be the centre. The portion thus enclosed—hardly one tenth
part of what lies within the bills of mortality—may contain half a
million persons. Allowing for the narrow streets of old Jerusalem,
we may reckon that the same area in that city would hold 100,000
more, thus very nearly verifying the statement of Tacitus. No doubt,
at the time of the Passover, vast numbers came from foreign lands,
and these found accommodation, as well as they could, in Jerusalem
itself, or in the environs. Many probably were lodged in outlying
villages, and many more, according to the common practice in the
East, slept in the open air. These would, of course, be driven into
Jerusalem by the approach of the Roman armies, and thus the numbers at the beginning of the siege might have amounted to a million
or thereabouts. But the notion of nearly three millions being
crowded into the area above described is simply preposterous.

But if Josephus's statistics on these two important points are to be
rejected as wholly untrustworthy, how are we to credit his assertions
in matters of very nearly the same kind ? He tells us that Galilee in
his time contained more than two hundred towns and villages, no one
of which held less than 15,000 inhabitants.[6] If this were indeed the

---

[1] Joseph., *Ant.* xi. 3, § 10.   [2] Ezra ii. 64 ; Nehem. vii. 66.

[3] Joseph., *Bell. Jud.* vi. 9, § 3.   [4] Tac. *Hist.* v. 13.

[5] This is the most probable explanation of the smallness of his estimate of the
numbers in the city during the siege. The ordinary population would probably
be about the amount he gives.

[6] Joseph., *Bell. Jud.* iii. 3, § 2.

case, that province, scarcely larger than one of the largest of our English counties, must have had a population of fully three millions, while that of the whole of Palestine would approach ten millions. Few readers will be found to credit this.

At the same time more than one trustworthy writer affirms that Palestine was a thickly populated country. The population to the square mile is said to have been larger in it than in any other portion of the Roman dominions. Diodorus,[1] Strabo,[2] Tacitus,[3] and Dion Cassius[4] all concur in this; and therefore, though we cannot accept Josephus's statements as being even approximately accurate, they may be admitted so far, as establishing the numerous population of Palestine at the time of the siege. Nor are we wholly without means of forming an estimate as to its amount, independently altogether of the above-named writers. Thus Hecatæus of Abdera (quoted by Joseph. Ap. i. 21) says that Jerusalem in his time (A.D. 312) contained 120,000 inhabitants. Presuming the average increase of population to have taken place, according to this reckoning, Jeru salem at the time of the siege would contain about 600,000—agreeing closely with Tacitus's estimate. According to Maccab. II., the city at the date of Antiochus Epiphanes, A.D. 180, had 160,000, or, according to others, 180,000. This would make the number of residents at the outbreak of the civil war somewhat less; but there would be no material difference. On the whole, we may assume that, by dividing Josephus's estimates by three, we approximate to the real number. According to this, the census of the Holy Land, A.D. 71, would be about three and a half millions, and the total of persons besieged in the Holy City something under one million.

It is still more difficult to estimate the total of the Jews in other countries of the world at this time. We may safely assume that they could not have been fewer than the inhabitants of Palestine. We have reason to believe that the bulk of the nation did not return with Zorobabel. Those who remained behind in the foreign countries to which they had been conveyed throve and multiplied in their new homes. There are grounds for supposing that, at subsequent periods, large emigrations from the Holy Land took place, probably at the date of King Ahasuerus's edict, more certainly during the persecution of Antiochus Epiphanes and the Roman invasion. We have the

---

[1] Diodor. Sic. xl. *Eclog.* 1.   [2] Strabo xvi. 2, § 28.   [3] Tacitus, *Hist.* v. 8.
[4] Dion Cass. lxix. 14. Dion makes the astonishing assertion that Adrian destroyed nearly 1000 towns κῶμαι ὀνομαστότεραι in Palestine, besides fortresses.

clearest testimony of contemporaneous writers as to the extent to which
the Jews in our Lord's time had spread into foreign lands, forming
everywhere a distinct people, as they do at the present day. Momm-
sen quotes the statement of a writer of Julius Cæsar's date, to the
effect that it would be dangerous for the Roman governor of his
province to offend the Jews, because, on his return to Rome, he
might encounter contumely from their countrymen there. Agrippa
I. wrote to the Emperor Caligula to the same effect, but more explicitly. 'Jerusalem,' he says, 'is the metropolis, not of Judæa only,
but of very many lands, on account of the colonies which from
time to time it has sent out into the adjoining countries—Egypt,
Phœnicia, Syria, Cœlo-Syria, Pamphylia, Cilicia, Asia Minor, as far as
Bithynia, and the remotest parts of Pontus; likewise into Europe—
Thessaly, Bœotia, Macedonia, Ætolia, Attica, Argos, Corinth, and
the Peloponnesus. Nor are the Jewish settlements confined to the
mainland. They are to be found also in the more important islands,
Eubœa, Cyprus, Crete. I do not insist on the countries beyond the
Euphrates; for with few exceptions all of them, Babylon and the
fertile regions round it, have Jewish inhabitants.'[1] This testimony
is confirmed by St. Luke's narrative of what occurred on the day of
Pentecost immediately following the crucifixion (Acts ii. 9, 10). It
can hardly be doubted that at the date of the commencement of this
history, there were fully as many Jews in other lands as there were in
Palestine—the whole nation numbering, at the lowest computation,
not less than seven millions.

Eighteen centuries have elapsed since that time, and the Jews are
still a distinct and peculiar people, intermarrying with other races
less than any other nation in the world. According to the rate[2] at
which population ordinarily increases, they ought to have doubled
their number more than seven times over, and to amount at the
present time to many hundreds of millions. The inherent vigour
of the race does not seem to be either intellectually or physically impaired. It is reported by those who have studied the question, that
their health, in the various lands where they are sojourners, is at least
as good, indeed, distinctly better, than that of the populations among
which they reside. It becomes, then, an interesting and curious
question—what the amount of their numbers is in the present day.

---

[1] Philo, *Legat. ad Gaium*, § 36.
[2] The increase of population is said by those who have made the subject their
study, to be $\frac{1}{37}$ annually, or according to others, $\frac{1}{33}$.

Nor does the same difficulty we have experienced in endeavouring to ascertain the exact sum of their population at the time of the fall of Jerusalem, meet us when we enter on that. Statistics have been given by trustworthy authorities, which are found, on examination, to agree very nearly with one another. I propose to give them here in detail.

To begin with Europe. Here the country in which they are most numerous is Russia. In that, the official return for 1876 was 2,612,179. In Austria and Hungary it was 1,372,333 ; in the German Empire, 520,575. In France their total does not exceed 60,000 or 80,000.[1] In England, the number is nearly the same. In Italy the total is 53,000 ; in Holland, 68,000 ; in Moldavia, Servia, and Roumania, about 300,000. In the remaining countries of Europe there may be 20,000. These returns show a total of some hundreds of thousands over 5,000,000 of Jews in Europe.

Proceeding to Asia, the Jews in the Turkish dominions (including both Turkey in Europe and Turkey in Asia) amount to about 200,000. In Persia, Bokhara, Samarcand, Central and Eastern Asia, it is more difficult to ascertain their real numbers ; but it is generally agreed that these may be approximately estimated at 50,000. In Arabia, there is a great difference of opinion, some affirming them to amount to as many as 200,000, while more trustworthy authorities place the total at one tenth that number. There are also the Jews of Syria and the Holy Land, of which the census has already been given. On the whole, the Asiatic Jews may be considered as amounting to 300,000, or perhaps 400,000.

Turning next to Africa, the Jews of Egypt are estimated at 80,000 ; those of Tripoli, 100,000 ; of Tunis, 50,000 ; of Algiers, 70,000 ; of Morocco, 300,000. Thus the total of African Jews in the Northern kingdoms somewhat exceeds half a million. If to these are added such as are to be found in Central and Southern Africa, the entire sum may amount to 600,000

Lastly, in America and Australia there is said to be a Jewish population somewhat exceeding that of Asia. Here their chief centres are the United States, Canada, and Brazil.

From these returns, which, it may be assumed, are neither much in excess nor much short of the actual amount, the total number of pro-

---

[1] This is probably too low an estimate. In a census taken in 1808, there were 80,000 Jews in France ; and there has been nothing to check their increase. Their number is more probably 100,000.

fessing Jews at the present time appears to be somewhat less than seven millions—the very number which, so far as it is possible to determine, was that of the Jewish people when the Lord became incarnate upon earth. Can any man realize this astonishing fact, and yet doubt the living miracle which the history of the Jews presents?

> ' How many generations of mankind
> Have risen and fallen asleep,
> Yet it remains the same ! '

THE word Talmud has several meanings, which are most nearly rendered by 'study,' or 'learning.' There are two books so called—the Jerusalem and the Babylonian. Each of these is made up of two parts—the Mishna, or repetition,—it being, as it were, a reissue of the Mosaic law,—and the Gemara, or complement, the critical expansion of the Mishna. The Mishna of both Talmuds is the same, the Gemaras different : that of the Babylonian being the larger as well as the more diversified. They are encyclopædias of the Jewish knowledge of their day, and deal with civil and criminal, as well as moral and religious questions, law, science, metaphysics, history, and general literature.

The Mishna was compiled by Rabbi Judah, called Hakkadosh, or 'the Holy,' who lived in the reign of Antoninus Pius. It is written in very pure Hebrew. But as many things are introduced into it which have foreign names, there is a frequent occurrence of Latin and Greek phrases. The Gemara of the Jerusalem Talmud, which is believed to have been completed about the end of the fourth century, is written in what is called the Eastern Aramæan : that of the Babylonian, which is at the least a century, and probably two cen turies, later, in Western Aramæan.

The origin of the Mishna is declared to be as follows. While Moses was with God in Sinai, He communicated to him a twofold law, written and oral.[1] The latter Moses repeated to Aaron, who delivered it to Eleazar and Ithamar; they to the Seventy Elders; they to the prophets; and the prophets to the synagogues. In this manner it was passed on from generation to generation, to the time of the great Jewish doctor Hillel, who lived shortly before the birth of Christ. He digested the great mass of precepts under six heads, still, however, without committing them to writing; which, it was believed, would have been contrary to the intention of the Divine Giver. Under the more formal shape which it had now assumed, the Oral Law was passed on till the time of the destruction of Bethor, and the final dispersion of the Hebrew people. Then, as we have seen, Rabbi Judah Hakkadosh, perceiving that the restoration of the Jews to their ancient status was not to be looked for, and fearing that the consequence of this would be the total loss of the ' Law of the Mouth,' as it was called,—conceiving also that the peculiar circumstances of the case justified him in breaking the rule that had been so long observed,—embodied the traditions in a volume which might be preserved for ever, secure from addition or change.

His countrymen endorsed this belief, and accepted the Mishna with the most profound respect. It had scarcely been issued, when commentaries began to be written upon it by learned Rabbins; which, about the end of the third century, were collected into a volume by Rabbi Jochanan Ben Eliezer, and called the Gemara. The style in which this is written is harsh, much inferior to that of the Mishna; and even the best Hebraists are unable to expound satisfactorily some portions of it. This obscurity was probably the reason why another Gemara was set on foot by the Mesopotamian Jews, about a century after the issue of the Jerusalem Talmud. The work was begun by Rabbi Asa or Asche, and carried on to the time of Rabbi Jose, about A.D. 500. There is some variety of opinion as to the date of its completion; but Laurence is generally thought to have proved satisfactorily that it cannot be later than the beginning of the sixth century. Christian commentators commonly prefer the

---

[1] The meaning of this is, that the development of the Law is contained in the Law itself. There must have been from the first difficulties in the interpretation of the Law. These were referred to Moses. His decisions were traditionally preserved, and called the Oral Law, this is figured by God's delivering the Oral Law to Moses. A Rabbinical fable further declares that God committed the Written Law to Moses by day, and the Oral by night. This symbolizes, first, that God's law is the true measure of time, and secondly, that the Written Law is to the Oral as the light to the darkness.

Jerusalem Talmud,[1] as containing less of fabulous and frivolous matter; but the preference of the Jews is for that of Babylon.

The Mishna is divided into six principal heads, or Orders, as they are called. Each Order is divided into a variety of titles or treatises, and these again into chapters and sections. The six Orders are : I. Zeraim, or Seeds; II. Moed, or Festivals; III. Nashim, or Women; IV. Nezikin, or Injuries; V. Kodashim, or Holy Things; and VI. Taharoth, or Purifications.

The First Order is subdivided into eleven treatises :—

1. Treats of the prayers and benedictions which are to precede and follow meals.

2. Of the gleanings of vine and olive yards, alms, and first-fruits to be given to the poor.

3. Of the purchased fruits of the earth, which may be lawfully used, if they have paid tithe, but are illegal if they have not paid.

4. Of mixtures of various kinds of grain, and the wool of animals.

5. Of the laws relating to the Sabbatic, or seventh, year.

6. Of the first-fruits, given to the Priests.

7. Of the tithes, given to the Levites.

8. Of the second tithe, to be sent up to Jerusalem.

9. Of the cake offered as a heave offering.

10. Of the fruits of trees to be counted as uncircumcised for three years.

11. Of first-fruits generally.

The Second Order contains thirteen treatises :—

1. Of the Sabbath day.

2. Of various Sabbatical rules.

3. Of the Passover.

4. Of the half shekel paid as tribute to the Sanctuary.

5. Of the great Day of Atonement.

6. Of the Feast of Tabernacles.

7. Of Pentecost.

8. Of certain things forbidden on Feast Days.

9. Of the New Year.

10. Of the Fasts and Days of Humiliation.

11. Of the Feast of Purim.

---

[1] The Jerusalem Talmud contains only four of the six Orders which make up that of Babylon, and a portion of the fifth. Whenever, it should be noted, ' The Talmud ' is spoken of, without any intimation *which* Talmud is referred to, the expression must be understood to mean that of Babylon.

12. Of the lesser Jewish Festivals.

13. Of the three great Festivals.

The Third Order has seven titles :—

1. Of the Law of Levitical Marriage.

2. Of Marriage Contracts.

3. Of Women's Vows.

4. Of the Vows of Nazarites.

5. Of Writings of Divorcement.

6. Of the Putting away of Wives.

7. Of the Ceremony of Espousal.

The Fourth Order has nine sections :—

1. Injuries inflicted by Violence, Wounds, etc.

2. Leases, Hirings, Loans, Exchanges, etc.

3. Succession to Property, Partnerships, Contracts, etc.

4. The Sanhedrin.

5. Stripes.

6. Oaths.

7. Witnesses, Evidence, also Idolatry.[1]

8. Decrees of Judges and Apothegms of Wise Men.

9. Record of Errors in the Decisions of Judges.

The Fifth runs to eleven treatises, which deal with :—

1. Sacrifices.

2. Oblations and Offerings.

3. Things Profane.

4. The First Born.

5. Valuations of Males and Females.

6. Exchange and Redemption.

7. Atoning Sacrifices.

8. Trespass Offerings.

9. The Daily Sacrifice.

10. Dimensions, Form, and Structure of the Sanctuary.

11. Offerings of Birds.

The Sixth and last Order contains twelve heads, relating to :—

1. Purifying of Vessels.

2. Tents and Tabernacles, and Pollution by Corpses.

3. Vestments and Uncleanness by Leprosy.

4. The Ashes of the Heifer Purifying the Unclean.

5. Purifications generally.

---

[1] Here introduced because idolatry is sometimes the subject of judicial proceedings.

6. Vessels containing Water.
7. Separation for Legal Impurity.
8. Legal Impurity generally.
9. Regulations concerning Uncleanness.
10. The Washing of Lepers.
11. The Washing of Hands.
12. Supplementary matters.

The Gemaras, it should be noted, are not so much commentaries on the Mishna, as a series of disquisitions on passages in Holy Scripture, or on the text of the Mishna, or possibly on some question of Jewish law. Great subtlety of thought is displayed in these discussions. Points of similarity are discovered between things which are, to ordinary observation, wholly diverse, and points of difference between things apparently quite identical. The ruling principle of the writers seems to be, that in the sacred writings, and more particularly in the Pentateuch, there is not a word, not a letter, that has not its special use and significance. Where this is not patent or easy of discovery, they hold that it is nevertheless latent in the text, and will be brought out when events have taken place, or opinions have been propounded, which were necessary to its development—as what appears to be a mere speck in a photograph may be enlarged until it is found to be in itself a complete picture. These lengthy and abstruse speculations are frequently varied by incidental anecdotes (called Haggadoth), which serve to illustrate the writer's meaning, by allegories, proverbs and parables, or sometimes by the wildest Oriental legends, myths, and romantic tales. Some of these are extremely touching and beautiful; others absurd, frivolous, and extravagant, bordering occasionally on the profane, if not the blasphemous. There is, in fact, a strange and bizarre mixture of heterogeneous subjects. Eastern fancies are intermingled with the speculations of the Greek and Roman moralists. A celebrated writer has described the Talmud as 'an extraordinary monument of human industry, human wisdom, and human folly.'[1] The probable explanation of this perversion of high intellect and patient study is to be found in the fact that the writers, being excluded by the

---

[1] Against this, however, may be set the opinion of the celebrated Buxtorf. He says, that 'it contains excellent lessons in jurisprudence, medicine, physics, ethics, politics, and astronomy; admirable proverbs, and apothegms and shining gems of eloquence, not less ornamental to the Hebrew tongue than are the flowers of eloquence to the Greek and Latin languages. Nor would the knowledge of Hebrew and Chaldee be complete without them.'

peculiarity of their social and political position from handling the topics on which literary men ordinarily employ their pens, they were driven to busy themselves with the only subjects open to them. Hence too, probably, the extraordinary respect paid to the Talmuds by the Jewish people. They have ever regarded these books, and especially the Babylonian Talmud, with the profoundest reverence and affection. Indeed, they have been charged with bestowing more of their regard on them than on their own inspired Scriptures. They have a proverb, that 'They who study the Scriptures do a virtuous, but not an unmixedly virtuous, act. They who study the Mishna perform a wholly virtuous act, and merit a reward. But they who study the Gemara perform the most virtuous of all acts.' And again, 'The Scriptures are water, the Mishna wine, the Gemara spiced wine.' [1]

As regards the history of the Talmuds, it is a singular fact that no notice is taken of either Mishna or Gemara by any of the Fathers belonging to the first four centuries of Church history, notwithstanding that they frequently handle the subject of Jewish tradition. Even Tertullian, when specially writing on this subject, while he speaks of the primal law given to Adam, and the laws of the Two Tables committed to Moses, makes no mention of the Mishna. Augustine, in the fifth century, does name the δευτέρωσις. or Second Law ; but even he speaks of it as containing the *unwritten* traditions of the Jews, transmitted from one generation to another by word of mouth. We can only suppose that, although the Mishna was indeed completed before the end of the second century, the knowledge of it was for a long time confined to the learned among the Jews, and for a still longer time to the Hebrew nation generally. The same was the case as regards the completed Jerusalem Talmud. There was, in fact, no recognition of the work by Christians until the time of the Emperor Justinian, who, about the middle of the sixth century, issued a Novella, or edict, against it. He allowed the reading of Scripture in the synagogues, but prohibited that of the Mishna, as being 'the mere invention of earthly men, who had nothing of Heaven in them.' From his time to the sixteenth century of

---

[1] Some persons might be inclined to remark on this saying, that it is a great deal truer than its authors were aware of. Yet its meaning has probably been misunderstood, and there is no intention of disparaging Scripture. It may only mean, that the Mishna is the knowledge of Scripture with more knowledge added, and the Gemara is the knowledge of Scripture and Mishna combined with a yet further addition of knowledge.

Christianity, popes and kings have put forth one manifesto after
another, warning men against its perusal, and ordering the book itself
to be suppressed, and even publicly destroyed. In 1286 Pope
Honorius IV. wrote to Archbishop Peckham, requiring him to forbid
the perusal of the Talmud as a 'liber damnabilis,' from which all of
manner of evil was certain to arise. Nor were the popes content with
prescribing it. In 1230 Gregory IX., following the example of his
predecessor Innocent, burned twenty cartloads of it. In 1553, during
the Feast of Tabernacles, all the copies that could anywhere be found
were committed to the flames by order of Julius III.; and a few years
subsequently, 12,000 volumes underwent the same fate by command
of Paul IV. During the last half of the sixteenth century the
Talmud was in this manner brought to the stake no less than six
times, and was burned, not by the single copy, but by the waggon-
load. The Hebrew copyists of those times must have laboured hard
to prevent the total disappearance of the book. But the establishment of the printing presses, and the declaration of Reuchlin, early
in the sixteenth century,[1] in its favour, in the course of a generation or
two put an end to the attempts to root out all traces of it.

The celebrated Maimonides, in the twelfth century, made an epi-
tome of the laws of the Talmud, which many prefer to the Talmud
itself, forasmuch as he omits the strange fables with which the
original work abounds, and preserves the really valuable matter. The
name of his book is Yad-ha-chazzak, or *The Strong Hand.* It is of
great use to those who wish to gain a knowledge of Jewish laws and
ceremonies.

---

[1] See p. 269.

THE TARGUMS, MASSORA, CABBALA, SEPHER-YETSIRA, AND ZOHAR.

THE TARGUMS.

THE Targums are expository paraphrases of the Books of the Old Testament. They are written in Chaldee, which was more familiar to the Jews after Ezra's time than the Hebrew. It would appear that after the return from Captivity it was the habit in the synagogue worship to read out some portion of Scripture in the Hebrew, and then give orally a Targum on the passage in question. But the *written* Targums—viz., those of Jonathan, Onkelos, Jonathan son of Uzziel, Jerusalem, and Joseph the Blind—were none of them composed, or at all events committed to writing, much before the era of our Lord. They come therefore within the scope of the present work.

The Targum of Jonathan is the most ancient, and is generally thought to have been drawn up in its present form about thirty years before the birth of Christ. That of Onkelos is somewhat later, and is concerned with the Books of Moses only. It is greatly superior to its predecessor in simplicity of language and purity of style. It is quoted in the Mishna, but does not seem to have been known to the early Christian Fathers.

The Targum of the younger Jonathan comments on the Books of the Prophets only. It resembles that of Onkelos in purity of style, but is less simple, and runs occasionally into allegory. It is believed

that additions have been made to it by doctors who lived long subsequently to its author.

The Targum of Jerusalem deals with the Books of Moses, or
rather with a portion of them. It is little better than a fragment of
an ancient paraphrase of the Pentateuch.

The Targum of Joseph the Blind is on the Hagiographa, viz.,
the Psalms, Proverbs, Ecclesiastes, Song of Solomon, Esther, Job,
and Ruth. The style is very corrupt Chaldee, containing many
foreign words.

There is no Targum on Daniel, Ezra, or Nehemiah, because these
books were already written in Aramaic. The Targums are of much
value in establishing the genuineness of the present Hebrew text,
proving it to be the same as it was when the Targums were written.
They are also useful in Jewish controversy, as showing the manner
in which the Jews, previously to the Christian era, interpreted the
great prophecies respecting the Messiah.

MASSORA.

This word properly denotes tradition; and those persons are called
Massorites who determined the meaning of the Hebrew text by
adding pointed vowels to it. There are in the Hebrew language
four vowels, but these were found insufficient ; and further, it was a
frequent practice in early times to omit these vowels, writing the
consonants only of the words. The consequence of this was, that the
meaning of a word was often ambiguous, its sense becoming different
according to the vowels inserted. Thus there is said to have been a
dispute between David and Joab as to the meaning of the word
זכר (Deut. xxv. 19). In one of his raids against the Amalekites,
Joab slew the men, but spared the women and children. David rebuked him for this, alleging that the command was ' to blot out the
memory of,' *i.e.*, to exterminate (זֵכֶר) the Amalekites. But Joab
answered that the word was זָכָר, ordering the slaughter of the males
only.[1] In order to put a stop to perplexities so caused, the Massorites[2] are said to have added the points, or pointed vowels, of

---

[1] This story may, or may not, be historical ; but any way it illustrates the use of
the Massoretic points.

[2] The Massorites were an inferior description of Scribes, whose profession it
was to write out copies of the Hebrew Scriptures ; also to teach the people the
true readings, as well as to comment on them. They called their work ' Massora,'
or tradition, because they believed that God gave the Law on Sinai, imparting to
Moses, at the same time, the true interpretation.

which there are fourteen. These are placed below or above the consonants, supplying the place of vowels, where these are wanting, and determining the pronunciation, when present.

The Massorites not only added the vowel points, but numbered the chapters, sections, verses, words, and even the letters of the sacred text. Thus they have noted the fact that there are in the Book of Genesis 1,534 verses, 20,713 words, and 78,100 letters. They have also marked the central verse, word, and letter of the book. They have done the same also in the instance of all the other Books of the Old Testament. The object is to preserve the inspired text from interpolation, mutilation, in fact, change of any kind, and also to give facilities for reference. Much of their work has been censured as 'laborious trifling;' but it has been of service to scholars nevertheless.

The age to be assigned to the Massorites is a matter of doubt. Some have affirmed that Moses himself communicated to the elders this method of elucidating and preserving inviolate the Sacred Writings. Others ascribe the invention of the Massoretic vowels to Ezra, and the Great Synagogue of his time. But neither of these opinions has much to support it; and the most trustworthy authorities place them in the fifth or sixth century of Christianity. The fact that there were many variations in the sacred text long subsequently to the time of Ezra, is clearly enough proved by the versions of the Septuagint writers, Aquila, Symmachus and Theodotion, none of which are in entire accordance with one another. This could not have been the case if, previously to the date of these translators, the Massorites had completed their labours. Jerome states that the text was not determined even in his time. The most approved view seems to be that of Walton. He thinks that the work was begun early in the fifth century, and came gradually more into notice, until it was completed, *circa* 1030 A.D. Maimonides appears to say that the final revision was made by the famous scholar Rabbi Ben Asher. The Massorites, it should be noted, have been charged with endeavouring to pass off erroneous readings favourable to their own views, and, in order to secure this object, preventing any recurrence to the original and genuine text.

CABBALA.

This word also denotes tradition, and originally included all the interpretations of Scripture, which the Jews professed to have received, in the first instance, from Moses, and in the second, from

Ezra. But subsequently it came to be used for an abstruse species of science, by which certain passages of Holy Writ are mystically explained. The Cabbala, in this sense, has many processes, of which the three best known are Gematria, Notaricon, and Themurah.[1] The first mentioned of these consists in assuming the letters of a Hebrew word to denote ciphers, or arithmetical numbers, and then explaining every word by the arithmetical value of the letters composing it. Thus, for example, the letters of the word Jabo-Shiloh (Gen. xlix. 10), that is, 'Shiloh shall come,' when reckoned according to their arithmetical valuation, make up the same number as does the Hebrew word 'Messiah.' Hence the Cabbalists infer that Shiloh signifies the same as Messiah.

Notaricon consists in taking every letter of a word as being in itself a complete word, and the letters, when put together, as a complete sentence. Thus, the first word of the Book of Genesis, Bereshith, resolved into its component letters, is understood to mean Bara, Rakia, Arez, Shamaion, Iam, Tehomoth, *i.e.*, 'He created the firmament, the earth, the heavens, the sea, and the deep.' Or again, the initial letters of every word in a sentence may be formed into a word, possessing, of course, a mystical meaning.

Themurah, is where the letters are transposed so as to form a new word—sometimes by the process known to us as anagram, sometimes by the substitution of one letter for another. The Cabbalists believed that the Scriptures contained endless recondite meanings, which might be brought to light by patient investigation. They were persuaded that the sacred writers had some special secret reason for their choice of every word they employed, and for its place in the verse, chapter, and book in which it is found.

BOOK OF YETZIRA.

Though some of the Chasidim professed a reverence for the Talmud, their system of theology is in reality antagonistic to it.[2] The basis of their confession of faith is, not the Talmud, but the Book of Zohar. This, together with the Yetzira, contains the fullest exposition of their views.

---

[1] Graetz says of the Cabbala, that it is a fungous growth, which since the thirteenth century has crept over the body of the Law.

[2] The Talmud is said to have been publicly burnt in Podolia, A.D. 1755, by some Sabbathain Cabbalists. On the other side, the Rabbinical Talmudists have repeatedly condemned the Cabbalism of the Chasidim.

The age of the Sepher-Yetzira, Book of Creation, is a matter of dispute. By many it has been assigned to the seventh or eighth century. More trustworthy authorities consider it to have been composed greatly earlier. In the Talmud there is the mention of a Sepher-Yetzira, a book older, apparently, than the Mishna itself. If this is the same work as that now under consideration, it must be referred to the first, or at latest the second, century of Christianity. The language and style of the book are in accordance with this notion, being those of the Apostolic age; and though there are passages suggesting a later date than this, scholars are inclined to coincide in the view of M. Adolph. Francke,[1] that the book belongs to the Apostolic age.

BOOK OF ZOHAR.

The Sepher-Zohar, Book of Light,[2] is of the more importance, because it is accounted the code and text-book of the theological system, as adopted by the Chasidim. It takes the form of a commentary on the Mosaic Books, and is extremely mystical and full of allegory. Its contents are thus described by Surenhusius: ' Veteris Ecclesiæ judaicæ fundamenta, prout Templo Hierosolymano stante secundo erant, non ex opere Talmudico, vel ab alio quodam auctore antiquo, sed ex Zohare tantum sunt quærenda. Cum in opere Talmudico, leges Ecclesiasticæ, forenses et politicæ exponantur, in Zohare autem loca scripturæ sacræ ad Theologiæ capita reducantur, in quibus de Existentiâ, de Attributis, de Epithetis, ac Nominibus Dei, itemque de Messiâ, de Angelis, tam bonis quam malis, de animâ humanâ, ejusdemque origine ac statu, atque, ut uno verbo dicam, de cognitione Dei nostri per Messiam genuinum Filium, agitur.'

Its authorship and date are even more a matter of dispute than those of the Yetzira. It is said by many to be the composition of Simeon Jochaides (Simeon ben Yochai), who is believed to have lived somewhere about the time of our Lord. Others, though they do not consider Simeon to be the actual author, yet are of opinion that it was written by one of his scholars, who embodied in it his master's teaching. The language in which it is written is that of the Palestinian Jews in the times immediately preceding the composition of the Talmud. 'The ideas and expressions also,' writes Etheridge,

---

[1] *La Cabbale*, par Adolph. Francke, Paris, 1843; a work of extensive research and profound learning.

[2] Daniel xii. 3. The word is there rendered by our translators, as ' brightness.'

'belong to that date.' It would be possible, however, perhaps not very difficult, to simulate that style, if it was the object of the composer to pass it off as the production of an early age; and it is difficult to believe that some of the contents of the book could be the work of any Jew of the date assigned. M. Francke's opinion here also is the safest to follow. He places it in the seventh century. The notion, however, that the Zohar is simply the composition of Moses de Léon, fully six hundred years afterwards, finds supporters even at the present day.

It is in form, as has already been intimated, a commentary on the Pentateuch; but in reality a heterogeneous mass of doctrine—the Aristotelian, Neo-Platonic, and Rabbinical conceptions being inextricably blended together. It professes to reveal great mysteries; but the revelation is conveyed in language so enigmatical and obscure that it is often difficult to arrive at any definite meaning. It recognises God as the Infinite, having no beginning, and no end of existence; and declares that He has revealed Himself under ten forms, or rather emanations, to which the Zohar gives the name of Sephiroth. These ten are Transcendency (the crown), Wisdom, Knowledge, Mercy, Justice, Beauty, Triumph, Glory, Basis, Dominion. In all these representations the Triune character of the Godhead is exhibited.[1] Hence, in the confession of faith adopted by the Zoharites, as the followers of Jacob Frank and others were called, the doctrine of the Blessed Trinity, as held by the Church Catholic, was distinctly professed.

---

[1] It is proper to remark that Jewish controversialists deny the existence of Trinitarian doctrine in the Book of Zohar. On the contrary, they affirm that they were wont to twit the Cabbalists with 'believing in ten gods, whereas (said they) even the Christians believed in only three.'

APPENDIX IV.

GRAVE doubts have been advanced, by one writer or another, of what may be called the ancient belief on this subject. It has been questioned: I. Whether the attempt to rebuild the Temple ever was really made; and II. whether, allowing the work to have been begun and interrupted, its interruption was not due to natural causes only.

I. It is argued, chiefly by Lardner,[1] that Julian did no more than project such an undertaking, which he never attempted to carry into effect. In his letter addressed to the Jewish people, he tells them, '*if* he returned from his Persian expedition, he would rebuild and inhabit with them the holy city of Jerusalem.' But, as he never returned, Lardner argues that he never made the promised attempt. The same appears to be the tradition of the Jews.[2] Thus, David Gans, in the fifteenth century, writes, 'The work was prevented from being accomplished, *for* Julian never returned, but perished in the Persian War;' and similarly Cassel: 'He made preparations for restoring the Temple, but, after a brief reign, fell in battle.' A passage from one of Julian's orations is, further, quoted by Lardner, in which he says that, 'he conceived the design of rebuilding the

---

[1] Lardner, V. iii. p. 603 ff.

[2] Cassel, I. § 53. Other Jewish writers, as Jost, admit the occurrence, but deny the miracle.

Temple.' But, as he does not add that he executed it, Lardner reasons that he probably did not.

It is almost needless to say that these arguments carry very little weight. The reader should note that Julian did not promise to rebuild the *Temple*, on his return from Persia, but *Jerusalem*. As that city was then standing, his meaning must have been, that he would restore it to its pristine magnificence. This would be a long and costly work, which might well require his personal presence. But he might commit the rebuilding of the Temple, the design of which was well known, to a deputy—an instalment, so to speak, of the greater work to follow. Nor can it be reasonably argued, that, because a man does not *say* that he put in force a design, *therefore* he *did* not put it in force.[1]

Whatever weight Lardner's reasoning might carry is lost altogether, when we take into consideration the testimony of the contemporaneous historians, and those of the age immediately following. The first include Gregory Nazianzen, Bishop of Constantinople, John Chrysostom, Cyril of Jerusalem, Ambrose, and Ammianus Marcellinus ; the second, Socrates, Sozomen, and Theodoret. All these record the main facts, viz., the repeated bursting forth of the fire, until the work was abandoned from the impossibility of persisting. Each adds some minor details, which do not affect the credibility of the occurrence itself.[2] The most important witness is Ammianus Marcellinus, a heathen and a personal friend of the Emperor. It will be better to give his account of the matter in his own words. 'The Emperor was meditating,' he writes,[3] 'the restoration, at an

---

[1] Lardner also insists much on the silence of Jerome, Prudentius, and Orosius. If facts of history are to be doubted because some historians of the time do not mention them how many would remain which could be regarded as certain?

[2] Thus, Gregory says that the doors of a church were miraculously closed against the fugitives, and a fiery flame issuing from it destroyed them ; that a circle and cross of fire were visible in the heavens, and crosses of fire seen on the garments of the spectators. Chrysostom states that the workmen had dug out the foundation, and begun to build, when the flames burst forth. Socrates, that the building tools and implements were consumed by fire, and were a whole day burning. He adds, what is important, that the earthquake occurred during the night, and the fires broke out on the following day. Theodoret says that the earthquake threw down some of the stones of the newly laid foundations, and shook some of the excavated earth back into the hole out of which it had been dug. Chrysostom confirms him in this.

[3] Ammian. Marcellin. XXIII. I. It has been suggested that he took his account without inquiry from Christian writers. So Gibbon, ch. XXXIII. But that a heathen historian and devoted friend of Julian should in this manner have

unlimited expense, of the Jewish Temple, and had committed the
care of the matter to Alypius of Antioch. When, then, Alypius
was vigorously prosecuting the work, and the governor of the province was rendering him his help, frightful balls of fire breaking
forth with continued outbursts near the foundations, again and
again consumed the workmen, and rendered it impossible to approach the spot ; and in this manner the element more obstinately
(*i.e.*, more obstinately than even the pertinacious persistence of
the workmen) driving them away, the attempt was abandoned.'

In the face of evidence like this, he must be a hardy advocate
who would maintain that the occurrence never took place.

But it may be contended that although it did take place, there
was nothing in it of a miraculous character. It may be alleged,—

(1) That there was simply an earthquake, to which the whole
was due.

(2) That there may have been an explosion of foul air, caused by
the sudden opening of the vaults under the Temple. These had long
been closed, and the noxious vapours, coming into contact with the
workmen's fires, exploded.

(3) That it is improbable that such a miracle *would* be worked,
there being nothing in the rebuilding of the Temple which *called for*
a miracle. Our Lord, no doubt, had declared that the Temple
should be utterly destroyed, but not that it should never be rebuilt.
Nor had Daniel (rightly understood), or any other prophet, ever
said so.

(4) That the age in which the miracle is related to have taken
place is one in which miracles are spoken of as having been of almost
daily occurrence—some of them frivolous and childish to the last
degree. In these no reasonable man can place any faith ; and there
is nothing to separate this miracle from them.

Let us consider these objections.

1. Earthquakes have always been of common occurrence in Palestine. Nor is it denied that an earthquake took place on the present
occasion. But a simple earthquake will not account for the bursting
forth of the fiery balls, *as often as the labourers attempted to resume the
work.* No other earthquake ever exhibited these phenomena.

2. This explanation was, I believe, unknown to Warburton, Basnage, Lardner, or Gibbon. It appears to have been first suggested

---

recorded what was at once unfavourable to his creed and painful to his feelings as
a friend, is too improbable to need refutation.

in a German magazine,[1] by the celebrated Michaelis, in the latter half of the eighteenth century. But, on inquiry, it appears more ingenious than probable. Who knows that the caverns under the Temple *had* been hermetically sealed for a long time previously to Julian's attempt? They were constantly opened at other times (as the story told by Benjamin of Tudela evidences), and no such result followed. The present was but one out of many occasions when foundations had been dug and buildings erected in the same spot ; but without any explosion or fiery outburst. How was it that Solomon's workmen, and Zorobabel's, and Adrian's, and I know not how many more—how was it that they escaped the fatal injuries that befell those of Julian ?

Again, the phenomena related by Marcellinus and others do not accord with the idea of an explosion of mephitic gases. These ignite instantaneously, and burn till exhausted. They could not be described by any writer as '*balls* of fire' breaking forth with continual outbursts, as often as the labourers attempted to resume the work. It is also evident that the fire did not break forth the moment the ground was opened, but only when the whole foundation had been laid and the masons had begun to build ; for Chrysostom says that some of the stones already laid were thrown down.

3. In dealing with this objection, we enter on new and more difficult ground. It may be true, and I incline to believe it is so, that the truth of Holy Writ was not, so to speak, imperilled by this enterprise. If it had succeeded, I do not see that any saying of Inspiration would have been thereby contravened.[2] But such an occurrence would surely have been at variance with the Divine purpose in setting up the Christian Church. Type and shadow were to vanish when the reality and the substance came. The rebuilding of the Jewish Temple would have been an unmeaning renewal of them. Further, such strange anomalies as the reconstruction of the Holy of Holies, with its veil unrent, and the renewal of the Temple sacrifices, fore-

---

[1] *Magazin von Lichtenberg.* Quoted by the editor of Ammian. Marcell. in his notes.

[2] Warburton argues that not only did our Lord never declare that the Jewish Temple should not be rebuilt, but that He even implied that it would be, when He said (St. Luke xxi. 24), 'Jerusalem shall be trodden down of the Gentiles, *until* the times of the Gentiles be fulfilled.' But this is to mistake the meaning of the Greek phrase Ἄχρις οὗ, ἕως οὗ. These denote a state of things up to a given point, but determine nothing as to what will follow. See Chrysostom on St. Matt. i. 25 etc.

C C

shadowing an event long past, would have disturbed the faith of large numbers of professing members of the Church, as well as deterred equally large numbers from entering its pale. It is a difficult—it may be thought a presumptuous—thing to attempt determining what would be a sufficient reason for expecting a miracle. But if there ever has been an instance in the history of the Christian Church when a miracle was, so to speak, demanded, it was the one we have under consideration. Almighty God had been directly challenged by the supreme human ruler of the earth, and in the sight of all Christendom, to show the right. Do we wonder that, as at Mount Carmel, He answered by fire?

4. These considerations make it easy to deal with the last of the four objections. It may freely be granted that the age of Julian was signalized by the endless recurrence of reported miracles—most of which must be regarded with grave suspicion, while many others are wholly unworthy of credit. Thus Gregory relates of Julian, that one day when he was sacrificing, the entrails of the victim were found to be impressed with the emblem of a cross within a circle.[1] On another occasion, when he attempted to build a heathen temple over the spot where a Christian had been buried, it fell down again as soon as it was put up.[2] These are two instances, out of many, of the idle tales current in that day. If the occurrence we have now under consideration is to be classed with these, no one could wonder at the unwillingness of men to lend it credit. But it stands entirely apart from them. It was not worked at the command or through the entreaty of any man. It was not manifested to prove the truth of any disputed dogma, or the sanctity of any theological leader, or the orthodoxy of any party in the Church. It was wrought by the finger of God directly and visibly ; and, unless we are prepared to affirm that since the Apostolic age He has never openly interfered in the affairs of men, we may reasonably believe that He interfered here.

---

[1] Greg. Naz. Orat. III.   [2] Chrysost. in Matth. Hom. IV.

APPENDIX V.

THE BLOOD ACCUSATIONS.

AMONG the many accusations which have been advanced against
the Jews, there are three, which may be distinguished from
the others as ' Blood Accusations,' and which have been the causes
of terrible suffering to them. The first of these is the charge of
crucifying boys, in parody of the Saviour's death upon the cross ; the
second, that of using Christian blood in the preparation of the Paschal
cakes ; the third, that of possessing themselves, by underhand means,
of the consecrated Host, for the purpose of insulting and stabbing it.
It might seem that this last was not a *blood* accusation. But, as it
was believed that they cut and pierced the wafer, as being the very
body of the Lord, which indeed bled like any human body under
their knives, it may be classed with the other two. The first is the
most ancient, and the one which has been most pertinaciously
adhered to ; though the other two have been continually repeated
and accredited. Our present object is to inquire when these charges
were first made, and what could have given rise to them.

As regards the time and origin of the notion respecting their
crucifixion of boys, I have at p. 73 suggested the probable source of
that accusation. Of all the Jewish feasts, the most mirthful, or rather
the most riotous, was the Feast of Purim ; of which it was said that
' the Jews were wont to drink, until they could not distinguish
between the blessings pronounced on Mordecai and the curses imprecated on Haman.' At this feast, in the earlier centuries of

Christianity, it was customary to introduce the effigy of Haman suspended on his gibbet; and the resemblance of this figure to a crucified malefactor soon engaged the notice of the Jews. Hence jests and innuendos against our Blessed Lord came to be a common topic among the revellers; on which ground the Jews were forbidden by the Christian emperors to celebrate this feast. Nor did the Jews confine their insolence to words. On one occasion, at Inmestar, they seized a Christian youth, whom they fastened to Haman's gibbet, and scourged so mercilessly that he died under their hands. This, of course, provoked a fierce outburst of indignation and horror; and we can well understand that the tradition of the outrage would spread far and endure for many generations.

The second accusation—that of mixing Christian blood with the Passover cakes, or, as some said, with the Paschal sacrifice itself, does not appear to have been advanced until some time in the 13th century, though the exact date cannot be determined. Now, it is at least remarkable in connection with this charge, that it was first made just about the time when the doctrine of Transubstantiation was beginning to take forcible hold on men's minds.[1] That was declared for the first time to be a doctrine of the Catholic faith, by a Lateran Council A.D. 1215. According to that belief, the eucharistic wafer became, after consecration, the actual body and blood of the Lord, so that men actually ate His flesh and drank His blood. It may be assumed as tolerably certain that the Jews would mock and deride this doctrine; which great numbers of pious Christians found themselves unable to accept. Even if the Jews did not openly satirize the Christians who upheld this extravagant conception, their opinion about it would be notorious enough; nor could the knowledge of what the Jews thought about it fail to exasperate still further the bitterness with which the extreme zealots of Ultramontanism already regarded them. It was an easy and obvious addition to the old charge of crucifying a Christian in mockery of the Saviour's passion, to say that the Jews further mixed the blood of their victim with the Paschal bread, in order to deride the holy rite whereby Christians became partakers of His very body and blood.

The Jews themselves allege other reasons for the circulation of

---

[1] 'These accusations began only 600 years ago,' writes De Virga in the *Shebet Yehuda* published in Amsterdam A.D. 1651. 'They commenced in the reign of Alphonso X. of Castile. In his time there was a priest in Spain who in his sermons declared that the Israelites could not sacrifice their Passover unless they had Christian blood to use in the performance of the rite.'

this slander. They declare the charge to have been first made in the earliest ages of the Church, and to have been levelled, nominally indeed at the Jews, but really at the Christians. A vague rumour of the words spoken by Jesus at the Paschal Supper, when He delivered the cup to the Apostles, ''This is My blood,' had spread among the heathen, and given the idea that the Christians actually drank human blood at their religious celebrations. It is true that the authors of these accusations attribute the offence to the Israelites ; but (say the Jews, and so far certainly truly) the earlier heathen writers continually confound the Christians with Jews, regarding the former as simply an heretical Jewish sect. Further, it is alleged that the calumny derived some support from the known practice of certain heretical Christian sects, notably the Cataphrygians, who mixed with the consecrated bread the blood of infants, which they extracted from them by puncturing a vein. This, however, is nothing more than a plausible theory. Granting that such reports gained currency in the first or second century of Christianity, the Christians, against whom they were really circulated, would know their monstrous falsehood, and entirely disregard them. It is impossible to conceive that they would have retorted such a charge on the Jews, or even countenanced its circulation.

Again, it is said that there is an imperative order in the Talmud,[1] that the Jews shall, at the Passover, drink a certain quantity of 'red wine,' and that this 'red wine' was supposed to mean really human blood, though the command was disguised under a metaphor. But independently of the extravagance of such an interpretation of very plain and simple words, the charge made against the Jews was not that of *drinking* Christian blood, but of mixing it with the Passover bread. No one ever supposed that for any of the four cups drunk at the Paschal Feast a cup of human blood was substituted.

If the idea above named has nothing but its likelihood to support it, at all events it has that. And the third charge, brought not long afterwards, of getting surreptitious possession of the consecrated wafer in order to treat it with indignity, tends to strengthen the likelihood. It is alleged that, not content with deriding the doctrine of Transubstantiation, they were eager to insult the body of the Lord itself. They would bribe with a large sum some official to purloin the

---

[1] Hierosolym. Talmudis, Fol. II. 1. 'Quæritur de mensurâ poculorum, quæ ebiberunt ad Pascha, aliaque convivia sacra ; et qualitate vini. Præceptum est. ut vino rubido præstat officium. Vinum rubrum requiritur in sacris.' See Lightfoot, *Index Talmud. Hierosolym.* Vol. X. p. 509 of his works.

Host, and hand it over to them—when they would stab it with their knives, and it would bleed, like any human body—they, it was assumed, remaining wholly unmoved by the sight of so tremendous a miracle, nay, only anxious, by multiplied evidence of it, to increase their own condemnation in the sight of Heaven ! It is beyond dispute that these alleged marvels were quoted in support of the doctrine of the Corporal Presence in the Eucharist. It is hardly too much to assume that the charges against the Jews were coined—partly, no doubt, in consequence of the bitter hate with which they were regarded, but partly also to establish the certainty of the popular dogma of the day.

I have not thought it necessary to advance any arguments to prove the falsehood of these accusations. No competent tribunal by which they have been tried has ever failed to declare them groundless. Indeed, no person who has the most ordinary acquaintance with the Mosaic ritual, but must be aware, not only of the falsehood, but of the absurdity and the impossibility of the charges. The touch, nay the mere contiguity, of a dead body, according to the Jewish law, rendered all persons in its vicinity unclean, so that they could not partake in, much less celebrate, religious rites until they were purged from the pollution. How then could the blood of a murdered person be used in the consecration of victims and offerings, which its very presence would *ipso facto* desecrate ? If nothing short of the most distinct statement on the subject will satisfy some minds, they have even that. The words of Moses, Levit. vii. 26, 27, are, ‘ Ye shall eat *no manner* of blood’ (πᾶν αἷμα οὐκ ἔδεσθε)—no blood, not even of beast or bird, how much less, of man !